New Approaches in Sociology

Studies in Social Inequality, Social Change, and Social Justice

Edited by

Nancy A. Naples
University of Connecticut

A Routledge Series

New Approaches in Sociology

Studies in Social Inequality, Social Change, and Social Justice

Nancy A. Naples, *General Editor*

Linking Activism
Ecology, Social Justice, and Education for Social Change
Morgan Gardner

The Everyday Lives of Sex Workers in the Netherlands
Katherine Gregory

Striving and Surviving
A Daily Life Analysis of Honduran Transnational Families
Leah Schmalzbauer

Unequal Partnerships
Beyond the Rhetoric of Philanthropic Collaboration
Ira Silver

Domestic Democracy
At Home in South Africa
Jennifer Natalie Fish

Praxis and Politics
Knowledge Production in Social Movements
Janet M. Conway

The Suppression of Dissent
How the State and Mass Media Squelch USAmerican Social Movements
Jules Boykoff

Are We Thinking Straight?
The Politics of Straightness in a Lesbian and Gay Social Movement Organization
Daniel K. Cortese

"Rice Plus"
Widows and Economic Survival in Rural Cambodia
Susan Hagood Lee

"Between Worlds"
Deaf Women, Work, and Intersections of Gender and Ability
Cheryl G. Najarian

If I Only Had a Brain
Deconstructing Brain Injury
Mark Sherry

Minority within a Minority
Black Francophone Immigrants and the Dynamics of Power and Resistance
Amal I. Madibbo

Gender Trouble Makers
Education and Empowerment in Nepal
Jennifer Rothchild

No Place Like Home
Organizing Home-Based Labor in the Era of Structural Adjustment
David E. Staples

Negotiating Decolonization in the United Nations
Politics of Space, Identity, and International Community
Vrushali Patil

Disability, Mothers, and Organization
Accidental Activists
Melanie Panitch

Judicial Reform and Reorganization in 20th Century Iran
State-Building, Modernization and Islamicization
Majid Mohammadi

Judicial Reform and Reorganization in 20th Century Iran

State-Building, Modernization and Islamicization

Majid Mohammadi

Routledge
Taylor & Francis Group
New York London

First published 2008
by Routledge
711 Third Avenue, New York, NY 10017

Simultaneously published in the UK
by Routledge
2 Park Square, Milton Park, Abingdon, Oxfordshire OX14 4RN

First issued in paperback 2014

Routledge is an imprint of the Taylor & Francis Group, an informa business

Typeset in Sabon by IBT Global

Library of Congress Cataloging-in-Publication Data

Mohammadi, Majid, 1960-
Judicial reform and reorganization in 20th century Iran : state-building, modernization, and Islamicization / by Majid Mohammadi.
p. cm. -- (New approaches in sociology)
Includes bibliographical references and index.
ISBN 0-415-96350-8
1. Justice, Administration of—Iran—History. 2. Law reform—Iran—History. I. Title.

KMH1572.M64 2008
340'.30955--dc22 2007025727

ISBN 13: 978-0-415-96350-3 (hbk)
ISBN 13: 978-0-415-51291-6 (pbk)

Contents

List of Figures

List of Tables

Notes on Transliteration and Dates

The system of transliteration used in this study renders consonants according to the system adopted by the *International Journal of Middle East Studies,* but omits diacritical marks, with the exception of the *hamzeh* (indicated by an apostrophe, ') the *ayn* (indicated by a grave,`), and Ā and ā for long *alef* (a in Persian). Vowels are rendered to reflect the sound in English that most closely approximates modern Persian pronunciation. Words commonly used in English are transliterated according to common practice. The common spelling of names such as Reza, Tehran and Khan has been retained. Personal names are rendered in accordance with the transliteration rules outlined here, except when cited in European language sources. I did not change the transliteration of the Middle Eastern names that have been already used in English. All Persian and Arabic words used in the text are italicized. All translations are by the author unless otherwise stated. All *ezāfeh*s (a noun governing the genitive or possessive case) are transliterated as–e or–ye, depending on the last character in Persian word.

In the text, dates are all in the Gregorian calendar unless they refer directly to Persian texts. Wherever a date is given in the Islamic solar (*shamsi,* A. S. *anno shamsi*) or lunar (*qamar*i, A. Q. *anno qamari*) calendar, they are followed by the corresponding Gregorian date. In the transliterating of common words used both in Arabic and Persian I have used their own system respectively, e.g. fiqh, 'urf, dhemmi, and Islam if they are used in Arabic and feqh, 'orf, zemmi, and Eslam (when it is used in the name of books or individuals) if they are used in Persian.

Chapter One
Introduction

1.1. PROBLEM

The Islamic regime of post-revolutionary Iran as a religious state is a unique political regime in the modern world. This regime, which is based on a special reading of Shi'ite political doctrine, entwines institutions of a modern state with religious institutions, and the clerics both as the political elite and Islamic jurists have the final say in different aspects of its politics and policies including law.

There are not many cases of judicial reform that have resulted from first a constitutional and then a religious revolution in the same century. The Iranian judicial system after the Revolution of 1979 purportedly based on jurists' law[1] in an authoritarian[2] state-with its different characteristics in different periods-makes this society all the more interesting for sociological studies. Authoritarian regime of Iran has transformed from hierocratic authoritarianism of 1981–1989 to hierocratic authoritarian sultanism of 1989–1997 and 2001–2006. This system attempts to give priority to jurists' law in the area of law making and makes it a public law by resort to the authority of an authoritarian regime. The subject matter of the *shari'ah*[3] that is partially codified in Islamic Republic of Iran has been totally politicized by the state and political factions, and its regulations have being executed in the public. Iranian law is claimed to be a divine law and the law of the state at the same time. Politicization of the judiciary in post-Khomeini era is a specific character of Iranian polity when judiciary branch is mostly acting in the opposite direction to the rest of the world in the last quarter of the 20th century. Judicial reforms also provide concrete examples, cases and events to be considered when discussing the tensions between the secular and religious institutions.

By studying developments in Iran's judiciary in the 20th century, I can contribute in explaining the interplay between law and society and gain greater insight and understanding of the intricacies of law and society, mechanisms for alteration, administration and enforcement of the rules, and transition from a traditional homogeneous society that rely on custom and religion as the sources of legal rules and resolves disputes through conciliation or mediation by village elders and mullahs to a more complex and heterogeneous society that needs regulatory and enforcement mechanisms. By focusing on the conflicts between legitimacy and coercion and between the state and society and pursuing legal developments within a broad historical and comparative framework I am going to study the development of constitutional law with respect to judiciary in a non-Western developing society. The story of legal and judicial development in Iran is the story of national development.[4] Judicial reforms in Iran, as in any other country, reflect the changes in values, interaction patterns, and ideologies because they all are embodied in law as substantive rules. Working in the framework of sociology and law, in this study I am concerned with the nature of legitimate authority, the mechanisms of social control, issues of democracy, rule of law and human rights, power arrangements, the relationship between different spheres of life, and intellectual, social, economic and political context of law and judicial system.

Studying Iranian judiciary system will let me compare different models and periods of the law/religion/society problematic that Iranian society has experienced during the 20th century. It will also construct the typology of contemporary Iranian politico-legal regimes on the basis of the varied historical experience of state building that ignores the civil society and squeezes the public sphere in that century. The appropriate ideal-types for politico-legal regimes in each period will be constructed on the basis of what has been happening in the judiciary and the strategies and policies selected for judicial reform and reorganization. I will use the extensive literature (Berkes, 1964; Devereux, 1963; Lambton, Lewis *et al.* 1965) and existing typologies of political regimes as applied to the contemporary Middle East, such as Chehabi and Linz's (1998) "sultanic regimes" or Crystal's (1994) locally inflected "authoritarianism," and comparative materials on Middle Eastern legal systems in the second half of the twentieth century (Brown, 1997) to update taxonomy of legal and political organization of Iran in the 20th century. The typological characteristics of each politico-legal regime have set the boundaries, the opportunities, the nature and the failures of the judicial reforms and reorganizations in this country in the 20th century.

This society has followed four different models of legal system in this century i.e. "dualistic judicial system" under Qājār dynasty even after the Constitutional Revolution of 1906 (Arjomand, 1988: 66), "state law system" of Pahlavi dynasty, overcoming "ideologized jurists' law" of the first decade after the Islamic Revolution beside another kind of dual judicial system, i.e. dual courts, in lower levels in the chart of the judiciary, and "formal jurist law" of post-charismatic era after the death of Khomeini.

It may be asked why the period of 20th century has been chosen for this study. To make an answer to this question a couple of points call for attention. First of all, it is during this period that most of the legal and judicial changes occur. It is also during this period that the society repeatedly endures social and political revolutions. In this period, the Iranian society was in the processes of state building, modernization, codification and transplantation, mass mobilization and Islamicization.

My subject in this study is the relationship between socio-political change, social revolution, and judicial reform in the case of Iran. In the discussions on politico-legal regimes, I will try to find the connections between legal institutions and political organizations in Iranian history, using a number of ideal-types. In this mostly problem-based case study, I mainly focus on foundations, causes, dilemmas and problems of judicial reform as a process and as a part of the package of reform, and take into account judicial projects that were planned and implemented to change the judicial system of Iran. The main questions of this study are: What are the possible causes and consequences of the secular and religious judicial reforms in 20th century Iran? How these two have been interacting? Are the causes internal or external or both? How have the two Iranian revolutions, i.e. 1906 and 1979 changed Iranian judiciary? What explains the sequence of dissolution and purging and then restructuring and recruitment processes in Iranian judiciary during 20th century? Why did different states restructure the judiciary and almost completely changed the judges after their consolidation? What factors account for the variation in the timing of the dissolution and purging processes? Who did what in the Iranian legal and judicial systems in the four periods of reforms that will be discussed in this study, and why? Who ran it? What are the basic principles of judiciary in these periods? What were the basic divisions of labor in the legal processes? Why did political elite in each period make the particular choices they did to adopt special judicial policies and make special judicial administrative decisions, and why did they succeed or fail? How have Iranian socio-political and judicial structures been interacting during the 20th century? What legal and political recognition is granted to professional associations and non-governmental organizations in the different periods of judicial reform?

To answer these questions I need to address some other questions like: What are the legal and judicial regimes in different periods of judicial reform in Iran and how these regimes are overthrown? Have legal administration, organizations and mechanisms been independent from legislative mechanisms and executive administration? What is the role of legal profession in the reform? Do laws including constitutional, statutory and ministerial regulations act directly under the influence of administrative change? Why and how judges decide as they do? Why did Iranian administrations choose the form of legal rules to accomplish their ends in each period of judicial reforms during 20th century? Have civil society actors contributed to reform of the judiciary? What are the achievements and limitations of state-lead judicial reforms in Iran? What did determine the timing, the extent, and the nature of judicial reform and reorganization? What was the relation between state law and the *shari`ah*? What was the place of the *shari`ah* and "jurists' law" developed by schools of jurisprudence in the legal system and judiciary organization of 20th century Iran?"

Understanding a judicial system and its practical operation with greater accuracy requires raising basic questions from the ground up: who does what, when, with what level of preparation and resources, and to what effect? What are the structure of courts and their level of accessibility? What is the manner in which law and courts are used as social control mechanisms? Without this kind of bottom-up understanding, we are likely to misunderstand the behavior of the collective system on a higher or even lower level. The failure to look at a judicial system from the bottom-up or the inside out carries significant peril in attempted reforms.

The mapping of the judicial patterns of 20th century Iran will dispose of the widely held harmful and ahistorical dichotomy between the traditional Islamic judicial system and the Western-inspired judiciary of the modern Iranian nation-state. My study is expected to show that the basic misunderstanding implicit in this idea is that modern judicial system replaced the Islamic law or the *shari'a* in Pahlavi era and Islamic judicial system replaced the modern one after the Revolution of 1979. In historical reality, modern formal judicial system replaced not the *shari`ah* courts, as it is explained[5] but the dual "'orfi or state + *shari`ah*" court system. The *shar'i* courts never attained that position of supreme judicial authority independent of political control, which would have provided the only sure foundation and real guarantee for the ideal of Civitas Dei (Coulson, 1964: 121). The substantial aspect was mostly kept in the same way. Many of the substantive provisions of the *shari`ah* were in fact incorporated into the Iranian Civil Codes of 1928 and 1935 ('Āqeli, 1990), as they were in the Civil Codes of Egypt in 1948 and Iraq in 1953 (Al-'Azmeh, 1998: 211–14), but these were henceforth enforced as statutory law by the modern state. Furthermore, the legal forms that reflect the contemporary Iranian society are not equal with the Islamic medieval jurists' law known as the *shari`ah,* although the government and Islamists claim to be so. These legal forms, even after the Revolution of 1979, are mostly reflecting administrative law. With this conceptual clarification, I can correctly assess the initial impact of European judicial systems on Iranian judiciary.

Therefore, this concrete, historically grounded, causal analysis of a series of specific cases of judicial reform in Iran is mostly focused on different periods, paradigms, policies, causes, successes, dilemmas, challenges, failures and consequences of the failures of one period of judicial reform in Iran compared to other periods during the twentieth century and explanation of political developments as the cause and consequence of judicial reform in relation to social revolutions. In this way, this study is also an important part of an inclusive study about revolution and reform itself and their different meanings in 20th century Iran. I prefer to chart the complexities of this distinct case and its sub-cases and to carry out careful comparisons with similar cases of revolutionary transformation and authoritarian regimes especially in the Middle Eastern countries in order to make particular inferences. My analysis will make the challenges of reform in Iran clearer and modify the possible theories of the relationship between political and judicial structures. The generality, visibility and frequency of judicial reform and reorganization will also provide useful insights into the study of nature of politics and state in Iran and the interaction of society and state.

I will try to do three distinct tasks in this study. First, I intend to show that throughout the twentieth century there has never been rule of law in Iran and in the situation of lawlessness it was very difficult for any administration to pursue a successful judicial reform, regardless of its goals and causes in different periods. No judicial reform by different governments has been able to establish an independent and effective judiciary. Second, judicial reform has been a real possibility but it mostly failed. During the twentieth century there was a real chance that judicial reform would "succeed" in the sense of producing an independent and effective judiciary due to opportunities brought about by social and political movements, the regime changes, and changes in the social settings. My third task is to show that the form of the judicial system varied from one period to another.

1.2. WHAT DO I MEAN BY JUDICIAL REFORM AND REORGANIZATION?

Judicial reform can be defined as the governmental measures designed to affect what is claimed to be a more equitable, impartial and effective judicial system in response to the perceived inadequacies of the existing one. It usually takes the shape of restructuring or reorganization and establishing new institutions on the basis of new ideas and ideologies to increase the power and authority of the government to control the public and/or increase its own legitimacy. Iranians have pursued judicial reform with measures and criteria like judicial performance and backlogs, enforcing law and order, the level of vindications of citizens' civil and constitutional rights, and enacting new laws and systems. The consistency and integrity of the reform plan can also be evaluated. The core of judicial reform typically consists of measures to strengthen the judicial branch of government for different reasons, for example, improve the legitimacy and/or efficiency of the government, to introduce internal control mechanisms to prevent corruption and abuse of power, to exert political control, to meet the challenges of democracy and the rule of law, and recently, to make the legal system more market friendly (Messick, 1999). These reasons are typical of different historical periods and depend on the dominant ideology of that period[6] and dominant ideology of the social movements, if any. It may include seemingly or implicitly opposite goals and ends like due process, improving access to alternative dispute resolution mechanisms, making the judicial branch more independent,[7] to speed the processing of cases, judicialization of politics and professionalizing the bench and the bar in liberal democracies on the one hand and judicial activism, political control and politicization of judiciary in states with dislocated legitimacy or democratic and welfare failure,[8] ideologization[9] of the procedures and laws, consolidation of the power structure, management of the information flow and human resources, politicization of the bench and the bar, and pursuing justice for some in authoritarian regimes on the other. Iranians have pointed to judicial reform in each of these periods with measures like increasing judicial independence,[10] recruitment of new judges by the government, judicial training, court- administration and case management, providing alternative dispute resolution, providing access to and availability of justice for all, and fighting corruption.

Change in the following areas is part of the judicial reform when and only when it is related to the measures mentioned above: 1) the legal order that includes basic norms, long term processes of normative reconstruction, customs, and the constitution. In explaining the pattern of socio-legal change, the concept of constitutional politics (Arjomand, 1992, 2003) will serve as a mechanism of social selection in critical historical conjunctures; 2) legal regime or legal school that makes clear how law is made, interpreted, changed, and developed, what are the sources of law[11] and what are the legal logic and legal reasoning; 3) judicial structure that includes legal institutions and organizations like different kinds of courts (primary, appellate and supreme), prosecution, division of jurisdiction, judicial research centers, civil or human rights NGOs that are focused on legal matters, attorney's offices, bar associations and law schools that objectify legal profession; 4) the relations of judicial institutions on one hand and political, economic, religious and cultural institutions on the other; 5) legal administration and mechanisms; and 6) laws including customary (Geertz, 1963: 220–246), constitutional, statutory and ministerial regulations especially laws related to judicial processes. These changes in different aspects of judicial system may be classified as procedural, organizational, disciplinary or professional, structural and supportive (Carey, 1981: 7). When sociologists usually talk about "law," as they discuss economy, politics or culture, they mostly mean the phenomenon of law as the order of human behavior (Kelsen, 1961: 3) that includes all those six realms mentioned above.

Judicial reform may include or overlap with court reform and reorganization of the judiciary (with the goals like facilitation of access to judicial arenas and decreasing the case load congestion and backlogs [Gambitta & May, 1982: 69]), legal reform (focusing on doctrinal substance and laws), administrative or procedural reform (Wheeler & Whitcomb, 1977: 12), rule-making procedures reform (Weinstein, 1977), politico-judicial reform (focusing on the relation between political and judicial institutions[12]) and manipulation in the ideology of the legal system (e.g. grounding all aspects of judicial and legal affairs in Islamic practices and principles)[13] -in this case, Islamicization-when these reforms are pursued by the government. Therefore, legal change (as is studied in *The Challenge of Law Reform* by Arthur T. Vanderbilt) that is not through the state will not be included in the subject matter.[14] Constitutional reform (as is studied in Zurcher, 1951; Smith, 1997; and Brown, 2002), where related to judicial reform, will be included in the subject matter. The studies of legal, constitutional and judicial reform have some overlaps and each one is an independent area of research. In this study I will only cover single idea of judicial reform in 20th century Iran and legal and constitutional reform will be discussed only when they have overlaps with judicial reform.

Legal change can be part of the ideological change or change of the laws that culminate to judicial reform, and it also can be the consequence of judicial reform when the change in political-judicial relation leads to legal change. Legal change is mostly studied in the areas of law and religious studies, as in Horowitz's study on Islamic law reform (1994), while judicial reform is studied in macro-sociology of law and political sociology. Legal change can also be considered as interlinked with social change and studied in sociology of law (Watson, 1983). Legal change only includes changes in constitutional and statutory law and judicial doctrine, while judicial reform includes legal change and 1) reconstruction of justice through change(s) in judicial policy making, 2) change in judicial system that entail establishing new relationships between different branches of power like legislative and judicial, 3) establishing institutions or ways for vindication or extension of the legal rights of citizens and implementing the dynamics of institutional change, and 4) realigning the court system.

Constitutional reform is more comprehensive than legal and judicial reforms and extends to political and social structure. Discussions on constitutional reform include judicial review, constitutionalism, ideologization of constitution, and constitutional jurisprudence (Brown, 2002). Judicial reform and constitutional reform may overlap with regard to legal change and the relations of judicial institutions on one hand and political, cultural, economic and social institutions on the other. I will consider constitutional reform in Iran especially in two periods of the Constitutional movement and Islamic revolution as far as creation or changes of the Iranian constitutions of 1907 and 1979 are related to judicial reform.

When I use the term 'judicial reform' in this study, I do not use it as a normative term. Hence, any considerable organizational, structural and procedural change in the judiciary, whether it is secular or religious, pursued by the law educated elite or revolutionaries, based on any legal regime, and with any consequences is considered a kind of judicial reform in my study.

1.3. FOUR PERIODS OF JUDICIAL REFORM IN 20TH CENTURY IRAN

This study is not a history of Iran's judiciary system but an interpretive and analytical sociological study of judicial reform and reorganization in 20th century Iran. I will focus on how political and social reforms or revolutions led to developments in the area of jurisprudence and judiciary. Judicial reform in Iran has always been caused and shaped by political developments.

The contemporary political and legal history of Iran can be divided into four different periods i.e. the post Constitutional Revolution era (1906–1925), modernization era (1925–1979), post Islamic Revolution era (1979–1989) and post Khomeini or post-charismatic era (1989-). Judicial reforms have usually happened a few years after the establishment of new regimes, dynasties or change of leaders. In this categorization, change in ideological developments, social movements, social revolutions, legal regimes, social and political processes and critical events are considered.

Each of these periods begins and ends (except the last one) with an important event: the victory of Constitutional Revolution (1906), transition from Qājār to Pahlavi Dynasty (1925) and its aftermath, victory of the Islamic Revolution (1979) and the death of Khomeini (1989). Judicial reforms began respectively in 1911, 1927, 1979 and 1994. Iran's judiciary system endures concurrent developments in Iranian polity, society and culture in those periods. Each of the political regimes of these periods has its constitution, totally new or revised.

In each period, the emphasis differs with the overcoming concepts, agenda and discourses of the public sphere in developing and developed societies. Developing societies have had different responses to those concepts or agenda propagated from developed ones: adoption, rejection or eclectically selection. Common elements of judicial reform under the influence of different elements of this responsive framework include instituting procedural reform, improving the administration of the courts, establishing alternative dispute resolution mechanisms, expanding access to justice, strengthening the role of bar associations, and developing and upgrading judicial training and legal education (Rowat, et al., 1995:3). Each kind of judicial reform is based on different synthesis of these factors and different policies to pursue them.

In each of these four periods, the emphasis of Iranian society and polity differs with the overcoming concepts and agenda of the official public sphere and political elite. Modernity, centralization and authoritative development, Islamism, and authoritarianism/partial democracy are the main agendas of the Iranian polity in these periods respectively. Modernization, rationalization, ideologization and politicization of all governmental bodies are different social and political processes parallel to those agendas.

The model of judicial reform in the first decades of the 20th century Iran is different in important respects from the judicial reform in the end of this century. The judicial reform in international arena in the first decades of 20th century was directed to state building, centralization and modernization of the judicial procedure and this is what exactly pursued in Iran in those decades. The motivations of judicial reform in international arena in the final decades of 20th century are to enforce clear rules, to promote good governance, to create an independent and impartial judicial system, to support legal reform, and to promote economic and social development[15] that are totally different from ideological judicial reform in Iran in the same period. An effective judiciary in the international paradigm is supposed to apply and enforce laws and regulations impartially, predictably and efficiently in its ideal form. In this period, the goal of developing and implementing judicial reform programs, as a part of larger packages of reform, with the help of international institutions is to achieve sustainable economic growth and social and political development based on empowerment, opportunity, and security for all citizens.

Judicial reform in Iran will be explained in the context of four widespread processes of modernization, state rebuilding, ideologization, and politicization of governmental institutions/personalization of power that each of them was going on in the mentioned four periods during 20th century Iran respectively. The period of 1906–25 is the modernization era. In this period, the main issue of the intellectuals and political elite is to modernize all educational, economic, social and political institutions, governmental or non-governmental (Qāsemi Pouyā, 1998: chap. 4). The main social and political process between 1925 and 1979 is limited to state building process that is only one aspect of modernization. The Pahlavis established a powerful centralized state and extended its functions. Islamicization is the crucial feature of Iranian society after the Islamic Revolution. This process extended to every aspect of Iranian society including educational, judicial, economic and political aspects and even life-styles. The post Khomeini era can be described by authoritarian politicization of governmental institutions like military, police, judiciary and intelligence and personalization of power. Dominant political cultures and ideologies in each of these four periods, i.e. modernism, secularism, Islamism, and authoritarianism respectively made the political elite perceive the existing system as inadequate and set in motion different reforms including judicial reform. This does not mean that ideology itself was actually primary cause. Social revolutions based on the mentioned ideologies are the engines of these reforms.

In transition from each of these four periods to another, the main characteristics of each period change: the agenda of the time and the main answer to it, the model of the judiciary to cope with, the goal, causes and consequences of the judicial reform, the ideal type of the law, the system of law, and the role of the judges. Each period has its critical social and political event.

Iranian judiciary has been suffering from a lack of administrative and oversight capacity, a poorly defined court organizational structure, partisan justice, deficient training, lack of funds, low level access to justice, case delays and backlogs, administrative inefficiency, outdated resource management system, the weak institutional capacity of the courts, slow pace of judicial reform in some periods, disregarding human rights, corruption and procedural problems in the whole 20th century. The real challenge facing the Iranian judicial sector in this century is resistance against or demonizing any kind of reform in a legal and professional way. Iranian reformers have always been crying for due process, judicial review, judicial training, respect for the independence of the judiciary and legal aid reform. The main question of this study is why the goals of judicial reform i.e. due process and rule of law have not been implemented in one century of social movements, state building and debate about the problems of and solutions for these goals.

With the study of the paradoxical, truncated and often flimsy manner in which judicial reform was pursued in Iran, I wish to highlight the place of judicial reform in the whole reform and revolutionary movements in Iran during the twentieth century. Iran's economic advances in this century have more or less occurred without the benefits of a vital and continuous tradition of political and legal reform. The economic developments could not create a social base for further political and social reforms.

This study also reminds us that ideas matter. The ideas of change and reform presented to Iranian society prior to real reform in the physical and social world are not of lesser significance than structure of classes or state. During a period in which the Iranians have been facing the rise of the Western civilization and experiencing its impact and decline or underdevelopment of their own society i.e. the 20th century, a study of the Iranian response to the development and power of the West in judicial respects has some significance. Iranian society has striven to internalize these developments and modernize but has not always been successful. Today Iranian intellectuals in Iran and abroad are less enthusiastic about the procedure and direction, causes and consequences, and prospects and limitations of reform in the whole 20th century Iran. They are mostly concentrated on the aftermaths of the reform movement that began in the 1990's, its strategies and tactics and a way out of the chaos that the authoritarian regime has sustained.

The mistrust of reason and the inclination to use its achievements as the output of an infidel or stranger civilization, while the public remains largely ignorant of its inherent features and consequences continues to de-institutionalize abstract and non-embedded ideas on any kind of reform. Iranian reformers have had great inclination to institutionalize those ideas but they lacked deliberated agendas, forums, policies and networks to do so. Institutions and policies that accomplish due process in courts and judicial procedures are good examples of this intention.

I will seriously take the political regime and social setting of each period seriously into consideration for explaining the trend and fate of the judicial reform, because judicial reform does not happen in vacuum. Independence and accountability are not only functions of horizontal political relationships among the branches of government, but also influenced by vertical relationships between state and society. For example, a free press and NGOs focused on legal issues simultaneously can establish greater accountability of judicial institutions to society, and cultivate greater public trust through publicity of the process of judicial determinations, itself a source of independence from the other branches of government.

1.4 METHODOLOGY

This study is concerned with understanding (in a Weberian sense) societal dynamics of an important social structure, i.e. Iran's judiciary and the interaction of the country's politico-social structure and judicial decisions and actions.[16] The subject matter of this study is not judicial structure as a timeless world of facts or judicial actions as a timeless world of meanings but social history of judicial change. I want to understand the relationship of personal judicial decisions and actions on the one hand and judicial organization on the other "as something that is continuously constructed in time" (Abrams, 1982: 16). The research strategy of this study is "case-oriented multi-causal/analytical interpretive comparative method." In this section I will elaborate on each aspect of my method.

Case-oriented. Every period of judicial reform in the 20th century Iran may be considered as a case and will be compared to other periods of judicial reform in Iran. The uniqueness and authenticity of a period of historical development define a case. Therefore this study is not a statistical, variable-oriented or simple case study. It does not also presume large range evolutionary scheme, uni-linear developments, universal stages and causal master keys. This study does not use parallels and analogies for the construction of ideal types and generalizations.

Multi-causal. In my empirical generalizations, I will use a combination of John Stuart Mill's method of agreement and the indirect method of difference in order to establish likely causes and to formulate theoretical conclusions by controlled comparisons. I will control for common social and political changes and administrative developments. Using method of agreement, I will consider several sub-cases having in common judicial reform and the hypothesized *n* causal factors of judicial reform like state building, economic development, importing ideas and social institutions, social movements, dictates from the West, administrative manipulation, and justice oriented reforms. These cases vary in other ways that might have seemed causally relevant. After elimination of n-1 to n-x explanatory factors, I will introduce the circumstance or circumstances (x) in which all the instances agree as the cause or causes of judicial reform. I will use this method to support my interpretation of a causal sequence in the case of Iran by taking into consideration different sub-cases as independent cases.

This study is basically inductive because initial theoretical notions about state building, rationalization, modernization and ideologization in 20th century Iran serve as guides in the examination of causally relevant similarities and differences. Examining empirical cases of judicial reform in Iran will allow me to determine which of the theoretically relevant similarities and differences are operative. I will focus on polity, state structure, social structure, and legal system in Iran to learn about the processes and mechanisms of judicial reorganization in this society.

Analytical. Considering historical and cultural turns of methodology of social sciences in the 1990's (Ragin, 2000), this study like any other case study will be a starting point for doing sociology in an analytical way and building or rebuilding theories sensitive to cases, not necessarily grand ones. To do this, I will try to uncover the cultural foundations of reform in Iran's judiciary system in all of those four periods of judicial development by unraveling and dissecting the specific structural conditions. In this historical analysis, the explanation of why these judicial reforms happened is inextricably contained within accounts of how judicial changes happened. "How it happened" question demands answers in terms of manifold, sequential and cumulative structuring (Abrams, 1982: 310).

Interpretive. This study is both historically interpretive–focusing upon the construction of concepts and reconstruction (Kalberg, 1994: 5) of my case—and causally analytic—testing of hypotheses or the formation of theoretical statements or causal models (Kalberg, 1994: 5). I will also offer limited historical generalization sensitive to context when possible, while individualizing the case focused upon, rendering it more visible and preserving its historical particularity (Kalberg, 1994: 6). I will pursue the dialectics between the logic of judicial reform and the actions of political elites, intellectuals and judges, where applicable.

This interpretive historical study examines the integrity, complexity, historical development and social context of judicial reform in 20th century Iran. The interpretive aspect of this study will not lead me to a highly abstract and non-empirical work that traditionally has been called interpretive. There is no necessary contradiction between doing empirically based causal analysis and interpreting cases historically (Ragin, 1987:35). Historical narrative and contextual comparisons across cases will provide a hope of discerning causes of judicial reform in the 20th century Iran. To delineate the causes of judicial reform, I cannot compare successful and failed judicial reforms in the Middle East because there is not any completely successful one in the region. I will adhere to causal analytical model to test my causal hypothesis and generate a new explanatory generalization. This does not mean that I will not pursue causality through a chronicle of events, if applicable. My goal is to achieve a reasoned interpretation of the design of long-term judicial change.

Comparative. I will use comparative materials to conduct parallel demonstrations of theory and to analyze causal mechanisms across sets of comparable cases, i.e. different periods of judicial reform in Iran's case, or universalizing, encompassing or variation-finding strategies to aid comprehension of diverse historical trajectories (Ragin, 1987: 34). This study differs from previous studies of judicial power, which have mainly relied on single case studies that address specific research interests and tend to stress the unique conditions that lead to judicial reform and reorganization in specific countries and specific periods. To achieve a better understanding of the judicial reform in each period, its magnitude and the conditions that facilitate or inhibit it in general and magnitude and conditions of judicial reform in 20th century Iran in particular, comparative analysis is a must. The fundamental characteristics of the judiciary and formal framework within which they operate are also considered. The number of cases is determined by the research questions. The cases selected clearly show sufficient similarities to make a comparison viable. They also display some crucial variations within the same country.

The logic of this study may be labeled as macro-causal analysis and not parallel demonstration of theory or contrast of contexts.[17] This kind of analysis manipulates groups of cases, if available, to control sources of variation to make causal inferences. I turned to this multivariate analysis in order to validate causal statements about macro-level structures, phenomena and processes for which inherently there are many factors and not enough cases. I will not use those comparative strategies that are centered on extensive use of ideal types to guide my interpretation of empirical cases.

There are two methodological questions that I will try to answer in my study: To what degree should or would my case-oriented study strive to use compatible orienting concepts like reform? And to what degree should I place my case(s) in a larger context and how far should this contextualization extend? Can it extend to the scale of formulating typologies or construction of historical types?

This periodization of judicial reform history suggests two sets of comparisons. The first set would compare the judicial development and reconstruction of judicial regimes that bear the mark of the ideologies of revolutionary social transformation under the differential impact of the revolutionary movements, i.e. Constitutional and Islamic Revolutions. The impact is maximal in the case of Islamic Revolution, which led to Islamicization of polity including the judiciary. The popular movement of 1979 expected to totally change the judicial affairs. The impact is much less strong in the case of Constitutional Revolution, where it was under the pressure of an elitist movement and an influential popular ideology was absent. Further comparisons derive from the diametrically opposite ideological foundations of these two sets of judicial reforms after 1906 and 1979.

The second set of comparisons would contrast these four sets of judicial reforms with the political and social reconstructions. My study focuses as far as possible on the observable relationship between politics, society and justice (Friedman, 1975), and attention will also paid to the description of their interactive development over time. Here the extent and character of transplantation as the model of the first and second period and Islamicization as the model of the third and fourth period of the judicial organization will be set in the typological context of two secular and Islamic state-building and further contrasted by assessing the relative strength of their "bearers," to use a Weberian analytical term, be they domestic or transnational, in relation to other domestic and external forces in the judicial politics of 20th century Iran. The two sets of comparisons can then be brought together within a unified analytical framework centered on the selective transformation of law, whether from the modern world (Watson, 1993; Tamanaha, 2001: 107–20) or traditional Islam. This study offers an opportunity for studying the variations in the pattern of judicial transplantation and transformation of distinctive judicial models of four different eras in Iranian history.

1.5 LITERATURE REVIEW AND THEORY

The interaction of law and society is rich with values, norms, ideologies, policies and agendas. As far as law defines the scope, powers and limitations of different elements of governance as the obligatory institutions of public agencies, and defines the permissible relations among legal persons and between legal persons and entities of governance, it is totally involved in any social and political action.

It is hard to find a theoretical point of view to explain successfully changes or reforms in all of those six aspects of judicial system in the four periods of judicial reform in the 20th century Iran. With respect to theory, I will try to find 1) a general theory to explain important aspects of the judicial reform in the 20th century Iran, 2) aspects which have been the most important or dominant ones in each period and 3) theoretical frameworks that will specifically present the best explanation of that aspect beside the general theory.

The theoretical framework of this study must help me to "determine how and in what way particular ideas, acts, and institutions sustain, fail to sustain or even inhibit" (Geertz, 1968: 1–2) a special context of law and legal system. The change of ideas, acts and institutions in the realm of judiciary can be explained by resort to the change in social and political structure and polity. The developments in the judiciary system are under the influence of the social and political changes in the whole society. The question is "to what extent judicial changes can be explained in terms of legal as well as non-legal factors.

To answer the questions presented in the first section of this chapter, I should have a theory of judicial reform and examine the dynamics and causes of judicial change by considering and examining different hypotheses about it. I am not only interested in the possible causes of judicial reform to answer the question of why judicial reform happened in Iran but also in the consolidation of new legal culture and legal structure in each period to answer the question of how judicial reform happened. In Iran's case, judicial reform first happens during the restructuring of power and then follows by establishing new judicial institutions. The state rebuilding process includes restructuring of power, judicial reform that follows by institutionalization of power and again another phase of judicial reform. The theory should help us to understand how and why judicial reform happens and how and why one phase of judicial reform is replaced with another one.

Literature Review

To have an understanding of the judicial reform and reorganization in a general way, we should look into theories of judicial change and social, political and cultural theories of law. To build a theory of judicial change we need to look at the interlinks and 'interactions' of three groups of theories, not these theories by themselves: 1) theories of social change, e.g. change from simple to complex, traditional to modern, undeveloped to developed, or vice versa, 2) theories of political change, e.g. from centralized to decentralized, from authoritarian to democratic or vice versa, and 3) theories of legal and judicial procedural change. The thematic links between first and third group of theories are changes in 1) judicial and legal procedures, 2) functions of the law like defining social relationships, 3) methods for taming naked force and maintenance of order, 4) disposition of trouble cases, 5) maintaining adaptability (Hoebel, 1954: 275), 6) social control, 7) and directing social change and dispute settlement. Enforcement procedures, codification, transplantation (usually from above) and judicial policies are some of the thematic links between second and third groups of theories.

Maine, Durkheim, and Gluckman build the links between the first and third groups of theories by classification of societies; the development of legal and judicial systems in these scholar's view are closely related to the differences between kin-based and territorially based organization (Maine, 1861), between mechanical and organic social cohesion (Durkheim, 1933), and between tribal and differentiated societies (Gluckman, 1965). Another way of building this link is to classify legal and judicial systems into a whole social series in which every legal and judicial development belongs to a specific stage of history (Diamond, 1935, 1951, 1965) or a specific stage of society (Hoebel, 1954). Hoebel emphasizes on the development of judicial systems as organs of government for law enforcement due to development of societies from simple to complex and from decentralized to centralized (Hoebel, 1954: 289). Malinowski explains the relationship of law and society by focusing on reciprocal obligations, complementary rights, and reputation. Law, for Malinowski, is embodied in all binding obligations and its main function is social control. Hence nothing but an account of change in social relations will adequately explain change in the content and workings of its legal and judicial systems. The underlying premise of these theories is that there is an intimate relationship between law and society, that law is part of social life in general and must be treated analytically as such (Moore, 1978: 218).

The socialist attitude is that law in its entirety is an instrument of ruling class and social policy and law, whether civil or common, Islamic or Jewish, Indian or Japanese reflect a capitalist, bourgeois, imperialist, exploitative society, economy, and government (Merryman, 1969: 4). The milder version of this attitude is that law embodies but does not clearly state capitalist ideologies.

Parallelism between political and judicial systems of dispute settlement and pursuing the role of legal authority in uni-centric and multi-centric political systems are some formal ways of linking second and third groups of theories mentioned above (Gulliver, 1963; Bohannan, 1967). Uni-centric and multi-centric political systems settle disputes through the exercise of political authority and multi-social authority respectively. Focusing on agency theory of action in the dispute settlement side of procedure, the role of the intermediary, the negotiator, the mediator, the conciliator, and the arbitrator will become more prominent on a scale of increasing authoritativeness. Law resides in the minds and practices of people in a society and in the compulsion imposed by statutes and commands of the sovereign. In this way, the relationship between political structure and procedure comes through clearly.

There are five different socio-legal theories for explaining the interaction between political and legal structures or systems. The first one is Hayek's theory of grown (spontaneous, endogenous) and made (organized, exogenous) *order* (Hayek, 1973). This theory studies developments of norms and orders while considering "a multiplicity of elements of various kinds related to each other" (Hayek, 1973, Vol.1: 36). Hayek's theory answers the question of origin of orderly structures, whether indigenous or exogenous. On the basis of Hayek's theory, we can ask what properties a legal system possesses so that the separate actions of the individuals do not produce an overall order. The state, in Hayek's view, is charged with keeping in order an operating structure, enforcing the rules (indigenous and exogenous) on which that order rests and rendering other services which the spontaneous order cannot produce adequately (Hayek, 1973, Vol.1: 48). Hayek does not discuss the dynamics of "made" or exogenous order-whether through national or foreign states-that is prominent in the developing states. Hayek mostly explains the mechanism of change in the legal order, one of six elements of judicial reform that were mentioned before.

The second theory is Habermas's theory of *legitimation*. Habermas believes in "internal connection of law with the political power" (Habermas, 1998: 133). He focuses on the sanctioning, organizing and executive power and protecting capacity of the state. The authority of a state-organized system of courts relies on the sanctioning power of the state (Habermas, 1998: 134). The administration and further development of this system draws on the organizational capacity of the state. This is the state that begets legitimacy for the procedure of lawmaking: "Legal community has need of both a collective self-maintenance and an organized judiciary" (Habermas, 1998: 133) that makes the state necessary. In Habermas's view "political power is not externally juxtaposed to law but is rather presupposed by law and itself established in the form of law" (Habermas, 1998: 134). Law and state, in his point of view, have a mutual transaction: law legitimizes the enforcement of power, and state makes use of law to fulfill its own functions (Habermas, 1998: 135); law authorizes the social power and the social power sanctions the law (Habermas, 1998: 143). Tilly goes in the same direction when he discusses the crisis, challenges and problems of modern national states like penetration, integration, participation, identity, legitimacy and distribution. Establishing legal system helps these states to "create loyalty to and confidence in the established structure of political institutions . . . and to ensure regular conformity to rules and regulations issued by the agencies authorized within the system" (Tilly, 1975: 609). This effort is directed to decrease the crisis of problems of illegitimacy.

The third theory is Mann's theory of *entwined development of social forces*. In his view, the interactions of social forces of power i.e. ideological, economic, military and political forces change one another's inner shapes as well as their outward trajectories (Mann, 1993: 1–2). Michael Mann sees the law as a phenomenon that occupies the ideological interface between church, state and commerce in the framework of nation-states (Mann, 1993: 38). Thus law has a dual role: expressing the state's will and embodying customary and divine law (Mann, 1993: 65). In Mann's theory, judiciary is not an independent social force but cement between other forces.

The fourth one is Weber's theory of *legal domination*. Law and state, in his view, are entwined only in the third type of general development of law i.e. imposition of law by secular or theocratic powers in the era of modern nation-state establishment. In the first and second stages of Western civilization, Western societies experienced "charismatic legal revelation through law prophets, and empirical creation and finding of law by legal notables" (Weber, 1954: 303). The fourth stage may be viewed as "systematic elaboration of law and professionalized administration of justice by persons who have received their legal training in a learned and formally logical manner" (Weber, 1954: 303). Secular and theocratic powers in the beginning of nation-state era and still in developing societies respond to administrative and political exigencies by imposition or enactment of laws. They may promote the rationalization of law-getting, free from administrative arbitrariness and disturbance by concrete privileges, and offering firm guaranties of the legally binding character of contracts (Weber, 1954: 268) through legal enactment. This rationalization does not merely imply the separation of legal institutions from political institutions in this stage. Imposition of laws by the state increases the formal rationality of legal procedure (Bendix, 1962: 399) and allows the establishment of a national law system and the curtailment of an arbitrary exercise of power. Weber's concept of legal change is mainly reflected in the shift from substantively rational to formally rational law (Sutton, 2001: 129).

The fifth one is Kelsen's *positivist* theory of law. Kelsen views the state as a legal person created by a national legal order: "the state as juristic person is a personification of this community or the national legal order constituting this community" (Kelsen, 1961: 181). In this view, "the community we call 'state' is 'its' legal order" (Kelsen, 1961: 181, quotations are Kelsen's).

These theories together, except Kelsen's, will help the researcher of socio-legal systems to discuss about the origins, dynamics and the roles of the judiciary system and judicial reform in the greater context of social and political order, and the impact of political development on the judiciary and legal system. Kelsen's theory makes the analytical borders between state, society, and community ambiguous and leaves no place for their tensions and interactions. The four important factors in the interaction of legal and political systems i.e. order, legitimacy, social forces and domination are recognized in those four theories on socio-legal structure. In the literature on judicial reform and reorganization and the case studies on this subject, one or some of the four mentioned factors are ignored. In this study I will also consider the changing nature of law, the changing nature of legislative bodies (Hayek, 1973, Vol.1: 72–90), the legal regime (Jacobs, 1996), the changing paradigms of law (Habermas, 1998: Ch. 9), the purpose and functions of law, judge and legislation

(Hayek, 1973, Vol.1: 94–121), different sources of law (Watson, 1998), and the dynamics of legal change (Fuller, 1964) to pursue the interaction of state and judicial system.

Theories of Judicial Change

What sociological state of play do I challenge? What historical interpretations do I contest? What concepts of judicial reform do I counter-pose to prevailing views? I will identify the issues at stake in this subject and the challenges in meeting them. I will set out my own theoretical point of view and will provide a brief overview of each of the contributions to this topic. To establish a specific theory of judicial reform, first we have to look at the theories on the logic of legal and judicial change in general. These theories can be categorized in four basic theories:

1) *Mirror theories*, whether strong or weak, and loose or tight, that depict legal and judicial changes as dependent to other forces of societies external to law and judiciary, like class relations, national spirit, power relations, and market (Ewald, 1995: 489–493);
2) I*solation theory* or autonomy of law and judiciary that depict legal and judicial systems as isolated islands-even in the same society-that their developments are more under the influence of internal forces of legal and judicial domain rather than external ones, and can be explained without reference to social, economic and political factors (this is the unspoken theory of most of the Iranian clerics and judiciary officials and what they understand from independence of judiciary[18]);
3) *Functionalist theories* that focus on the functions of law instead of legal structure and explain the judicial change by resort to functional changes. Fuller's functionalist conception of law is helpful for explaining the dynamics of legal change. In his view, nothing can count as law unless it is capable of performing law's essential function of guiding behavior. To be capable of performing this function, a system of rules must satisfy the following principles: (P1) the rules must be expressed in general terms; (P2) the rules must be publicly promulgated; (P3) the rules must be prospective in effect; (P4) the rules must be expressed in understandable terms; (P5) the rules must be consistent with one another; (P6) the rules must not require conduct beyond the powers of the affected parties; (P7) the rules must not be changed so frequently that the subject cannot rely on them; and (P8) the rules must be administered in a manner consistent with their wording. Fuller's principles express the internal

logic of functioning laws (Fuller, 1964). This is not enough. For a law to be functioning, it must be 1) responsive to the serious needs and desires of the citizens of the state, 2) comprehensible, and 3) comprehensible to the persons affected by it;[19] and

4) *Inter-societal isolation theory* that views the judicial changes as the result of interactions between judicial systems of different societies rather than interactions between different aspects of one society. Watson's transplantation theory is a good example of inter-societal isolation theory of legal and judicial change. Watson thinks that rules can be readily transported from society to society and law is, at least sometimes, isolated from social and economic changes (Watson, 1983). In his theory, "there is no close, inherent, necessary relationship between legal rules and the society in which they operate" (Watson, 1983: 1136). The ups and downs of judicial reform after the Islamic Revolution based on return to traditional Islamic law showed that planned transplantation is not the only cause of judicial and legal reform.

My theory in this realm is a combination of *weak and loose mirror theory* (legal and judicial changes are closely related to legal and non-legal/social and political forces, and various interests of groups and individuals are represented in the legal and judicial systems according to their strength in the society), *weak isolation theory* (judicial system in any society is peculiar to it and reflects the desires and needs of a specific society; it is the result of social engineering and exists to institutionalize dispute situations and to validate decisions given in the appropriate process which itself has the specific object of inhibiting unregulated conflict in a special society) and *transitional transplantation* theory (transitional societies borrow some sections of their judicial and legal systems from others and internalize them) in the case of societies under modernization project. These elements explain interactional (law-society), institutional and epochal aspects of my theory. The functional theory cannot help me in this special case because it is a key that opens every door in theoretical issues and hence cannot open any. I will try to find out how legal change in Iran is directed to satisfy Fuller's functional principles (Fuller, 1964). In this study, I want to know if law-making in Iran satisfies these principles and if the approved and enforced laws and legal reforms are consistent with the legal regime.

Weak and Loose Mirror Theory

My theory of judicial structure is based on legal realism. In this theoretical framework, researchers urge more attention to the social context of the law. Based on weak and loose mirror theory, I will place the legal and judicial systems in their larger social and political context. I want to understand how courts and judicial systems relate to their social and political environment. Laws and courts are firmly embedded in social and political structures and practices. In this study, I want to emphasize on the role of law and legal institutions in consolidation of the political regimes and maintaining social order, the ways legal professionals stand as gatekeepers to legal institutions, the links that judges have with politics and the manner in which courts are policymakers and become entangled in political challenges.

The process of modernization or Islamicization in a society cannot be limited to special aspects of life. When it begins for example in economic or political domains, cultural and social and legal domains will be influenced. Judicial modernization or Islamicization also extends to and includes modernization or Islamicization of the legal order, legal regime, judicial structure, politico-legal relationship, judicial administration and laws.

Superficial modernization (oil exporting countries experience), reactionary modernization (Nazi German experience), authoritarian modernization (some of Asian Tigers like South Korea), and totalitarian modernization (Soviet experiencc) are alternative processes for explaining the political and legal developments in early 20th century Iran. There are also popular, authoritarian and totalitarian Islamicizations in late 20th century Iran. Calling some developments superficial in the case of modernization imply that these developments were only objectification of imported ideas, and the changes in the social, political and economic structures were not internally motivated and pursued. In this kind of development, imported ideas and institutions have no root in the society. Ralf Dahrendorf pointed out that Nazi Germany shows the future of the less developed societies. Using Dahrendorf's idea, Jeffrey Herf believes that "as long as nationalism remains a potent force something like reactionary modernism will continue to confront us" (Herf, 1984: x). The common base of analyzing Iranian society on the basis of reactionary modernization and reactionary Islamicization are ideas like anti-modernism, politics of cultural despair, longing for a simpler and pre-industrial life, strife for return to glorious past, gap between ideology and praxis, seeking cultural revolution and irrational ideas present in both German nationalism (Herf, 1984: Ch. 1) and Iranian authoritarianism and Islamism.

Totalitarian and authoritarian modernizations are mostly defined as industrial and economic developments without democracy and liberalism (Arendt, 1973). The differences between Iranian authoritarianism and other kinds of local or regional authoritarianisms lie in different facts like

Shi'ite religion as the religion of majority, authoritarian political culture, lack of industrialization, and ongoing social movements in different periods of the 20th century.

Iranian society confronted with the early phases of superficial modernization in Qājār period. It then transfers to an authoritative modernization in Pahlavi dynasty and harsh reaction to modernization in the era of hierocracy under Khomeini's rule. It then goes back to authoritative modernization in post-charismatic era. Each of these traditions of modernization and anti-modernization consists of a coherent and meaningful set of metaphors, familiar words and phrases, agendas in public sphere, and emotionally laden expressions.

Different social movements in contemporary Iran were not motivated only by rejection of modernity. We can always observe a mixture of superficial and reactionary modernity combined with dreams of the past. State building, codification and secularization are the most important elements in Iranian modernization. Iranian inwardness that is directed to solve the identity problem in the nation-state era co-exists with Iranian outwardness that is directed to overcome the challenges of underdevelopment.

Weak Autonomy Theory

Among Weber, Marx, Maine and Durkheim as the main theoreticians of legal change (Appendix B) whose theories can be categorized as weak isolation theories of legal change, Weber's theory of legal change is the most relevant theory to explain the development in legal order in 20th century Iran. Weber does not identify different or evolutionary stages of legal change; he sees only tensions among formally irrational, substantively irrational, substantively rational and formally rational stages that are different spheres of life in a specific society. Those two stages of Maine i.e. no law, customary and era of codes, two stages of Durkheim i.e. repressive and restitutive law, and five stages of history in Marx historical point of view that is imposed on legal system by infrastructure cannot explain different periods of legal order in Iranian society. Weberian model also will help me to explain the pathology of legal culture in Iranian society in the time period of study. Hayek's theory on spontaneous order and constructivism (Hayek, 1973) may help me to study developments of norms and orders.

The developments in the Iranian judiciary system are comparable to the social and political changes in the whole society. As the social and cultural patterns change among urban population, both civil and *shari`ah* law change to internalize those developments. During different periods of secularization (substantive and formal) and Islamicization (substantive and formal) state and *shari`ah* laws conform to the changes of power structure.

The change of power structure has direct effect on judiciary system. Courts often reflect the degree of centralization, specialization and accessibility of the government they are a part.

As the state becomes more centralized and authoritarian, the judiciary becomes more and more dependent to the state and part of the state structure. The dynamic relation of the *shari'* and state courts and increasingly dependence of these courts to the state shows this direction. This challenge leads to a point where all *shari'* courts become part of the bureaucracy of the judiciary after the Constitutional and Islamic Revolutions.

The form that judicial policies take is strongly under the influence of elites of different periods of judicial reform but influences the ability of state elites to legitimize their policy choices and actions, and legitimize the political regime. Before the fourth period of judicial reform, Iranian public was not so sensitive to the decisions of judiciary but in the 1990's judicial decisions could directly change the public support of each group in the elections. There have also been important power structural and institutional constraints at work within the state political culture that establish the threshold and direction of change. Divided political elite has not let the judiciary to have a progressive change in the whole 20th century.

Transitional Transplantation

I will not assume, as Watson mentions, a simple mechanical and automatic relationship between law and society with a few admitted but unimportant exceptions (Watson, 1983: 1137). I will study the influences of Western legal and political systems on Iranian one, especially in the first and second periods of judicial reform. Legal and judicial borrowings are the most fertile source of legal and judicial changes in Iran supported by the social and political changes. While transplant bias of Western legal systems was grounded in the legal profession (Ewald, 1995: 499), transplant bias of Iranian legal system in 20th century was grounded in the nature of a transient peripheral society. Iranian lawyers in the previous century could not constitute an elite law-making and law-enforcing group within society. Iranian clergy had this status, while most of its members opposed any transplantation. Legal profession has never been an independent social variable in Iran's social and political developments.

I need a multiple norms model to explain what is happening in Iran's judiciary during 20th century. I am also looking for the socio-economic and political changes that result from the alterations in judicial system and legal rules. In the Iranian legal tradition that most important forms of social rule-making and rule-enforcing (law, politics and religion) are not separated (there is no specific actor in each of these domains), political and legal processes cannot be separated. In this tradition, we can consider hundreds of cases where political processes have moved to determine the outcome of the legal process and vice versa. In other words, law is not absent but is extremely marginalized and weak before other sources of social rule making, i.e. political power. The professional law in Iran cannot be considered the hegemonic pattern of social rule making. Political and social relationships usually determine the legal process, a process that Mattei calls it "rule of political law" (28) opposing rule of traditional and professional law. Formal law in this legal system cannot exert binding on the government. Surrounding circumstances and the need to keep power usually justify the disregard for formal and substantial laws. The outcome of the litigation totally depends on "who is who" in the political world, especially when the clash occurs between the government and individual rights.

What contributions do I hope to make? I hope to contribute to politico-legal approach to judicial reform. The four cases examined in this study fall within different wave of state-building process in the world[20] and are oriented toward different models.[21] I also hope to contribute to the increasing application of the political process approach to explanation of judicial reform.[22] The modest goal of this study is to shed some light on the variation in the trajectories of judicial reform and reorganization in 20th century Iran. I attempt to sketch a framework that may be useful to scholars studying judicial reform in transitional societies. I also attempt to illustrate how legal characteristics and political context interact to influence the trajectories of judicial reform. I hope this study would be provocative to motivate some scholars to undertake other comparative analyses of the judicial reform in intra- and inter- regional scales.

Alternative Specific Theories

Other than my specific theory on Iran, there are five possible alternative theories for explaining the judicial reforms in societies like Iran: 1) dependence theory that explains the reforms in the first and second periods as the dictates of Western colonial powers pursued by a puppet or close-handed regime[23] and ignores the internal dynamics of local society, 2) efficiency theory that illustrates the reforms as mere administrative manipulation of a bureaucratic system (Dubois, 1982) to improve the accountability and efficiency of the judiciary, and mostly ignores the role of ideologies and political culture, 3) materialist theory that puts law on the shelf of superstructure, looks at the change in class structure and ignores the interaction of judiciary and legal profession with the state and society, 4) development theories that emphasizes on economic development as the main cause of social reform, and 5) justice orientation of revolutionaries that focuses on the claimed ends instead of means and usually ignores the due process as the main victim of revolutionary justice.

In dependency theory point of view, Western imperial powers had and continue to have the control over communication technologies and the military might to define less powerful nation's legal system. According to this point of view, states in the modern international system based on market economy are responsible for clarifying and enforcing legal and property rights within their territories. When an exchange occurs across state borders, each state expects the other to provide information about legal rights and to enforce them. Western states demanded that non-Western countries clarify and protect the legal and property rights of individuals (citizens and foreigners alike) within their territories as a precondition for the abolition of colonization and capitulation. It concludes that as non-Western countries codified their rules to clarify legal rights and consolidated the legal authority to enforce these legal rights—a process which I call the institutionalization of a state-based legal system—Western countries abolished capitulation. This argument could be falsified by referring to endeavors of different administrations and parliaments to annul the capitulation. In 1918, Samsām ul-Saltaneh Bakhtiāri annulled the capitulation by issuing a decree. Nullification of capitulation was one of Iran's demands in Paris Peace Conference. Seyyed Ziā cabinet annulled it with a declaration (Zerang, Vol. I, 2002: 353). These annulments did not go into effect until Dāvar's reform that facilitated the official annulment of capitulation.

In efficiency theory, judicial reform is explained with respect to some changes in the chart and high-ranking officials of the judiciary and manipulation of some mechanisms to get rid of backlogs, to expedite the process, and to fight against corruption. Although almost all of the goals and purposes of reform elaborated by different administration and presented in public rhetoric express objects like providing justice and efficiency[24] directed toward efficiency, none of the judicial reforms was successful in expediting the process, reducing backlogs or corruption (even the successful one of Dāvar's), and bringing about rule of law. The Islamic revolutionaries were very successful in the political and cultural arenas and "the administrative, judicial, and coercive apparatuses were reorganized and used for vicious attacks on the life-styles" (Farhi, 1990, 107), but they have always complained about their failure to totally Islamicize the society including the judiciary. Due to this failure Islamicization process has been an unending process in Iranian society.

Materialist theory looks at judicial reform as part of superstructure (Sutton, 2001: 71) and hence, something secondary with subsidiary importance because it considers all laws as an instrument of economic and social policy and reflection of a capitalistic, bourgeois, imperialist, exploitive society, economy and government (Merryman, 1969: 4). Marxian deterministic theory holds that underlying economic forces cause legal phenomena. Although this theory is usually shaped in a non-falsifiable manner, the endeavors of different political regimes to change the judicial system denote the importance of legal and judicial systems for any political regime in Iran. Judicial reforms in different periods are reflections of the given distribution of power and identification of the interests of the powerful with the general interest and to make sure they are never merged. Power groups exercised their domination in terms of legitimating arguments through change in the judiciary system.

Economic development, more or less, has always been going on in Iran from early 20th to early 21st century and is not a characteristic of specific periods. In the highest points of economic development, i.e. 1960's and 1970's, there is no significant judicial reform or reorganization. When the rates of economic development were low in 1980, the endeavors for judicial reform were at their highest points.

Justice oriented explanations were only effective after the Constitutional and Islamic Revolution to justify the reforms in the judiciary and to address some of the grievances but they never paid a crucial role in elaborating the reforms. Almost all decisions for judicial reform immediately after the Islamic Revolution, as it is discussed in the section on revolutionary justice, were to ignore due process that is the core of justice in any judicial system. Even the expected and planned judicial reforms after the Constitutional Revolution were to formally reform the organization framework of the judiciary the administration was not successful to implement the reforms.

Judicial reform in 20th century Iran was 1) the result of internal politics and have to be explained by the necessities of stabilization and/or integration of political organization, and the change in the state structure in the long time-spans, not merely the pressures or dictates of external forces, even it is inspired by changes in other societies that is explained by transitional transplantation, 2) not usually confined to bureaucratic change and relates to the ways of the overall system to maintain itself or disintegrate over time and regulate conflict, and to provide more autonomy for the judicial institution and disengage it from the influence of the high ranking *'ulamā*, whether in secular Pahlavi regime or Islamic regime (Moslem, 2002: 81), 3) not the effect of mere social and economic change but in most circumstances the effect of political developments and changes, 4) the outcome of interaction between state, legal and economic developments and conditions of social order and disorder, and 5) more directed toward social and political control rather than justice. The logic of change, as I showed in previous chapters, is based on the dynamics of political regimes, social settings and legal regime, and not copying reform from other societies.

1.6 BASIC ASSUMPTIONS

My underlying assumptions about law, judiciary and judicial reform, based on my theoretical point of view, are:

1) Law is analytically an independent, autonomous and separate sphere of life like politics, culture and economy that is clear in Weberian tradition of thinking. Economic situations do not automatically give birth to new legal forms; they merely provide the opportunity for the actual spread of a legal technique if it is invented (Weber, 1968: 687). The concept of law, in this study, has no moral connotation and designates a specific technique of social organization. Law and justice are also two different concepts (Kelsen, 1961: 5). Jurisprudence is also an autonomous area of enquiry (Kelsen, 1992: 1). I will not reduce jurisprudence in this study to deliberations of legal policy, as I will not reduce law to social facts (Green, 2003: 385) or to "governmental social control" (Unger, 1976: 127). This, of course does not deny the interactions between different social forces and legal and judicial systems. Law can be the expression of political domination (Appendix II) as well as the social structure. The center of gravity of legal and judicial change lies "not in legislation, nor in juristic science, nor in judicial decisions, but in society itself" (Ehrlich, 1975: Foreword). All spheres of life interact and sometimes change each other. Law in this study will be considered something more than mere reflection of the material interests of social classes or the mirror of society that functions to maintain social order (Tamanaha, 2001: Ch. 5). Most of the Iranian scholars who have been thinking in the framework of Marxist tradition and have written Iran's social history (like Morteza Rāvandi, 1977) have implicitly considered law as part of the superstructure, and legal system has not a significant place in their studies. I will implicitly criticize this Marxist tradition in my study and analyze Iranian society and polity in a multi-factor approach. I will also consider the interaction, in some cases opposition, of law and government in the Middle East (Bozeman, 1971: 78);
2) Law in real life is a subclass of a category called legitimate or normative order (Trubek, 1972: 724). Without denial of metaphysical, mythic or theological understanding of law and jurisprudence, which seek to elevate law or the state into something above and beyond modes of social structures, I will only focus on sociological approach to law and jurisprudence. Law, in this study, is a system of

dynamic norms that its validity has to be simply assumed (Kelsen, 1961: 113; 1992: 56). Laws maintain the *status quo* and provide the impetus for change (Vago, 2006: 1).

3) As Weber write, "when we are concerned with law, legal order, rule of law, we must strictly observe the distinction between a juristic and a sociological point of view."[25] Sociology of law, as the disciplinary base of this study, describes law and jurisprudence in terms of real rules and jurisdictions, not of ought-rules or the validity of rules. In this study, I have nothing to do with validity or non-validity of judicial reforms or laws; I am only concerned about what has been actually happening in the realms of judiciary and law. Using Weber's definition of sociology, we can define sociology of law as the interpretation of judicial and legal actions, which have already been subjected to an interpretation by the acting individuals.
4) The relation between law and state can be well explained in terms of the rise of centralized states and state building process (Appendix II); two major concerns of modern states are stability and legitimacy. The courts are tugged to a greater or lesser degree on the one hand by the value the regime places on stability and on the other by its desire for legitimacy (Jacob, 1996: 391).
5) I will regard legal rule as "a component of an empirical reality" (Albrow, 1975: 17) and concern myself with sociological approach and not mere juristic interpretation;
6) The dynamics of society and law relationship in 20th century is based on the rise of capitalism as the main reason of the rise of legal rationality (Appendix II);
7) I will not found any of my arguments on believing in evolutionary stages of legal change that can be found in the works of Hoebel (1954); I will mostly emphasize on tensions among and interactions of different spheres of life like law and politics and tensions between formally irrational, formally rational, substantially rational and substantially irrational (Appendix II) aspects of law;
8) This study cannot be reduced to the interactions between different branches of government. This study is about the interactions between different facets of society, i.e. interaction between law and politics, law and culture, and social movement and law, especially influence of interest groups on legal order;
9) Political culture, social movements, the structure of the state and social processes like modernization, secularization, and Islamicization effect the content and form of judicial reform in the society;

10) Law is a process. I consider law-making, law-enforcing and social and political orders as human phenomena "matched only by the manipulation, circumvention, remaking, replacing, and unmaking of rules and symbols in which people seem equally engaged" (Moore, 1978: 1);
11) Judicial reform, other than political and social structures, is shaped by ideologies and ideas, indigenous or exogenous. Iranian intellectuals and political activists were under the influence of different intellectual paradigms in different periods of 20th century. When accomplished, judicial reform as part of the baggage of the new judiciary is a new entity that has its own functions and effects.
12) Legal institutions, other than ideologies and ideas, are also vehicles for the expression of interests (Moore, 1978: 238). They are reflections of a social order and instruments for controlling society (Clifford-Vaughan and Scotford-Norton, 1967). Therefore non-legal institutions can be used for airing legal controversies. Law resides not only in the people's minds but in their practices (Austin, 1954). Law is both a prescriptive and descriptive device.
13) Focusing on immediate local causes that impel any legal and judicial change, contrary to Watson (1983: 1122), would not cause one to overlook similar changes in other systems and in other times; similar changes logically would have different causes. Concentration on one legal system, again contrary to Watson (1983: 1122), does not necessarily mean that it is easy to overlook the extent to which that system is indebted to another.
14) As Watson correctly mentions, "legal historians tend to concentrate on change and innovation" (1983: 1122–23) and they usually ignore this question that why a legal and judicial change did not occur when society changed, or when perceptions about the quality of law and the expectations toward judiciary changed. Other than explaining the judicial reforms and reorganizations in different periods, my task in this study is to explain why an intended judicial reform was not successful and why a social movement with public support could not influence the direction of change in the judiciary.
15) I will focus on law-in-action beside changes in the law when I study judicial reform and reorganization. This is the well-known distinction between law in books and law in action (Pound, 1910). A focus on law-in-action, i.e. actual behaviors of legal officials, clerks and lay persons, does not necessarily lead to a

discounting of the importance of the role of legal rules or law-in-books, i.e. juristic writings, judicial decisions and verdicts, and the authoritative pronouncements of legislatures in the framework of judicial reform. Legal rules are sometimes dysfunctional. I will also dwell on the gap between promise and performance in the legal and judicial systems.

16) Legal tradition itself plays an enormous role in the development of legal rules and approaches to law, and largely determines the pattern of change (Watson, 1983: 1134). Iranian legal system mostly falls in the category of civil law tradition (Appendix III). This tradition has its own dynamics of change, usually through change in the polity and state.

17) The relationship between law and society is not the same as the relationship between the judiciary and society. The former, as Watson mentions, "is not as close as existing theories of legal change and law and society suggest" (1983: 1135). The legal rules are sometimes in obvious conflict with the best interests and desires of the public, but nonetheless continue in existence. The judiciary, especially in authoritarian regimes, is directly under the influence of political and, periodically, social changes and it is always changed to adapt the dynamic situation. There is a close relationship between the needs and interests of the ruling elite and the judicial reform, especially in authoritarian regimes in which judiciary is not independent and reform is supposed to fulfill the new elite's perspectives and interests. Instead of divergence of law and society in some cases, we can talk about convergence of judicial system and politics in authoritarian regimes. While it takes years for the law to catch up with the social changes, even in democratic societies and where civil society institutions are powerful, judicial system is immediately changed to respond to the needs of the political regimes. Judicial change may be rooted in social, economic, or political factors as well as transnational aspects of the legal tradition. Judicial reform in post-revolutionary Iran showed that transplant and codification are not the only cause of reform in developing societies. The influence is not always direct and through transplantation and codification; it may be through social movements that are under the influence of social and political developments in other societies. Society has almost no choice other than tolerating a great deal of inappropriate law and judicial decisions and policies. The most important requirement of judicial change is social revolution and thereafter,

the change of political regime in societies with no or short periods of democratic experience.

18) I do not view society as an undifferentiated whole or as a series of interest groups utterly dominated by a monolithic ruling class. Iranian society has been including many recognizable groups; these groups' interests may often be very different with regard to what the law should be and how the judiciary should function, though within a weak civil society. Rules that are unsatisfactory for the majority may suit some powerful groups and therefore maintained in any judicial and legal reform.
19) In this study, the concept of judicial reform does not necessarily signify progress and move toward justice. It can be toward due process or more violations of individuals' rights; it can be directed toward rule of law or direct political control; it can follow the path toward judicial independence or its dependence to political expediencies.

Chapter Two
Socio-Historical Background

Despite most of the Middle Eastern societies, nation and state building processes in Iran does not begin in the early 20th century. These processes go back to more than two and a half millennium of social and political changes. During these millennia, administration of justice has come along with consolidation of new dynasties and centralization of power. Iranian dynasties did not overlook any effort to monopolize judicial system and undertook as legal capacity as possible under their authority. This includes two waves of transplantation: one during Elamites and Achaemenids, and the other in the post-Islamic conquer up to the end of the 19th century and three periods of judicial reorganization during Seljuqs and Qājārs. By transplantation, Iranian kings were addressing the social, political and economic demands for administration of justice by the government. By judicial reforms and reorganizations, they were addressing increasing grievances of their subjects. Judicial reforms during Qājārs were part of a greater and general change of the society and polity under the influence of ideas and thoughts coming from Europe.

Due to the weakness of the central government, system of political and judicial delegation, unending challenges between religious and state judicial systems, no system of checks and balances, and unification of the judicial and executive powers, Qājārs failed to establish a centralized judicial organization and hence could not deliver justice in their territory. Almost all of the six waves of judicial reform and reorganization during Qājārs before the Constitutional Revolution of 1906 did not lead to institutionalization of reforms. Plans and actions of reformist prime ministers like Qā'em Maqām-e Farāhāni, Amir Kabir, Mirzā Hosein Khan Sepah Sālār proved abortive due to the power of the shahs' court, and control of the state judicial system by the provincial governors who were not accountable to the central government in judicial affairs.

2.1. STATE BUILDING: TOWARD CENTRALIZATION OF THE ADMINISTRATION OF JUSTICE

During the pre-Islamic dynasties of Achaemenids, Selucids and Parthians, all the powers and authorities including jurisdiction were in the hands of kings (Rāvandi, 1961, Vol. I: 436). The difference in social and legal status between slaves and non-slaves was so sharp that it is these two categories that predominate in Iranian private law, although the slaves had a very limited right of property, practicing their own religion, and some elements of legal personality like legal capacity in relation to procedural matters (Perikhanian, 1983: 635 & 637). On the basis of agnatic structure, the members of the family possessed unequal degrees of legal capacity (Perikhanian, 1983: 642). Juridical acts, like weddings, were performed before an assembly of the adult members of the agnatic group (Perikhanian, 1983: 643–44). The texts from Susa (Shush), the royal city of Elamite, show the tradition of written contracts among private citizens. These contracts were witnessed, signed by the scribes, and sealed (Harper et al, 1992: 267–268).

The important judicial development in Achaemenid era was transfer of judgeship from elders and chieftains to judicial system of the state. The expansion of the kingdom and the diversity of subject nations necessitated a complicated governmental system. The king as the highest official of the state was considered as the chief justice and legislative in the country (Pirniā, Vol. II, 1983: 1462). He was the last resort in legal disputes (Dandamaev & Lukonin, 1989: 117) but it was his custom to delegate this function to some learned elder in his retinue. The decisions of the king were not subject to change but had to rule in accordance with the traditional practices and customs of Persians and had to seek the counsel of the representatives of leading noble clans who played a major role in the legal life of the country (Dandamaev & Lukonin, 1989: 117). Below him was a High Court of Justice with seven members, and below this were local courts scattered through the realm. The members of the judicial board were a prosecutor, a public attorney, and a judge selected from the board of the temple (Herodotus, Vol. III, 1954: 134: Amin, 2003: 90). The clerics and, in some periods, laypersons sat in judgment. Appeals from the decision of local judges might be carried directly to the *satrap*'s court located in local kings' governorships (Olmstead, 1948: 71).

The other development was Darius legal reform based on codification and transplantation to create a new law to be enforced upon the whole empire (Olmstead, 1948: 119). The institution of evidence was established in Iran in this era (Olmstead, 1948: 129–130). The Persians also inserted in the subordinate offices of the empire; they sat with natives on the bank of judges (Olmstead, 1948: 133–134). In military cases, disputes might be brought before regular judges, though the higher officers normally settled them (Olmstead, 1948: 245).

Achaemenid courts accepted bail in all but the most important cases. The court decreed occasionally rewards as well as punishments, and in considering a crime weighed against it the good record and services of the accused. The law's delays were mitigated by fixing a time limit for each case, and by proposing to all disputants an arbitrator of their own choice who might bring them to a peaceable settlement. The precedents were gathered to help the judges to conduct their cases. Oaths were taken, and occasionally used as a part of an ordeal.

The administration of the law was partly financed by commuting stripes into fines. More serious crimes were punished with branding, maiming, mutilation, blinding, imprisonment or death (Pirniā, Vol. II, 1983: 1488). Death was procured in cases like rape, treason, sodomy, murder, or alike by poisoning, impaling and crucifixion, hanging, stoning, burying, crushing the head, and smothering. With these laws and the army, the kings sought to govern their twenty satrapies from the capital.

The highly developed law of obligations emerged in Sasanian period. The practice of its features, i.e. the fixing of the agreement in written form, different ways of ensuring the fulfillment of obligations, and judicial protection of the interests of the parties (Perikhanian, 1983: 670), led to the working out of precise formulas for contractual bases of social relationships. Setting up law-courts in nearly every chief town and rural division and documenting judicial proceedings, time limit between the beginning of an action and the trial, the division of labor between the plaintiff's judge and the respondent's judge, and the hierarchy of the courts were the fundamentals of judicial administration (Perikhanian, 1983: 676–680).

There are two traditions of commentators occurring in *The Book of Thousand Judgments* that based on canonic precepts and official regulations embraced both private law and the norms of judicial procedure (Perikhanian, 1997: 14). The main practical problem in jurisdiction has its roots in the tension between the precepts of religious books intended for a long vanished society on the one hand and massive influx of new norms and official regulations intended for the guidance of judicial bodies which could not find adequate reflection in commentaries on the legal *nask*s (Avesta's teachings) on the other (Perikhanian, 1997: 14). The regulations related to judicial proceedings in *The Book of Thousand Judgments* have no reference to religious sources (Perikhanian, 1997: 14); this shows that at least some of them were drafted by the secular officials, although numerous regulations regarding legal procedure including the order of appeals emanated from the heads of the clergy (Perikhanian, 1997: 15). In this period, the judicial offices were set up. They had a secretariat staffed with four scribes in each district (Perikhanian, 1997: 16).

Certain legal decisions during Sassanids were recommended by the legal authorities and commentators of legal *nasks* of the Avesta, written down precisely by those who heard these decisions from those commentators (Perikhanian, 1997: 216–245). There were also certain formulae, which it is said that must be adhered to in judicial proceeding and are set down in *The Book of Thousand Judgments* (Perikhanian, 1997: 266–277). Some examples of these formulae are equality before the law (A13, 2–3), sealing the documents regarding an ordeal (A13, 7–8), and time limits for the appointment of a court session (A15, 7–8).

The expansion of Zoroastrian religion and its influence led to judicial incumbency of *mubadān,* Zoroastrian clerics. Their verdicts were final. The judicial organization of Sassanids was the result of tight relationship between state and religion and centralization of power. The judicial authority belonged to the king and, similar to Achaemenid dynasty, he was the chief justice in the land (Ghirshman, 1954: 311). Religious crimes like atheism and blasphemy had the most severe punishments (Christensen, 1989: 216–217) and they and other civil cases were dealt with in religious courts (Bulsara, 1937).

After being conquered by Muslims, the jurisdiction in Iranian territory was based on Islamic doctrine. According to the classical concept of Muslim law, which developed under the influence of Byzantine and Persian thought, the state system is autocratic (Tyan, 1955: 236). The ruler himself, like pre-Islamic era, holds all powers and all officials act only by virtue of a delegation conferred upon them by the ruler. In this system, the judge is essentially a lieutenant, the delegate-representative of the ruler or his appointed governors. He does not have an independent or even autonomous position. Whenever the ruler or his governors appointed a judge as the chief-justice, the latter could sub-delegate power to a third person who could, in turn, delegate his powers, and so on. The higher authority could force a person to accept a judicial function and the appointment might be terminated by the sole desire of the appointing authority. In some cases, even the delegated officials could deputize a private individual, one of his assistants or a formerly appointed *qāzi* to deal with a specific case (Tyan, 1955: 237–9). The expansion of *qāzi*s' duties to such unrelated functions as supervision of the public treasury, endowments, coining, and police was based on the concept of delegation (Tyan, 1955: 241).

This practice of substitution became permanent in most part of the Islamic world to the end of the fifth century A.H. (12th century A.D.)

when *qāzi*s were forbidden to delegate their powers to their own accord (Tyan, 1955: 240). This development granted more independence to appointed judges.

The dispute settlement in Islamic empire was the job of a judge. If plaintiff or accused was not consent with the judgment, the next step could be the chief justice (Ensāfpur, 1977: 315). *Mazālem* court was the last resort in some cases and stemmed from the absolute authority of the sovereign and from his fundamental competence to deal with all litigations and to right all wrongs (Tyan, 1955: 263). The existence of the office of *qāzi al-qozāt* was not part of appellate jurisdiction. The *mazālem* judge usually the king himself or his direct appointee was not bound by any rules of procedure (Tyan, 1955: 267). The law according to which the *sultān* gave his judgment was not *shari`ah* but *'orf*[1] or the state law usually based on custom (Morgan, 1988: 36) and arbitrary will of the king.

There is no distinction between various degrees of jurisdiction in Islamic judicial organization. Judicial organization in Islamic world was based on delegation; every appointee was responsible in front of the higher official who has appointed him. This is totally different from considering the right of people to appeal. Islamic judicial system was based on the principle of a single judge in the court and judicial procedure. The delegation principle cannot explain the single judgeship.[2] The caliph or his appointed *vālis* (governors) could appoint more than one judge as their delegates-representatives. Since the principle of collective decision-making was totally absent in the administrations, judgment in the court could not be an exception. The political foundation of judicial assemblies, i.e. democratic organization of the city-state could not go hand in hand with the principle of personal authority in the Muslim world.

Abbasids continued the centralization policy of Ummayids but elaborated the administration. Al-Mansur separated judgeships from governorships, making their personnel and functions discrete, and it is said that he was the first caliph personally to appoint judges in the important cities (Mottahedeh, 1975: 69). Hārun al-Rashid appointed the first chief judge and later provincial judges were subordinated to him (Mottahedeh, 1975: 81). The main judicial development in this era was the extension of chief-justice office. His office included the positions of 1) doorkeeper, 2) introducer, 3) deputy, 4) scrivener, 5) helper, 6) just people, 7) interpreter, 8) hearer, 9) trustworthy, consultants etc (Ibn-e Abi al-Dam, 1975: 64).

In Islamic tradition, judges were originally responsible for settling the disputes. If plaintiff or the defendant was not satisfied with the verdict, he/she could complain to the *mazālem* (ruler's) court. *Qāzi*s' court usually dealt with family or civil cases on the basis of the *shari`ah*. The next step was the chief judge (*qāzi al-quzāt*) and the last one, the caliph or the king. The caliph or king had unlimited power with respect to judicial decision making (Sāket, 1986: 99). The judge of the military (*qāzi askar*) was to consider the cases in which the defendant was a military staff (Ensāfpur, 1977: 315). Courts were instruments in the hands of caliph or *sultān* to confiscate the lands and wealth of people by profiling.

The permanent members of a court in Sassanids and early Islamic era are as follows: 1) the judge, 2) secretary of the court or the consultant, 3) overseer, 4) security and execution officers, and 5) documents clerk (Ensāfpur, 1977: 317 & 369).

The establishment of a general body of law out of Qurān and *hadith,* known as *shari`ah,* contributed to the establishment of certain separation of powers and relative autonomy of the *qāzi*s. This body of law was superimposed upon the judiciary officials as well as the ruler. The authority could not ignore all the principles of Islamic system by recourse to its will or expediency. This body weakened the bonds of subordination and gave *qāzi*s more independence.

Saffārids and Ghaznavids kept their links with masses through the Islamic institution of sessions in which people could lay complaints of oppression or wrongdoing (*mazālem* court, established during Umayyid era) before the ruler (Baihaqi, 1945: 39; Bosworth, 1975 (a): 127; Bosworth, 1975 (b): 184). The important judicial development in Saffārid era was the de facto independence of judicial system from Caliphate and its integration to local dynasties.

Buyids were effective in establishing the bifurcation of the Islamic structure of domination into caliphate and rulership (Arjomand, 1984: 94). The traditional rights of caliph were severely infringed by Buyids when they dismissed and exiled the supreme judge who was located in Baghdad. This position was transferred to Shiraz and had four representatives in Baghdad (Busse, 1975: 271). Buyids like Dailamite leaders and Sāmanids displayed considerable reverence for the Iranian royal past and embraced Iranian monarchy and its absolutism. Buyids were convinced that the coexistence of caliphate and monarchy would provide a solution for the political and religious problems of the period. 'Azed ul-Dowlah's dismissal of the chief justice in Baghdad might therefore appear as incomprehensible negation of this theory of coexistence (Busse, 1975: 278).

During the Seljuqs, i.e. between 11th to 13th centuries, the rulers and their appointees in provinces would personally hear and investigate every complaint of injustices (Bosworth, 1968: 86). The caliph in Baghdad was the supreme authority in matters relating to legal administration but he had authorized the *sultān*'s assumption of power. The *sultān*'s absolute and centralized authority was justified with resort to political expediency and secular justice of Iranian absolutism rather than the charismatic theory of imamate (Shi'ism) or the universalistic theory of caliphate. A diploma issued by the *sultān*'s *divān* for the chief *qāzi* of a town or district, called the *qāzi al-quzāt,* was enough for him to exercise and administer his own ways of justice (Lambton, 1968: 209). The chief *qāzi* of the empire, *qāzi-ye jumla-ye mamālek* was entrusted with the care of mosques and *awqāf* (endowments), and was instructed to hear the *shari`ah* cases and to take good care of the documents. The *sultān* as the shadow of God and the center of the universe was not to neglect the ordering of the affairs of the world and the interests and protection of the people (Lambton, 1968: 208–211). In this period, the political and religious institutions were drawn more closely together, under the authority of sultan (Lambton, 1968: 211).

Many cases in Seljuq's era, under "*amir-a'yān* system" and the "military-patronage state" (Hodgson, 1974, Vol. II), were settled by a mixture of arbitration, local custom and equity, and the decisions of such ad hoc tribunals were sanctioned by *shari`ah* judges (Lambton, 1988: 69). Judges were part of the historical bureaucratic empire (Arjomand 1999). The *qāzi*s enjoyed certain independence and prestige deriving from their status as the administrators of the divine law and deputies of the prophet, a position that was supposed to be independent of the ruler's will. Nomination by the ruler, the possibility of being dismissed by him and no power to enforce their judgments limited the judges' independence.

The *mazālem* court was the main channel of contact between the *sultān* and his subjects during Seljuqs, usually delegated its function to the vizier, *amir* or the provincial *qāzi*. In this court, the administration of justice was exercised on the basis of custom, equity, and governmental regulations (Lambton, 1968: 269) through which sanction could be given to *'orfi* courts (Lambton, 1988: 72). This court could try governmental officials and settle administrative disputes (Sāket, 1986: 217 & 273). The procedure of this court differed from that of *shari`ah* courts; the man who presided over the *mazālem* court possessed the power to exercise his functions and to apply the rule of justice, which was not the case with the *qāzi* who presided the *shari`ah* courts. The immediate source of the judge in *mazālem* courts was the *sultān,* but his functional authority was derived from the *shari`ah* (Lambton, 1968: 270). The *qāzi* in both courts normally applied the *shari`ah* according to the rite and school of canonical law to which most people in the area under his jurisdiction belonged (Lambton, 1968: 269). The *qāzi*s were subject to dismissal by the *sultān,* or by those to whom the *sultān* had delegated authority in the provinces. The *mazālem* court, superceding the *qāzi*'s court, became an everyday application to *sultān*'s representative to be dealt with according to a settled practice (Lambton, 1968: 227, 248 & 269–270). The *qāzis*' decrees were not subject to review, though in some cases an appeal could in theory be made to the *mazālem* court (Lambton, 1968: 270). The position of *Qāzi* was usually inherited (Petrushevsky, 1968: 510). The main function of *qāzi* under Seljuq was political control, to watch over the religious institutions on behalf of *sultān* (Lambton, 1968: 271).

During the judicial reform under the management of Khājeh Nezām ul-Molk, Malekshāh issued an order to limit the duration of litigations to thirty years (Ja'fari Langroudi, 118). This order may have led to stabilization of ownership and prevention of fraudulent litigations (Tabātabā'i, 1966: 603).

The independence of judges was more violated during Khārazmshāhids (Zerang, Vol. I, 2002: 85), and there were more and more violations during Moguls. The Moguls, Timurids and Safavids inherited from the Seljuqs a tradition of patrimonial monarchy and sought to centralize the power of the state, while they all needed the tribal institutions to defend the land against foreign invasions. Between 13th–14th Centuries, Muslim religious leaders served the conquerors (Ilkhānids and Timurids) as *qāzis*, diplomats, advisors and tutors (Lapidus, 1988: 280). They helped these conquerors rally support from both nomadic and town populations as well as to legitimize these new regimes. The important judicial developments in these dynasties were 1) new provisions governing civilian life gathered in collections called Yāsā (Spuler, 1964: 6; Ja'fari Langrudi, 116), 2) registration of properties during Moguls to terminate the land disputes (Amin, 2003: 306), and 3) establishing special courts for settling the cases that both sides were Moguls (*yārghu* and *olus* Courts). Ghāzān ordered that only people who are expert in *shari`ah* being offered the judicial positions; he waived any taxes for judges and prevented them to charge any side of litigations; he also reconfirmed Malekshāh's limitation on litigation periods. According to his order, it was only the court who could issue titles and indentures (Fazlollāh, 1989: 197–200 & 218–22). He tried to establish uniformity and the regular conduct of legal affairs throughout the Mogul empire, but his reforms remained on paper (Lambton, 1988: 94).

During Safavids, the governors had the right to oversight administrative and judicial organizations in their provinces (Rohrborn, 1978: 92). When lower level executives did not have enough power to settle a dispute, the governors were involved in the trials. Legal disputes that were even in the jurisdiction of *shar'i* courts were reviewed in governors' presence. *Shar'i* courts did not have jurisdiction over criminal cases (Rohrborn, 1978: 95). It was only the king who could order execution (Rohrborn, 1978: 167, 169);

divānbigi and governors who was directly appointed by the king had the authority to try cases related to four common crimes known as "*ahdāth-e arba'eh*" namely murder, sodomy and rape, high way robbery, and injuries like blinding and breaking of teeth (Rohrborn, 1978: 95–96).

Safavid's state building program was parallel to creation of a religious establishment, i.e. Shi'ism as the official religion of the state, which lend its authority and administrative services to the support of the regime (Lapidus, 1988: 295). Shi'ite jurisprudence that had been unofficial as compared to Hanafi and Shāfe'i jurisprudence before Moguls and Ilkhānids, promoted to the official religion in these periods and paved the way for Safavids to resort to it as the ideological cement and legitimizing factor of their new state. They organized the Shi'ite *'ulamā* into a state-controlled bureaucracy. The administrative and political authority of the shahs over the religious establishment disposed Shi'i *'ulamā* to stress those elements of the Shi'i tradition which affirmed the state order as a historical necessity (Lapidus, 1988: 296). *'Ulamā* exchanged the acceptance of the political authority of the Safavids for imposing Twevler Shi'ism as the official religion of the state. This was done through a wave of persecutions and violent suppression of Sufis, Sunnis and non-Muslims by the state. During Safavids, 16th and 17th centuries, and their struggle to centralize political power, a chief religious bureaucrat (*sadr*) supervised judicial appointments (Mirzā Sami'a, 1989: 2; Lapidus, 1988: 289, 296). The chief judges of each province were formally appointed by the Shah's order (Qā'em Maqāmi, 1969: 45 & 46). The office of *divānbigi* was created as a high court of appeal to oversee customary courts, and the incumbent rose to the status of last resort in judicial decision-making and somehow equal to that of army generals, thus bringing the administration of law under direct governmental control. *Shar'i* documents were to be registered with the divānbigi.

Shah Safi divided *sadr* office to two specific and general *sadr*s. Sadr-e khāsseh was in charge of crown lands (*phasseh* or *khāleseh*), the other was *sadr-e māmalek*. The *sadr* was the highest functionary in charge of clerical administration, one to be the consultant of the Shah in Justice Department (*divān 'edālat*) and the king's endowments, and the other to watch over the public dispute settlements and public endowments (Amin, 2003: 338). Sadr al-Sodour had the oversight over the *shari`ah* courts. In some periods of Safavid dynasty like Shah Tahmāsb, specific judges (*sadr-e khāseh*) were representatives of the *shari`ah* law in *divanbigi* courts (Rāvandi, 1961: 480). The position of *qāzi* in some provinces was inherited. Military institutions had their own military judges (*qāzi askar*) (Turkamān, 1971: 149) in the last years of Safavids' rule. There were also temporary judges (*qāzi ahdās*) for taking care of emergency situations and when the speedy process was necessary (Turkamān, 1971: 308).

Another important judicial development in Safavid era, besides concentrating all the judicial powers in the hands of the government, was submission of judicial capitulation to European powers. Shāh Abbās issued an order that gave immunity to the Britain tradesmen (Amin, 2003: 411). Russians got this immunity after the Fat'h Ali Shah defeat to them in 1828 in the framework of Turkmānchai Treaty (1828). Judicial capitulation dictated that cases between Persians and foreign subjects and also between foreign subjects were removed from the jurisdiction of Iranian courts.

Afshārids in the 18th century called Ja'fari school equal in status to the four Sunni schools. They weakened the Shi'i *'ulamā* by confiscating properties, abolishing clerical positions in the government, and canceling the jurisdiction of religious courts (Lapidus, 1988: 300). Zandids like Afshārids limited *'ulamā* to their religious deeds and did not let them to consolidate their power through administration of justice, trust funds and endowments (Nafisi, 1965: 39). The destruction of the Iranian state in the 18th century led to the latent Shi'i claims to autonomy in the 19th and 20th centuries and the withdrawal of *'ulamā* from engagement in public affairs.

The Qājār dynasty that ruled Iran between 1779 and 1925 resembled its Safavid predecessor in that it represented a weekly centralized regime faced with strong provincial tribal forces, and an increasingly independent, autonomous and centralized religious establishment (Amin ul-Dowlah, 1962: 166, 242–243). Competition and in some cases cooperation (Arjomand, 1984: 224) of the state and hierocracy as the two organs of polity facilitated the resolution of normative problem of legitimacy of political and hierocratic domination. The legitimacy crisis of Qājārs pushed them to resort to Shi'ite hierocracy "whose power and independence had grown imperceptibly but tremendously during the intervening decades of civil strife" (Arjomand, 1988a: 89–90).

In the new constellation of hierocratic and temporal power, *'ulamā* claimed the right to exercise independent judgment while the secular courts of the state were not able to investigate litigations, to settle the disputes and to persecute crimes (Amin ul-Dowlah, 1962: 167; Nafisi, 1965: 39, 53, & 58; E'temād ul-Saltaneh, 1966: 684). This began from late Safavids, when their power was on decline and clerics could independently execute *sharī`ah* penances (Dowlat Ābādi, 1992: 87ff.). They consolidated their ties with the common people through the administration of justice and other religious affairs (Lapidus, 1988: 572).[3] They were killing the apostates, cutting the heads of heretics and Babis, and were not accountable in front of the government. They were always breaching the government's monopoly over enforcing the law and punishment. *'Ulamā* even did not believe that their role is to issue verdicts and the government has to execute those verdicts. They were publicly criticizing the government for being loose on acts against the orders of *shari'ah* (E'temād ul-Saltaneh, 1966: 697, 785 & 876). In some periods of Qājār era, *mazālem* courts were active and the king opened the court for hearing complains (Denbali, 1827: 139; see Arjomand 2005:31); it was reformed into divān-khāneh as the royal court of appeals (Schneider, 2005).

The benefits of these judicial actions for clerics who were involved in this kind of career were to gather more wealth, have their hands over the endowments, put pressure on governmental officials, get waiver for their land taxes, have benefices for their family members and children, and improve their rulership domains (Ravandi, 1961: 508, citing Yahyā Dowlat Ābādi, *Hayat-e Yahya,* 50ff.).

Tribes and nomads, who beside urban and village settlers had their own social structure and hence judicial administration, could settle the disputes through arbitration of the elderly. Village headmen (*kadkhodā*) in the ladder of power were under the landlords and above the subjects (Ghaffari, 1989: 150–152).

2.2. RELIGIOUS AND STATE JUDICIAL SYSTEMS: UNENDING CHALLENGE

Secular and religious authorities have always intertwined in Iran. The centuries-old rivalry between the royal court and the religious communities (Dandamaev & Lukonin, 1989: 122) could not be dealt with or end in judicial affairs. Due to the theocratic element in adjudication, a practically complete parallelism of religious and secular law existed. Both authorities have had their own special institutions of power including legal ones. State and religious courts have had symbiosis with interference of areas of jurisdiction and function. This extends to the end of 19th century.

Iranian kings and rulers were less concerned with the idea of justice than with enforcing the political allegiance and obedience of their subjects through the state-imposed religion, i.e. Zoroastrianism during Sassanids, Shi'ism during Safavids and Islamism during the Islamic Republic, or state-supported religion, i.e. Islam during Seljuqs, and Shi'ism during Qājārs. The clerics, in cooperation with the monarchical courts, presided over minute forms of etiquette designed to create the charisma that under-girded monarchical authority.

Under the reigns of Cyrus and Cambyses, the Persian *satrap* appointed the judges and high civil and temple officials (Dandamaev & Lukonin, 1989: 122). The position of judgeship in Sassanid era was involved with religious authority. Kartir, as the chief judge of the empire, during the reign of Varahrān II, also received the rank of nobility, and the headship of the religion. He first came to power under Shapur-when he was a *herbad* and a *mubad*. Under King Hormizd, he was given the title '*mubad* of Ahura Mazda,' probably the first to hold this later well-attested title.[4]

The bond between religion and law survived side by side with a highly developed state and a broader range of secular legal institutions, though in some periods the legal sections of Avesta were no longer satisfactory for the stage of development reached by Iranian society. The new legal and procedural regulations developed by social practice during the centuries made imperative an extensive commentary upon the *nasks* (teachings) of Avesta (Perikhanian, 1997: 13).

Zoroastrian clerics in the third order of clerical hierarchy had to run the judicial affairs during the Sassanids. The customary and religious courts were separated and clerics were usually responsible for private and penal law cases (Christensen, 1989 (1944): 420; Amin, 2003: 123), but the centralization, as the main task of the state, did not harm incorporation of these clerics to be part of the government. They were working under the authority of *magupat* or *mubad* who was under the authority of *magupatanmagupat* or *mubadan mubad,* the highest-ranking cleric of Zoroastrian establishment ('Abdollahi, 1990: 176). Magupatanmagupat was actively participating in the realm of legal procedure. There were an obligation for keeping court records during the trial of a series of crimes, and attaching these records to the document containing the text of the sentence (Perikhanian, 1997: 15).

Shar'i jurisdiction was subordinated to the *'orfi* jurisdiction during Seljuqs. Provincial governors were responsible for the proper conduct of the *qāzi*'s courts (Lambton, 1988: 79). *Shar'i* matters were to be referred to the *qāzi*'s court, and customary matters (*rasmiyāt*), disputes which arise in social life (*mu'āmelāt*), and official affairs to the Ruler's Court (Divān-e Riyāsat) (Lambton, 1988: 80). The distinction between *'orfi* and *shar'i* jurisdiction was more sharply drawn under the Moguls, who brought with them their own laws and customs (Lambton, 1988: 82). Mogul custom and *shari'ah* law existed side by side throughout the period of the Ilkhānids and later the former assimilated to the procedures of the *mazālem* courts (Lambton, 1988: 96).

During the Safavids, *'ulamā* could not run their own courts without the enforcement of formal judicial appointees. Safavids could concentrate all the judicial powers in the hands of the government to the level that *'orfi* courts succeeded in limiting *shar'i* courts to settlement of disputes in private matters like will, marriage, divorce and inheritance, transactions and contracts (Minorsky, 1965: 71). 'Orfi judges were called *qāzi ahdās* (judges for public safety cases). It seems that *shar'i* judges' jurisdiction could extend from civil to penal cases (Ja'fari Langroudi, 132) while other cases were tried by *'orfi* judges (Ja'fari Langroudi, 142). In this period *'ulamā* who traditionally had this position in their families stopped doing judgeship (Turkamān, 1971: 155). While accepting the duality of customary and *shari`ah* courts, the Safavid kings had always the upper say when confronted with *'ulamā* and sometimes had harsh reaction toward some of them for what they have done and said in the areas of religious conflicts (Turkamān, 1971: 214–215). The decrease of the power of state led to the weakening of customary courts in late Safavid and later Qājār eras.

Qājārs' patrimonial regime tolerated more powerful religious institutions. The unstable governments of Iran in this era defaulted nearly all their judicial authorities to the *shari`ah* courts. As a result *'orf* or state system of courts did not develop and, before the Constitutional Revolution, consisted only of the Divān-khāneh-ye 'Adliyeh (Court of Justice) in Tehran (Banani, 1961: 68). Nevertheless, the shah appointed the highest judge of *shar'i* court in each district. The governmental officials enforced the verdict of this court (Curzon, Vol. I, 1982: 590).

In general, Iranian kings were considered as the highest judicial and legislative authorities and had the right to issue judicial orders. They could also sit in the position of the highest judges in the state and even make decisions against custom and *shari`ah*. *'Orfi* law had mostly precedence over *shari`ah*. Having its root in the king's power over judiciary power, the confrontation between the *'orfi* and *shar'i* judgment intensified in Mogul period and continued to Safavids. According to Minorsky, "jurisdiction of *shar'i* and *'orfi* courts were ambiguous and the shahs and their ministers did not want to make them clear because that ambiguity could increase their power" (Minorsky, 1965: 76).

Shari`ah* law in Qājār era, in many of its parts, was much more substantively rational and more highly developed on the formal side than *'orfi* law of the state. *Shari`ah law could reflect the general pattern so characteristic of all theocratic law. It was the mixture of substantive legislative and moral ends with formally relevant elements of normation, what Weber ascribes to canon law (1968: 829).

The jurisprudence is considered a collective obligation (*wajeb-e kefā'i*) by most of the *mujtaheds* from *usuli* school for which no specific delegation or designation is necessary (Montazeri, 1988: Vol. I, 139, Vol. II, 141, 145). In this school, the jurists greatly varied in defining the scope of the authority of the jurist. This theory did not challenge the judiciary authority of the king as the higher arbiter of the subjects' appeal in all matters. This supreme judiciary authority was granted to the king in the political ethic of patrimonial monarchy which required him to be fully accessible to his subjects and to hear their appeals concerning wrongdoings in all areas of life, including the rulings of religious courts (Arjomand, 2004: 31). The king could decide where a case should be referred, a religious or a state court (Zabihi & Sotudeh, Vol. VI, 1976: 166–8, 170, 120–121, cited in Arjomand, 2005; 31).

With increase of the *'ulamā*'s power, theoretically and practically some tensions between hierocracy and monarchy was inevitable. *'Ulamā* had the power to declare Shi'ite rulers' decisions unlawful without authorization of *mujtaheds* (Algar, 1991: 715–716).[5] The intermeshing of royal and juristic authority within the judiciary led to lots of unresolved legal struggles, while the *shar'i* and *'orfi* court orders presented the rulings of the *mujtaheds* and *qāzis* as fully binding respectively, although both hierocratic and state judges were ineffective; hierocratic judges were dependent on the state to enforce their ruling, and the importance of the office of state judges had sharply declined after the establishment of Shi'ism by the Safavids (Arjomand, 1984: 127).

2.3 CODIFICATION AND TRANSPLANTATION: TOP-DOWN APPROACH

Iranian society has experienced three waves of legal and judicial transplantation and codification during Elamites and Achaemenids, in the post-Islamic conquer, and between 19th to 20th centuries. Elamites as the first Iranian dynasty in around 3200 B.C. established a legal system in Iran. The main development in this era was the invention of written language in Sumer (Hinz, 1973: 101). Elamites used written language to create a system of writing for keeping legal records. Transplantation of Hammurabi code was another development in this era (Hinz, 1973: 104; Olmstead, 1948: 121). Their legal system had a close relationship with religious beliefs. Comparing the Akkadian texts of certain portions of Darius' inspections with the prologue and epilogue of Hammurabi's law book reveals many parallels in vocabulary and phraseology that convinces the readers that the younger copied from the older (Olmstead, 1948: 122).

Intensive work on the codification of the laws of the conquered peoples was carried out during the reign of Darius I (Dandamaev & Lukonin, 1989: 117). The Achaemenid administration utilized the local law during contact with the Babylonians, and the Persians who had begun to take an active part in the business life of the country were guided by Babylonian laws. The laws of Hammurabi continued to be written and studied during Achaemenid times (Dandamaev & Lukonin, 1989: 121, 123).

In the next round of transplantation, Islamic law replaced pre-Islamic rules. The conquer of Iran by 'Omar's troops facilitated the transplantation process (Zarrinkoob, 1975: 29) and it was extended to a degree that Iranian jurists composed *shari`ah* law books and established Islamic legal schools. The third wave of legal transplantation began in 19th century and extended to 20th century, when Iranian intellectuals and political elites strived to modernize different aspects of the society and culture including judiciary and law. I will talk about the third wave in detail later in this work.

Prior to being converted to Islam in the second half of the 7th century, Zoroastrian Persia had developed its own legal system. It possessed no codified law or formal legal code (Perikhanian, 1997: 12). The important legal development in this era was codification in the framework of collections of legal cases and decisions that could serve as guides to judges and others, gathered in collections out of which, *The Book of Thousand Judgments* has survived. The law in general formed a part of religious ethics, and social ethics was similarly sanctified by religion (Perikhanian, 1997: 13). The legal *nasks* of the Avesta were used in legal proceedings, but not directly (Perikhanian, 1983: 628). Written commentaries on the legal *nasks* provided the basis for legal proceedings as early as the middle of Sasanian period. There were law schools that composed of followers of one or other of commentators (Perikhanian, 1983: 629).

With being conquered by Arabs, there was no need for codification; Islamic law promulgated in the Arab world was declared as the law of the land. This situation persisted for centuries till the introduction of Western civilization to Iranian intellectuals from early 19th century.

In early Qājārs, the law was rarely codified and barely stood out from its ethico-normative context (Arjomand, 2004: 22). Codification came to the scene in mid-Qājār era, when there was the need for new laws to adjust with the waves of changes instigated from communication with industrialized world. Other than translation of text related to legal matters, there were some endeavors toward promulgation of laws. In 1871, Mirzā Hosein Khan Moshir ul-Dowleh (Sepahsālār) created six courts and offices, one of them a court for drafting bills (*majles-e tanzim-e qānun*) (Amin, 2003: 427). Promulgation of Department of Judiciary Code to create regulation regarding due process, scientific investigation and prison reform in 1872 (Mahboubi Ardekāni, 1999, Vol.2: 5) was a prominent move in codification process.

Another example of codification in this era is promulgation of the Code of Tanzimāt-e Hasāneh (beneficent reorganization) (*Ketabcheh-ye Tanzimāt-e Hasāneh-ye Dowlat-e 'Aliyeh va Mahrouseh-ye Iran)* in 1875, if enforced, could remove the judicial authority remaining to the governors by transferring control of the jurisdiction of the *'orfi* and partially *shar'i* courts to the Majles-e Tanzimāt. This Majles specified that the *shar'i* court had to be approved by both sides, and Majles-e Tanzimāt had to be notified of the choice, and only the ruling of that court would be binding (Nashat, 1982: 53).

2.4 JUDICIAL REFORM AND REORGANIZATION: ADDRESSING GRIEVANCES AND SATISFYING THE ELITE

There are two periods of prominent measures of judicial reform and reorganization in Iran's history before the 20th century. Addressing grievances of the subjects and satisfying the elite, although sometimes contradictory, were both on the table and both Seljuqs and Qājārs could not please their subjects. The first period was during Seljuqs. The important actions toward judicial reform during Seljuqs were 1) principle of lapse in financial disputes, 2) establishment of law schools for training judges in big cities like Baghdad, Basreh, Balkh, Naishābur, Herāt, Isfahān, Marv, etc by Nezām ul-Molk (Mohit Tabātabāii, 1968: 23–24), and 3) the installation of Justice Pillar that people who endured injustice could stand beside it, wearing their letter of grievance (Amin, 2003: 282).

Second period was during Qājār era. The expected changes in the judicial system of Qājār Iran were part of a greater and general change of the society and polity under the influence of ideas and thoughts coming from Europe. There are six waves of taking actions toward judicial reform and reorganization during Qājārs before the Constitutional Revolution of 1906, some of them totally fruitless and some, short lived, did not lead to institutionalization of reforms. In the first wave that began early in the nineteenth century, the Crown Prince 'Abbās Mirza tried to ensure that honest and capable judges were appointed to the *shar'i* court. He also established a new *divān-khāneh* in Tabriz, his own seat of government, which supervised *qāzis* who where appointed to the other towns in Azerbaijan (Najmi, 1958: 29 & 198). In this wave, Fat'h Ali Shah created a central *divān* or court of justice in the 1830's, later abolished due to running counter the interests of influential members of bureaucracy (Floor, 1983: 118).

In the second wave, Mirza Abu al-Qāsem Qā'em Maqām-e Farāhāni, the first prime minister of Mohammad Shah, took action to establish a *divān-e 'edālat* or court of justice that dealt with customary law cases. Other than *amir* or the head of the *divān,* this court had seven members: the representative of *'ulamā,* a eunuch chosen to deal with cases involving females, *amir-e nujabā* or representative of the nobles who was responsible for settling disputes among Qājār princes, *amir-e lashkar* or the head of military tribunals, *mustowfi-e divān* or the comptroller of the fiscal affairs, *nazem-e 'edālat* or attorney general, and the *munshi bāshi* or secretary who was the head of the department's office (Floor, 1983: 118).

The third one occurred during the administration of Mirzā Taqi Khan Amir Nezām (Amir Kabir) who was the first to attempt to bring about a structural reform of the judicial system. The measures that were headed to organizational changes include 1) Amir Kabir's decree for prohibition of torture in judicial procedures (1850) (Adamiyyat, 1969: 302–3), 2) restriction of the number of places of asylum (*bast*), 3) abolition of harsh punishments like blinding, firing at people by cannon, burying people alive, and placing people alive in a wall,[6] and 4) establishment of the Department of Justice. This department was to try cases related to four common crimes known as "*ahdāth-e arba'eh*," and to settle disputes between the state and individuals, between foreign citizens who were working for Iranian government and also between foreigners and Iranians, and customary (*'orfi*) disputes between Iranian citizens (Divān-khāneh-ye 'Adliyeh) (1850) (Ādamiyyat, 1969: 302–3). Divān-khāneh could actually settle disputes in all areas of life. By 1870, the old informal Divān-khāneh had become the ministry of justice and employed fifty people, although it was still part of the Ministry of Interior (MacDaniel, 1974: 27).

His measures toward reform aimed at extending the control of the state over courts, *shar'i* and *'orfi*. He reorganized the Divān-khāneh-ye 'Edālat and extended its jurisdiction. Cases had first to be referred to this *divān,* which had to select the *shar'i* court that would deal with the case. The decision taken by the *shar'i* court was only valid when the Divān-khāneh-ye 'Edālat confirmed it. He also abolished the *nāsekh* judgments (reversing earlier decisions).[7] By giving precedence to a particular *shar'i* court in Tehran, the decisions of which had force of precedence for all other *shar'i* courts, he tried to streamline the functioning of the *shar'* courts and centralized government's control over these courts (Floor, 1983: 119; Sheikholeslami, 1997: 26).

The fourth wave came through during the Ministry of Mirza Hosein Khan Moshir ul-Dowleh that led to the reforms in the Ministry of Justice. His reforms were to enhance the authority of the central government by creating central control in the judicial process. Using two earlier decrees issued in 1858 and 1862, he continued effort to centralize the judiciary system by strengthening the central Divān-khāneh, founding independent tribunals, and to establish a unified code of laws, reclaiming the right of the central government to legislate. His goal was to administer both state and religious courts under one Ministry of Justice and get rid of overlaps of jurisdiction. He tried unsuccessfully to lay down the fundamental principle that the power to exercise jurisdiction was restricted to the Ministry of justice in Tehran and its representatives in provinces. The Minister of Justice had no power over the provincial courts, mostly under the influence of landowners and the holders of *toyuls*,[8] and merely supervised the Divan-e 'Adliyyeh A'zam, the High Court of Justice.

Divān-khāneh consisted of a high court in the capital and an independent presiding judge in each province, who was only responsible to the Ministry of Justice. The 'Edālat-khāneh (literally, house of justice) constituted part of a reorganization of the Ministry of Justice and aimed at prohibiting provincial governors from interfering in judicial affairs (Martin, 1989: 76). A court of appeals, an executive court, a legislative court to draw up regulations, and three specialized courts for dealing with criminal, commercial, and property cases were established in the Ministry of Justice (Arjomand, 1988: 32).

The fifth wave came through during the Prime Ministry of Mirzā Hosein Khan Sepah Sālār. He gave priority to judicial reform and set up the Ministry of Justice. His Minister of Justice, Mostashār ul-Dowleh, put forth endeavor to reorganize the judiciary in four different judicial offices, i.e. the Office of Prosecution and Investigation (Majles-e Tahqiq-e Da'āvi) to receive petitions, Criminal Court (Majles-e Jenāyat) to investigate cases of assault, identify the culprit and nature of offense, and deal with the decisions issued by the judge, Commercial Court (Majles-e Tejārat) to supervise commercial transactions and disputes, and Land and Property Court (Mahkameh-ye Amlāk) to investigate old leases and land claims. There were also expected to be two executive sections, Executive Office (Dāyereh-ye Ejrā-ye Ahkām) to carry out all decisions proceeding from the Ministry of Justice, and Drafting Bill Office (Dayereh-ye Tanzim-e Qavānin) to draw up regulations equally applicable to every case and to all classes (Amin, 2003: 427; Nashat, 1982: 45–47) and propose a new codified system. The purpose of judicial reform in this administration was to centralize the administration of justice, to limit the authority of provincial governors and *'ulamā* (Ādamiyyat, 1973: 81; Lambton, 1987: 291–2) and hence ensure the independence of the judiciary from the executive, and consolidate the state courts, setting a clear demarcating line which *shari'ah* courts had to accept (Bayat, 1991: 39). Sepah Sālār established tribunals throughout the provinces under a central body in the capital to which the government administration was accountable for (Martin, 1989: 77).

The sixth and last unsuccessful wave of judicial reform attempts before the Constitutional Revolution occurred by Amin ul-Dowleh's measures in 1893. He gave an order to the Ministry of Justice to set up an *'edalat-khāneh* to deal with trials and to protect the subjects' rights. In this context, *'edalat-khāneh* meant a system of tribunals under the Ministry of

Justice with the function of watching over the provincial authorities and obtaining grievances against them (Martin, 1989: 77).

Most of these plans and actions proved abortive due to duality of judicial administration and overlap of state (*'orfi*) and religious (*shari`ah*) courts, executive interference in the judicial procedures, no hierarchy of the courts, handicapped *shar'i* courts due to their lack of power to execute their decisions, and control of the state judicial system by the provincial governors who were not accountable to the central government in judicial affairs. The division of labor between these two courts was murky; the *'orfi* or state courts dealt primarily with offences against the state and law and order of the society such as rebellion, embezzlement, theft and drunkenness, while the *shar'i* courts were mainly concerned with affairs of a civil nature, especially those of personal status (Floor, 1983: 113). In the area of *shar'i* courts, in spite of signing an *eltezām* (obligation) paper to honor the judges' verdict, a case could always be reopened before another judge. Although *'orfi* courts were administered by the state and the highest *'orfi* court was located in Tehran, the governors could delegate their presupposed judicial powers to an *'orfi* judge. These courts had different ways of punishment,[9] laws and sources of law,[10] and prosecution. In both of these courts, neither court archives nor records were kept.

There is no evidence of a legal profession as law practice before the Constitutional Revolution despite the flourishing business for the entrepreneurial class, the rise of trading and banking and increasing expenditures in the late 19th century Iran (Issawi & Polk, 1971). People could work as lawyers for others, but in a case-based manner. Mullahs were serving as notaries and the scribe usually wrote for pay anything from a will to a madrigal, in a society that a vast majority was illiterate. The plaintiff mostly preferred his own plea. Litigation was socially and legally discouraged; in many cases, if the accuser could not prove the charge, e.g. in an adultery case, she/he would confront severe punishment like being lashed.

Qājārs instigated and promulgated some judicial reforms through 1) sending students to foreign countries, mainly Western Europe during Nāser ul-Din Shah era[11] to study law (Ardekāni, Vol. I, 1999: 399–400), 2) establishing new law schools in 1898 (Ardekani, Vol. I, 1999: 401), and 3) establishing the Ministry of Justice in 1858 and its re-establishment in 1871 by Sepah Sālār, even before the Constitutional Revolution (Ardekāni, Vol. II, 1997: 5).

2.5 CHALLENGES AND DILEMMAS: DUALITIES, LACK OF INDEPENDENCE AND WEAK STATE

There are some common features in all Iran's judicial history before 20th century. Firstly, the judiciary was never an independent and impenetrable power. The judiciary, when had an independent institution from the king's court, had a meager role compared to it. Access to the king was almost impossible for general population. Writing petitions of grievances (*'arizeh*) was a substitute for to be heard in the kings' courts (Ensāfpur, 1977: 193–4). During Nāser ul-Din Shah, *'arizeh* boxes (*sanduq-e 'edālat;* boxes of justice) were installed to gather people's grievances directly for the shah (Nezam-Mafi, 1989:52) but local authorities were vigilant over the boxes with leashes to not let people to reach them. (Curzon, Vol. I, 1982: 603; Schneider, 2005) Although the letters reaching the central government through these boxes were given serious attention by a committee that included Mirzā Husein Khan, the reluctance of the local authorities to send the boxes back to the capital led to quietly removal of them after several months without giving specific reason for withdrawal (Nashat, 1982: 58).

The consequence of the concept of delegation in post Islamic era was the complete lack of separation between the judicial and executive powers (Tyan, 1955: 239). The judges were subordinated not only to the central executive authority, but also to the various regional and local authorities. Subjects could rarely protect themselves against the whim and extortion of local representatives of the government (Hāji Sayyāh, 1967: 137–138). Justice was administrated by the governors and their representatives and the clerics (Sykes, 1910: 61).

As a result, laws and judicial procedures were mostly and most of the time for securing the interests of the ruling class working on the basis of politico-legal characteristics of the Iranian "patrimonial monarchy" extended to the first half of the nineteenth century (Arjomand 2004e), and other strata had mainly no other rights other than working, paying taxes, and providing men for the wars (for Sassanids see Rāvandi, Vol. I, 1961: 691; for Qājārs see Bozorg, Vol. I, 2002: 128–132 & 237–39 and Nezam-Mafi, 1989: 61).[12] Judgeship was a privilege for ruling elite that ordinary people were deprived of. Judges were appointed from among the nobles for life with hereditary transfer of their posts (Dandamaev & Lukonin, 1989: 118); this was somehow true for *shar'i* court judges. Most of the social movements in the late 19th century and the 20th century Iran have been addressing these issues.

In this situation, the king was always the last resort; a final appeal should be carried to the king himself. The king ruled and reigned. The power of Persian kings, from Elamites era to the Constitutional Revolution of 1906, was theoretically absolute; he could kill with a word, without trial or reason given. Few even of the greatest nobles dared to offer any criticism or rebuke; there was nothing such as public opinion or organized public pressure. Although in theory all had a right of appeal to the shah, yet few availed themselves of the privilege, knowing that in such a case everything would be in all probability be swallowed up by the royal judge and his courtiers (Sykes, 1910: 62). In such a state, the only law was the will of the king. According to the Persian-sultanate theory, the king was supposed to be inspired by the god in his edicts and judgments. The law of the realm was the Divine Will, objectified in the king's person, whoever he may be. There was nothing that can be considered as civil society aura in judicial profession and judicial procedures.

In the absence of powerful and independent judiciary, it was important who did the crime. The court could change the decree on the basis of the record of the accused, how he/she confronts the court, and discretion of the judge. Individuals were not equal in the courts and were not treated as equal. "Both sides bribe to the extent of their resources, and he who has the longest purse will usually win his case unless he is so obviously in the wrong that the governor fears public opinion or the priesthood" (Sykes, 1910: 61–62).

There was nothing in the codes about the rights of the individual against the state. No rights were sacred against the absolute will of kings, and no precedents could avail except an earlier decree of the king. Some articles of *sharī`ah* provided, if not political, at least economic protection.

Thirdly, judiciary has been an area of cooperation and conflict between state and religious institutions. In Sasanian period, breach of an agreed obligation was regarded as a religious offence and the fear of divine wrath helped to ensure the fulfillment of an obligation (Perikhanian, 1983: 670). Religious and political elite performed judgment in the whole Iranian legal history; the state had never total power in appointing and deposing the judges, and controlling their actions (Ensāfpur, 1977: 315). Any intent by the government to create a strong centralized judiciary in the age of nation-state, i.e. after Safavids, confronted the resistance of *'ulamā* who were thinking government was going to curtail their power. On the other side, most people continued to refer their disputes to religious courts to the point that these courts were working due their low cost and quicker decisions than the state courts.

Fourthly, the judicial system was dual, run by the state and religious courts. In some periods, like Moguls, this duality was intensified, and in some periods, like Safavids, it was reduced. The judicial duality almost handicapped both courts during Qājārs. Shari' tribunals did not have enough power to execute their decisions, and state courts were usually limited by provincial governors and religious leaders to issue and enforce their verdicts. Because of the notoriety of state courts, the *sharī`ah* courts and other rival procedures, such as the courts of arbitration, continued to dominate the judicial system (Floor, 1983: 132). Provincial and district governors ignored most of the orders of central government regarding reform in the judicial procedure; the orders of the Qājār shahs to establish provincial courts whose presidents were supposed to be appointed by the Ministry of Justice were rendered ineffective by the local authorities who appointed their own men to these functions. (E'temād ul-Saltaneh, 1877–80: Vol. I, 460 & Vol. III, 188) Almost all of the ideas related to reform in the judicial system, brought about by the shahs, prime ministers and ministers of justice during Qājārs came to naught because no measures were taken to implement and if implemented, no measures to supervise the implementation of the decrees for the reforms.

Fifthly, there was no central judicial organization to oversee and check what was happening in the judiciary all around the country. There was no unified procedure to guarantee the integration of judicial affairs and similarity of verdicts in similar cases in the whole country (Ja'fari Langrudi, 181). There was also no hierarchy in the court system (Ja'fari Langroudi, 181). Mazālem courts were supposed to overcome the irregularities created because of disorder. The sacredness of the *shar'* and the sanctity of those who administered decisions based upon it made it impossible to dispute the decisions of that tribunal. Even after the establishment of Ministry of Justice by Qājārs in 1858, there were specialized courts outside this Ministry such as the commercial court in the Ministry of Trade (Floor, 1983: 124). The trial of foreign subjects was also relegated to the Ministry of Foreign Affairs (1868) (Nashat, 1982: 44).

Ordinary people usually had no access to justice. Only people who had enough wealth and lands like landlords and big business holders had access to the king's court to complain. Some *qāzi*s took fees from those who referred to their courts[13] (Lambton, 1988: 75). Ordinary people had no rights to claim something as plaintiff (Ensāfpur, 1977: 190). Until the rapid growth of commerce in the second half of the nineteenth century most villages and tribes (more than eighty percent of the population) remained virtually self-contained, practically self-sufficient, economically autonomous, and predominantly self-governed (Abrahamian, 1982: 11). Only the urban population had access to the state and *mazālem* courts.

And at last, other than hearing cases and dispute resolution, judges had other duties like acting as a notary public, assessor, writing documents for landed states, supervision of the *hesbah* (enjoining of the good and forbidding evil) unless there was a *muhtaseb* (the official who enforces the vice law and oversees the public) appointed by the ruler. Other than these, they were expected to give consult to local authorities, to be associate governors in law and order issues, to recite the *khutbeh* (in Friday sermon, that was delivered in the name of the ruler in the *masjid-e jame'* and therefore in major cities), and to write marriage and divorce settlements and bonds concerning inheritance.

Chapter Three

First Period: Post Constitutional Revolution Era

In chapter 2, discussion was focused on forces pushing for effective judicial administration and forces working against it. My second chapter was built around addressing, amplifying, and evaluating the dynamics of judicial administration in pre-Constitutional Revolution era. The Constitutional Revolution of 1906 was a reaction to failures of plans and actions toward the reforms in the second half of the 19th century.

The rise of new thoughts and ideas in the academic and practical areas of judicial system, extension of economic and cultural interactions between Iran and European countries, and unaccountability and brutality of the political leaders were the driving forces for the Constitutional Revolution that led to establishment of a new legal base for judicial organization, and passing of the judicial regulation in judicial committee[1] of the newly established parliament. 'Adliyyeh (independent judicial branch of the government) was the main agenda in the Constitutional Revolution.

Due to the powerful religious establishment and embryonic situation of secular forces, only formal secularization and organizational change were the agendas of the constitutional revolutionaries. They began transplantation and codification with procedural law and regulations regarding judicial organization. The public demand for more effective administration of justice, pressure of a social movement for justice and the necessity of the time to centralize the government in the nation-state era were the pushing forces for reforms. The strong alliance of the royal court and traditional *'ulamā* could not be defeated by a very new strata of Western educated individuals from well off families.

Although Mokhber ul-Saltaneh, Moshir ul-Dowleh and Foroughi tried to centralize the judiciary system, draft new laws, strengthen judiciary personnel and establish due process, the international and national, theoretical and practical, and organizational and procedural challenges and dilemmas led to the failure of the judicial reforms. The upper hands of the powerful religious forces, which were coming out of the ashes of Qājār failures to deliver, led to small gains of the reformers in some areas and their failures in others.

The new waves of reform supported by the European powers and the news from and consequences of reforms in the Ottoman Empire were encouraging and positive enough to make reformers confident of victory to try hard. Despite the governments' failures, the alternative for traditional forces of religious establishment and kings' court did not have a powerful social base to build their agendas on their demands and push for real and sustained change.

The reform movement got as far as it did to pass new laws, encroach on Shari'a Courts and to establish a whole new court system, but it failed to enforce the new laws, expand the system to the whole country and institutionalize it. The Constitutional Revolution that was limited to some big cities and some sections of the population was not enough forceful to push for more change when its flames diminished.

3.1 STATE BUILDING BASED ON CONSTITUTIONALISM

The Qājārs (1795–1925) attempted to revive the Safavid Empire and in many ways patterned their administration after that of the Safavids. They lacked the claims to religious legitimacy available to the Safavids and failed to establish strong central control, and government bureaucracy and functions were limited (Keddie & Amanat, 1991: 176). Due to the spread of the quasi-feudal land tenure[2] system based on *toyul* that strengthened the regional power of tribal and other military leaders, the strength of central government was crucially damaged. In the absence of increased sources of revenue, the expansion of the central bureaucracy set the stage for the bankruptcy of state finances and fragmentation of power (Arjomand, 1988: 32). In traditional despotic rule of Qājārs, the king was the source of law and hence he was above the law, even the laws that were issued by him. His will was the law and there was no institution to put limit on his action.

Although the incorporation of Iran into the international system of sovereign states introduced attempts at modernizing the state and the idea of modern state gained currency and became the ideal of the reformers (Arjomand, 1988: 29–30), the developments before and after the Constitutional Revolution led to a weaker state. The entrenched diversification of power and delegation of state authority and other matters of state, such as maintaining local order, applying justice, and tax collection, to local authorities chosen from amongst powerful notables and tribal leaders throughout the country made state-building extremely difficult. As a consequence, the Qājārs were not able to create the foundation of an effective administration and failed to centralize the institution of the state.[3] Even the Constitutional Revolution of 1906 did not succeed in disengagement of the state from dynastic, proprietary, and social inter-linkages and setting up a strong modern state (Arjomand, 1988: 27). Being neither a grassroots nor a widespread phenomenon, the Revolution did not aim to build a strong state and, in fact, was largely a reaction to the gradual strengthening of the state. Instead of establishing justice, the rule of law and some sense of order, it led to chaos and disorder.[4]

Qājārs also faced an external threat from superior European powers, primarily Russia and Britain. Foreign interference in Iran, Qājār misrule, and new ideas on governance and social change coming from Europe led to protests and eventually to the Constitutional Revolution (1906–07), which, at least on paper, limited royal absolutism, created a constitutional monarchy in Iran, and recognized the people as a source of legitimacy.

The Constitution of 1906—coming to life in the second wave of constitution-making in the world (Elster, 1995: 368)—expressly declared the abolition of the traditional doctrine of sovereignty that was based on the prerogative of the ruler to exercise his will for the enACTment of custom. It also and referred to legislation or passing an ACT by Parliament in the legal literature within the areas left free by *shari'ah*. Like other constitutions written in this period under the influence of European revolutions in 19th century, it recognized the separation of powers, civil rights of the individuals and low levels of independence for the judiciary. The Constitution of 1906 was to make the sovereign an executive bound to the laws made by the parliament. Now that the nation (*mellat*) was declared the source of the three powers and of sovereignty (Articles 26 and 35 of the Supplement to the Fundamental Law, approved in Oct. 7, 1907) the members of the parliament as its representatives were theoretically invested with a power parallel to the king's power.

The pre-constitutional political regime was fundamentally based on patronage. The shah was considered the sole source of power, the pivot of the universe (*qebleh-ye 'ālam*) (Amanat, 1997) and shadow of God (Arjomand, 1984). The patrimonial regime of Qājārs was operating on the basis of personal and tribal loyalties. These loyal bonds usually gave a bargaining power to the actors of the political arena, i.e. Qājār family, tribal leaders, and bureaucratic elite. The *ra'iyyah*s or lower classes did not in practice have access to the officials and justice, and had to turn to brokers; *'ulamā* were the most influential group among these brokers.

The Qājār state before 1906 was a non-ideological, courtly state that was based on non-politicized masses. The main social pattern of lord-vassal-peasant was translated to king-court-subject model in the polity. There were no hierarchical or contractual relations in governmental offices: personal relations were the cements of official relationships in the polity. There was also no system of rule constituted of impersonal, official roles. There was no right for even some individuals to resist prevaricating ruler. Fragmentation and a low degree of institutionalization and fragmentation of authority and system of rule made the scene ready for sporadic social uprisings and rebellions. The state had already lost its military significance to tribal leaders due to defeats and foreign encroachments, and non-successful reforms of the military structures (Ādamiyyat, 1969). Public prerogatives of the ruler were no longer enough for social and political control.

In the nineteen century, cultural influence of the West, the rise of a new bourgeois class and economic penetration of Europeans polarized state and society in Iran. This led to the Constitutional Revolution of 1906 that was not based on a demand for the transfer of power to a group with new ideology, but simply for the restoration of righteous or just government. In this revolution, a coalition of intellectuals, *'ulamā,* merchants, urban wage earners, trades people, and artisans attempted to create a parliamentary monarchy, while landowners were allied to the establishment, i.e. the bureaucracy, courtiers (*darbāris*), large fief holders (*toyuldārhā*), the hereditary state accountants (*mostowfihā*), the royal family, the titled officials, and the tribal leaders (Keddie & Amanat, 1991: 174–179, 192, 202; Abrahamian, 1982: 33). In the first and second constitutional periods, i.e. 1906–7 and 1909–1911, two coalitions were shaped: coalition of the Shah, disillusioned *'ulamā,* wealthy landowners and their clienteles on one side and the coalition of merchants, artisans, some of the tribesmen and some clerics. The majority of the *'ulamā* confronted the reformers' programs for secular education, secular judicial administration and land redistribution and did not usually exercise any effective role in the parliament and in judicial affairs (Hairi, 1977: 216). This culminated to a weak and fragile state, susceptible to coup and dynastic change.

In this period, social order was maintained through an agrarian system of absentee landlordism. Qājār dynasty rulers, after consolidation of their power, gave tracts of the land to their valiant chieftains, and exempted such estates from taxation; these men kept order in their territories and in theory provided soldiers and supplies for the exploits of the king. Livestock husbandry necessitated its own social relations rooted in nomadic military power.

In the period of 1907–1925 urban masses (a small portion of the population (Rāvandi, Vol. III, 1961: 9–12), that had been politicized and prone to ideology during the Constitutional Revolution, were depoliticized and de-ideologized[5] after 1911. The elite remained ideological in this period. Within the limits of the arbitrary rule of the king, the central and local landlords and the administrators appointed by the king, mainly carried on the government. These people were randomly advised and checked by the provincial high-ranking officials and elders of the tribes. Due to the lack of centralized state and anarchy and disintegration followed by the constitutional Revolution from 1906 to 1921 (Arjomand, 1988: 58) the government had no authority over its territory and could not enforce law and order.

The constitution of 1906 and its supplement of 1907 established the basics of popular sovereignty, monopoly of the state over legislation and punishment of Iranian citizens, separation of powers, rule of law and civil rights for all citizens, i.e. the most crucial elements of modern nation-states in Europe. Based on the Constitution, the courts were to be free entirely from outside interference. The basic rights and duties of Iranian people were clearly defined in the section of the Supplement to the Fundamental Law on people's rights (Articles 8–25). Subjects were guaranteed complete inviolability of their domiciles except with the authority of the courts and according to law (Articles 9, 13 & 16). The government could not thereafter examine and seize private letters and publications in the mails and telegraphs (Articles 22 &23). Freedom of press and political associations and gathering were guaranteed (Articles 20 & 21). The Constitution provided that judges are independent in the conduct of trials and in rendering of their judgments in an indirect way (Articles 28, 81 & 82).

Articles 71, 73 and 74 of the Supplement of the Fundamental Law were crucial in establishing one of the basic elements of modern nation-states, i.e. monopoly of the state in exercising legitimate violence against the citizens (Weber, 1968: 901). Article 71 states that "the Supreme Court of Justice and courts of justice are official authorities to hear and settle disputes." According to Article 73, "'*Orfi* Courts can only be established by law and no one in any position and rank cannot establish a court against the law." Article 74 laid down this rule that "no court would be held except by law." According to Article 12, "no one could be punished other than by virtue of law." This article together with Articles 16 and 17 of the Supplement established the rule of legality of defining crimes and punishment that is accomplished through powers of the state. These Articles were to concentrate the judicial power in the hands of the central government. They also obligated the state to settle any disputes among citizens and between citizens and the state. These articles set forth the principle of rule of law and equality of citizens before the law.

During the Constitutional Revolution, Moshir ul-Dowleh Pirniā,[6] who became PM in the early 1920s, believed that only one system of law should be enforced in the whole country (Zerang, Vol. I, 2002: 192–193). Marginalizing the opposite approach, i.e. considering different laws for different part of the country,[7] it could pave the way for establishing the legal foundations of a modern and unified nation-state.

The royal power, during Qājārs, was limited in practice by the strength of the aristocracy that mediated between the people and the throne. This class had exceptional privileges and was consulted in all matters of vital interest. Most members of the aristocracy were attached to the throne by receiving their estates from the king; in return they provided him with men and materials when he was in war. Within their fiefs they had almost complete authority-levying taxes, enacting laws, executing judgment along with *sharī`ah* courts, and maintaining their own armed forces (Shaikhulislami, 1971).

In the late Qājār, the landed aristocracy gradually turned some of its power over to a commercial plutocracy helped to maintain social control and served as intermediary between the people and the king. Every Qājār king, and later Pahlavis and even Islamic jurists in post-Islamic revolutionary era, formed a clique of supporters and used them to oppress any dissident, if suppression was not possible through bureaucracy of inflicting fear and obedience.

The Constitutional Movement led Iranians of all classes, merchants, clerics and tribal leaders who demanded a limited monarchy and the creation of an elected parliament to a new era. For the Islamicizing elites, the doors of *ejtehād* was open for founding a constitution on Islamic *sharī`ah*. For secularizing elites, the partial hegemony of the West was the key for promoting their democratization and secularization project.

In pursuing their goals of establishing a constitutional regime and get rid of despotism, the different groups that were active in the movement ignored the many inherent contradictions in their programs and social plans. Achievement of the immediate goals ended the loose coalition of divergent interests and ideas, and old hostilities were revived.

'Ulamā were not by any means united. There were generally three groups of them: 1) conservatives that desired to retain their existing privileges in any political regime, 2) the group that in retrospect might be called Islamists who had a maximalist reading of *sharī`ah* in public affairs and saw the Constitutional Movement as a step towards the establishment of the Islamic state (*mashru'eh*), refused democratic principles like equality of individuals in front of the law and elections, and were pursuing conformity of every regulation and policy with *sharī`ah*, and 3) Constitutionalists who had a minimalist reading of *sharī`ah* in public affairs and their aim was " not the adoption of Western civilization, but only its techniques, in order to establish the supremacy of law, interpreted to be *sharī`ah*, and to prevent foreign encroachment" (Lambton, 1987: 299–300). This group

was pursuing the goal of not having regulations and policies contradictory with Islamic ordinances in the framework of the Constitution (*mashruteh*). The second group believed that there is no need for enactment of new laws while *shari`ah* expresses the verdict in any case. The members of this group repeatedly cried this idea that "our law is Quran.[8]"

In Qājār era, even after the Constitutional Revolution, there was almost no concentration in most of the governmental and bureaucratic affairs of the state. Clerics had no doubt in any case not to refer disputes to state courts.[9] In local areas, the khans and chiefs of tribes hardly cared about the government agents, and had their own government and judicial officers (Hairi, 1977: 13–14).

The separation of power as the basis of the new political structure was violated by the executive and legislative powers in this period. Most of the governors and executive officials still interfered in the judiciary affairs after the victory of Constitutional Revolution.[10] Mohammad Ali Shah killed a bunch of freedom fighters, like Malek ul-Motakallemin, Sur Esrāfil, Ruh ul-Qodos, and Ardāqi Qazvini without trial after cannoning the Parliament. Sometimes beside executive and shah's interferences, legislative power proceeded trial of writers and political activists.[11]

Even a few years past from the Constitutional Revolution, the judges could not call their decisions "rule" or "decree"; they had to call it "report to the Ministry of Justice" (Amin, 2003: 496). Nobles and chieftains of the tribes were other sources of interference in the judicial procedure (Amin, 2003: 498). The Constitution of 1906–7 had recognized these difficulties but did little to address them. It professed general principles that everyone's rights should be protected, the judges should be partially kept independent of the government control, and separation of power should be recognized. This was left to the Parliament to elaborate on these principles, but any reform was left to the Shah.

3.2 RELIGIOUS AND STATE JUDICIAL SYSTEMS: FORMAL SECULARIZATION

The post-Constitutional Revolution governments lacked stability and homogeneity, although the prime ministers and ministers were all conspicuously secular in outlook. The secularizing and Islamicizing Iranian elites had been contesting over the state power from the onset of the Constitutional Revolution, and this contest had been going on for about a century.[12] In some periods and some issues, the contest was actually between two schools of *shari`ah* jurisprudence rather than a struggle between secular intellectuals and *'ulamā*. The Constitutional Revolution of 1906 transformed the debate from a philosophical and theological one between tradition and modernity to a debate between two interpretation or reading of Islam itself, i.e. democratic and authoritarian, reflected in the writings of pro- and anti-constitutionalist *'ulamā* (Nā'ini, 1955 [1909]; Zargarinezhād, 1998).

Although the political elite were eager to secularize the judiciary and to transfer judicial affairs from *'ulamā*'s hands to the state and they were aware of the obstacles, the legal, political and social structures played a deterring role in judicial secularization. They picked a gradual secularization program not to mobilize traditional forces against it. The pre-nation state nature of Islamic law, the complications in the structure of the courts, accessibility of *shari`ah* courts compared to state courts, and the specific prerogatives of *shari`ah* courts as opposed to the secular courts contributed in the failure of the judicial secularization in this period. It worked in some sections of the judicial system, like constitutional bases for an independent judiciary and due process, because of the cooperation between new elite and reformist *'ulamā* through bridging the jurisprudential gap between Islamic *shari`ah* and the state law.

The formal structure of judiciary and its relationship with other branches of government in the Constitution of 1906–7 was bound to create the difficulty of reconciling statute laws with a number of practices derived from the *shari`ah*. Complete legal equality was a modern concept that could not be matched with the necessities of *shari`ah* which recognized inequalities cutting across religious boundaries and inequalities between *'ulamā* as the God's representatives and hence privileged on the one hand, and laymen and laywomen as herd of the God on the other. Art. 32 regarding the right of everyone to litigate against any governmental office, Art. 8, of the Supplement, regarding complete legal equality, and Arts. 9 & 13–17, of the Supplement, regarding protection of life, property, dignity, and residence of every individual were to guarantee this legal equality. This idea was to limit the arbitrary rule of the king, though there was no mechanism to enforce it at the time.

Islamic law was not, traditionally, state law, and the whole movement to codify it and make it part of the state law begins only in 19th century. Every administrator and the king himself acknowledged the guidance and authority of the *shari`ah*. The legal development was from sacred to secular sanctions, from severity of religious codes to lenience of more humanized codes, and from physical to more financial penalties. In the framework of *shari`ah*, an appeal to god was taken through trial by ordeal.[13]

The financial independence of the *'ulamā* prevented the government to exert control over religious courts that in turn led to chaotic decision-making in the judicial affairs and courts. For the similar cases in *shari`ah* courts, there would be totally different decisions from different judges; this chaos usually directed people from one *shari`ah* court to the other to get what they were looking for at the end. If there was only Shari`ah Courts in the country, there was no chance for a unified system of judiciary. This has its roots in the plural religious authority system of Shi'ite tradition.

The structure of the courts in this period is complicated. Two separate court systems, religious or *shari`ah* courts and secular state courts, were operating side by side. This cohabitation, that has its roots in the long history of judiciary in Iran, is one of the main characteristics of the judiciary in this period. The structure was decentralized. Nevertheless, within this largely archaic structure the judiciary should settle complex conflicts generated by the twentieth century life. The administration of justice in this period was divided between *shari`ah* courts, run by the *'ulamā,* and "state courts in secular matters" (*mahākem-e 'adliyyeh dar 'orfiyyāt;* referred to in Article 27.2 of the Supplement) or state courts presided by the state officials. The term for the new judiciary consisting of state courts, i.e. *'adliyyeh,* if we think of it in terms of traditional theory of kingship based on justice (*'adl*), supports this idea that the authority of judges has to be derived from the king. The former had the more extensive network and was the basis for judiciary in the country due to the extensive network of clerics (Zerang, Vol. I, 2002: 174).

State courts were located in big cities and large towns, and people who were living in small cities, rural areas and villages had difficulty to access to them, while *'ulamā* were easily accessible all over the country. Some tribes had also their own customary law or *'orf.* In general, the Shari`ah Courts dealt with family and personal status law, with wills, contracts, and other legal documents, and with breaches of Islamic law, while magistrates' courts concentrated on criminal cases and rebels against the state. In the case of commercial litigation, the parties involved might choose between secular mediators or religious authorities (Keddie & Amanat, 1991: 178–179). Shari`ah Courts were not bound by any higher court other than the ruler's court (Arjomand, 2005). There was no appeal system for the religious courts.

The Articles 27 and 71 of the Supplement recognized both state and *shari`ah* courts. The Law of Judiciary Organization and Shari`ah Courts and Reconciliation Magistrates (LJO) of 1911 was a context for bringing these courts together and define their different jurisdictions in a more unified judicial system. In both civil and penal areas, two different organizations were promulgated for *'orfi* and *shari'* judgments. There were two radical approaches to interpret the Constitution and its Supplement: 1) the ideology of *mashruteh-ye mashru'eh* (religiously legitimized constitutionalism) which only recognized *shari`ah* courts as the base of the judiciary (Zerang, Vol. I, 2002: 2000) and 2) the ideology of secular *mashruteh* which only recognized state courts as the base of the new and modern judiciary (Zerang, Vol. I, 2002: 201).

According to Article 3 of LJO, the Ministry of Justice should recognize the *mujtahed* who is introduced by two sources of emulation to be the judge of *shari`ah* court. The *shari`ah* courts did only review the cases that were referred to them by the primary courts (Article 29 of LJO). The decisions of these courts could only be effective if the primary court issued its verdict considering the verdict of *shari`ah* court.

In spite of some limitations for *shari`ah* courts, wherever it was not clear that a case should be referred to a *shari`ah* or state court by considering their jurisdictions in virtue of law,[14] and plaintiff and defendant could not agree on a specific court, the case should be investigated in a *shari`ah* court (Kasravi, 1944: 152). *'Ulamā* also enjoyed lots of power in the state judiciary system. The Attorney General and the Attorney General of the appeal court were to be appointed by the Minister of Justice with confirmation of *'ulamā* and order of the king (Article 83 of the Supplement, and Article 153 of LJO). Beside the magistrate in reconciliation court, there was a sitting cleric who had the authority to investigate and settle dispute in *shari'* affairs (Article, 20 of LJO). At least one of three judges of the primary courts and the head of the criminal court and his deputies had to be from *'ulamā* (Articles 37 and 417 of LJO). In the *shari`ah* courts, one *mujtahed* presided the court and he had two assistant who should be near to *ejtehād* (near to be graduated from a Shi'ite seminary as *mujtahed*) (Article 3, LJO).

In this period, most of the judges were still mullahs, and the courts were for the most part located in the *'ulamā*'s houses (Rāvandi, Vol. III, 1961: 507) or their *mahāzer* (offices) (Rāvandi, Vol. III, 1961: 495 & 496). The penal law was mostly based on *lex talionis,* or the law of equivalent retaliation (*qesās*).[15] The penal law of the *shari`ah* was in abeyance in 19th century Iran, as it was in earlier periods and in many parts of the Muslim world, and the death penalty was the exclusive right of the Shah. Death was formally supposed to be decreed for a variety of crimes: incest, adultery, sodomy, treason, and murder, and only the king could decree it; and he never did it for sodomy or adultery, but for murder, highway robbery and bodily injuries-"the four crimes" (*ahdāth-e arba'eh*).[16] These traditions and habits of enforcing law and order, political and social control, and self-restraint have been part of the unconscious basis of Iranian legal-political culture. The writers of Iranian Civil Code had the ability to bridge the jurisprudential gap between Islamic *shari`ah* and the state law.[17] They could find strong appeal among Shi'ite *'ulamā.*

The most challenging aspect of the judicial reform in this era was judiciary's lack of unity. The difficulty of the reform management was the different Qājāri administrations' tendency, both before and after the Constitutional Revolution, to create new institutions to deal with new problems without destroying the old or relating them one to another. The Constitutionalists, instead of making an effort to rationalize the judicial process by merging the two systems of courts into a new judicial organization, recognized the dual court system.[18]

In this period, *shari`ah* courts still had the specific prerogatives as opposed to the secular courts. Despite provisions to bind *shari`ah* courts by state courts, which appeared to make *shari`ah* judges subordinate to the state judiciary, *shari`ah* courts retained most of their autonomy. The vast majority of cases decided by the shari`ah courts did not involve state questions, and *shari`ah* court judges, i.e. *'ulamā,* ruled upon them according to their own traditions. The religious leaders as well as secular court judges dealt with judicial affairs side by side and, at times, passing opposing judgments on the same case (Hairi, 1977: 14). Competition between the two court systems ensued from their overlapping jurisdiction. The constant interference of the *'ulamā* to exert their greater influence and authority and also their contradictory judgments and decisions led to paralysis in the judiciary's regular functions. While the Ministry of Justice ignored the religious courts' ordinances when they were incompatible with the workings of the Ministry, these tensions decreased the impact of the judicial reforms. This duality almost killed the reforms because those sections of *'ulamā* and guilds who were pro-reform need to maintain a united front against the Shah and could not fight over judicial reforms.

State courts in this period were functioning on the basis of three-stage/hierarchy judicial procedure but in a handful of regions and mainly in the capital, while Shari`ah Courts, widely scattered in all provinces, had no such thing and the decisions were final. The central government did not have enough power to enforce this three stage judicial procedure in small cities and hinterlands. In judicial arena, instead of two kinds of courts, there were at least three court systems operating in the country. Different authorities with different educational background were supervising these courts. Shari`ah Courts were in the hands of *'ulamā* and were issuing decrees based on *shari`ah*. The Criminal Courts were in the hands of *'ulamā* and secular judges and were issuing decrees on the basis of a dual legal system, produced out of *shari`ah* and secular laws. Commercial Courts were totally out of *'ulamā*'s domain of judgment and were functioning on the basis of a totally secular law and were working under the authority of Minister of Commerce, although with no friction with *shari`ah* (Zerang, Vol. I, 2002: 162–178). Each of these courts was dispensing justice to different groups of people according to different methods and different laws.[19]

The judicial reform would bring *'ulamā* into conflict with many of their potential and active followers and collaborators. Every reform that could threaten their privileges and authority would end to resistance. Some of the *'ulamā* supported the despotism, fearing the consequences of the reforms for the religious establishment. They thought that legal and judicial reforms would lessen the judicial power of the *'ulamā*. It was clear that the *'ulamā* would be compelled to try their cases in the courts of justice (state courts), as defined by the Article 71 and the succeeding articles of the Constitution, not in informal tribunals held at their private residences or elsewhere. Even Constitutionalist clerics did not want any bill or action to impair their judicial powers. They reserved the judicial power almost completely to the *'ulamā*.[20] *'Ulamā*'s resistance against the state and centralized rule of law was so severe that state courts for a long period did not have courage to call their decisions "verdict" and referred to their verdicts as "report to the Minister of Justice" (Sāleh, 1969: 231). Any discussion about law and order could instigate strong reactions from *'ulamā* that the officials want to legislate against *shar'* (Sāleh, 1969: 233).

'Ulamā did not have a homogeneous position and carried ideological challenges among themselves. Minimalist and maximalist reading of Islam and *shari`ah* were competing each other from the onset of the Constitutional Revolution. Maximalists have believed that the laws at any time should conform to the *shari`ah* but the minimalists have believed that the laws should not conflict with the *shari`ah* in principle. The powerful clerics who mostly had the maximalist approach were supported by the sentiments of the masses and safeguarded by the provisions of the Constitution. The minimalists backed by the intellectuals and new elite could not do anything and had to wait for a powerful government to pursue their approach.

The reformists wanted all cases referred initially to the Ministry of Justice, which would then decide whether they should go before a State or Shari`ah Court (Martin, 1989: 139[21]). The struggle over the judicial reforms highlighted the divergence between the interests of the *'ulama* and the interests of the new class of intellectuals who were crying for centralized government and a uniform national legal system. This struggle is part of the internalization of conflict between modern and traditional, as they were understood at the time.

Second Article of the Supplement to the Fundamental Law or the Constitution gives priority to *shar'* over the state law when it states that all laws should not be in contradiction with Islamic ordinances and authority of Islamic jurists. This was the main ideological and theoretical challenge for any secular reform in any state affair especially judiciary. The change of substantive laws like Civil, Trade, and Penal Laws was mainly postponed (Sāleh, 1969: 235) in this period due to this priority.

Legal reforms, such as those enacted by the constitutional governments in post Constitutional Revolution era, could have profound effects on all aspects of Iranians' political and social life, transforming even those features that revolutionaries and reformers intended to leave untouched. The prominent consequences of judicial reform in post-Constitutional Revolution era were transformation of sacred texts into worldly governmental regulations, deepening the gap between *'ulamā* and state, increase of the power of intellectuals graduating from new educational system, and increasing tension between mimimalist and maximalist readings of Islam.

When secular or state courts were established, *sharī`ah* courts were unwittingly transformed into either state courts or religious institutions; When reformers codified parts of the *sharī`ah,* they transformed sacred texts into worldly governmental regulations with consequences in law and order areas of life. The rich tradition of *sharī`ah* jurisprudence continued to shape people's lives and concerns. The unintended consequences of codifying were mixing the areas of religion and state, and rationalizing exchanges in the areas governed by irrational principles, i.e. religious decrees.

Due to the need of the judiciary and other governmental offices to hire more foreign educated individuals to run the state affairs the power of *'ulamā* to lobby in the political circles diminished. There was a great shortage of personnel with adequate legal training. The personnel were generally unfamiliar with the exact procedure prescribed by the new codes. The new judiciary system had only partial effect in Tehran and virtually none in other parts of the country. As a result, most cases were relegated to the *sharī`ah* courts where they were delayed or misjudged owing to incompetence and lack of legal discipline (Banani, 1961: 70).

The judicial reform and its dilemmas show that the main opposition is not between modern and traditional, i.e. between human reason and religious superstition, but between two types of religion: a minimalist religion that recognizes the separation of governmental and religious institutions, not separation of religion and politics as it is usually mentioned by clerics to misdirect or deceive the public and legitimize their rule, and an ideologized maximalist religion that is supposed to be the foundation of legitimacy of total and authoritarian power. The internal open, detailed and extended debates over the proper role of religious values and decrees in political life did not begin until the victory of the Islamic Revolution that led to the rule of clerics.

3.3 CODIFICATION AND TRANSPLANTATION: ORGANIZATIONAL CHANGE

To prevent an inconsistent and unsystematic reception of European laws in late 19th century, political elite resorted to codification for some areas of the law, including commercial laws where *shari`ah* was almost silent. They began transplantation and codification with procedural law and regulations regarding judicial organization in years immediately after the Constitutional Revolution. This was mostly the case in regulations regarding procedures that could trigger less opposition from *'ulamā*.[22] The pressure of foreign powers and their interference in internal matters had a double edged sword effect: they expedited the transplantation in some areas especially in procedural laws and at the same time caused the resistance from traditional sections of the society who were totally against military presence and occupation of part of the country by superpowers.

In 1908, the Office of Drafting Laws was established with the missions of translating laws, providing the regulations for the Office of Attorney General, setting forth the attributes and levels of heads and members of the courts and judiciary staff, establishing the reconciliation courts, and answering the judicial questions of the courts.[23] The Commercial Code was promulgated later in1915. This was based on the idea that although religious laws and decrees are necessary, they are not enough for regulating modern life.

The recruitment of foreign law teachers and consultant expedited the translation and transplantation process. The influence of French legal regime on Iranian judiciary is mostly due to the teachings of French teachers in Law and Political Science School (Zerang, Vol. I, 2002: 222–223). *'Ulamā* were quick to reject any law that they considered contrary to *shari`ah* (Sadr, 1985: 212).

The constitution of 1906,[24] mainly translated from Belgium and French constitutions (Sāleh, 1969: 265), contained no hint to the independence of the judicial function. Its separation from executive and legislative powers was later secured in the Supplement (Art. 27)[25] that was drafted out of Belgium Constitution and French laws.[26] Articles 81 and 82 of the Supplement provided a firm basis for independent of the judges in their verdicts.[27] The old concept of the judge (*qāzi*) that was a delegate of the ruler, now appointed through the Minister of Justice, persisted. This was to create difficulties when the reforms were really extended to the judicial organization and, especially, during the establishment of procedural laws and regulations.[28] The Constitutional Revolution did not require a negation of the old legal order.

The values that underlie law and society discourse and the heterogeneity of these values in the matter of the cause of this heterogeneity were based on Iranian traditions and Shi'ite Islam. Islam, in the context of the Constitutional Revolution, was "a" source of law, not "the" source of law.[29] *Shari`ah* that was believed to be beyond the power of human enactment or codification was the main source of the civil law, but the Constitution had European roots. The idea of *qānun* (law) was transformed from traditional law to the state's law. The concept of *'edālat* (justice) in this period is transferring from "giving each person his due in interests of order and stability" to "the promulgation and juridical execution of rules by the state" or "administration of justice in terms of equality before the law."

Transplantation and codification in this period were about organizational reform. Fundamental and substantive laws were out of discussion due to the balance of power between secularist and Islamist sections of the parliament. Even the Penal Code that was passed by the cabinet between sessions of Third and Fourth Parliament could not be enforced due to the discontent of *'ulamā* (Zerang, Vol. I, 2002: 226).[30] The LJO that was crucial in shaping the structure of new judiciary was modeled out of similar European laws.

It was the judiciary and not the Bar Association who licensed the lawyers (Arts. 237 & 240, LJO). In the legal textbooks of Political Science School, law was divided to private internal and public internal law. As defined in these textbooks, public internal law includes the regulations relating governmental offices and the relationship between the state and its subjects. Private internal law includes the regulation relating the relationship between the subjects of the state (Forughi, 1906: 11). As it can be seen, there is nothing about institutions between the top of the pyramid of power and the bottom, although the idea of constitution and constitutional rights was a progressive idea for state building at the time.

The Constitution approved dual courts system (Sec. 2, Art. 27 of the Supplement).[31] As the result of the policy of having both *shari`ah* and state courts, these two operated side by side. State or secular courts were justified by this argument that these courts are not only compatible with Islam but also were necessary to it.[32] In spite of creation of a court to settle disagreements between the state and *shari`ah* courts (in 1908) (Shāyegan, 1945: 30), the struggle between the clergy and state continued. Attempts to remove the conflicts between the two systems of law and courts continued throughout the post-Constitutional era to the point that Dāvar wound up the judiciary, and again revived after the Islamic Revolution of 1979. Secularizing bureaucrats avoided direct challenges to Islamic authority by setting up alternatives to Islamic schools and courts rather than replacing them in this period, because the central state had not enough power to enforce a completely secularized system of law.

Due to the pressure of modernization and state building from outside the country and demand for reform from inside, stage by stage, increasing areas of life had to undergo legal redefinition and even reorientation, and areas used to be under the control of *'ulamā* had to be removed from the sacred sphere and delivered to secular. Religious opposition to judicial and legal secularization continued until the Civil Code was drafted totally on the basis of *shari`ah* and codified the family, marriage, and inheritance laws which were the core of the *shari`ah*. But with the extension of the state courts (penal, commercial and civil), the scope of the functions and jurisdiction of the *shari`ah* courts was severely contracted. Before this era, Shari`ah Courts had no limitation in jurisdiction and decision-making. The jurisdiction of the Office of Justice (Divān-khāneh-ye 'Adlieh) that was directly working under the shah's authority was already and totally curtailed in favor of the new Ministry of Justice that was gradually taking over the judicial affairs (Zerang, Vol. I, 2002: 129, 145). The state courts did not have jurisdiction over cases to be judged according to non-codified *shari`ah*.[33] It was a challenge for the government to demarcate the scope of the jurisdiction of *shari`ah* courts. Much of this demarcation was not immediately enforced. The destruction of the *shari'* courts was gradually pursued by the government (Banani, 1961). The public demand for reform and the chaotic system of Shari`ah Courts gave enough leverage to the government to pursue its reform agenda, but 'ulamā, especially in rural areas, had enough power to neutralize the governments' actions. The illiterate and poor masses had no one other than mullahs to improvise basic services in the total absence of central government.

With reception of the European law, an enormous range of diverse social relations came to be legally regulated in ways that often differed widely from those of the traditional law that had sometimes elaborated and modified by Islamic jurists. The commercial law was one of the most important parts of this story. Enforcing this area of law was less challenging because it had no clash with *shari`ah*,[34] while it was the foundation for establishing new institutions like insurance companies and banks. The needs of commerce and the interests of merchants and European commercial laws, not the compilation of *shari`ah* laws, were the main sources of the new commercial law. Before the Constitutional Revolution, trades and commercial affaires were subject to *shari`ah* and the custom (*'orf*). Under

Nāser ul-Din Shah's rule and after the establishment of Department of Justice, an independent court was allocated to settling disputes in the area of commerce. This court, called Commercial Court, had many of the tradesmen as its consultants. The establishment of this court was due to economic growth of the late 19th century that culminated to the increasing power of tradesmen. In 1892, the representatives of tradesmen established the Iranian Trade Association that had representative all over the country. This association had the capacity to settle dispute between its members.

The Constitutional administrations confirmed this capacity, and the Commercial Court was recognized as one of the courts in new judicial organization (Mansur ul-Saltaneh, 1911: 373–374). After the Constitutional Revolution, the Commercial Code including 387 articles was ratified by the Parliament in 1915. There was also interplay between legal changes and the growth of commercial agriculture that led to the Registration of Deeds Act of 1921 and later Registration Act of 1932.

In the absence of the bar association in this period, all the affairs usually accomplished by bar associations like bar exam, licensing, disbarring, and prosecution of relevant transgressions were taken care of by the Minister of Justice[35]. The Law Exam Regulation of 1917 reasserted the authority of the executive power to license lawyers. This set of regulations put more limitation on practice of law by mentioning ambiguous terms like "honesty, religiosity, piety, dignity, and comportment" as the attributes of a lawyer and giving the authority to the state to verify these conditions and qualify or disqualify the lawyers. The first Iranian bar association was established in 1921 by the Ministry of Justice. This association had no financial and legal independence. Even the constitution of this association was written by the appointed board members and ratified by the Minister of Justice.[36] The new judiciary born after the Constitutional Revolution could not tolerate an independent bar association.

3.4 JUDICIAL REFORM AND REORGANIZATION: PROCEDURAL LAW AND CENTRALIZATION

There were two crucial causes for judicial reform in this period. The first one was a demand for more effective administration of justice and pressure of a social movement for justice. The government in post-Constitutional Revolution era had to respond to the demands for establishment of *'edālat-khāneh,* the house of justice that was the main demand of the participants in that movement. These are the governmental actions in the area of judiciary in this period to respond to that demand:

- Creation of four skeleton civil courts: the Court of Property and Financial Claims, the Criminal Court, the Court of Appeals, and the Supreme Court of Appeals (*divān-e tamiz*) in 1907,
- Centralization of the judiciary system by the Minister of Justice, Mokhber ul-Saltaneh (1908) (Arjomand, 1988: 47),
- Approval of the Judiciary Organization and Shari`ah Courts and Reconciliation Magistrates Law in 1911 dividing the courts to three levels of primary, appellate and cassation courts (Amin, 2003: 497),
- Formulation of a civil code under the guidance of a French jurist, Adolph Perni in 1911 (Banani, 1961: 69), and
- Issuing the decree for law practice exam as a condition for getting license for this profession by the Minister of Justice, Foroughi, in 1914.[37]

The second cause was the necessity to centralize the government. Centralization of the government was the driving force behind most of the political reforms in the region in the second half of the 19th and first half of the 20th century. The wave of nation and state building processes coming from Europe and implemented by the superpowers was so powerful that no subject state could resist against it. The necessity for trade and progress were also pushing for the new political structure. The new elite were totally aware of this wave and its consequences and they adopted policies and reforms to respond to it. Even the *'ulama* did not want to stay behind the forces of fragmentation and disintegration but they had their own ideas of nation and state building. The new elite was active during the Constitutional Revolution to represent the new idea of nation-state and its implications but it was frustrated when their former ally, i.e. *'ulama,* could not accept the consequences and implications of the new system of governance. On the other hand, *'ulama* were activated during the Constitutional Revolution to address their ignored role in the polity but soon were frustrated by the rise of the new elite to key positions of the state.

The judicial reform was headed to decrease the power of *'ulamā* and local chieftains and landlords in the area of judicial affairs. The creation of the Supreme Court of Appeals (1907), enactment of the Law of Registration of Deeds passed by the Majles on May, 1911 (Arjomand, 1988: 47), and approval of the registration of documents and property by the Majles and its amendments (1921, 1923 and 1925) (Mahbubi Ardekāni, 1999, Vol.2: 170; *Official Magazine of Justice Department,* Vol. 1, No. 10, 1928, p.6) were to reduce the influence of the Shari`ah Courts in criminal proceedings and property titles.

The Constitutionalists temporarily established Revolutionary Courts after conquering Tehran to try anti-Constitutionalist figures like Shaikh Fazl ul-Allah-e Nuri (Nāzem ul-Islam-e Kermāni, 1982: 535–537). Penal Courts were branches of Primary Courts. The Criminal Court was the highest primary court in the hierarchy of Penal Courts. The Police Courts were mostly established in small cities where there was no Penal Court. In these courts, the police commissioner or the village master (*kadkhodā*) played the role of the public attorney (Mansur ul-Saltaneh 'Adl, 1911: 382). Parallel to judicial courts and in spite of separation of powers, the executive power had its own special courts like Administrative Courts including General Auditing Office (Mansur ul-Saltaneh 'Adl, 1911: 386–387).

There were different goals for these reforms at this specific time of Iran's history. The first goal was to establish the House of Justice and access to justice for all. This was the most important demand of revolutionaries during the Constitutional Revolution and any administration after the Revolution had to respond to it. The second goal was to limit the direct intervention of *'ulamā* in judicial affairs. Article 27 of the Supplement to the Fundamental Law of 1907 clearly legitimizes the Shari`ah Courts beside customary (*'orfi*) ones, affirming the separation of *'orfi* and *shari`ah* courts that was a tradition in Iranian judiciary system from Safavids. By stating that "all courts are established by law," Article 74 closed the way for direct and illegal intervention of *'ulamā* in judiciary affairs. The constitutional administration in one of its first actions for judicial reform tried to clearly differentiate between *shari`ah* and *'orfi* courts' capacities. Mirzā Hasan Khan Moshir ul-Dowleh made the *'orfi* Courts' capacity clear in a statement: "bureaucratic disputes, customary affairs under the specific disciplines of the country and all commercial tasks."[38] Article 145 of the Judicial Organization and Procedure Law limited the capacity of *shari`ah* Courts to the following tasks: " 1) Disputes relating to ignorance of the provisions of *shari`ah* laws, 2) disputes relating to marriage and divorce, 3) in absentia decrees involving *shar'i* affairs, 4) cases in which decree of insolvency or incapability of insolvent or confiscation of property impedes compensation of debt or retribution writs, 5) cases in which disputes cannot be settled except with presenting evidence or inviting witnesses to the court or undertaking oath, 6) cases in which religious ordinances of both sides or one side are contradictory or concise and ambiguous, 7) cases in which the disputes are over the nature of endowment, the nature of will, trust of trustee, or testament of the executor, and 8) a case necessitates appointment of a trustee of endowment, a *shar'i* proctor, executor, or legal guardian is involved.[39]"[40]

According to Article 80 of the Supplement to the Fundamental Law of October 1907, this is the king who appoints all the judges.

Due to the weakness of the central government and its limitation to some big cities like Tehran and Tabriz, most of these provisions were not immediately enforced. Although the new procedure was completely different from what came before, in practice the government did not have enough trained personnel to change the routines. The new elite who were the main forces pressing for this delineation did not have enough power all over the country to marginalize the *'ulema* and local authorities as the main opposition. The relative strength of the new elite was in their familiarity with the modern world while the relative strength of *'ulama* was in their roots in the society. Iranians could ignore neither of these forces and hence pushed them to work together and resolve their seemingly irresolvable differences.

The third goal was to establish a three-stage judicial procedure. The point behind this idea was that justice is not the outcome of an individual decision but the outcome of a procedure. By establishing Appellate Court, Article 86 of the Supplement to the Fundamental Law of October 1907 confirmed two stages judicial procedure. This was a completely new development in Iran's judiciary. According to Islamic jurisprudence tradition, the verdicts of *shari`ah* judges could not taken to a higher court for judicial review. Establishment of Cassation Court in the Capital three years earlier, in 1908, had opened the way for three-stage judicial procedure.[41] The new system, if implemented, could reduce the authority and jurisdiction of the religious courts. The procedure part of the 1911 law was never passed; according to Sadr al-Ashrāf (quoted in 'Āqeli, 1990: 319), it was vetoed by Seyyed Hasan Modarres on behalf of the five *mojtahedin-e tarāz-e avval* (high ranking religious experts).

The by-product of the mentioned goals was secularization of the judiciary. Although the duality of courts is recognized in the Constitution of 1906–7, all of the judicial reforms were headed to secularize the judiciary, strengthen the state (*'orfi*) courts and weakening the *shari`ah* courts. All the new established courts, i.e. Primary, Penal, Appellate, and Cassation Courts, were customary courts.

There were three waves of judicial reform between 1908 to1925 that mainly happened because of separation of powers, and division of labor and missions between them. The first wave between 1908 to1911 was mainly headed to separation of religious and state courts' jurisdiction and clear definition of religious courts. The Minister of Justice, Mokhber ul-Saltaneh, tried to centralize the judiciary system in 1908 (Arjomand, 1988: 47). He also established the Office of Drafting Laws (1908) with the missions of translating laws, providing the regulations for the Office of Attorney General, setting forth the attributes and levels of heads and members

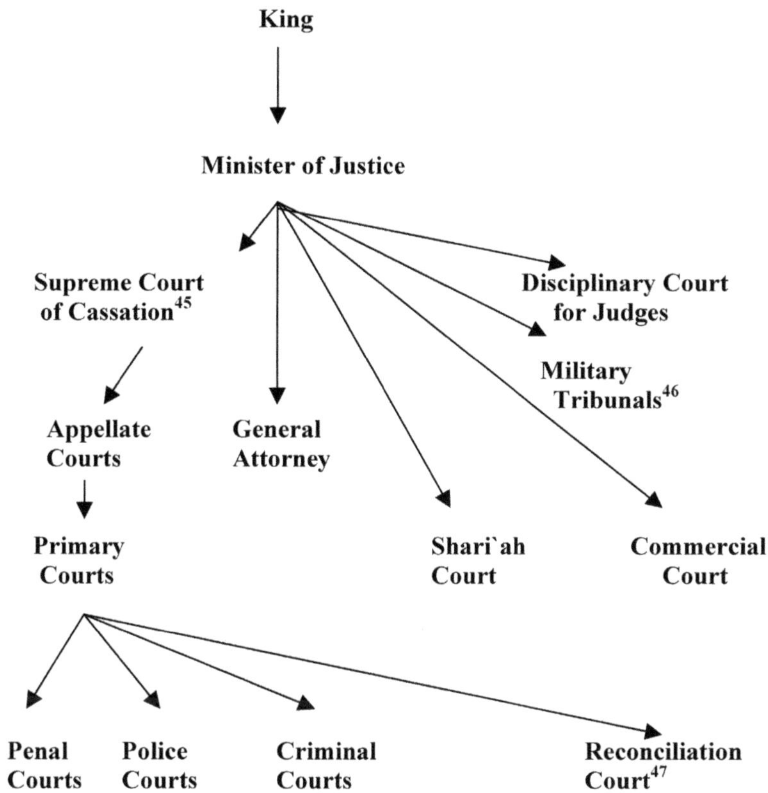

Fig. 3.1. The Chart of Iran's Judiciary, 1910–1927

of the courts and judiciary staff, establishing the reconciliation courts, and answering the judicial questions of the courts.[42] The second Minister of Justice in this period, Mirza Hasan Khan Moshir ul-Dowleh Pirniā, was successful in the areas of judiciary personnel reform, creation of due process law, recreation of the office of Attorney General (*modda'i ul-'omum*) in the Cassation Court (1910) (Mobārakiān, 1998: 363) and allocation of a specific budget for the judiciary (1909)[43] and revising some statutory laws.[44] He could also draw up the Judicial Organization Principles Law (1911).

His most important work was the approval of the Law of Judiciary Organization and Shari`ah Courts and Reconciliation Magistrates. According to this law all the heads and consultants of the Cassation Court, the heads and members of the Appellate Courts, the heads of the Primary Courts, were nominated by the minister of Justice and appointed by the king (Art. 149, LJO, 1911). As it can be seen in Fig. 3.1, all judicial powers are centered in the hands of the king and the Minister of Justice who is appointed by the king. The new judiciary organization, as it is presented in Fig. 3.1, was established by the Law of Judiciary Organization, Shari`ah Courts and Reconciliation Magistrate, 1911 to centralize the judiciary power in the hands of central government. It was also to prevent the interference of other powers of the government and local authorities in judicial affairs. Before LJO of 1911 and in spite of the approval of the Constitution and its Supplement, the judiciary similar to other pillars of the government was administered by a feudal political system. This law was to overcome the weakness of central government in judicial affairs.

The centralization of the judiciary could lead to more limitation of Shari`ah Courts. This did not happen in this period. Any move in this direction could potentially motivate protests of anti-Constitutionalist *'ulamā* who insisted on the unimpaired judiciary authority of the Shi'ite hierocracy. Even the constitutionalist *'ulamā* opposed the judicial reform. When the bill for reform of the judiciary came up for discussion during the last sessions of the First Majles in early 1908 the proponents of the judicial reform incurred excommunication by Behbahāni (Arjomand, 1988: 57).

In spite of drafting and passing of procedural and formal laws and laws regarding the judicial organization, almost no substantial law passed in the judicial committee of the parliament while the Constitution forbade any decision-making and punishment without invoking the law (Article 12 of the Supplement). As before, the ordinances of *shari`ah* were the bases of issuing verdicts.

The second wave between 1911 to1921 came through during the Ministry of Mohammad 'Ali Foroughi.[45] Issuing license for the judges, creation a test for getting in the judgeship career, and pushing courts to reason out their verdicts and document them with reference to the articles and principles of the law in accordance with which they are delivered were important developments in the judiciary in this period.

The main development in the third wave between 1921 to1925 was the formation of a new drafting commission in 1921 to draft new laws relating to the judiciary.[46] This commission prepared the draft of the Civil Code (passed 1928 and later in 1935), the Civil Procedural Law (passed in 1939),[47] Public Penal Code (passed in the cabinet in 1916 and annulled in 1922), Criminal Procedural law (first drafted in1912), and Bar Association Law (passed in the Parliament in1927). Experimental commercial code was introduced in 1924 (Banani, 1961: 70). Other developments in this wave are

- Establishment of law school in 1921 (Mahbubi Ardekāni, 1999, Vol.1: 404)
- Dissolution of the judiciary by Seyyed Ziā in1921 (Amin, 2003: 529). After Seyyed Ziā's coup of 1921, the most important measure of his administration was to dissolve the judiciary (Zerang, Vol. I, 2002: 230). The judiciary was dissolved once during Moshir ul-Dowleh's Ministry of Justice. This measure that was to reform judiciary led to more instability in the judicial system. Other than dissolution,[48] fiscal problems,[49] lack of communication in the governmental structure, corruption, weakness of central government, rebellion and riots, and insecure transportation system had important role in the instability of judicial organization. Judicial decisions were not protected by sanctions.
- The first election for Iranian Bar Association, Majma'-e Vokalā in 1921 ("Complete History of Law Practice in Iran" (*Tārikhche-ye Kāmel-e Vekālat dar Iran*) in official website of Iran's Bar Association),[50] and
- Approval of the registration of documents and property by the Majles and its amendments (1921, 1923 and 1925) (Mahbubi Ardekāni, 1999, Vol.2: 170; *Official Magazine of Justice Department,* Vol. 1, No. 10, 1928, p.6)

The registration of deeds was to deprive the *'ulamā* of an important function. This was part of the trend that began before the Constitutional Revolution of 1906 deepened the gap between the *'ulamā* and the state from the one hand and between the bourgeois strata and the hierocracy from the other. It did not happened in this period. Even in 1929, most of the public notary offices (*mahāzer*) were left in *ulamās*' hands. This only happened with the Registration of Documents and Property of 1932 (Banani, 72). After implementation it gave legal sanction to unconditionally held private property in land and thus constituted the legal basis for emergence of a new class of landlords who from now on would hold their title independent of the state (Arjomand, 1988: 47).

3.5 CHALLENGES AND DILEMMAS: LOW ACCESS OF THE NEW JUDICIAL INSTITUTIONS TO THE PEOPLE, JUDICIAL SERVICE FEES AND CORRUPTION

As it can be seen in the goals and causes of judicial reform in this period, reform was a serious task for different administrations but due to short-lived administrations and dilemmas mentioned below it could not fully be implemented. It would have produced an independent judiciary because of the rise of a new bourgeoisie class and the basics for an independent judiciary in the Constitution but it failed. The challenges and dilemmas could be categorized as international and national, theoretical and practical, organizational and procedural.

The most important international judicial challenge was the capitulation. The immunity from arrest that was given to foreigners resident in Iran and the right of trial by their own consular representatives, were both harmful to the authority of the judiciary. The operation of state courts were hampered and complicated by this system that permitted foreign consulates to interfere with the courts. This immunity was up to 1928.

The crucial theoretical challenge was the belief in self-fulfilling and reforming character of law. Iranian intellectuals and political activists in the second half of the 19th century believed in the self-fulfilling and reforming character of the law. They did not take into consideration the role of organizing people, cultural change, political pluralism, good governance and economic development in democratization process or establishment and effectiveness of the house of justice. They usually ignored the real political regime as opposed to legal political regime.

There were three practical challenges in front of the reforms: low access of the new judicial institutions to the people, judicial service fees, and corruption. The reformers had to deal with vested power from the traditional institutions, the very low literacy rate (Appendix VII), poverty, the lack of trained staff, and lack of facilities to have access to people. On the other side there was no popular conviction that the national government was an appropriate vehicle for furthering popular goals like justice, prosperity and stability, growth and distribution of income.

The judiciary system charged both sides of the dispute a percentage of the claim: 10 and 2.5 percents from the parties winning and losing the case respectively (Amin, 2003: 491).[51] This was totally against the principle of "justice for all." Other than non-accessibility, the country did not possess a single, centralized judiciary with suitable degree of specialization. A willingness to mobilize the law and judiciary to challenge the actions of government, i.e. the ideal of *'edālat-khāneh,* depends not only on the perceived legitimacy of such a challenge but also on such particulars as the availability of legal assistance, the presence of alternative forums for hearing complaints, and the costs, risks, and benefits associated with making complaints.

The public attorney offices were extensively corrupted, and this was worse in provinces compared to the Capital. It cannot be said that *shari`ah* courts were free of vice, since those who could pay their religious taxes to specific clerics were often favored. This is also true about corruption of the courts presided by clerics in the third and fourth eras of judicial reform in Iran.

The most crucial organization challenges had something to do with plans and procedures and jurisdictions. There was no pilot project, strategic sequencing, and procedural innovations. Judicial reform in this period was directed to change system in increments. Incremental reform was less costly and more easily controlled to render success, and tended to manage expectations by postponing the ambition for systemic reform. There was no pilot project, strategic sequencing, and procedural innovations. The selection of gradual approach was not based on research or consideration of consequences, but inability for systematic change. However, incremental reform failed for systemic reasons. Systemic reform was extremely difficult to carry out in practice. The new personnel were not available; the old personnel could not learn the requirements of new system quickly enough, and it was hard to change the internalized behavioral patterns.

Due to slow secularization and nationalization of the judiciary, different waves of reform in post-Constitutional Revolution era did not lead to extension of due process and secularization of the courts in national arena. The unsuccessful reform process in the judiciary and in the whole government led to Seyyed Ziā's coup of 1920.

It was not clear in the Constitution and in judicial system to which court a case was to be referred, and which cases came under what jurisdiction. Article 27 of the Supplement of Constitution merely states that *shari'* cases were to be tried in the *shari'* courts and *'orfi* cases in the governmental tribunals. Articles 71 and 82 dealing with the powers of the tribunals of justice and Court of Appeal respectively did not state the way of division of labor in the dual court system. The jurisdiction of individual judges of religious courts could not clearly be fixed as the parties might choose from among a number of competing judges. Weber explains this phenomenon as the charismatic character of "juridical prophets" (1968: 823). This jump from jurist to prophet is a very big one. The prophets reveal the law directly from God or a supernatural or sacred source. The jurist finds the law in the *feqh* books, and the Kadis administer the same. Neither is a 'prophet,' which is a special Weberian ideal type.

Chapter Four

Second Period: Modernization Era

When Qājār could no longer rule the country, political elites mostly educated in Europe who had ambitious plans for modernizing the state found an unprecedented opportunity to pursue their plans and ideas for modernizing Iran. Centralization and substantive secularization were at the heart of their plans that paved the way for Pahlavis to exercise rule in a more purposeful, continuous, and self-conscious manner. Judicial reform as an up-down reform is almost impossible without a centralized and powerful state.

Despite Dāvar's illegal dissolution of the judiciary, erosion of the judicial independence and occasions for frustration and backsliding, judicial processes were institutionalized and traditional laws were codified in new frames. Even after the Islamic Revolution of 1979, most of the codified *shari`ah* law were kept intact by the Islamic regime. With respect to the expectations and declared goals of the judicial reform, Dāvar's reforms were the most successful judicial reforms in the 20th century. A standard of efficiency and rationality unequaled in the Iranian history was established for all subjects of the state regardless of their ethnicity and locality. Although political activists confronted with brutality of the regime, regular cases benefited from the formal procedures and easier access to the courts.

Due to the gaps between the aspirations of intended design and the negative consequences of actual performance and local-capital unfilled space, the judicial system could not respond to the increasing expectations of urban strata in the second half of the 20th century. In spite of the early success of the ministers of justice during Reza Khan, political instability during 1940's and 1950's and autocracy and the necessity for political oppression during 1960's and 1970's closed the windows for more structural and institutional reforms.

4.1 MODERN STATE BUILDING

The state-building process in Iran during Pahlavi dynasty did not culminate in the institutionalization of power through depersonalization of rule, i.e. rule of office instead of rule of individuals, formalization, and standardization of expectations. In this period, authority is exercised by and through elite whose members are not representatives of interests and concerns of the majority of population. The practice of government addressed a bunch of new and distinctive concerns but in an exclusive way. Although the government increasingly took into account some aspects of the social processes like differentiation and urbanization, it failed to recognize their significance and made less and less contribution to their persistence.

The authoritarian modernization had to develop a balance between the extremes of a king with absolute power and the new educated elite, deal with the consequences of bureaucratization and transfer of technology, digest the demands of the weakened landed aristocracy, and prevent a coalition between new elite and aristocracy of the previous dynasty. The general conditions that favored the rise and survival of a new dynasty were: 1) protection by the superpowers, i.e. Great Britain and later the U.S., 2) continuous supply of political entrepreneurs, educated in European countries, 3) strong coalition of the central power with major segment of technocrat elite, 4) the availability of extractible resources, and 5) a population that had got used to being subjects (*ro'āyā*) of the government, not citizen with defined rights.

Political elite in Reza Shah era (1925–41) had ambitious plans for modernizing the state and society of Iran including the modernization of state. These plans included developing large-scale industries, implementing major infrastructure projects, building a cross-country railroad system, establishing a national public and secular education system, reforming the judiciary, and improving health care. A rural police organization, gendarmerie, was established and its control was transferred from the Ministry of War to that of Interior, again strengthening the civilian authorities in the provinces. The elite who believed in a strong, centralized government managed by educated personnel could carry out these plans.

The whole process of social, economic, cultural, and political modernization created unprecedented opportunities, problems, strains and conflicts, only some of which the state could adequately deal with in view of their emergency. The rapid growth of oil revenues especially during Mohammad Reza Shah (1941–79) played an important part in broadening the province of the state. Nevertheless, due to the lack of party system and democratization process, the state could not expand its reach to the influential groups and activists. The expansion of the state was not balanced with the demands of the social and economic enfranchisement, and creating occasions for patronage was not the answer for demand for participation. The authoritarian rule of Reza Shah worked against the democratic process in Iran.

The state, in this period, gradually got out of religious business through a complex of changes often referred to as secularization. Iran did not experience polity-separation but rather polity-expansion secularization, where the government "extends its jurisdiction into areas of social and economic life formerly regulated by religious structures." (Smith, 1974: 8) In the early Pahlavis, the power of *'ulamā* was in serious decline and their charisma which could claim *sharī`ah* as the only source of law and having all the high ranking judicial positions in their hands had dissipated by the first quarter of the 20th century, both politically and doctrinally. It is around this time that the government was centralized in Tehran, and institutionalized state structures such as a standing modern army were developed.

In this period, the state was considering what should be done to overhaul the structure of its administration. It was prompted to do so by scattered centers of power that did not follow the policies of the central government. Reorganization of the judiciary as part of the whole package of state building was sold on the basis of dissatisfaction of the people with the judiciary ('Āqeli, 1990: 111) and correction of the judicial procedures ('Āqeli, 1990; 108), and not political responsibility, popular control of the government, efficiency or cutting costs of the government. This had also little to do with economy.

In 1928, Ali Akbar Dāvar[1] abolished the capitulations under which Europeans and some other countries[2] in Iran had, since the nineteenth century, enjoyed the privilege of being subject to their own consular courts rather than to the Iranian judiciary. This was to strengthen the national pride of Iranians in the age of nationalism. For two decades, between the Constitutional Revolution when Iran had virtually no trained lawyers and judges and no institutionalized procedure of law enforcement and legal decision making, and the 1920's when some advances were finally being made, the hope that the regular courts would some day replace the capitulatory jurisdictions prompted nationalist Iranians to accept or at least tolerate this kind of jurisdiction. One of the main goals of judicial reform was to make Iran's judiciary a state-of the art system to persuade Europeans to end their judicial privileges based on capitulation.

During the Qājārs, generalized social status was the main criterion for the holding and exercising of political and administrative offices. During Pahlavis, appointment from above was added to the previous criterion. The state was not able to increase the rationality of bureaucratic and productive processes and to replace the negotiating conditions of employment based on formally equal contractual partnership for the forcible imposition of working duties upon subordinate individuals. At the same time bureaucratization including the bureaucratization of the judiciary was the inexorable fate of the authoritarian state building in the early 20th century. Judicial reform in this period was also directly pointed to make the bureaucracy more effective as an important element of modernization.

Due to the historical novelty of statism and state-building, the institutional principles of the state were very difficult to implement. The social processes at work in the everyday reality of political arrangements revealed the resilience and persistence of practices, which belonged to pre state-building era. The state in this period of Iran's contemporary history gradually became sluggish, top-heavy, insensitive, and incapable of perceiving and reacting to the multi-faceted changes occurring in the societal environment, let alone of initiating change itself. Other than incapability of state, social breakdown through reduction of the cohesion of the traditional society, disjunction between economic and political development, and rising expectations, religious values, politicization of social conflicts between advantaged and disadvantaged groups, and international pressures are said to have played some roles in destabilitization of the political structure.[3] This situation paved the way for a victorious revolution in 1979.

The state had to stand in opposition both to the autonomy of classes like clergy, *bāzāri*s and landowners, and to every kind of power outside the state like tribes (Cronin, 2000; Tapper, 1997; Beck, 1986; Oberling, 1974) to get centralized. The construction of a modern, centralized state, with a culturally homogenized population and unmediated power was against the interest of local and traditional powers. The state tended to be the only source of law, claiming sovereignty for itself both internally and internationally, but powerful social forces saw their interests in risk if the state would become the only source of law. The process of building a national law in Iran did not take place under conditions and on the basis of "assumptions that presaged European legal positivism" (Merryman, 1969: 20). These assumptions include distributed law making, temporal or spiritual superiority of the state, and inclusion of laws of local origin, while clergy had influence on the form and content of law making.

State centralization, economic modernization and secularization of the education helped to create an elite of army officers, bureaucrats, merchants, contractors, doctors, lawyers, engineers, writers, university teachers, and artists who adopted Western values and Western lifestyle in Pahlavi era. The secularization process was a socio-cultural process that enlarged "the areas of life-material, institutional and intellectual- in which the role of sacred is progressively limited" (Madan, 1998: 5). In the Iranian secularization process of early 20th century sectors of society and culture were "removed from the domination of religious institutions and symbols" (Berger, 1973: 113). The new government developed a minimum core of technically trained men capable of maintaining order, collecting taxes, and organizing the staff work required for the inevitable substantial role of the government in the economy, education process and settling the disputes.

The goal of officials in the Pahlavi regime was to exercise rule in a more purposeful, continuous, self-conscious manner, vesting various aspects of it in differentiated offices, manned by expressly trained, appointed personnel, operating according to stated rules, and controlled in those operations by the superior offices. But due to strong authoritative approaches in the polity and lack of civil society institutions, except the press and political parties during 1941–53, the state never worked as a rational bureaucratic machine.

Independency of different branches of power in post-Reza shah period was due to lack of a political power that could cover most of the social forces; there was nothing to bind all social groups and institutions, i.e. army, landed proprietors, *'ulamā,* new class of rich merchants, old bazaar and craft guild groups, bureaucracy, intellectuals and professionals. Some of the opposition parties like nationalist parties, as well as government bureaucracy and modern business circles, had some support coming from the judiciary. The charismatic, non-military figure of Mosaddeq functioned as the social cement for mustering most of these groups between1951 to 1953 under the flag of a nationalist movement. Instead of putting his energy into the construction of a strong political movement, he purged the judiciary and attempted to place his men in the important administrative posts (Binder, 1962: 114).

Iranian legal regime in the first half of the 20th century was headed toward a national law system, which was based on absolute sovereignty of the state. In this model, nothing outside the state could make law effective on or within the state without the state's consent (Merryman, 1969: 22). Counting the specifications of the new judiciary, Dāvar refers to the principle of monopoly of judicial affairs in the hands of the government ('Āqeli, 1990: 143). In this national system of law, the Constitution was supposed to be the main source of law and regulate all legislation; a statute was perceived to prevail over a contrary regulation; both a statute and a regulation were supposed to prevail over an inconsistent custom, when there was a misfit between the national legal system of the central government and the values of the local custom. The strong movement toward constitutionalism led to the assertion of its superiority, at least on paper, as the main source of law. The hierarchy of sources of law now must read "constitution, legislation, regulations, and custom." The dogma of separation of legislative from judicial power did not let a court to decide whether a statute is void because it was it was considered in conflict with the Constitution.

Rules and laws have justifiably valid functions in state building process, not as arbitrary impositions by unresponsive actors, but as a channel to abstract people's trust. State building process involves in the creation of institutions empowered to hold officials to account over and above criminal investigations for malfeasance. In this process, the state claimed exclusive jurisdiction over all people within its territorial boundaries. Pahlavis wanted to enforce their administrative law but without accountability. The state that was being built was not going to balance between security and civil rights, between effectiveness and rule of law, and monopoly of violence and rule of law.

The absolute external and internal sovereignty of the state led to a state monopoly on lawmaking. Because of the separation of powers, judicial decisions were not law, though issued and enforced by the state. In the framework of civil law tradition, copied from the European continent by the Iranian elite, the legislature transferred its power to executive branch to promulgate regulations (Āqeli, 1990: 107 & 153), turning over the force of law to administrative organs of the government (Appendix III). Such administrative regulations were effective as law only within the limits of the power transferred by the legislature. Dāvar used this transferred power to do his reforms in the Iranian judiciary and justify treating something that was not created by the legislative power of the state as law.

Dāvar's reforms in the judiciary were based on the idea of administrative justice. The law, in this approach, was supposed to be one of the engines of radical change in the society and an instrument for social and political control enforced by the administration. The administration wanted to use the force of law for pre-determined social transformation. It was believed that change and enforcing public law could effect controlled radical change when it distributes power on the basis of new ideologies like nationalism and developmentalism. Sweeping politicized administrative measures were pervasive and politicized exercise of administrative law was always directed towards guarding the transition. State employment in this period was based on education, and almost everybody with modern education got a job in the new bureaucratic state under Reza Shah. Patronage was also used to organize public administration. Transformative judicial practices revealed the pervasive uses of public law to define a new polity.

The role of law in Reza Shah era was to modernize state and society but like in any regime, the imperatives of power intervened with normative and ideological goals of the regime. The latter reduced the role of law in some aspects and periods to balance political forces that shaped the onset of regime change from Qājār to Pahlavi. Law's function was to advance the construction of political regime and to consolidate the political power. The legislation in this period does not follow "the principles of legality as regularity, generality and prospectivity" (Teitel, 2000: 215), i.e. the essence of the rule of law, but the principles of authority. Those principles of legality, whenever recognized, were vividly in conflict in Iranian context.

The shah in this era was identified with the state, and it was apparent that the primary duty of bureaucracy, judiciary and other public offices was to serve the shah (Binder, 1962: 65), although governmental branches of power were separated. It was impossible to secure the shah's position unless he could achieve complete control of the administrative, judicial and military machinery of the state (Binder, 1962: 88).

One of the consistent features of the Iranian government during Pahlavis was the subordination of the judiciary to the executive (Graham, 1978: 136). Judicial decisions reflected the will of the government. The area of competence of the judiciary gradually eroded by the military tribunals[4] and by special civil service tribunals.[5] Under both Reza Shah and Mohammad Reza Shah the judicial system was based on the principle that the government can do no wrong (Binder, 1978: 136). This was even more the case when the restricted sphere of Islamic personal status law came to be applied by secular courts (Binder, 1962: 99). The discrepancy between the asserted character of the courts and their actual subordination becomes clear if we look at the resistance of the independent judges against the pressure from the police, the Minister of Interior or the Minister of Justice (Binder, 1962: 291). The area of competence of the judiciary gradually eroded by the military tribunals and by the civil service tribunals (Graham, 1978: 136). In the whole Pahlavi era, it was presumed that the state could do no wrong.

The law is positivized in this period. Modern law is not just guaranteed, but created by the state itself. This legal process filters out of juridical discourse questions of justice and natural law (Poggi, 2003: 252). The law in this discourse is produced and promulgated by the appropriate state organs according to their own procedural rules. But the state law did not apply to the state itself, its structure and operation. This can be called "rule of law for the ruled" and not for the rulers. The politically accused activists had no right to have access to lawyers and their files especially after 1953. Political activists were kept in jail for a long period without clear accusation and some prisoners were kept in prison even after completing their original sentence (Zerang, Vol. I, 2002: 396–398). The political trials were only shows of justice[6] (Montazeri, 2000: p. 23 of Ch. 6). The Military

Courts were concerned with all cases affecting national security-a blanket term that was loosely interpreted (Graham, 1978: 136; Zerang, Vol. II, 2002: 176; Binder, 1978: 136).

An essential component of political-legal change during the Pahlavi dynasty was a new body of public law. This body of law was especially concerned with the construction and operation of the administration system (Poggi, 1978: 74; Rosenberg, 1958: 47). This legal system simply means ruling the governed through law (Rosenberg, 1958: 47) and not rule of law. In Arjomand's view, the political system of this period is neo-patrimonialism (Arjomand, 1988: 64 & 72) that fits in with the model of government through law. According to Weber, patrimonialism refers to forms of government that are based on ruler's personal-familial authority (Weber, 1978: 1013). Due to the administrative obligation of a nation state, patrimonialism had to be manipulated and the patrimonial regime should change its way of rule from rule through coercive force or tradition to rule through law.

In the process of registration of lands and properties, some landlords were pushed to sell their properties to the king in very low prices (Sadr, 1985: 310). The authoritarian state during Reza Shah era acted as all country was property of the king and his clique and all citizens were his subjects. There was not rule of law, but rule of a few powerful figures who had the military and police in their hands. The judiciary could not preserve its independency against a few powerful groups.

Under the 1906 Constitution, Iran could enjoy a modern judicial system, headed by the Supreme Court, the highest court of appeal, presided over by a Chief Justice. On paper, it had eleven branches, each of which had four associate judges. In addition, there were courts of appeal in every province, and civil and criminal courts of first instance at the town and district levels.[7] Finally, there were a civil service tribunal, a number of courts dealing solely with religious matters, military courts, whose competence extended to civilians accused of anti-state activities, armed robbery and serious narcotics offences. These provisions never implemented outside of Tehran.

Legal regulation of state activities and governmental intervention through general laws did not exclude exceptional, particular and individual forms of intervention by the state; legal regulation was directed toward disciplinary order, not rule of law. Public law was not mostly coupled with forms of private power and authority. The state's rule did not prohibit arbitrary forms of state activity with no internal principle of limitation. The lack of participation of the governed, and lack of the representative parliamentary democracy opened the way for politicization of the judiciary and impeded an effective system for providing a rational check on governmental activity within a unified framework of legal-political sovereignty.

Rationalization of the government in this period did not premise on the rights and free initiative of individuals.

Judicial reform usually happens during the consolidation of new leadership. This phase of consolidation in early and mid-20th century Iran has five outstanding features: 1) the assertion on the part of political elite of the determination to modernize (Tilly, 1975: 606), 2) an effective and decisive break with the institutions associated with the past, in our case, *shari`ah* courts, 3) the creation of a national state with a centralized government and tamed local powers, 4) upbringing a new elite in the new institutions, in our case, judiciary, and 5) transplantation, in this case, of new codes and judicial institutions.[8] These features have more to do with penetration and legitimacy of the government and less to do with participation and distribution (Tilly, 1975: 609). Most of the transformations that the state accomplished in the first half of the 20th century, including judicial reform, were by-products of the consolidation of central control.

What the courts do or what is the nature of adjudication matters because it influences greatly the content of the substantive law and the costs of dispute resolution. In the mid 1920s at the time of Ali Akbar Dāvar's reorganization of the ministry, Kasravi rose to be chief of the Courts of First Instance for the District of Tehran. In that post he constantly annoyed Dāvar with his manner of administering justice and frequently ruling against the interests of the power elite. In one case, for example, the Royal Court wanted to confiscate some villages near Tehran (Evin), to hand over to a fractious mullah. The farmers sought judicial assistance and Kasravi found for the peasants—unprecedented in Iran. The same day he went to Evin to make sure that his decree was enforced.[9]

The rules whose observance served to formalize the practice of rule in modern Western states were chiefly judicial rules (Poggi, 2003: 251), whereas in the case of Iran during Pahlavis they were administrative rules. In post revolutionary Iran, they changed to ideological rules.

In the textbooks of law schools in this period, when private and public laws are defined, neither public nor private law includes regulations regarding non-governmental institutions (Khal'atbary, 1933: 3). The institutions of the society presumed in these definitions are family, economic corporations (*sherkathā*) and state, nothing in between.

There were two kinds of ordinances in this period: ordinances based on statutes whose function was to execute the law, and ordinances which were not directly on the basis of the Constitution or statutes but issued in place of statutes by the executive power or the king (the leader, in post-revolutionary era). The significance of ordinances based on executive order and decree-law as opposed to statute law is due to the peculiar position, which the administrative authorities occupied in the legal system of the nation. The administration, especially the king's court (bait of the leader in post-revolutionary era) had its capacity as law-applying organ, the same rank as courts. The administrative act had the same legal effect as a judicial decision, sometime more. The administrative authorities, especially higher ones like the king (the leader in post-revolutionary era) had the power to issue general legal norms, and these general legal norms or the administrative ordinances had the same legal effect as statutes.[10] The king was over the three branches of the government and was free to create law. In this legal system, there was not such a step or action as judicial review of ordinances to decrease the danger that administrative organs would exceed the limits of their power of creating general legal rules. There was no organ to monitor and check the personal responsibility of the organ, which has enacted the unconstitutional norm, and non-application of the constitutional norm.

Articles 81 and 82 of the Supplement to the Constitution of 1906 specify that the judges could not be temporarily and permanently removed or transferred to other districts or other judicial positions. The Article one of the interpretational Act of Article 82, ratified on August 1931, annulled that article with this arrangement that in transferring of the judges their ranks should not be changed. This was the only article of the Constitution that was redefined or violated in the course of reforms of the judiciary system and was to allow the government a greater freedom in the rotation and removal of judges.[11] The interpretation of Article 82 of Supplementary Constitution by the Judiciary Committee of the Parliament gave this power to the administration to remove judges, whether temporarily or permanently from the post they occupied without trial and proof of their guilt, or in consequence of a violation entailing their dismissal, and to transfer or re-designate judges without their consent, even in cases the interest of society did not necessitate them. Mosaddeq nullified this interpretation by the September 1952 Bill and Amendment of the Justice Department Act of September 1957 (Sāleh, 1968: 283). The specific *shari`ah* reservation, though ignored, remained unchanged.

A half-century of the autocratic rule of the Pahlavis eroded the independence of the judiciary and dismantled the positive developments pursued by the judicial elites. The Shahs' secret police intimidated judges, and the Military Courts tried dissidents. Dāvar himself was not without controversy. He was criticized for promoting Shah's repressive regime.

Crying for independent judiciary through legal provisions by some sections of the intellectuals, and execution of some provisions like securing terms of office provided no guaranty of independence. The mere existence of a disciplinary system provides no assurance of ethical compliance. Data on case disposition rates and times do not measure efficiency and the value of the social good produced by the particular time and investment. Thus, independence, impartiality, and efficiency depend on some combination of less frequently postulated factors that were ignored by different administrations during Pahlavis. The will of the shah was mostly over the independence of the courts.[12]

The Judiciary was in track to get more independence during Dāvar to the point that in some cases Reza Shah was convicted for forceful confiscation of people's properties. This did not last; some judges or heads of the Supreme Court would have been fired, if they issued decisions the king did not like (Firoez, 1994: 27, 35 & 54). Laws were violated against the people whom the regime had any sensitivity for. Reza Shah wanted executive power to rule over the judiciary. The police and security forces were not under the control and disciplinary actions of the judiciary.

The Judiciary in Reza Shah era was supposed to politically control the dissidents and support the Police and security forces; when it did not cooperate, it was punished. When judiciary could not be as active as the regime expected it to be, political dissidence was responded by sending activists to exile or jail without open and fair trials (Bahār, Khājeh Nuri), slaying them in prison or exile (Seyyed Hasan Modarres, Taymurtāsh, Sardār As'ad Bakhtiāri, Farrokhi Yazdi) ('Āqeli, 1990: 269–272; Amin, 2003: 558), while they were spending their sentence in prison, or killing them in the society (Mirzādeh 'Eshqi, Shaikh Mohammad Khiābāni, Mirzā Kuchak Jangali, Shaikh Khaz'al, Abdul Hosein Dibā, Haidar Khan 'Amoqli, Arbāb Kaikhosro Shahrokh) or abroad (Taymur Bakhtiār in Iraq) (Musavi Zādeh, 2001; Saifi Fami Tafreshi, 1988).[13] Mohammad Reza Shah did the same thing when he consolidated his power after the 1953 CIA supported coup: kidnapping and slaying Afshar Tus, Police Chief of Mosaddeq administration (1953), execution of Dr. Fātemi (1954), jailing or exiling political figures (Mosaddeq, Ahmad Razavi, Ali Shāyegān, Mehdi Bazargān, Seyyed Mahmud Tāleqani, Yaddollah Sahābi), slaying university students (1953), political prisoners (Bijan Jazani, 1975), and political activists (Karimpur Shirāzi), suspicious slain (Mohammad Ali Khonji), and trial of and jailing lots of political activists ignoring due process

4.2 RELIGIOUS AND STATE JUDICIAL SYSTEMS: SUBSTANTIVE SECULARIZATION

Many of the Reza Shah's measures were consciously designed to break the power of the religious hierarchy in public domains.[14] His educational reforms ended the clerics' near monopoly on education. The state even encroached on the administration of *waqf* (religious endowments). His administration gradually excluded the clerics from judgeships, created a system of secular courts, and transferred the important and lucrative task of notarizing documents from the clerics to state-licensed notaries. The parliament passed a law concerning the employment of judges by requiring all of them to hold a degree from the Tehran Faculty of Law or a foreign university (1936). The new Civil Procedural Law was passed in 1939. The Registration of Deeds and Property Law (passed in1932) (Arjomand, 1988: 66; Banani, 1961: 72) required that the registration of legal documents, of ownership, and of other transactions concerning property be carried out only in secular state courts.

The secularization and centralization of legal administration was part of a larger program of state-controlled economic modernization (Tabari, 1977: 75–78). A new custom office was developed in 1920s and 1930s as parts of the infrastructure of a modern economy. Reorganization of judicial administration was a damaging blow to the *'ulamā*. The judiciary became increasingly divorced from the *shari`ah* as its *'ulamā* constituents began to be replaced by a new type of educated staff-the product of the European schools or domestic secular learning institutions.

Though civil and criminal courts had been set up in the constitution of 1906, and new civil commercial codes promulgated in 1911 and 1915, judicial administration remained in the hands of the *'ulamā*. The new regime introduced new codes in 1928 which replaced *shari`ah*. The Organizational Principles Law of 1928 eliminated the reconciliation judge of the Reconciliation Court who was responsible for *shar'i* adjudications (Zerang, Vol. I, 2002: 325). In 1932 the parliament enacted a new law, which turned registration of legal documents over to secular courts and removed the most lucrative functions of the religious courts. A law of 1936 required all judges to hold a degree from the Tehran Faculty of Law or a foreign university, making it impossible for the *'ulama* to sit in courts of law (Lapidus, 1988: 582).

The institutional making of this reform was a transition from jurisdiction in the hand of the landlord-master-mullah triangle applying *shari`ah* law in local courts to the state law enforced by the central ruler. With dissolution of the Specific Criminal Court that was a *shar'i* court the way was opened for enforcement of General Penal Law of 1925 (Sāleh, 1968: 238). The Specific Criminal Court's jurisdiction was limited to cases that their supposed punishments were to be *qesās* (retributive justice), *had* (a fixed punishment based on *shari`ah* law) or *ta'zir* (a variable punishment based on *shari`ah* law or the discretion of the judge). The key material component of the entire process was a given center's ability to threaten or exercise overwhelming and monopolistic military violence to such an effect that other centers submit to it and surrender their autonomy.

Reza Shah suppressed the independent clerical courts and turned their jurisdiction over to state judicial system. The judiciary officials from 1926 expanded and professionalized system of courts and this made the judicial power of clerical courts less significant even at the provincial level and in religious cities like Mash-had and Qom. The process of decreasing the *Shai'ah* Courts jurisdiction that began in 1922[15] when Reza Khan was Prime Minister expedited after his taking over the title of the kingdom. Article 40 of the Organizational Principles Law of 1928 subdued Shar'i Courts to the State Courts and at the same time made the former ones official and part of the formal judiciary. A modern state can no longer submit part of its authority to other centers of power in the society. While the Law of Judiciary Organization and Shari`ah Courts and Reconciliation Magistrates (LJO) of 1911 had been a context for bringing Shar'i and 'Orfi Courts together and define their different jurisdictions in a more unified judicial system during Moshir ul-Dowleh, Dāvar's measures were headed to limit and then totally diminish the jurisdiction of Shar'i Courts. The first Article of Amendment of 1928 to LJO limited the jurisdiction of Shar'i Courts to three subjects: "1. disputes regarding marriage and divorce, 2. those disputes which could not be settled except by resort to witness or oath, and 3. cases which necessitate appointment of guardian, executor, or administrator." This amendment made Articles 143–149 which gave upper hand to Shar'i Courts void (Zerang, Vol. I, 2002: 369). A circulation in 1931 made this totally null and void (Zerang, Vol. I, 2002: 369–370). The Shar'i Court Law of 1931 limited the jurisdiction of these courts to family matters and appointment of guardian or administrator. Later in 1939, another law suspended the second area of jurisdiction of these courts. The Non-Litigious Act of 1939 transferred all matters of guardianship to the state courts for cities (*dādgāh-e shahrestān*) (Zerang, Vol. I, 2002: 369–370).

Redefinition of the status and jurisdiction of Shari`ah Courts by the Majles in 1931 led to the complete submission of Shari`ah Courts to the State Courts. The Special Penal Court that was a Shar'i Court was dissolved in 1931 (Zerang, Vol. I, 2002: 368). Article 2 of the new law stated that "no cases may be referred to Shari`ah Courts without authorization from state courts and the office of the Attorney General" (*Record of Parliamentary Legislation, Eighth Parliament,* 158; Banani, 1961: 78). According to this law, Shari`ah Court's jurisdiction was narrowed to disputes involving family relationship and the appointment of trustees and guardians, what is considered the jurist's realm in the traditional reading of *shari`ah*. Hence, Shari`ah Courts were forbidden from pronouncing sentences. The provisions of 1939 and 1940 Civil and Penal Codes put an end to the Shari`ah Courts in Iranian legal system.

Foundations to care for properties belonging to orphans were transferred to the authority of the Ministry of Justice; the religious courts were subject to review by the secular Appeals Court (Banani, 1961: 79). In the dual system, *qāzis* of the religious courts were not appointed, supervised, transferred, and dismissed by the Ministry of justice and Iranian *'ulamā* were not placed under direct government control. By gradually unification of the judicial system, the final vestiges of authority was removed from the clergy in such a way as to make no provision for *shar'iah* courts (Banani, 1961: 79).

Enforcing the new laws and reorganization of the judiciary decreased the role and the power of the clerics in the judicial affairs. Even in the areas like marriage and divorce that were in the *shari`ah* court jurisdictions, clerics had to get license from the government to run their business. Each step in the judicial reform was headed to erode the power of *'ulamā* and local chieftains and landlords. The new Civil Law of 1927 reduced the influence of *shari`ah* in criminal proceedings and property titles, restricting the jurisdiction of lower level clerics to personal matters such as marriage, divorce, and wills.

While the government gradually abolished the Shari`ah Courts, and transferred their jurisdictions to secular courts, *shari`ah* laws were partially replaced by new secular codes of civil law, criminal law, and commercial law based on European codes. The religious titles were limited, and the wearing of *hejāb* in public was discouraged and in some periods was prohibited. Polygamy was formally abolished during Mohammad Reza Shah in 1967, and divorce by court action gave women extensive grounds to divorce their husbands. The wearing of turbans in public was prohibited and the hat was made the official headgear. Civil marriages were made compulsory for all, though almost all people still had religious marriages as well. Women allowed to vote and to be elected. They were admitted in the public schools, the civil service, and most of the professions. Selling, buying and drinking alcohol were made legal.

Before Dāvar's reforms, punishments came from a mix of the Quran and ancient tribal customs. He was responsible for reforming the laws of Iran in 1927 during the time of the first Pahlavi. A legal code developed in that year did away with extreme Islamic punishments such as stoning and lashing. These developments shocked the religious establishment. All of these were directed toward undermining the religious classes indirectly by an authoritative modernism.

The process of legal and judicial secularization encountered difficulties in defining the boundaries between the secular and sacred when it reached to the stage of codifying the civil law. This was because of 1) the presence of *shari`ah* law in the realms that private and public law in Muslim communities encounter, and 2) the interconnections between areas of law, i.e. commercial cases that have criminal or civil implications (Berkes, 1964: 165).

Quran-oriented discourse of some religious scholars like Reza Qoli (Shari'at) Sangelaji's[16] (p.6) and their legal promulgations gave doctrinal legitimation to a new wave of *ejtehād* that was no longer in tune with Shi'ite orthodoxy. Scholars like Sangelaji found great appeal among the new generation of secular intellectuals who wanted to be a true Muslim, in the context of Islam as a culture, and a modernist at the same time. This new way of thinking and interpreting Islam could not tune in with the reforms to base them on tradition and decrease the tension between modernity and tradition, though it was successful in denying the traditional Islam that was preached and interpreted by the clergy.

Rising of a new elite who isolated traditional judges and limited *shari`ah* courts and judgeship was part of a process of secularization that was supposed to consolidate the regime and at last helped its fall by an Islamic Revolution. Similar to the first period, the reformers had to deal with vested power from the traditional institutions, the low literacy rate, poverty, the lack of trained staff, and lack of facilities to have access to people. On the other side there was no popular conviction that the national government was an appropriate vehicle for furthering popular goals like justice, prosperity and stability, growth and distribution of income.

The pursuit of individual interests compromised collective values, and the pursuit of collective aims was in the individual (at least short-term) interest of the system's primary participants. Judicial reform at least as a triggering decision, was determined by one person, the Minister of Justice, while in an organized, complex social system, the views, practices, and interests of each participant are critical, particularly in their interactions with others. In the latter system, each actor exhibits an individual and collective sense of self-awareness, assessment of the problems, openness to change, level of creativity, commitment to consensus building, courage, sense of personal and professional dilemmas in making a commitment to change, and strategies (including tough value choices) for dealing with these dilemmas. Even the most passive followers may lead by creating an implicit demand for (or lack of interference with) a particular direction they are willing to traverse without a fuss.

4.3 CODIFICATION AND TRANSPLANTATION: CIVIL LAW TRADITION

Dāvar presented 120 drafts on judicial affairs to the parliament. The shah, his court and the majority of the MPs completely supported him. Most of the laws codified during this period were directed to increase the power of state in the judicial process. For example, most of the changes in the Civil

Code that allowed greater jurisdiction to lower courts increased the powers of state attorneys and prosecutors.

To limit further the power of the clerics, the judiciary under Reza Shah's rule undertook a codification of the laws that created a body of secular law, applied and interpreted by a secular judiciary outside the control of the religious establishment. Watson's theory on the context of codification is true in this case when he says "the impetus towards codification of the law in the interest of clarity or simplicity often does not come from lawyers or legislatures and traditional lawmakers but dictators or other powerful leaders who have made their reputation in other activities" (Watson, 1983: 1156). Among the codes comprising the new secular law were the Civil Code, the work of Justice Minister, Ali Akbar Dāvar, enacted between 1927 and 1932, the General Accounting Act (1934–35), a milestone in financial administration, a new tax law, and a civil service code.

The traditional Islamic jurisprudence was not able to cope with new needs of the Iranian society. Other than theoretical and practical inadequacies, the struggle between *shari`ah* and state courts usually could not be easily settled. The interpretations of the law by the *mujtaheds* not only conflicted with the decrees of the state courts, but also differed among them; none of them usually enforced by the state, as it was in the first quarter of the 20th century. The solution for this problem, in the eyes of new elite, was transplantation; both the Civil Code and the Penal Code as the backbones of the new legal system as well as the organization of the courts reflect the influence of Western judiciary models, i.e. Belgium, France, Italy (Banani, 1961: 74). New elite did not mind to borrow laws, and people like Dāvar who knew the history of law presumed that "history of a system of law is largely a history of borrowings of legal materials from other legal systems and of assimilation of materials from outside of the law" (Watson, 1974: 22). This development caused a whole generation of Iranian students, lawyers and judges to look to Europe as sources of inspiration for legal principles and practices.

Half a century later, immediately before and after the Islamic Revolution, most of the elites pursued the path of purification of culture and governmental systems from what was considered as Western. The post-Constitutional Revolution elite believed that legal rules are not particularly devised for the particular society in which they operate. The elites of Reza Shah era had an organic point of view on transplantation; they thought that "a successful legal transplant-like that of a human organ-will grow in its new body, and become part of that body just as the rule or institution would have continued to develop in its parent system (Watson, 1974: 27). Therefore, when the Ministry of Justice considered any question of major reform, the first instinct was to look at the solutions in other jurisdictions, and took account of the foreign hegemonic systems of law because, according to Watson, this was easy in this kind of situation (1974: 95).

At the time, European continental systems had considerable influence on the conceptual structure of reform of the law and judiciary for legal and judicial acts. Little attention was directed toward Dutch or English law system primarily because none of the high-ranking consultants could read English or Dutch, and French language was understood by most of the educated men at the time. Another factor was that the continental systems fitted more with the authoritarian political regime during Pahlavis. The third factor was the detail and written aspect of continental law that fitted more with the expected coerced judicial reform enforced from above by a centralized government; the elite had this idea in mind that "law which is not written has far less chance of spreading" (Watson, 1974: 93). English law was incapable of being imposed; the educated people in law considered English law as a system of jurists' law, and not containing something approaching a code.

Due to the neo-patrimonial regime of Pahlavis, legal transplantation was an imposed one, not solicited imposition, penetration, infiltration, crypto-reception, or inoculation. Iranian people did not voluntarily accept a large part of the European legal system because they had no say in these matters. The hegemony and authority of the Europeans in the region played an important role in this legal borrowing. A law or a system of law is usually adopted because of the authority and hegemony of its model or promulgator; the authority of the government usually maintains the transplanted law.

In pursuing judicial reform, Iranian elites were looking directly at the judicial and legal achievements of the Western civilization. To prevent an inconsistent and unsystematic reception of European laws, political elite resorted to codification for most of the laws, including civil, commercial and penal laws. The Civil Code based on Twevler Shi'ite jurisprudence,[17] Due Process Law, Public Penal Code, Trial Principles Law, Military Due Process Law, Ministry of Justice New Organization Law, and New Commercial Law were composed and passed between 1927–1933. These were different sections of codification process. The codification was based on the idea that religious laws and decrees are not enough for regulating modern life. Other than codification, simplification and unification of *sharī`ah* were considered in drafting the Civil Code. The codification of Dāvar's reforms was mostly directed to expedition of trial and protection of public law in front of private law.

The social and political structures of Iran were more receptive to the civil law system, and its legal system was mainly copied from European countries with this legal tradition. This led to the long process of codification that is, as Watson notifies, "a typical attribute of civil law systems" (1983: 1132). The ideology of codification at work that reflects the ideology of the Constitutional Movement was based on secularism, statism and glorification of Iranian nation-state. The drive toward a centralized state made it important to bring some unity out of the diversity of legal systems and materials, even in the Iranian capital. The secular legal and judicial systems were expected to support the emergence of the monolithic nation-state. The political elite's assumption was that by feeding religious law into the framework of a secular legal system, one could derive a legal system that would both meet the needs of the new society and the new government in the beginning of the 20th century, without motivating dissidence among traditional strata.

Iranian elite of this period could not think about transplanting a common law system because the conservative tendencies of this tradition stood in marked contrast to the ideology of revolution held by Constitutionalists and ideology of up-down secularism held by Pahlavi ruling elite, while the spirit of civil law codification that emerged from the ideology of Constitutional Revolution could better fit into the new regime. The elite were also educated in countries where civil law system was considered the most rational and modern. At the same time, the regime could not trust to deliver legislation and molding the law to the judges as it goes in common law tradition. The role of civil law judge is generally much more restricted and modest than that of the common law judge. This restriction was the main reason for the absence of judicial review in the whole 20th century. This is generic to civil law system[18] and not specific to Iran. The Islamic regime, later in the last quarter of the 20th century, replaced the preeminence of the scholar in the civil law tradition with the importance of the Islamic jurists.

The radical nature of the social revolutions like Constitutional Revolution together with the interest of new elite who proposed new models to exaggerate the failures of the old texts convinced many not only that the *shari`ah* was inadequate but also that a simple re-styling would not be enough. This of course does not necessarily means that the state of law is principally to be explained by the transplantation of legal rules, as Watson does (Ewald, 1995: 489). As Watson mentions, transplant can be due to number of factors, such as economic conditions and religious outlook (1974: 97) that, in case of early 20th century Iran, were not susceptible and ready for basic legal and judicial change. The main divisions of the law, the major institutions, and the boundary lines between one institution and the other were totally adopted from the European systems of law; there was still a wide divergence from Islamic and Western classification in the new eclectic system.

The *shari`ah* principles persisted more in civil law than criminal law. From 1920's to 1940's the laws regarding marriage, divorce, and family relations changed four times, each one a further departure from the strict *shari`ah* rules, yet preserving the original principles. Some of these departures are setting a legal age requirement for marriage (Articles 1041–43 of the Civil Code), requiring marriages and divorces to be registered in civil bureaus (*Record of Parliamentary Legislation, Eighth Parliament, 133–134*). Permission for the breaking of an engagement, even after the arrangements for depositing the *mehr* (the prenuptial sum given by the groom to the bride) are completed (Article 1035 of the Civil Code), requiring the government's permission for Iranian women who want to marry aliens (Article 1060 of the Civil Code), and requiring medical certificates before marriage (passed by the Majles on Nov. 1938; *Record of Parliamentary Legislation, Eleventh Parliament, 61–62;* Banani, 1961: 80–84).

Iran adopted family law supporting women's equality. Major changes introduced in area of family law under Pahlavis with passage of Family Protection Law 1967 (significantly amended 1975) supporting women's equality and granting them new rights in marriage and divorce, among others, and abolishing extra-judicial divorce and requiring judicial permission for polygamy and only for limited circumstances (Mir-Hosseini, 1993; Pakzad, 1994; Ramaz, 1993). Family Protection Law gave women almost equal rights in divorce, custody of children and marriage settlements, and granted limited rights of guardianship; it raised the age of marriage for girls to eighteen, recognized women's equal rights with men to hinder their partners from undesirable occupations, and subjected polygamy to certain restrictions. This law ordained men to get the court's license for their second, third or fourth marriage, that was totally against *shari`ah* law.

The developments in family laws were more prominent during Mohammad Reza Shah. The continued advocacy and awareness-raising efforts of women's rights activists, strong backing by government leaders, and the public support of Mohammad Reza Shah's action in favor of women's rights contributed to the decisions in favor of a reformed Iranian Family Law. Iranian modern Family Law was consistent with the more tolerant reading of Islam and lifting the iniquity imposed on women, protecting children's rights, and safeguarding men's dignity. The law regarding family included in the Civil Code included various reforms with respect to equality, divorce, polygamy, and enforcement of law. Husband and wife shared joint responsibility for the family; the wife was no longer legally obliged to obey her husband; the adult woman was entitled to self-guardianship, rather than that of a male family member, and may exercise it freely and independently; and the minimum age of marriage was increased to18 for both men and women.

The right to divorce was considered a prerogative of both men and women, exercised under judicial supervision; the principle of divorce by mutual consent was established. Polygamy was subject to the judges' authorization and to stringent legal conditions, making the practice nearly impossible; the woman had the right to impose a condition in the marriage contract requiring that her husband refrain from taking other wives; if there was no pre-established condition, the first wife should be informed of her husband's intent to remarry, the second wife should be informed that her husband-to-be is already married, and moreover, the first wife may ask for a divorce due to harm suffered. The Family Law assigned a key role to the judiciary in upholding the rule of law and provided for the public prosecutor to be a party to every legal action involving the enforcement of Family Law stipulations. The woman was given the possibility of retaining custody of her child or children even upon remarrying or moving out of the area where her husband lives; the child's right to acknowledgment of paternity was protected in the case that the marriage had not been officially registered (Zerang, Vol. II, 2002: 168–170).

4.4 JUDICIAL REFORM AND REORGANIZATION: ADMINISTRATIVE JUSTICE AND EXPANSION

4.4.1 Under Reza Shah (1925–41)

One of the most important goals of judicial reform in this period was correction of the judicial procedures. In the proceeding of the Parliament about Dāvar's bill on dissolution of the judiciary in Feb. 16, 1927 (27 Bahman, 1305 S.), the dissolution of judiciary and its reform are justified on the basis of people's grievances and necessary corrections ('Āqeli, 1990; 111). Another goal was administrative reorganization. Judicial reform in this period was part of a state-building process. This process was mainly focused on administrative reorganization that was feature of the time[19] and the intellectuals and political elite were talking about it in their circles. In spite of administrative reorganization in Europe and the United States, this procedure in Iran was not urged upon by the democratically elected legislatures; it was not motivated by investigations and reports of efficiency and economy commissions or similar bodies; and it was not accomplished by the laws actually passed or taken into consideration in constitutional revisions providing for reorganization.

The main goal of the judicial reform in this period was to form adaptable, complex, autonomous, and coherent organizations and procedures in the area of jurisprudence. This goal was partly directed to legitimize political roles and structures of the new dynasty and the new king. The new political regime had to respond to the diffusion of political forms from the West to the East and international structures of domination. International structure and internal obligations were for up-down reform, especially in governmental institutions. Dāvar declared these two goals for his judicial reforms: 1) removing the deficiencies of existing and experienced laws, and 2) correcting judiciary organization with respect to staff and ranking officials' competency[20]. Mosaddeq had the same goals in reforming the judiciary when he got the power in his hands (Amin, 2003: 641–646).

Among the four periods of judicial reforms and reorganizations, the second is the most prominent one. Comparing the changes and measures in judicial affairs in chronological calendar of Appendix I shows that the judiciary had a more viable program for reform in this period and elite were more serious about it. The number of basic codes related to judiciary passed by the parliament, number of courts established, and the number of international covenants joined are higher than other periods, while this period was longer than others. The judiciary was completely reorganized in this period. The codes and laws, approved in this period were completely effective and have largely survived the minor touches of Islamization process after the Islamic Revolution.

One of the important aspects of judicial reform in this period was a division of work between the state courts. The structure of courts was designed in a way that division of work between them was symmetrical and provinces had identical court structure. Tiers of state courts were supposed to hear cases with different levels of importance: felony trials where the defendant may be sentenced to a short and long prison term or execution and civil suits that involved a greater sum of money. Courts were ranked on the basis of the levels of expected sentences and suits. Depending on the level of importance, courts were located at the rural, township, provincial and state levels. In some provinces several townships shared a single court, which normally sat in one and visited by people in others. Many provinces had a set of specialized courts, which fitted somewhere between the major and minor trial courts. Some of them dealt with family matters, some with monetary claims, and some with handling the administration of wills and estates.

There were two waves of judicial reform during Pahlavis. Dāvar's reforms were mainly directed toward reorganization and codification, while Lotfi's and Hey'at's[21] reforms were directed toward a more independent judiciary and judicial-related organizations (Appendix I). Dāvar's

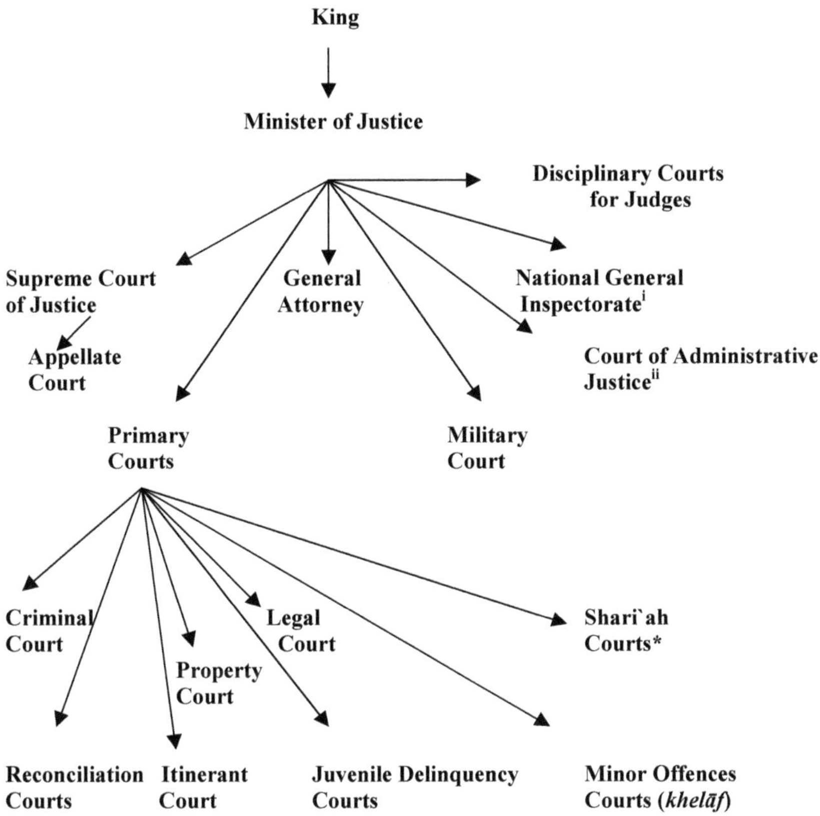

Fig. 4.1. The Chart of Iran's Judiciary, 1927–1979

* These courts were gradually phased out of existence in the 1920s and 1930s.

reforms were more stable and lasting compared to what were done during Mosaddeq administration, though almost all of them were annulled after the coup.[22]

Iran's judicial system between 1927 to1979, modeled after that of Europeans, was based on a hierarchy of courts from the district courts on the lowest level up to the Supreme Court, i.e. the court of final appeal that was not the body to determine the constitutionality of current legislations and judicial decisions (Fig. 4.1).

Articles 75 and 76 of the Constitution gave this opportunity to Dāvar to upgrade the position of the Supreme Court. This court was the highest court in appealing procedure. Dāvar increased the number of primary, appellate and cassation courts and established itinerant appellate courts and limited reconciliation courts. Hence there was more access to justice.

In 1936, Reza Shah stripped the state judicial system of most of its clerics when he required that all judges presiding over government courts hold a degree from the secular Tehran University Faculty of Law or a foreign university (Mackay, 1996: 179). In the first round of judicial appointments after the dissolution of the judiciary in 1927 (1305),thirty seven people were appointed as judges, General Attorney, DAs and other high-ranking judiciary officials. Of this number at least 5 of them were clerics. In only two years from 1926 to 1928, the number of high ranking judicial appointees increased to 260 including judges, DAs and prosecutors; out of this number, 42 were prosecutors (*mostanteq*s), and 37 were district attorneys (*moda'i ul-'omoum*); at least 10 of them were clerics ('Āqeli: 1990: 161–184). However, most of the clerics were in the highest court, the Court of Cassation, which had 7 clerical jurists out of its 20 members. There were no cleric judges (*hākem-e shar'*) among those judges who were appointed in 1927. In 1929, three judges were appointed as the Shari`ah Courts' judges and three *hākem-e shar'* in Rasht province's Primary Court and Isfahān and Fārs provinces' Appeal Courts ('Āqeli, 1990: 179, 132, 183). However, in the early 1930s, the clerics were forced to discard their clerical robe and become civilians or lose their jobs.

The presupposition for the change of judicial staff in this period and other periods studied in this work was based on this postulation that the judicial organization can be more easily changed if it is staffed by younger, supportive, loyal and competent (as it was defined by the reformers) personnel. Dāvar, like his successors, believed that the change agents must be introduced in sufficiently large numbers and at one more echelon in the hierarchy. This belief made them to underscore the role of general characteristics of the judiciary and general judicial organizational network. Dāvar recruited inexperienced judges and staff. In this situation, the judiciary could not simultaneously assure the quality of judicial performance, secure the accountability of judges, and protect the tradition of judicial independence.

Dāvar was aware of not sacrificing justice for expedition of judicial procedure. When he was asked about his point of view on legitimacy of court of appeal and cassation court, he promised to make the judicial procedure more simple and easier for different sides without ignoring people's right to appeal ('Āqeli, 1990: 131).

Addressing the members of parliament on the organizational aspects of his reform, Dāvar mentioned these points: "1. the principle of multiplicity of judges is replaced by singularity of judges in courts [in Primary Courts[23]], 2. increase of the cassation courts from two to four, 3. dividing the Primary and

Appellate Courts to itinerant and stationary courts, 4. establishment of reconciliation court, . . . 6. separation of for Primary and Appellate Courts, . . . , [and] 7. increase of the Appellate Courts from 4 to 6." (Āqeli, 1990: 143). Dāvar made registration of properties obligatory and ordered the judges to issue verdict on the basis of law and not their own Islamic jurisprudential opinions (Āqeli, 1990: 143).

In spite of a vast judicial reform by Dāvar, the civil society institutions in the realm of judiciary like the courts had no way to be independent. It was the Ministry of Justice that composed all the regulations for legal profession associations.[24] Transgressor lawyers and judges were tried in the same court, i.e. Judges' Disciplinary Court. Article 113 of the Judiciary Organization Law ratified in 1927 deprived lawyers to have any independent association for pursuing their professional interests and concerns. The Circular Letter regarding Art. 107 gave the upper hand to the general attorneys with respect to lawyers.

The state-run Bar Association, similar to the1906–1925 period, was founded by the state and it was totally under the control of the state. This bar could not even select its board of directors' members. This was not the bar association who could be responsible for developing, promoting, coordinating and strengthening professional disciplinary and regulatory programs and procedures throughout the nation. According to the Organizational Principles Law of 1928, all lawyers had to receive their licenses from the Ministry of Justice ('Āqeli, 1990: 189)

The Law Practice Code of 1935 only gave financial independence to the Iranian Bar Association. The Law Practice Code of 1936 secured the total dominance of the state over lawyers; according to Art. 20 of this law, the Minister of Justice could choose the board of the association, and lawyers are obliged to follow the regulations determined by the Ministry of Justice for their professional tasks.

4.4.2 Under Mohammad Reza Shah (1941–79).

When Reza Shah was out of the office, the way opened for a more independent judiciary and more independent bar association. Some judges even ruled against the Royal family.[25] Other minor developments between 1941 and 1950 were the decrease of special courts'[26] and Military Court jurisdiction[27] (Zerang, Vol. II, 2002: 43), and dissolution of the Supreme Council of Judiciary that was a threat to occupational security of judges (Zerang, Vol. II, 2002: 47). In spite of a more democratically elected parliament and weaker king's court, the promised reforms could not go through due to instability of the different administrations, declaration of extraordinary situation and trial of citizens in the Military Courts (Zerang, Vol. II, 2002:

64–69), occupation of the country by foreign military forces from 1942–1946 and interference of foreign countries in Iran's interior affairs. In about 10 years, 16 cabinets and 19 Minister of Justice were sworn into office (Zerang, Vol. II, 2002: 59).

In 1946, for the first time, the members elected the Bar Association board of directors. In 1952, during the Mosaddeq administration, the Bar Independence Bill was ratified and enforced.[28] According to this law, the Iranian Bar Association (Kānun-e Vokalā-ye Dādgostari) is a financially and legally independent institution. The Iranian Bar Association could not achieve this goal even after the Islamic Revolution of 1979, although it asked for elected judges and budgetary autonomy in the constitution in 1979 (Bakhash, 1984: 77).

There were many occasions to instigate frustration and backsliding, ways in which judicial procedures were diverted to sterile or disruptive goals. The obliteration of the division between sacred and customary law by the Civil and Penal Codes of 1939 and 1940 which finally omitted all reference to the sacred law and to religious courts was the most important reason for frustration of *'ulamā*. They lost one of the strongholds of their economic, social and political powers to the new class of technocrats and intellectuals educated in Europe. The law of registration of documents and property of March 1932 that required legal documents to be registered by official state notaries also deprived the *'ulamā* of one of their most lucrative functions. Leading to the decrease of *'ulamās'* power, these developments deteriorated the hierocracy-state relations.

The Governmental Officials Penal Law of 1928 established the Organization of Administrative Justice to deal with corruption and embezzlement of governmental officials (Zerang, Vol. I, 2002: 342). Although the judicial reforms improved the efficiency of provincial governments, it could not put an end to tribal judicial procedures. These procedures extended to the Islamic Republic and tolerated if they were no in contradiction to Islamic *shari`ah*.

Some of the reforms like total dissolution of judiciary were illegal. Dāvar used an illegal comprehensive, as opposed to piecemeal, method to reform the judiciary, while there was a trend for the legislatures to give closer surveillance to administration and its reforms. On the basis of the Constitution of 1906, no one can shut down the judiciary. The parliaments in this period handed over the legislation authority to the Minister of Justice or the Judiciary Committee of the Parliament. Therefore the parliament as a whole did not have a role in drafting and passing the laws related to judiciary. There was also no public debate on the legislation or legislation process.[29] Mosaddeq administration took the right of legislation and violated the separation of powers and the principle of ceaselessness of foundation of Constitutionality of the state.

Mosaddeq, as a lawyer, believed that a competent and honest judiciary was an essential element in promoting rule of law and democracy in Iran. Hence, the reform of the judicial branch and rooting out of corruption was a high priority for his administration (Ladjevardi, 1988: 85). Using his limited legislative powers, he revised the law pertaining employment of judges, abolished the special courts and the Department of Supervision of the Ministry of Justice, and in its place created the Office of the Disciplinary Prosecutor of Judges (Dādsarā-ye Entezāmi-e Quzāt). This office would prosecute alleged misconduct of jurists before the High Disciplinary Court (Dādgāh-e 'Āli-ye Entezāmi), providing for judicial rather than administrative review of alleged wrongdoing by jurists. He also approved the bill regarding the reorganization of the administrative structure of the Ministry of Justice (Ladjevardi, 1988: 85–6).

Mosaddeq was more committed to the piecemeal approach compared to Dāvar. The piecemeal approach to reorganization has always had as one of its advantages that it may bring about a structural improvement when the circumstances are promising (Perkins, 1951: 514). Davar's comprehensive reform could not bring structural improvement in the judiciary as it was expected, while political circumstances during Mosaddeq administration were not promising. Dāvar's reorganization was hurriedly planned, without careful study and with no reference to the general philosophy or concept of previous organization. Political mismanagement and the crises of nationalization of oil did not let Mosaddeq to scatter the opposition of special interest groups. The reorganization in this circumstance could not meet the wishes of a clientele group with which the expected reform was affiliated.

Mosaddeq's reforms in the judiciary were focused on neutralization of what have been done by resort to authority of Reza Shah regarding the judiciary. His goal was to fight against corruption (Zerang, Vol. II, 2002: 80), to have more independence for judges, and dissolve or decrease the jurisdiction of specific courts (approved by the parliament in 1952). He tried and somehow succeeded in purging the judiciary from corrupted judges.[30]

There were minor reforms after the U.S. supported coup of 1953 against Mosaddeq administration. In the immediate years after the coup, different administrations nullified what was being done during Mosaddeq: fired judges were recruited (1954), the Military Judicial Organization went back to its structure before 1950 (1954), the Supreme Court was re-established, and specific courts were re-established (1955) (Zerang, Vol. II, 2002: 117–122, 137). The number of state courts in different levels of *bakhsh* (region), *shahrestān* (town) and *ostān* (province) increased (Zerang, Vol. II,

2002: 128). In 1967, the Family Protection Court as a specific civil court was established to settle down family disputes (Zerang, Vol. II, 2002: 135). Since the so-called White Revolution of 1963, the "Houses of Equity" (*khāneh ha-ye ensāf*) was added to the court system through which minor offences and disputes were supposed to be settled by courts of village elders, thus avoiding the inconvenience and expenses of referring them to often distant town courts in the cities. "Arbitration Councils" (*shourāhā -ye dāvari*) also fulfilled a similar function in settling minor disputes (Sāleh, 1968: 298–299). The revival of capitulation in 1964 was another important development in post-coup era (Zerang, Vol. II, 2002: 208).

Shock therapy of Dāvar underestimated the need to prepare for sudden change. The administration did not spend ample time preparing the roads and population for the sudden switch to a new system of judiciary. The impact of Westernization upon the institutions of Iranian society was more apparent in the reforms of her educational, lifestyle and judicial systems. For *'ulamā,* this giving away for Western secular educational, lifestylish and legal concepts was an unspoken admission of the inadequacy of the social institutions of Islam for modern times and consequently decrease of traditional authority, and hence they could not theoretically accept it, although a large number of mullahs practically accepted this and became civilians.

4.5 CHALLENGES AND DILEMMAS: DESIGN/PERFORMANCE AND LOCAL/CAPITAL GAPS

Not all the abuses and injustices were removed from the Iranian judicial system during Pahlavis any more than they have been from those of other states in the region. But a standard of efficiency and rationality unequaled in the Iranian history was established for all subjects of the state regardless of their ethnicity and locality. Under the direction of Ministers of Justice like Dāvar the new laws were put in practice, judicial processes were institutionalized and traditional laws were codified in new frames. Although some prominent figures suffered from Reza Shah and Mohammad Reza Shah interventions and rights of the individuals were violated,[31] the formal justice was dispensed to the mass of the people, whose rights were protected far more extensively than in the past. The judicial system, despite modeling after Europeans, could not respond to the increasing expectations of urban strata in the second half of the 20th century. It could not provide adequate protection for abuses of the individual rights who now had more information about their rights. Accordingly, Iranians did not hold the judicial system in high esteem (Wilbur, 1963: 153).

Judicial reform was a serious task for Dāvar but due to the gaps mentioned below it could not fully implemented. It would have produced an independent judiciary because of the huge support for Dāvar by the king and the parliament but it partly failed and partly succeeded. The achievements like concentration of power, unification of courts, and codification should be considered in the general picture of the reforms that contains different dilemmas and challenges.

There was a gap between the aspirations of intended design and the negative consequences of actual performance. In the practical operation, judicial system encountered the profound problems and the limits of many reform proposals and strategies—particularly those that do not involve or address the motivations of key participants in the legal process, i.e. the landlords, king's court and new class of bureaucrats. The Iranian judicial system in the second period reflected a growing gap between the aspirations of its intended design and the negative consequences of its actual performance.

The common problems of political interference, corruption,[32] and delay were systemic, the barriers to reform were high, and the dilemmas facing reformers were perplexing. Ostensibly responsive reform proposals (especially those drawn from foreign sources or hatched by high-level government officials) were easily deflected. The judiciary failed to dedicate itself to the primary goals of the judicial reform in any modern state, i.e. peaceful resolution of private civil conflicts, enforcement of laws, restraint upon governmental intrusion and acting as a safety valve for the amelioration of repressive orders and laws. The second gap was the local-capital unfilled space that continued to function in this period. Law was designed to apply uniformly over the territory of nation-state but the legal and judicial systems were mostly changing among the urban population, ignoring rural areas. In the villages and among nomads, the age-old practices of law showed no signs of change.

The result of these gaps was frustration with the pace and effectiveness of judicial reform that inspired two original contributions: first, highlighting the systemic nature of common problems, the internal barriers to reform, and the promise of bottom-up reform processes, and second, underlining the limits of externally determined or hierarchically imposed solutions, a maze-like series of unsatisfactory choices or dilemmas. The perceived conflict between judicial independence and accountability (a design dilemma), incremental and systemic change (a method dilemma), or short-term individual self-interest and longer-term systemic objectives (a social dilemma), each represented additional obstacles to effective reform.[33]

Although this top-down or outside-in way of looking at judicial reform provided useful frameworks for capturing a mass of complex and detailed information form the West, it had a very limited perspective of external views that could be transplanted. By a strong dose of bottom-up and internal observation, the different and diverse world of ideas about judicial reform would be opened up to reformers. Reform of legal and judicial institutions and processes was not integral to the promotion of civil rights, democratic development and good governance. Most of the inventions were not produced through direct transplantation, but by internalization of what is going to be transplanted.

In the wide field of comparative characterization, binary distinctions of impartial/partial, adversarial/inquisitorial, civil/common law, or fast/slow systems provided frequently misleading views of the entire legal process for people involved in the judiciary. While no state including Iran could ignore the increasingly strong judicial role in managing adversarial processes, Pahlavis did not pay enough attention to frustrations resulted from dualities.

The Judiciary was discredited by three factors during Pahlavi era: 1) the collapse of centralized government of Reza Shah in 1941, 2) declaring extraordinary situation and interference of the military in civil affairs time to time (1941, 1948, 1953, 1978), and 3) arrest, interrogation, prosecution of Iranian citizens and sending them to exile by Allied Forces who occupied the country between 1941 to 1946 and did not care about national judicial procedures. These realities sometimes led to anarchy (Sadr, 1985: 420–421).

Chapter Five

Third Period: Post-Islamic Revolution Era

Alongside with the centralization of the state and secularization of the society and polity, the authority of the religious leadership was also centralized and the ideology of the traditional opposition gradually Islamicized. The increasing expectation of the masses, failure of the Pahlavis to deliver and the increasing power of the clergy led to the collapse of the Pahlavi regime and grab of the power by the religious establishment who had a revolutionary agenda and a revolutionary method to found the bases of an Islamic Republic.

Instead of institutionalizing a powerful judiciary, the revolutionary and parallel judicial system weakened the theoretical and practical bases of judicial establishment. The ideologization of *sharī`ah* could not respond to the demands of the revolutionaries, although the clerics wanted it to legitimize their rise into power and monopolize it. The revolutionary judiciary that realized with characteristics like populist-discriminatory, anti-Western, ignorance toward strategic planning, duality of the judicial system, and anti-routinization to consolidate the revolutionary regime and its hierarchical charismatic nature and clean the society that comes with the priority of the end rather than procedure. These characteristics later dismantled the structure of the modern judiciary that was built by Dāvar and other reformist elites in the judiciary.

Due to the pretense of greater knowledge of *'ulamā,* indifference of the high ranking ruling clergy toward the technical aspects of law, *sharī`ah* or state law, lack of any mechanism to address judicial accountability, the substantial Islamicization process could not reach to its ideal. Other important factors in this regard were backlogs, profound internal impediments to religious reforms especially in the bureaucracy, and reluctance of the public against some harsh punishments of the Islamic Penal Code. Its ideal was to establish an Islamic society through enforcing Islamic codes and ordinances.

5.1 REVOLUTIONARY AND CHARISMATIC STATE BUILDING

When Mohammad Reza Pahlavi, despite his massive military, huge oil export revenue, fearsome security police, and superpower support was overthrown by a popular and largely peaceful revolution, a popular and Islamic state substituted the regime that it was doomed to be mostly alike in only one decade. Among the clergy, clear and irrevocable option for the Revolution and overthrowing the *shahanshāhi* regime took a century to develop. During this time, religious questions increasingly became political questions as well.

The main characteristics of Islamic Revolution of 1979 are as follows: 1) loose organization of the revolutionaries in schools and mosques, 2) tactically mainly based on peaceful and non-violent demonstrations, 3) cooperation of clerics and religious intellectuals, 4) a national and effective network of communication, 4) addressing grievances of all strata, 5) unity of leadership, 6) widely supported by middle, lower middle and upper middle class, 7) based on a new militant and ideologized reading of Islam, 8) combination of mass mobilization and charismatic leadership, and 9) solidarity of different social groups including *bāzāris,* clerics, university students, technocrats, and blue and white collar workers (Keddie & Richard, 1981; Arjomand, 1988; Ladjevardi, 1985; Mottahedeh, 1985; Milani, 1988; Parsa, 1989).

The image of the shah as the benevolent, sympathetic, wise, and efficient administrator was quite overshadowed by the image of a distant, corrupt, and egomaniac dispenser of arbitrary decisions. Pahlavi aristocracy was the beneficiary of state policy to a significant extent and the members of this caste almost hold most of the high administrative, legislative, judicial and military positions.

Within months of the Revolution in 1979, the clerics took control of the country's most powerful institutions. The Islamic leadership executed former members of the shah's army and secret police[1] and neutralized or eliminated all opposition groups without destroying the repressive apparatus connected to the old regime (Farhi, 1990: 107). When they got rid of all oppositional parties who participated in the toppling of shah's regime they took over coercive apparatuses of the state. They first excluded Nehzat-e Āzādi (the Freedom Movement) in 1979 and then Shurā-ye Hamāhangi-ye Enqelāb-e Eslāmi (the Solidarity Council for the Islamic Revolution led by

Bani Sadr) and Mojāhedin-e Khalq in 1981 and wiped out all communist parties and groups who represented ethnic minorities from the public.

The characteristics of the state in this period of Iran's contemporary history, 1979–1989, can be explained as mobilizational but not highly organized, participatory mostly based on religious duty and not based on rights politics, increasingly ideologized polity, and consensual politics in a mass society. The Iran-Iraq war amplified these characteristics that were established during the Islamic Revolution.

Religion and politics were entwined in three different aspects: first aspect in that the domains of religion and politics were not necessarily separated; they had their ties in two ways: one the one hand, institution of religion did not relinquish political power and did not leave politics to go its own way. Religious leaders needed political power to strengthen their ever-declining positions and statuses in the society. On the other hand, it is right that the political domain set itself as a religion, somehow as a reaction to *shahanshahi* ideology with its own calendar, sacred symbols and rituals to compete Marxist and socialist ideologies that were popular among some sections of young people. Based on the second aspect, religious institutions were merging into governmental institutions. The independence of religious institutions was no more an ideal for religious elite. These institutions wanted to be the top rentiers of the state and public resources. The third aspect was the legitimacy crisis of the state after the sunset of revolutionary excitements. The politicians needed religion to justify their lifelong staying in power, e.g. by resort to the theory of rule by the deputies of hidden Imam. The guardianship of the Islamic jurist (*velāyat-e faqih*) was supposed to compensate the increasing illegitimacy of a non-elected and unaccountable government.

The problem of multiple centers of power and of revolutionary organizations not subject to central control persisted to plague Abu al-Hasan Bani Sadr, the first president of the new regime. Like Mehdi Bāzargān, the first provisional prime minister, Bani Sadr found himself competing for primacy with the clerics and activists of the Islamic Republic Party (IRP). The struggle between the president and the IRP dominated the political life of the country during Bani Sadr's presidency. Bani Sadr failed to secure the dissolution of the Pāsdārān and the Revolutionary Courts and Committees. He also failed to establish control over the judiciary or the state-run radio and television networks. Ali Akbar Hāshemi Rafsanjāni as the Parliament Speaker, Mohammad Beheshti as the Head of the Supreme Court and member of the Supreme Judiciary Council and Abd ul-Karim Musavi Ardebili as Attorney General and member of the Supreme Judiciary Council were on the other side of the political isle. Bani Sadr's appointees to head the state broadcasting services and the Pāsdārān were forced to resign within weeks of their appointments.

The main criterion for holding and exercising of political and administrative offices in this period is the possession of revolutionary background and being a student of Khomeini between 1962 to1981 and then mainly kinship relationship with the ruling clerics and being completely obedient to the Revolutionary Leader. Latter criterion turns to be the only one to get a high-ranking position in the Ali Khāmenei administration, as the second leader after the Revolution. During Khāmenei, appointed bodies of government have had always the upper hand, while election from below has had a very limited impact on the configuration of polity.

The state in this period tended to involve itself in a greater and greater number and variety of social tasks, ranging from those associated with the welfare state to those required by the Islamicization process and Islamist political ideology of the state. These tasks were extended from execution of and enforcing *shari'ah*[2] laws especially judicial ordinances to taking care of ethical and social values, and from obliging individuals to observing the ordinances of *shari`ah* in their personal life to uphold and lift up clerical lifestyle. They also put aside an eight decades long record of the involvement in the constitutional politics (Hairi 1977; Arjomand 1988: ch.2; 2000a) and got involved in grabbing the absolute power. Ruling clerics put aside the traditional division between *'ebādāt* [acts of worship] and *mu'āmelāt* [transactions], ordinances regarding the expectations of God from individuals and ordinances related to civil affairs. By resort to formal categorization of *shar'i* legal precepts into five areas, i.e. acts commanded, recommended, reprobated, forbidden, and left legally indifferent, they claimed that Islamic law is perfect and there is no necessity for borrowing law from other countries. By focusing on punitive approach to law and justice, they had enough rules in *shari`ah* to enforce: harsh punishments for adultery, drinking, sodomy, theft, robbery, and others through courts and they did not discriminate between private and public affairs; even acts of worship was used against or for the defendants or accused in the courts. The agents of the Department for Preservation of Virtue and Prevention of Vice illegally and unofficially punished people routinely.

The ruling clerics had to give civil affairs the sacredness of prayers, and give social aspect to purification and prayer to support the Islamicization process, to establish the foundations of Islamic state in the new wave of state building and to respond to the legitimacy crisis. The state in this period claims to lead men to heaven by legislative enactments that are supposed to be based on *shari`ah*. The dichotomy was no longer expected to exist in the Islamic Republic.

The other radical change in Shi'ite jurisprudence after gaining and monopolizing the power was digesting the idea of *maslahat* (public interest) which was always totally rejected in Shi'ite jurisprudence (*feqh*).[3] This was far from the idea of *zarurah* (necessity), *'osr va haraj* (hardship and chaos), or necessity that has been sparingly applied in Shi'ite jurisprudence. Some of the clerics totally rejected the idea of legislation during the Constitutional Revolution because they believed making law is equal to reduction of God's power.[4] Public policy or the expediency of the public and the political regime was never an important factor in extracting God's ordinances from Quran or *sunnah* in Shi'ite tradition. While expediting the routinization of Khomeini's charismatic leadership and Islamic ideology as presented during the Revolution , this departure-later institutionalized in the Expediency Council-helped the clerics to respond to some of the demands of the mass which could not be totally ignored in the years immediately after the Revolution while the power struggle was still under way.

Islamicization of the polity is to take one side in the quintessential religious questions and to oblige the government to sponsor religious activities with its discretion in any public setting by resort to the popularity and authority of a charismatic leader. The plurality of Shi'ite jurisprudence was going to be replaced by the absolute monopoly of the state in religious affairs including interpretation of sacred texts. This is what I call charismatic state building in this period. In this framework, supporting a special set of religious beliefs and acts becomes simply patriotic acknowledgment of "the nation's formal religion," i.e. ruling clerics' version of Islamic ideology, and not the nation's religious history or the plurality of *fatva*s in seminaries. Islamicization does not stop to this point that the nation was founded by individuals who believed in God and the Constitution declares Shi'ite Islam as the official religion, but it requires the government not to be neutral in religious challenges. Islamity (*eslāmiyyat*) of the state, in this sense, is a normative statement that poses no threat to the separation of religious and governmental institutions. This Islamity was presented as part of the renovation or revival of Islam by interpreting it in the light of modern conditions, in this case modern nation-states.

New wave of Islamic interpretations and "ideological Islam" (*eslām-e maktabi*) that was fresh and productive, from the victory of Islamic Revolution onwards, became increasingly slate and uninteresting for the public. This was because of the rigidity of ideologized *shari`ah* (*eslām-e feqhi),* whether traditional *(feqh-e sonnati*)[5] or "innovative" *(feqh-e pouya)*[6] as the two schools of political Islam in 1980's in Iran) and its setting in the final mould. In many respects, the revolutionary clerical rule represented the consummation of tendencies, which were present between two religious groups: followers of Islamic intellectual ideologues and followers of the traditionalist clergy both loyal to Khomeini. While the rigidity of traditional Islamic law helped it to maintain its stability over the centuries of decay of political institutions during 'Abbasids (Schacht, 1964: 75), the rigidity of ideologized *shari`ah* did not help it to stabilize due to its total dependency to political power and the transitional situation of a developing country like Iran. In spite of claimed openness of gate of independent reasoning (*ejtehād*) in Shi'ite tradition[7] that closely interrelate law, society, religion and politics, ideologized *shari`ah* (both static and dynamic ones) has been rigid and strict. This is due to the priority of private law (marriage, divorce, maintenance, property, inheritance, intimate relationships, etc.) to the public law (taxation, constitutional law, war, corporations and law of contracts, remedies and obligations and rights) in Islamic tradition.

The Islamic *feqh* did not historically develop with the expansion of governmental activities and increasing importance of public law; this is also true after the Revolution due to shortage of jurists who may work in seminaries as their career; almost all of them were engaged now in state affairs in a way or another. The number, length, and variety of commentaries, and treatises written by Islamic jurists in the areas of public life are not comparable to what they have done in private law. This underdevelopment seriously altered the view of elite and intellectuals, even religious ones, toward *shari`ah*. The idealist view that was created by ideologues like Ali Shari'ati and Mortezā Motahhari that Islam includes any solution for social, political, and economic problems evaporated in only some month after the Revolution and new generation confronted with deficiencies of clerics and their doctrines. Much of the public law, particularly constitutional and administrative law, was mostly a product of the developments of Iranian nation-state and secular nation-state building process during Pahlavis that only a very small section of clerics were involved with it. Some of the achievements of the Constitutional Revolution were formal separation of governmental powers, regarding judicial offices not as personal properties, more centralized governmental system, and abnegation of divine origin of state law. The Islamic revolutionaries reaffirmed all these except the worldly nature of law.

Less detailed law of contract and obligations could facilitate a greater flexibility and adaptability, if the clerics' view of the politics was more practical and formally rational. The observance of the letter rather than of the spirit did not let the clerics to see beyond the text, although "the laws which rule the lives of the Iranian Muslim have never been [fully] coextensive with pure Islamic law, if it exists" (Schacht, 1964: 85). The project of adapting Islam to a series of modern conditions replaced with and reduced to the project of adapting Islam with the necessities of a clerical or hierocratic authoritarian, and in some respects totalitarian state.

Most of the terms of the Constitution of 1979 have distinctively religious cast. The ruling clerics attempted to make the *shari`ah* as the basis of the politico-legal order in the ideological constitution of the Islamic Republic of Iran (Schirazi 1997). There are numerous examples of religious references scattered throughout the Iranians' civic life, if any. The phrases like "absolute sovereignty of God" (Preamble, Article 56) support the concept of unlimited government, serving as a reminder that government is the highest authority in human affairs because of inalienable rights of the Islamic jurists coming from God.[8] While "absolute sovereignty over the world and man belongs to God" (Article 56) and "the direction of affairs is in the hands of those who are learned concerning God" (Preamble of the Constitution), the elections will function as a decoration for the state to be presented as democratic in the modern world. These words in the Constitution of 1979 have not been brought up in vain; they are not there to proclaim Iranians' reliance on God or their seeking of the wisdom and blessing of divine providence; they are to create a religious state in favor of the privileges for religious ruling caste. While "the government of the Islamic Republic of Iran has the duty of directing all its resources to" eliminate "all forms of despotism and autocracy and all attempts to monopolize power" (Article 3) by groups other than clergy, it gives over absolute power to the Guardian Council (Article 4) and the leader (Articles 5, 107 and 110).

Every religious act mentioned in the Constitution of 1979 is a coerced one. It is with resort to these words that the clergy led obligatory prayers at public schools, military bases and governmental offices. Clerics were invited to any commencement ceremonies in universities on the ground that the graduating students were effectively coerced into participating in a public life that should be colored with Islam. The Expert Council who selects the leader only includes Islamic jurists; the Guardian Council disqualifies nominees who are considered non-true believers to Islam and non-loyal to the leader and the guardianship of the jurist; and people are denied to be recruited in public offices on the basis of their different beliefs and ideas. These are all parts and parcels of building a new Islamic state in the modern world. People who did not take part in these obligatory religious and state ceremonies were considered as outsiders and deprived of most of their political and civil rights as the second order citizens of the new state.

In this ideological prospect, if people are doubtful about the truthful of the guardianship of the jurist, not the existence of God, they are of doubtful loyalty to both the nation and the state. The mobilization process and the entry of the masses into politics were not associated with the emergence of coalitions or party politics, development of adversary politics and thus rotation of elite. It was just *bai'ah* (confirmation of the only candidate for the highest public office) and not political participation.

According to the Constitution of 1979, all the powers of the state were concentrated in the leader. They include appointment, dismissal, and acceptance of resignation of the *fuqahā* (jurists) on the Guardian Council, the supreme judicial authority of the country, the head of the radio and television networks of the Islamic Republic of Iran, the chief of the joint staff, the chief commander of the Islamic Revolutionary Guards Corps (IRGC) and the supreme commanders of the armed forces. He endorses the President after his election, delineates the general policies of the Islamic Republic of Iran after consultation with the Regime's Expediency Council (according to 1989 amendment to the Constitution), supervises over the proper execution of the general policies of the system, issues decrees for national referenda, assumes supreme command of the armed forces, and declares war and peace and the mobilization of the armed forces. He also resolves differences between the three wings of the armed forces and regulation of their relations, resolves the problems which cannot be solved by conventional methods through the Expediency Council, dismisses the President of the Republic, with due regard for the interests of the country, after the Supreme Court holds him guilty of the violation of his constitutional duties, or after a vote of the Islamic Consultative Assembly testifying to his incompetence on the basis of Article 89 of the Constitution, and pardons or reduces the sentences of convicts, within the framework of Islamic criteria, on a recommendation [to that effect] from the Head of judicial power (Article 110). Even this vast spectrum of power has not been enough for the two leaders of the IRI and they have violated this article on the basis of absolute guardianship of the jurist.[9] The violations are justified by the creation of a new category in Shi'ite jurisprudence, claiming the power of the supreme jurist to issue governmental orders (*hokm-e hokumati*). *Hokm-e hokumati* is neither an executive order/decree-law on the one hand nor a statute law. It is an afterthought to create a *feqhi* (jurisprudential) category, first to justify public law and later to put the *vali-ye faqih* (ruling jurist) above the law.

All three branches of government operate under the Jurist's supervision (Article 57). In spite of the expected nature of the regime that was supposed to be a republic, clearly the new Constitution was not a republicanized version of the 1906 Constitution, but its Islamicized version, as the authority does not originate in the nation and centrality of the parliament is reduced (Bashiriyeh, 1984: 168). The process of concentration of power and overcoming the problems of fragmentation of authority[10] ended with the revision of the Constitution at the end of this period. This let the ruling caste to get rid of division of authority in most of the political bodies of government, i.e. president and prime minister in the executive power and the members of the Supreme Judiciary Council. Bani Sadr failed to adapt with the implications of these divisions in the first years of the Islamic Republic.

The Iranian revolutionaries, later ruling caste, did not believe that the gate of *ejtehād* was closed. They, whether traditionalist or populist, believed that the sacred law of Islam was an all-embracing body of religious duties, not rights, for the subjects of the Islamic state (Soroush, 1996).[11] It comprises ordinances regarding worship and ritual, as well as political and legal rules. While theology and mysticism were the basic frameworks of revolutionary doctrines (*maktab*) drawn up by the Islamic ideologues as Ali Shari'ati and Mehdi Bāzargān, Islamic *feqh* took place of the previous Islamicized ideology as the ideology of the state and facilitated another phase of ideologizing Islam, i.e. ideologizing *shari`ah*. The clergy was the carrier of *shari`ah,* and no tradition even the love-based doctrine of mysticism was strong enough to challenge the ascendancy of the Islamic law over the minds of revolutionary Iranian Muslims. In this way, the Islamic law that was never supported by an organized power (Schacht, 1964: 2) found a total support by its ruling carriers. But the Islamic law was not as unified, uniform, original[12] and radical breakaway from the Arab way of life, as the revolutionaries had expected.

The Islamic law in the hands of seminary students still embraced what Schacht represents as duality of legal subject matter and religious norms, dualism of religion and state, discordance between the sacred law and the reality of actual practice, outward variety of legal, ethical, and ritual rules, and tensions between theory and practice (Schacht, 1964: 2–4). The revolutionary ignored not only all elements of historical Islam that were not in accordance with the narrowest possible interpretation of Islam, i.e. reducing the material sources of Islam to Quran and *Hadith* (*Sunnah,* precedent or normative custom), but also the elements that were not in accordance with the necessities of an Islamic state. This state was not based on rule of law, democracy and human rights. At the same time, Islamic law did not enjoy the highest degree of actual efficiency, even in post-revolutionary Iran.

Although Islamic law was by no means essentially irrational, ideologization of *shari`ah* in a transient mass movement, lack of moral rules, the unprincipled use of expediency principle, and irrational method of interpretation by revolutionaries made it substantively and formally irrational. As a consequence of inadequacy of formal rationality of juridical Islamic thought, systematic lawmaking, aiming at legal uniformity or consistency was impossible (Weber, 1968: 821). In this system, predictability of decisions of kadi justice system is at minimum (Weber, 1968: 823).

Once Islamic Revolution prevailed, religious authoritarians reasserted themselves in the polity. The patrimonialism and authoritarianism of religious authorities found their expression in the idea of Islamity of the government. Islamic ideology, the innovation of Shari'ati and Bāzargān,[13] had to open the way for ideologized *shari`ah* that was partially based on enforcing all Islamic ordinances through judiciary as part of the state. Even among the clerics who were influential in drafting the Constitution of 1979 and setting forth the idea of guardianship of the jurist as the main element of Islamity of the state, there was not a complete agreement. Montazeri and Beheshti were the most influential members of the Expert Council for Drafting the Constitution who added the guardianship of the jurist to the draft and defended it in the floor of the Council.[14]

Technical aspects of law, *shari`ah* or state law, were a matter of indifference to the high ranking ruling clergy. By establishment of the Guardian Council they were sure that they would always have the power of vetting any law passed by the parliament and the leader can always interfere in any affair by resort to the power of the guardian or governmental order (*hokm-e hokumati*). In spite of the endeavors of early Muslims to adopt legal and administrative institutions and practices of the conquered territories, Islamic revolutionaries of the late 20th century could not adopt these institutions due to the obstacles they could create for consolidation of the new clerical elite and filtration of the old one. The identity challenges were pushing them to gett everything from the new militant Islam, not the West. Although the new regime internalized most of the so-called non-anti-Islamic routines and regulations, it pretended to avoid retention of the old institutions. Different administrations tried to close the doors of the country to what was coming from Western civilization, and as far as the leaders never believed in the accomplishment of the consolidation those doors stayed closed to prevent the loss of legitimacy of the regime by new measures and ideas coming from the West.

The main concern was not with religious law itself but with political administration; enforcing religious laws in their ups and downs was a way for consolidation and legitimization of the new regime(s). Almost all the religious intellectuals and political activists who were advocating the return to so-called Quranic values were eliminated from the polity in only three years and *feqh* or clerical reading of Islam was replaced as the ideology of the post-revolutionary government. Clergy transferred the term "Islamity," as it was used by the intellectuals, from its political and theological context to a juridical context with only one alternative, i.e. *shari`ah*. In this transfer, the practice of Islamic local community, ethically inspired opposition to the status quo, and the doctrines of Islamic theologians and mystics were completely ignored. As far as the pristine Islamic law did not include anything about organization, centralization, and bureaucratization of the government, the revolutionaries picked the dual structure as the best way to deal with new and old parts of the government; they created a new organization beside any old one with similar missions and functions. The new ones were mostly modeled out of the authoritarian regimes of the Communist Bloc.

The future subjects of Islamic regime regarded Khomeini a charisma before the victory of the Revolution, someone "endowed with supernatural, superhuman, or at least specifically exceptional powers or qualities" (Weber, 1968: 241). He got this feature through revolutionary actions. Khomeini, in the heyday of his charismatic era (1979–81), knew no formal and regulated appointment or dismissal, no supervisory of appeals body, and no local and technical jurisdiction. He was self-determined and set his own limits. His charismatic justice figure was mainly based on juridical, political and judicial discretion. With transfer from charismatic regime to an authoritarian one, these characteristics began to fade.

When the tide that lifted a charismatically led group out of ordinary life in revolutionary era flew back into the channels of workaday routines, the charismatic domination of Khomeini turned into an authoritarian regime claiming political authority of the Muslim ruler who is not necessarily deputy of hidden Imam. In some texts, this charisma is called *saltanat-e mosalmān-e zi showkat* (kingship of the authoritative Muslim).[15] The ruled were not in the position to acclaim their political rights, and hence regular electoral system did not develop. In a society that half of the people were illiterate, 40 percent were living in villages without access to healthy water, electricity, modern transportation and communication, and cities were surrounded by the ghettos, standard suffrage, legal equality, direct or indirect election, rotation of elite, majority or proportional method, and rule of law seemed idealistic and remained on the paper. The three important preconditions of these factors, i.e. strong civil society, extension of market economy and effective bureaucracy were absent. At the time, the process of differentiation and appropriation among and within organizations had not advanced and had not extended to most of the communities, individuals were not simultaneously members of several organizations, and the relative degrees of power of officials and governmental officers were not subject to fixed and increasingly rational rules.

Islamic government born out of the ashes of 1979 Revolution tried to establish a community of faith in the whole country. In Pahlavi era, the nationality tie replaced the blood tie of Qājār era. The community of faith was supposed to replace the community based on nationality. In spite of the popular Islamic Revolution, this could not happen. Iranian society could not be a mere Muslim community because the so-called "true believers" were only a minority, now ruling the country, and their ideology and lifestyle could not be the ideology and lifestyle of most of the Iranians under the umbrella of Iranian nation-state.

In the eyes of Muslim revolutionaries of Iran, this community of faith (*ummah*) as the base for Islamic state would be created, ruled and protected by an Islamic government, more probably authoritarian and totalitarian, and less probably democratic, first in a national framework and then in a global arena. This new *ummah* that was the product of a social movement was modeled out of the idea of mass society in which the informal systems of loyalty and ideological affiliations take place of impersonal bureaucratized relationships (Gusfield, 1962: 20). In this situation, representative nature of intermediate structure and independent groups (Kornhauser, 1959: 78) is undermined, and autonomous public opinion arising from public discussion does not exist. This society is based on a disorganized mass which is acted on by an elite, as Mills states (1956: 304), through the mass media thus shaping the nature of "public opinion."

The disputes in this society would be settled by *shari`ah*-as-it-was-read-by-the-leader as the highest rule of the state. The leadership of *ummah* was supposed to be the last ring of *imāmah* chain. This community was expected to be different from any other: it was chosen; it included holy people; it was based on the holy land (*umm ul-qurā'*), the holy leader (*imām*), and the promised state (*dowlat-e mow'ud* or *hokumat-e 'adl*).

The conception of law in the community of faith-read it Islamic mass society- is determined by communal brotherhood controlled by the source of authority. This concept is based on God's expectation from men and women as understood by the ruling clerics, be it the norms of the pristine community of believers as understood by different generations of believers, the interaction of revelation and public weal (*maslahat-e 'omoumi*) or will and expediency of an authority justified by faith, or different readings, interpretations or reconstructions of the sacred texts. The community of religious and piety minded people[16] has been shrinking from the day after the victory of the Revolution later included only a very small portion of the society. Submission to the law of this community is a religious and social duty; people who infringe this legal order have committed a crime and a sin at the same time. In this perspective, crime and sin are two kinds of looking at the same phenomenon. Jurisprudence is not a civil act but a religious practice that points to theology and eschatology as its ultimate bases.

In this point of view, human society would not be possible without some limitations on appetites and actions of every individual defined by the Islamic ideology. According to this view, God has set a bound to human activity through assigning five categories according to their values representing the whole body of positive law, i.e. things indispensable or expressly commanded (*wājeb* or *farz*), things absolutely forbidden, prohibited (*harām*), things reprehensible (*makruh*), things recommended or desirable (*mostahab* or *mandub*), and things admissible, permitted or indifferent (*mobāh* or *jā'ez*).

In 1979, Iran became the modern world's first theocracy due to the success of the Islamic revolutionaries in political and cultural arenas and using administrative, judicial and coercive apparatuses to get rid of all "outsiders." The outsiders were considered to be remnants of the old regime, leftist groups who participated in the shah's overthrow, and even militant and non-militant Islamic groups with different readings of Islam and *shari`ah*. The voices of change in Iran coming from women, university students, and even clerics who have been disenfranchised and instrumental in modifying the system, were all labeled as mercenaries of Imperialism and hence outsiders. The new regime could ride on the waves of change and remold people's lifestyles by demobilizing the masses, neutralization of the old elite, and pacification or elimination of all rivals, especially socialists and liberal-nationalists who were effective in consolidation of Islamic regime immediately after the Revolution.

There was a challenge between the clergymen about the application of *shari`ah* in post-revolutionary Iran. Traditional clerics believed that if *shari`ah* is applied as the state-law, it changes the nature and function of religion in the society. In their belief, separation of *shari`ah* and state law takes out religion from politics and saves it; it does not withdraw it from the public life but safeguard it.

While the secular state and polity was going to be Islamicized in post-Revolutionary era,[17] the continuing secularization process that was going on before and after the Revolution extended to different strata of the society. This process was not merely limited to the secular governments of Iran from the beginning of the 20th century to the time of Islamic Revolution. It implicitly extended to the religious community and other independent groups and institutions. After the Revolution, Iranian secularization process extends from one dimensionality of secularization of state to tri-dimensionality of secularization in the frameworks of religious traditions, enlightenment and sociological and political thoughts.

Islamic Revolution was only a social fever for about three years. After consolidation of the new regime, mass rallies gradually disappeared. The government adopted a policy of demobilization. State economic policy of intervention was gradually abandoned. Upward mobilization and the change of the elite were stopped. All the revolutionary institutions were bureaucratized; ban on the interest abandoned; mechanisms of social control integrated; and massive purges of the bureaucracy, confiscation of property, and nationalization of foreign assets and trade and the government control of much of domestic trade were over. Hence what was left was only the change of the government, with new names: *vali-ye faqih* for king, office or house (*bait*) of the guardian for court of the king, turban for the crown (Arjomand, 1988), Revolutionary Court for the Military Tribunal, Mustaz'afān Foundation for the Pahlavi Foundation, etc. The most important change was from the *shahanshahi* ideology to Islamic one that led to a more authoritarian regime and less social and cultural freedom for individuals.

However, the fact that the Revolution did not end the monarchical hierarchy of power[18] has been commented by many scholars and politicians as diverse as Mohsen Kadivar,[19] Abdollah Nouri,[20] Akbar Ganji[21] and Majid Mohammadi;[22] they allude that what has transpired in post-revolutionary Iran is some sort of monarchical order reconstituted in the absolutist clerical rule. Shahs in Qājār period and the Leaders (jurists) of I.R.I and even some of their oppositional leaders have claimed to be the guardian of justice and equity for the people[23] and in some periods people have bought this idea. According to Amanat, the ruler is responsible for maintaining a causal cycle, i.e. cycle of equity that interplays between the ruler, the government and the subjects (Amanat, 1997: 9, 72) to discharge his duty in defending the kingdom and administration of justice. This cycle has been crisis-driven and crisis-ridden due to the instability, grievances, belittling of individuals and resulting revolutionary situations from one hand and rulers' despotic way of governance in creating poverty, unemployment, inequality, economic and political insecurity and marginalization from the other. This cycle has been producing bloated bureaucracies, inefficient public management and over-protected public sector that extend to industry and agriculture. The resultant institutions were more preoccupied with self-preservation than performance. The micromanagement usually leads governments either smother or marginalize non-governmental views, arrogating a monopoly on truth, and cling to their accustomed strategies of regulation and subsidy. This strengthens pressure on those who sympathize with extreme views and presents potential extremists with a range of attractive options. If a reformist alternative is desired (true both in case of Nāser ul-Din Shah and Khāmenei[24]), the alternative is for the shah or *faqih* to micro manage everything, including instructing his goons when and where to attack his opponents. Due to different ways and means for micromanagement, the nature and structure of authoritarian regime varies. A micro manager naturally begets personalization of power, which in turn leads to the consolidation of oppositional movement against him. Even someone with a deep knowledge of Shi'ism may even claim that the leader and his manipulations are outside the bound of the *shari`ah*.

All the manipulations could be compared to the manipulations occurred during the shift from Qājār dynasty to Pahlavi dynasty. The economic and political structure of the state did not eminently change. The old and new regimes were both clientalist and authoritarian. Changing the ideology of the state does not mean a social transfer from secular to Islamic society, even when the Islamic ideology was as worldly as the previous one. The process of Islamicization was limited to the areas of Islamists' powers. The society soon returned to the idea of secular state when Islamicization did not function as it was promised and brought more limitation instead of relief. Although the Islamic state changed the pace of social secularism and pursued the process of Islamicization as previous state followed the secular process of state building based on *shahanshahi* ideology, the society in both periods did not completely accompany these trends, though did not negate them from the beginning.

The religious institutions shifted from the civil society to political society. This shift monopolized the power and hence involved more in the business affairs of modern governmental institutions. This led to routinization of the religious tasks that religious organizations were conducting. The new wave of governmental Islamicization, in spite of the early Islamicization of second century of Islam was not accompanied with the complementary tendency to reason and to systematize. It was mainly done through consideration of improvising and impromptu situations and on an ad hoc basis to go beyond the existing laws and principles of *ejtehād*. Individual reasoning, though, scarce, was purely discretionary and personal or inspired by an effort to survival of the revolutionary regime and its ruling class. Discretionary (*maslahat*) reasoning, even based on public interest, convenience, or similar considerations, beside *estehsān* (appropriate personal choice) and *qiyās* (analogy) had no precedent in Shi'ite tradition.

Iran in the 1960's and 1970's saw the emergence of the notion of the perfectibility of man, not by praying alone but by praxis and social action. The teachings of religious intellectuals like Ali Shari'ati were strengthening the engagement of believers in social and political life and their responsibility to take charge of their lives based on their beliefs (Shari'ati, 1979). These ideas facilitated involvement of believers in objectifying perceived utopia in real world through ideologized politics.

In spite of religious state at work in every area of life in post-Revolutionary era, using Peter Gay's words, "religious institutions and religious explanations of events were slowly displaced from the center of life to its periphery" (Gay, 1966: 336). After the revolution, the emphasis was no longer on the sacred phenomena beyond, but on *shari`ah* that has always been a worldly framework for organizing human life. In this period, routinization and then secularization deeply encompassed everything including art, history, morals, social science and politics that were not under total control of the government. Natural science was already secularized during the Pahlavi era. Separation of commitment to ideology (*ta'ahhod*) and professionalism (*takhassos*)- that was originally meant to Islamicize the human resources- and at the same time the need to administer the country in a modern world expedited the routinization process. The intensification of clerics' engagement in daily activities through taking official governmental positions routinized most portions of the religious community, clergy's life and bureaucratized revolutionaries, although clerics themselves would hardly approve of. Although religious ideas contributed to the strengthening of the religious state, the latter in turn, ironically, contributed to the erosion of the public presence of religious beliefs, practices and authority especially in civil society and family. The establishment of religious state created a sacred void in Iranian society, for it demanded a worldly and secular reality within the gestalt of God's grace.

If we define secularization as separation of church and state, separation of laws and morals, and neutrality of state in religious and ethical matters, the state has experienced a high level of Islamicization, as opposed to secularization. However, Iranian society unlike its governments resisted these three measures especially after 1981. The institution of family and non-governmental institutions have headed toward separation of laws and morals and they generally believe in separation of religious institutions and state and neutrality of state in religious and ethical matters. As far as NGOs are involved, this could also be described as the dissemination of secularism in the public sphere, which leaves the individual to be as secular or non-secular as he or she pleases in private life. This is secularization of the social life, especially the sub-society of believers, not secularization of Shi'ite clergy as a whole that had already been secularized during Safavids.

By secularization in the framework of religious traditions, I mean the progress of an underlying idea of duality of domains of action that is repeatedly stated in Islamic texts. We read about the things that are God's (*elāhi*) and things that are worldly (*donyavi*). The latter is the fundamental of two domains of life and Islamic clerics have never avoided engaging in it. The clergy of Islamic world has always been secular in this sense and Islamic Revolution invigorated this secularity and made it clearer and stronger. The conflict between religious faith and human reason has always been part of the background of the Islamic tradition and its secular clerics. Different Islamic theological schools, even mysticism, did not negate engaging in worldly affairs by all Muslims.[25]

Before the Islamic Revolution, the *'ulamā* (religious scholars) and *fuqahā* (Islamic jurists) were private individuals and religious institutions like mosques, seminaries and endowments were part of the civil society institutions, singled out from the governmental institutions by their special concerns and interests. After the Revolution, in only one decade, all aspects of independency, i.e. social, economic and political were gradually abrogated.

The separation of religious institutions and state and neutrality of state in religious disputes inside religious groups and among religious and non-religious groups as two criteria for secularity of state were institutionally violated. As far as the state was not neutral on the question of which religion is correct and was engaged in promotion of one religion over another, it could not be considered secular. In reaction to totalitarian face of the new regime, now some Iranians began to think about this idea that belief in God should be stripped from official expression altogether.

The structure of authority/domination and the place of religious authority within them are at stake here. The relevant dimension of what I refer to as the "*'orfi-shodan-e din*" (secularization of religion) is not the domination of religious authority over the state but the domination of state over the religious authority and the merge of religious institutions into governmental institutions. As this process goes so on, some sections of religious establishment distanciate itself from the state. As a reaction to this domination, a new secular religion has been coming to the public sphere that keeps its distance from the state. Although passing of the *hodoud*, *diyāt* and *qesās* laws was a further step in Islamicization, the increasingly negative public responses to these kinds of steps and pushing them out of public sight were signs of social secularization. If we want to focus on authority defined as religious, or better as "clerical" and the degree of its extension over the legal and the political spheres, the state was Islamicized, and at the same time family and other independent social institutions were secularized. To keep the state Islamicized while society was going to be routinized, the state took the policy of destruction of institutions and classes before they reach the level of serving society as part of the social structure and before playing the roles of representation in the polity.

The judiciary in post-revolutionary era was being Islamicized. This Islamization can be explained through establishing an ideology using all elements of Islamic theology and *shari'ah* that suitably respond to the needs and demands of the modern world as understood by the ruling clerics. The success of this ideology is not the subject at hand because Marxism, Leninism,

Fascism and Anarchism were ideologies created for modern times, while all of them could not survive as ideologies in power. The idea of enforcing all books and articles of the *shari`ah* law by resort to state monopoly of power and violence is totally modern. There is no such idea in *shari`ah*.

5.2 RELIGIOUS AND STATE JUDICIAL SYSTEMS: SUBSTANTIVE ISLAMICIZATION

After consolidation of power, the Islamic leadership pursued its agenda of Islamicization. In this project, the justice system was to institute a strict version of Islamic law. Of particular interest to the ruling clerics was the judiciary, which—given that Islam is considered to be an elaborate body of laws in clerical point of view of Islam[26]—would be the most important branch of government (Bashiriyeh, 1984: 168) to reverse the social control disintegration during the revolution. They brought back harsh punishments and denounced everything Western, subjected the public to the same methods of surveillance and control that it was under the previous regime (Farhi, 1990: 107), made women wear the veil and excluded them from judgeship.

Islamicization was the continuation of state building process, i.e. the project of state as personification of the national legal order, this time national Islamic order enforced by the coercive forces under the control of clergy. In order to differentiate themselves and their revolution from the ruling class of Pahlavi dynasty, which they had superseded, the ruling clerics exaggerated the differences, and in opposition to their predecessors proclaimed their program of establishing the rule of God on earth. When they got rid of religious intellectuals and other Islamic dissidents in power struggles, they recognized the *shari`ah,* now upgraded to the ideology of the clerical state, as the only legitimate norm in Islam. Although the office of *qāzis* was separated from the executive power it became bound to the office of leader that led to a floating system in substance and procedure. The centralized tendency of the new regime which was responsible for appointment of the qāzis all around the country by the central government, in opposition to *shari`ah* courts of Qājār period, did not lead to the creation of dignity of high ranking officials of the judiciary. New regime gave priority to the *shari`ah* courts, now part of a hidden double administration of justice, one religious and exercised by the *qāzi* or *hākem-e shar'* based on *shari`ah,* the other one secular-superficially Islamicized- and exercised by the political authorities based on custom, equity and fairness, sometimes arbitrariness, and governmental regulations. Part of these secular laws were drafted and passed by the so-called non-Islamic legislators.

The rule of jurist cut the distinction between *shari`ah* law and some sections of the *'orf* (custom). The line between these two was recognized by *'ulamā* in Iranian society after Islam. The religious establishment replaced the *'orf* with *maslahat-e nezām* (the expediency of the regime) after the Islamic Revolution of 1979. The *'orf* and necessities of governing of the ruling caste, i.e. *maslahat-e nezām* substituted the dynamic custom of the society. The Expediency Council was established on Feb. 6, 1988[27] to see what was allowed to limit a text, but the survival of the regime was prior to considering the *'orf*. A general or specific *'orf* could not supersede a general or specific rule of *shari'ah*[28] as presented by a jurist, but it is the power of government vested in the Expediency Council that can supersede the Islamic rules and beliefs, any of them even unity of God (Khomeini, 1991: Vol. 20, p. 170), presented by the Islamic jurists. This substitution was headed to solve the crises of legitimacy and efficiency, while custom as a source of law was accepted to match the law and the changing necessities of social order. The ruling clergy in most cases ignored changing local customs that were embodied in *shari`ah* for centuries and declared their reading and version of *shari`ah* as the pure Islam. The ideologized Isalm (*maktab*) gave this new version of *shari`ah*, i.e. *shari`ah* as the ideology of the state, lifestyle and state law, the same sanction that was given to *'ebādat,* laws regulating rituals and religious observances. This sanction was given to this ideologized *shari`ah* by the actual power of the state, not the actual or supposed practice of the prophet or imam. Believers of the theory of jurist's guardianship and rule used the impossibility of clear definition of these two jurisdiction to upgrade one, *mu'āmelāt,* to the level of the other, *'ebādāt* with respect to sanctity and *'ebādāt* to the level of *mu'āmelāt* with respect to worldliness.

Islamic revolutionaries believed that the exercise of the *qazā'* (adjudication) was no longer simply as fulfillment of a public or social duty but a religious task, a devotional act and accomplishment of a religious obligation (Khomeini, 1991: Vol. 20, 99) that needs religious knowledge. Adjudiction was believed to be a principle of religion. The Therefore the *qāzi* should be a *mujtahed* (expert in *feqh* as the scientific study and elucidation of the shari`ah, or the science of Islamic jurisprudence and rulings) that can only be chosen from among the *'ulamā*.[29] This accomplishment was an important part of the Islamicization process. Adjudication in the framework of ideologized or political Islam (*eslām-e siāsi or eslām-e hokumati*) is a *vājeb-e kafā'ii* (conditional obligation based on adequacy of observance), one of those religious obligations, which is imposed upon every male believer when called upon and when he finds himself to be the only one to possess the necessary qualifications.

In spite of a functioning Ministry of Justice and an extending organization of Revolutionary Courts in provinces' capitals, Khomeini as the religious leader kept appointing *shar'i* judges even one year after the establishment of the Islamic regime.[30] These appointments did not follow a pattern in the whole country and were stopped after the establishment of the Supreme Judiciary Council based on chapter 11of the Constitution.

The strengthening of the religious character of the *qāzi*'s office in post-revolutionary era enlarged the scope of the *qāzi*'s functions by conferring upon him certain duties essentially political in nature. The founders of the Islamic republic like any jurist of the Islamic world rejected any possibility of a collegial formation.[31] Hence the judicial tribunal was composed of a single judge.[32] Even jurists who believed in the idea of council of *eftā'* (issuing decrees and legal statements for the believers) did not believe in collegial formation of the court.

The Islamic Republic introduced *shari`ah* law as the state law. Before the rule of jurist, *shari`ah* was believed to cover all aspects of believer's life and administered by the *qāzi* in the *shari`ah* courts. After the ideologization of *shari`ah* and making it as part of the state law, *shari`ah* was believed by the ruling caste to cover all aspects of believers' and non-believers' public lives. Now *shari`ah* was supposed to regulate all aspects of public and even private lives of every individual in the state. The state as the arbiter of the custom, manipulated it to be the custom of ruling clergy as the only accepted lifestyle and framework of thinking. *Shari`ah* as a system of law in a society that its majority did not know anything about it and cried for a new system of law after the Revolution could supercede the custom that was unwritten and there was no institution to represent it. The idealistic, and at the same time, unknown law of the mass society of clerics' followers overcame the state law of an overthrown regime.

The formal juridical and judicial character of this new ideology, i.e. ideologized *shari`ah,* was not developed; the main concerns of the Islamic ideologues was overthrowing the regime and they were not expecting to win soon, while the main concern of the traditional clerics whom were supposed to be the future judges was enforcing *shari`ah* law. The new judges took the *shari`ah* law seriously and were trying to ideologize it, while the revolutionary generation took Quranic norms seriously. The followers of the Islamic ideology, a huge number of revolutionaries, as was drawn up by Shari'ati did not believe in this post-revolutionary produced ideology, i.e. ideologized *shari`ah*.

The new regime suffered lack of an organized judicial system, while revolutionaries needed an organized system to consolidate their power and use it as part of a new ideology in the modern time. Islamic traditional law was used to represent an extreme case of a jurist law (Schacht, 1964, 5) while the revolutionaries wanted a judiciary to be controlled by the leaders, not the judges. An imagined judiciary based on jurist law could not be used as a political instrument for control. Iranian revolutionaries wanted to entwine a supposedly common-law system of pristine Islam[33] with a long civil law tradition of the Iranian state. In real world they leaned toward civil law tradition. As evidence, I can refer to the role of judges in the courts; judicial interpretation was relegated to the Supreme Court, not the judges. *Qāzi* was supposed to present a sovereign ordinance, either of God or of the Prophet and Imams, with no need for a legal system in the narrow meaning of the term, and with no need to lay down legal rules regulating the form and controlling and dealing with the effects of these transactions.[34]

After a victorious revolution with Islamic agenda, *shari`ah* enjoyed a prestige that was denied to *'orf*. *'Orf* was considered to be the arbitrary decisions of illegitimate governments or people's opinions and lifestyles that could be totally against Islam. *Shari`ah* as a legal system, that was not being tested in the same society for a long time, could easily challenge those arbitrary decisions. Now this was *shari`ah* which was enforced by the strong hand of the government, and any opposition was muted. In practice in the courts, cases were still settled by a mixture of arbitration, local custom and equity, and this was justified by the principle of *maslahat* or necessities of time (*moqtaziāt-e zamān*).

The creation of the Guardian Council by the Constitution was directed to end the conflict between the *shari`ah* law and the state law and exclude groups that are considered "outsiders" from the polity. This Council has vetted all the bills that headed to routinize the judiciary and rationalize the judicial procedure. Barring women from the judiciary, and their legal marginalization were another important section of Islamicization of the judiciary.

Judiciary was of particular interest for the clerics. This branch of power could give the clerics the opportunity to Islamicize the society and state from above. The judiciary also was considered the most important branch of government in an Islamic state. The judicial system had in fact been the stronghold of the clerical power before the Constitutional Movement of 1906 and secularization of society. Judiciary, if Islamicizing could go on, could be a major domain of clerical power and change the secular lifestyles brought about by the secular states.

The Constitution of 1979 in Articles 156 to 174 aimed to reverse the secularization process of Pahlavi era. It not only based the judicial system on Islamic law but also put it totally in the hands of *faqih* not only as the highest authority of the country but an Islamic jurist that blurs the relationship of state and religion. For solving the tension between diversity of opinions among the Islamic scholars (judges-to-be) and the necessity of the modern state to have a unified legal system,[35] the priority was practically given to the opinion of the ruling jurist, although there was nothing about this priority in the Constitution.

The project of Islamicization of judiciary was focused on two crucial elements. The first element was Islamicization of the laws and regulations as it was perceived by the revolutionaries and clerics. The annulment of the Family Protection Law was an important part of Islamicization of laws in immediate years after the Revolution. When the new regime could overcome its different rivals and consolidated its monopolistic power, there was no obstacle for Islamicization. In July 1982, Khomeini issued an order to void all the laws that are contradictory to Islamic *shar'iah*. After this order, the Supreme Judiciary Council issued a circular and ordered all the courts to use authentic Islamic texts and reliable *fatvas*[36] mainly Khomeini's main jurisprudential book, i.e. *Tahrir al-Wasila (Drafting the Means)*. This gave the force of state law to Khomeini's teachings and writings, transferring the right of the state in making law to a person. This was an important move by the government to Islamicize the judiciary and at the same time routinize Khomeini's charismatic leadership. This move showed the Islamicization's requirement of making jurists' law the law of the state that was totally against the rule of law which necessitates any law to be drafted and passed by the representatives of the citizens. According to Articles 71 and 74 of the Constitution, the law must be of the legislative branch or its participation, and executive branch must process by the law. While independent for its jurisdiction, judicial branch must also draft judiciary bills appropriate for the Islamic Republic (Article 158 of the Constitution) and present it through the cabinet to the Islamic Consultative Assembly (the parliament) to be passed. Article 170 obliges the judges of courts "to refrain from executing statutes and regulations of the government that are in conflict with the laws or the norms of Islam" that is the justification for using *Tahrir* (*Tahrir al-Wasileh,* one of Khomeini's pieces on Islamic jurisprudence) as the base of judicial decision making . Although Article 170 mainly and implicitly addresses the laws passed and enforced during Pahlavi regime, as it is not limited to the laws passed before the establishment of the Islamic government, it is contradictory with the presence of the Guardian Council which reviews all laws passed by the parliament to ensure its compatibility with the criteria of Islam and the Constitution (Article 94).

The most important laws that were approved by the Majles in the Islamicization process were Hodoud (Penal) and Qesās (Retributive Justice)

Law (Aug. 25, 1982), Islamic Punishment Law (Oct. 13, 1982), Blood Money Law (*diāt*) (Dec. 15, 1982), and *Ta'zirāt* Law (Aug. 9, 1983). Procedural laws were not as important as the substantive laws in this phase of Islamicization. The most important development in this regard was more limitation on appealing to higher courts (Zerang, Vol. II, 2002: 296). The Procedural Law of Ordinary and Revolutionary Courts of 1999 was an endeavor to bring Revolutionary Courts under the umbrella of ordinary Courts with regard to procedures.

The second element of Islamicization project was the injection of thousands of clerics and revolutionaries to the different positions, from the judicial to administrative positions. The graduates of seminaries soon filled the positions that were opened due to vast purge of the governmental offices including judiciary. This led to shortage of religious jurists for different governmental positions. The Shi'ite seminaries soon ran out of qualified religious jurists for the judiciary, and the leader opened the way for unqualified ones by a governmental order (*hokm-e hokumati*) (Khomeini, 1991: Vol. 19, 245). This was totally against the doctrines of Shi'ite school and Khomeini's own opinion that the judge should be a *mujtahed* (1978: 64–7). The Shi'ite seminary never expected to be the base for ruling clerics and did not program to train the future personnel of the Islamic regime. Even the judges who were recruited from seminaries continued to be private individuals, singled out from the revolutionary mass by their special interests. There was reluctance among the law educated to accept positions in the new judiciary and to enforce all decrees of Islam. Most of these judges were not looking at judgeship as their lifetime career.

Islamicization was to solve all the social problems. Iranian Revolutionaries believed that one of the distinctive features of Islamic law, as part of the Islamic ideology, is its ability to solve all the problems of mankind. They, like the followers of other ideologies, believed that implementation of Islamic laws will put an end to all crimes and injustices of the world (Khomeini, 1942: 274). This law, in their viewpoint, was all-inclusive and embraced all aspects of human life and endeavor, private and public, spiritual and secular, civil and criminal. During the Islamicization process in post-revolutionary Iran, the ruling clerics and their followers believed that *shari`ah* deals with rituals as well as with such matters as commercial activities, property, marriage, divorce, inheritance, personal conduct, personal hygiene, diet, and almost all aspects of life. They believed that the best cure for crime prevention is to have sincere faith in God and to exercise all decrees of *shari`ah* law in private and public. In their beliefs, adhering to the tenets of the Quran and *Sunnah* in all walks of life is the only way to keep an individual away from sin and crime. The only preventive policy of Iran's judiciary has been preaching the *shari`ah* law by the clergy and state run media, and pressing public to be at least a good pretender. Although most of the Iranians were Muslim before the Revolution of 1979, few of them were applying in its totality the code of behavior which was provided in *shari`ah*.

The legal regime of post-Revolutionary Iran was introduced only with respect to its origin, i.e. divine; before and even after the Revolution, nothing was said about subject matter of this legal system, how human beings have had or can have impact on this system and how this system will change. Law in this outlook is part of religion's affair and a social fact at the same time. The rules governing the division of labor, patronage, matrimony, kinship, and reproduction as the base of the constitution of the family, and the various needs of the individuals, as Arnold suggests (1931: 291), give rise to that net of relations and exchanges to which the jurists refer under the general name of legal transactions.

Islamic revolutionaries in power wanted to enforce a system of rules that comprise every part of an individual's life, from humblest details up to the principles of his/her moral and social existence, presuming every individual a believer or a would-be believer. People who are expert in the science of this discipline of human activity (*feqh*) are in charge and have the authority to enforce it through theory of the guardianship of the jurist (*velāyat-e faqih*) and the real power that is in the hands of *fuqahā* (jurists).

The Islamicization of the judiciary went hand in hand with increasing the number of title of crimes by the Islamic ideology. Some examples are producing, bootlegging and consuming alcoholic drinks, dress code, etc. After the consolidation of clerical rule anything other than what is routine in clerics' lifestyle were declared illegal. This includes producing, bootlegging and consumption of alcoholic drinks, selling, possessing and using VCRs and videocassettes in 1980's and possessing and using satellite receivers and dishes in 1990's and 2000's, selling, buying and having audio-cassettes containing music, Iranian, Arabian, Indian, Turkish or Western, selling, appearing in public without *hejāb* for women, intimate relationship out of wedlock, holding parties. When one of these items was absorbed in clerics' lifestyle, e.g. VCR, it was declared legal.

5.3 CODIFICATION VS. TRANSPLANTATION: IDEOLOGIZING SHARI`AH

The Islamic regime tried to replace the secular legal norms of the Old Regime with the religious norms as soon as possible. Religious norms as the legal norms could threaten the violators with punishment by both a superhuman and human authority. The sanctions which the religious norms laid down had a worldly and transcendental character; they were politically organized sanctions, and in this case, not more effective than the regular legal sanctions. Their efficacy did not presuppose belief in the existence and power of a superhuman authority. The politically motivated religious sanctions were acts of coercion of the state which a group of individuals, i.e. clergy and its loyalists now in power, determined by the political order directed against other individuals responsible for any conduct contrary to that order. The Islamic Republic defined sin as a crime with special punishments, and sinner as criminal.

In spite of enormous difficulty of codifying the Shi'ite sacred law, ruling clerics tried to codify the state law to fulfill the requirements of ideologized *shari`ah*. Nevertheless, re-codification could not be a successful and effective program because firstly most of the *shari`ah* private laws were codified during Dāvar's reform, and secondly the ruling clergy was bare handed when confronted with challenges of public life at the last quarter of the 20th century.

Codification in this period is mostly Islamicization, i.e. transforming the secular substance of the law as it was perceived, to an Islamic one. Shi'ite *'ulamā* who had refused to consider law as a system of commands enforced by the sanction of the state during Pahlavis forgot any other way for enforcing law other than state when they got the power. Considering law as the God's affair, whether enforced or not, they had been separating the domains of the state and God, represented by the clergy. In this framework, the *mujtaheds* are the only expounders and architects of the law. *Mujtaheds* only have the power of interpreting laws, of deducing new principles and applying them to new facts and events, and the right of enlarging and vivifying the law by their re-interpretation. Therefore Iranian society was living according to local, and somehow, national customs completely at variance with the varying divine ordinances, while revering the God's law for its divine character. This is one of the reasons for non-critical approach to Islamic law during Pahlavis while there was no political obstacle for it in front of law scholars and political activists.

The law's validity was seen as resting ultimately on the superhuman agency of God, operating through the ideologized tradition and custom and preached understanding of the legitimate holders of faculties of rule. The law as the product of revolutionary charismatic leadership could not bind the leader or set boundaries to that power. This charisma was not charisma of office or charisma of reason and natural rights, and hence could not be falsified. We should understand the charismatic leadership in the Islamic Revolution as a domination framework that deals with legitimation and administration in the triangle of ruler, *bait* (literally, the members of his office; his crony), and unorganized population at large. The structural source of conflict among these three sides of the triangle is of great importance. Islamic revolutionary charisma like any other charisma was based on emotional consociation, well-developed and well-funded ruling organization of religious institutions, ethic of conviction, and crisis of legitimacy on the part of the Old Regime rooted in the long-range structural changes (Roth, 1979: 129–132).

Law in this system of belief is supposed to protect and safeguard Islamic creed and moral values. Laws are evaluated based on the criterion of conformity with the teachings of Islam and Islamic injunctions. As a result, any man-made law poses a challenge to Islamic principles and constitutes a serious hurdle in the way of performing Islamic duties.[37] According to Islamic ideology of Iranian revolutionaries of 1970's, man-made laws were based on temporal objectives of governments and rarely based on religion, ethics or morality (Khomeini, 1991: Vol. 16, 254).

Although the sacred law of Islam was probably never, except for brief periods of some religious movements, been enforced as a whole, it had never been without powerful influence on the framework of Islamic society. In those periods, rules like stoning and amputation which were felt to be against the public taste were replaced by more softened decrees of *mujtaheds* or left in abeyance. Although *sharī`ah* professes to be a single logical whole (Vesey-Fitzgerald, 1955: 110), there is an immense diversity of opinions, decrees and ordinances, not only between the different schools of law but even between different jurists in the same school.

Authoritarian regimes resting on personal loyalty have usually created a non-formal type of law (Weber, 1968: 811). Formal or procedural justice is repugnant to all authoritarian powers, because it diminishes the dependency of individuals upon the grace and power of the authorities (Weber, 1968: 812). The non-elected rulers of the Islamic Republic refused to be bound by formal rules, even by the rules they have made themselves. Presenting the theory of absolute guardianship, Khomeini solved the problem of government being bound by sacred rules. The judges were bound by rules, administrative expediencies, and the will of the leader. If a judge's verdict was against his will, he could no longer occupy the position. Judicial decisions were reached based on concrete, political considerations while in Khomeini era they were partly based on feelings oriented toward social justice.

In traditional Islamic political thought and in the Islamic world, all officials including judges act only by virtue of a delegation of jurisdiction conferred upon them by the ruler (Tyan, 1955: 236). This delegation can be direct, as in the case of chief justice whose investiture was received directly from the head of the government, or indirect, as in the case of local judges. The entire structure of the Islamic state, as it is presented by most of the Iranian clerics, was constituted by a series of up-down delegations.[38] The authoritarian faction of the Iranian polity did not even want to see the elected bodies and put lots of efforts to change the nature of elected bodies to delegates of the leader.[39] The judges as well as the MP's and cabinet ministers are essentially considered as delegate-representative of the leader, back to the caliphate system of governance. They were not expected to have independent or even autonomous positions. Although the judiciary is more independent from the executive power, as compared to Pahlavi era, it is not independent from the leader's office and the leader has every power over it, even to overturn the decisions of the chief justice. The revival of the Islamic state for the ruling clerics meant this kind of the state leadership organization.

The reorganization of the Ministry of Justice in 1936 had removed the final vestiges of authority from the clergy and made no provision for the *shari`ah* courts. If this reorganization was based on considering *shari`ah* incompatible with the developments in the real world, why it came back to the scene forty three years later? Weber's typology of sacred law and his typology of political regimes provide some insights to answer this question. If I use Weber's term, during Pahlavi era in spite of endeavors of some sections of elite to make a transition from traditional to legal authority, the polity and society remained traditional. The regime could not solve the problems of tensions between sacred law and state law, traditional leadership and the bureaucratic one, and thus the social order could not be a legitimate one in the eyes of the majority. The legitimate order in Pahlavi era could not be provided by tradition, by virtue of effectual attitudes, its rationality, or its legality.[40] While distancing from personalized dispensing of justice by wise leaders or elders or clerics, the society was not in a course toward the codified, rationalized, and impersonal justice of the modern world. The problem of legitimate authority was linked to the problem of legitimate order and legitimate norms since norms and authority represent the basic forms of ordered social relationships. The legal and judicial regime was suspending above these orders and norms and Islamic Revolution helped it to land on the rigid land of tradition as it was conveyed by the *'ulamā*.

The Judiciary was the stronghold of the authoritarian faction after the injection of hundreds of clerics into this branch of power as judges, prosecutors, and public attorneys; the judiciary was taken over by the clerics, and the former secular judges were largely eliminated.[41] The clerics who took over had no legal training and what's more, they were suspicious of anything that had to do with the previous era when they began to Islamicize the courts. They believed that the application of the pure *shari`ah* would prevent the crimes. In only some years these people disillusioned that the applying of *shari`ah* cannot prevent the criminal. Islamic penal code was passed by the Parliament and changes in keeping with Islamic law were made in the Procedural Code (Bakhash, 1984: 247).

The Islamic regime gave back the religious character of the judicial function to the judiciary, what was denied during the Pahlavi dynasty. This religious character stems from the religious character of the regime and religious character of the leader who is an Islamic jurist. The essential mission of the leader and his appointees are to apply the *shari`ah* as it is laid down in the sacred texts (Arts. 4, 12. 91). In the definition of the judicial branch responsibilities in the Constitution (Art. 158, Sec. 2) in counting the characteristics of the head of judiciary (Art. 157), and in the definition of the judge's method of issuing verdicts (Art. 167), the religious character of the judiciary is clearly pronounced.

According to Khomeini and other clerics in power, justice consists in the application of the religious principle (Khomeini, 1991: Vol. 18, 237; 1984: 356–7). In this *'ash'ari* approach to justice, religion or any other ideology is not evaluated by resort to general principle of justice or other general principles like freedom, fairness or morality but anything that has been issued by the religion is justice *per se*. This was totally against rationalist *(mu'tazeli)* approach of religious intellectuals like Shari'ati[42] and even Motahhari (1989: 74) toward justice. In this view, justice was considered a general principle and every religion or ideology could be evaluated with respect to it. While radical Islamists had a *mu'tazeli* approach to justice, i. e. justice as expression of reason *('adl-e aqli)*, this was the traditionalist or orthodox theological (*'ash'ari)* approach, i.e. justice as the expression of God's will (*'adl-e shar'i*), that got the power in post-revolutionary Iran. As Khomeini says, "the exercise of the *qazā'* (adjudication) is a vital principle of the religion" (Khomeini, 1991: Vol. 18, 96–7; Vol. 19, 192) and "maintenance of justice in the society is a duty in Islam and is regarded as a sublime act of adoration and worship."[43]

5.4 JUDICIAL REFORM AND REORGANIZATION: REVOLUTIONARY JUSTICE[44] AND IDEOLOGIZATION

Revolutionary Justice

evolutionary justice is a special kind of transitional justice and is engaged with its legality dilemma. The dilemma of legality, i.e. rule of law when a legal system is in flux arises during periods of substantial political change (Teitel, 2000: 22). This dilemma is not related to judicial activism that interferes with democracy or retro-acts in judicial decision making, but legality in a transition from a real legal system to an imaginative one. Transformative adjudicatory practices usually do not bear the burden of the transformation of the rule of law. Although the revolutionaries usually believe in natural law, they do not assume a transformative role for adjudication.[45] Iranian Revolutionaries did not recognize transformative adjudication as self-regarding; they did not think that by changing adjudicatory principles and practices, institutions compromised by their officials' decision-making under prior rule can transform themselves.

Within transitional democracies, there is a place and a role for bounded political judgment and legal processes enable measured rational changes but in transition from one kind of authoritarianism to another kind of authoritarianism, there is no place for bounded political judgment, and law totally collapses in politics. While revolutionaries usually do not have a transformative understanding of the rule of law, they totally bypass it. Revolutionaries had little to say about the judiciary or other public institutions. Their main concern was to topple the Old Regime, establish a completely new one and consolidate it. They were looking at the new judicial system as an instrument for accomplishing revolutionary justice. After the trials by secret revolutionary tribunals resulted in instant execution of old regimes' high-ranking military and security officials, the new regime could be more confident in the survival of the new regime. The legitimacy of the state was also dependent upon responding to the pressure of a social revolution and increasing expectations for justice, and satisfying the revolutionaries who were adamant in purging the judiciary and other governmental organizations. Even the revolutionaries who were democrat had no idea about democratic management of the judiciary. There was almost no question of whether people should elect judges or whether there should be juries in criminal cases during the discussions on different drafts of the constitution and the process of its approval.

The activities of the Revolutionary Courts became a focus of intense controversy when hundreds of members of the Shah's different administrations including cabinet members, military staff, and high-ranking officials having just been prosecuted and executed by the infamous hanging judges like Sadeq Khalkhāli without any provisions of due process. Left-wing political groups and populist clerics pressed hard for "revolutionary justice" for miscreants of the former regime. On the other hand, lawyers and human rights groups protested the arbitrary nature of the Revolutionary Courts, the vagueness of charges, and the absence of defense lawyers. Bāzargān, the provincial Prime Minister after the Revolution, too, was critical of the courts' activities. At the Prime Minister's insistence, the Revolutionary Courts suspended their activities on March 14, 1979. On April 5, new regulations governing the courts were promulgated. The courts were to be established at the discretion of the Revolutionary Council and with Khomeini's permission. They were authorized to try a variety of broadly and vaguely defined crimes, such as "sowing corruption on earth," "crimes against the people," and "crimes against the Revolution." The courts resumed their work on April 6, 1979. On the following day, despite international pleas for clemency, Amir 'Abbās Hoveydā, the shah's prime minister for twelve years, was put to death. Attempts by Bāzargān to have the Revolutionary Courts placed under the judiciary and to secure protection for potential victims through amnesties issued by Khomeini also failed. Most of the early revolutionary leaders assumed that the Revolution should deal a death blow to the barbaric and inhumane Old Regime judicial practices, while the New Regime was doing worse.

Numerous active and resolute so-called enemies of the new revolutionary regime escaped serious punishment after being subjected to careless investigations and prosecutions. Some of them escaped the country. Parallel to the people who favored an acceleration of revolutionary momentum, there was an endeavor to reconcile and reassure royalist elements and non-revolutionaries to feel safe and secure. The traditional clerics who were active during the Revolution and at the same time had their community relationships as prayer leader made considerable effort to counsel those bent on vengeance to be patient and to make sure to observe at least Islamic laws in pursuing their enemies, and not hang and exterminate them before discussing and judging. They tried to present themselves as popular spokesmen and cutting-edge revolutionary politicians and always introduced themselves as committed to Islamic Revolution, and at the same time did not hide their fear and mistrust of the popular masses and revolutionary justice, though never declared their commitment to meaningful legal guarantees for defendants and observation of strict legal formalities. Most of the members of the Revolutionary Committees (Komiteh-hā) were quite willing to resist being relegated to a subordinate role in the judicial system.

Executions of military and police officers, SAVAK[46] agents, cabinet ministers, Majles deputies, and officials of the shah's regime followed on an almost daily basis. Beginning in August 1979, the courts tried and passed death sentences on members of ethnic minorities involved in anti-government movements. Some 550 persons had been executed by the time Bāzargān resigned in November 1979.[47] He attempted, but failed, to bring the Revolutionary Committees under his control. The committees, whose members were armed, performed a variety of duties. They policed neighborhoods in urban areas, guarded prisons and government buildings, made arrests, and served as the execution squads of the revolutionary tribunals. The committees often served the interests of powerful individual clerics, revolutionary personalities, and political groups, however. They made unauthorized arrests, intervened in labor-management disputes, and seized property. Despite these abuses, members of the Revolution's Council wanted to bring the committees under their own control, rather than to eliminate them. With this in mind, in less than a month in February 1979 it appointed Mohammad Reza Mahdavi Kani as the head of Tehran Revolutionary Committee and charged him with supervising the committees countrywide. Mahdavi Kani dissolved many Revolutionary Committees, consolidated others, and sent thousands of committeemen home. But the committees, like the Revolutionary Courts, endured, serving as one of the coercive arms of the revolutionary government.

Iranian revolutionary justice had its own specific characteristics plus characteristics that are common in any revolutions. These characteristics can be explained in ideas that were behind revolutionary action and approaches taken by revolutionaries. Populist-discriminatory, anti-Western, ignorance toward strategic planning, and anti-routinization were the most important approaches. Consolidation of the new government, dual judicial system, cleaning the society that comes with the priority of the end rather than procedure, and hierarchical charisma were the ideas behind religious revolutionary justice in Iran.

Populist discriminatory approach was a crucial approach for revolutionary judicial system. This approach begins with the idea of justice for all and then shifts to justice for true believers. One of the premises of revolutionary Islamic law was availability of justice for all Iranians but in practice, it could only provide justice for a few. This concept of justice does not require any provision for individuals' rights; what the revolutionaries do is justice per se. Hence the only way to provide justice is to have revolutionary judges and get rid of so-called *tāquti* (related to Old Regime) judges. This justice is focused on internal aspects of law, i.e. substantive justice, and totally ignores the procedural aspects of justice. Certain discrepancies between substantive and procedural justice in the Islamic world (Khadduri, 1984: 149), trusting in the *'edālat* of the judge (just judge) (Khadduri, 1984: 145–147) and necessities of the revolutionary situation invigorated the ignorance toward procedural justice.

The way that the revolutionary government treated the prisoners and especially political prisoners shows that there has been no respect for individuals' rights. According to some internal reports, the situation of arrested people and political prisoners in the years after the victory of Revolution was a disaster.[48] Due process was usually ignored and if it was required under the pressure of international forces, the judicial process was a show trial in which the defendant were coerced into making bogus confessions.

Xenophobia was the basis of the second approach behind revolutionary justice in Iran. By avoiding exposure to foreign systems and transplantation, reform models were less likely to be successful in post-revolutionary era. Between 1906 and 1979, the argument of the reformers was that transplants are easy and common. This argument profoundly undervalued the relationship between law and internal social objectives and forces. Islamic judicial reforms, in reaction to "perceived wholesale transplantation" conceived as blunt negations of the secular judicial reforms that were more likely to be successful. The revolutionary judicial reform proposals based on reaction to or negation of foreign systems also ignore the domestic needs and problems. Reforms usually require careful adaptation to local circumstances and conditions. Revolutionary proposals justified themselves with this argument that Pahlavi regime was not familiar with the tools of adaptation and tended to think of foreign models as package deals to accept or reject. Revolutionary regime had the same idea and ruined the whole system with an ideal type, i.e. Imam Ali's justice in pristine Islam that had no chance to be realized in late 20th century. The content of Imam Ali's justice was supposed to ride on the Communist or Robespierrian type of formalities. Revolutionary alterations tended to graft one institution onto another and modify the charts of the judiciary without comprehensive consideration of the system as a whole.

The third approach implicit in the revolutionary action is to ignore strategic planning. The revolutionary judiciary was inexperienced with strategic planning and implementation; it confronted with deep financial need coupled with the demands of the community for immediate action, scarcity of revolutionary judges, and personal and professional security concerns. The Iranian legal culture accustomed to exclusively top-down reform tended to be passive in developing its own views and complacent in holding authorities accountable to plans for implementation. Furthermore, actors in a collapsed judiciary system hindered by chaos were likely to feel threatened by anti-corruption reforms and their consequences. These conditions undermined the ability of revolutionary regime to develop and apply an effective reform implementation strategy.

The fourth approach is anti-routinization view. Between 1979 and 1982 there was almost no law enforcement because judiciary was in revolutionaries' hands and the judiciary officials did not want to enforce laws that could routinize the public affairs. Most of the non-political prisoners who escaped the prisons immediately after the victory of the Revolution never came back. The administrative structure of the judiciary, like other governmental offices, was broken up. In this period oppositional parties and independent newspapers were banned and closed down directly against the Constitution. Like the other appointed bodies of government, the entire judiciary is ultimately accountable to no one but the leader, the *vali-ye faqih,* or the Islamic jurist.

Ignoring the law enforcement makes the judiciary redundant. Revolutionaries were thinking about the creation of a community of believers; if this community could be established, the judicial system would not be so important and hence was not basically part of the picture of nascent Islamic society. They did not care about human rights[49] and looked at it as the conspiracy of Imperialists. The Islamic Revolutionaries did not want human rights to be manifested in codified laws; hence Iranian individuals were left with no other choice but to stage rebellion against tyranny and oppression and the regime was ready to oppress it: infinite cycles of violence.

Consolidation of the revolutionary government was the first and foremost goal. Instability of the new regime was the main justification of ignoring the due process. The revolutionaries could not go with so-called "turtle-court style" procedures that would unfold in a court system based on protection of defendants' rights. In contrast, they preferred "kangaroo-court style" that would let them to get rid of their dissidents as soon as possible.[50] Almost all the brutalities and massacres of Iranian regime in this period can be explained by its concern for consolidation.[51]

Another aspect of consolidation was the change of elite through confiscation. Confiscations were directed to degrade the economic status of people who were related to the previous regime and upgrade the economic status of members of the new elite. In any case, the judges put the utmost endeavor to find some reason for confiscation. When there was no reason for confiscation, they would follow the line of ascendants and ancestors to find a non-Muslim or someone related to Iranian dynasties to justify the confiscations (Montazeri, 2000: pp. 26–27 of ch.8).

In revolutionaries' eyes, all the wealth of Old Regimes' high-ranking officials was coming from illegal acts and monopolies. Hence the mission of Revolutionary Courts was to confiscate all their wealth and transfer them to deprived people (*mustaz'afeen*). The first part of this mission was accomplished but due to absence of any oversight the wealth was transferred to ruling clerics, their family members and some sections of revolutionary people. If we compare Khomeini's letter for amnesty (July 8, 1979) with his order to the Revolution's Attorney General regarding the amnesty (July 15, 1979), we will see the importance of this transfer for the new regime. In the letter, only people who have killed others or tortured others to death are exempted but in the order, just one week later, people who are misused and possessed the public expenditures (*bait ul-māl*) are also exempted from the amnesty (Khomeini, 1991: Vol. V, 111–113, 179).

Incoherent dualism is an inevitable idea of revolutionary justice. The company of idea of continual revolution with the consolidation of new regime let the revolutionaries have a dual judicial system. Although the Islamic constitution constructed a unified judiciary controlled by the clerics and based exclusively on Islamic principles, in contrast to its predecessor which created two distinct tribunals for *shar'i* and *'orfi* matters (Milani, 1992: 144), the regime created its own dual judiciary by (illegal) routinizing of the Revolutionary Courts and Special Court for Clergy. This duality dictated that the codes, legal system and procedures be incoherent, ambiguous and inconsistent. The prevailing spirit of Islamic utopia persuaded those in its spell that it was possible to draft unsystematic legislation that would have those characteristics to such a degree that the judiciary would have chaotic and ordering functions at the same time. Revolutionary Courts and Revolutionary public prosecutors with high level of jurisdiction, established by the approval of the Extraordinary Courts for Anti-revolutionary Crimes Law by the Revolution's Council in June 17, 1979, were parallel institutions outside the authority of the three branches of the government. Even the definition of these courts' jurisdictions by the parliament in 1983 could not limit these courts because of vague terms like "crimes against national security" or "plunder of public properties and funds" (Zerang, Vol. II, 2002: 226–277) incorporated in this approval. They were in the hands of the ruling clergy and were representative of the *shar'i* aspect of the state which was taking the place of the secular one. The legal procedure in these courts was not unified and legalized. The Constitution was silent about these courts. Because of duality of the courts and legal frameworks there was no unified legal procedure and legal decision making in the country. The civil and the criminal courts had counterparts in the Revolutionary Courts headed by clerics completely loyal to authoritarian camp. In the first years after the victory of Islamic Revolution, this court used to try subversive crimes considered to be challenges to the establishment, usually in closed door proceedings, but later its jurisdiction extended to most areas of Iranians' life. The Supreme Court was totally unsuccessful to implement unified judicial procedure and enforce the law of the nation all over the country.

The Revolutionary Courts took the place of the military tribunals which in Pahlavi era had the power to try all cases affecting national security and even some of the offences in the anti-profiteering campaigns (Graham, 1978: 137). The attempt to integrate the Revolutionary Courts into the

Ministry of Justice by the Supreme Judiciary Council as the Islamicizing force of the Judiciary that was approved by the Second Majles (on May 1983)-prominently in the hands of true believers of Khomeini and clerical reading of Islamic ideology- was overruled by Khomeini. He believed that the integration would demolish the revolutionary nature of the court that was necessary for taking actions against counterrevolutionary moves (Arjomand, 1988: 166), and could be a role model for Islamicizing the whole judiciary and other public institutions. In spite of the integration of Ministry of Justice and the Revolutionary Courts in 1984, the latter did not merge into the judiciary system and kept its independence inside the new judiciary. The Revolutionary Courts had their specific Public Prosecutors, specific jurisdiction,[52] specific offices, specific procedural law (before and in some aspects,[53] even after ratification of a unified procedure for General and Revolutionary Courts in 1994[54]) and specific judges all over the country.

The Revolutionary Courts did not observe the rights of people to have attorney for almost twelve years. In addition to the laws which have been in force since Pahlavi regime by which everybody had the right to an attorney in every law court so long as it was not against Islam and hence was not annulled after the Revolution, and further to Article 35 of the Constitution which has recognized the right for everybody to have an attorney in every lawsuit, the Expediency Council in 1991, while ensuring everybody to have an attorney in the court, obliged the Revolutionary Courts to receive the attorneys. There was lots of resistance against this rule in the Revolutionary Courts. To overcome this resistance, the Expediency Council specified that if the judges do not observe this rule, this should cause them to stand for trial in the Judges Disciplinary Court that could end with firing from the judicial position. It also specified that the judgment of a court for which either party to the lawsuit had been prevented to benefit from services of an attorney should be legally invalid.[55]

The elimination of the offices of the public prosecutor in the Revolutionary Courts increased the possibility that an error occurs. It also provided a good context for the judgments to be delivered and decisions be made contradictory. Some of the decisions of the General Board of Supreme Court regarding unitary procedure address this issue.[56] Some examples are the decisions regarding the right to appeal even when the defendant is acquitted, prohibition of reference to the General Courts Law in Military Tribunals, and deliberation of the appeallable cases.[57] Most of the decisions of this board is rewriting or reaffirming the Articles of the General Courts Law of 1994.[58] In later development, reinvestigation of decisions of Revolutionary Courts was recognized but reinvestigation was not the right of individuals; reinvestigation was totally dependent on the decision of the Public Attorneys of the Revolutionary Courts. Reinvestigation was also applicable in specific cases: the judgments which fall within cognizance of reinvestigations were those delivered for death penalty, imprisonment of more than 6 months, lashes, penances, retaliation (*lex talionis*), confiscation and appropriation of property. In this period, the Supreme Court acts as a court of cassation in recognizing the decisions of the Revolutionary Courts. In case the Supreme Court quashed the judgment it shall assign another court of the same category to reinvestigate the case.

Revolutionary Courts could not initially and essentially act on the basis of a unified procedure. No two regions had similar sentences for similar crimes. Revolution in each region had its own necessities and obligations and there ware no central guiding elements to unify the procedure. The judges of these courts had unlimited power. High expectation of the judicial change, and the push for revolutionizing the judiciary, even with shock therapy, limited the practical perspective of the changes.

Naser's revolutionary courts in Egypt had the same precepts and functions after the Free Officers' successful Revolution of 1952. A series of new constitutions and basic laws after 1952 granted extensive authority to the executive to rule by decree and created a weak parliament (Brown, 1997: 76). From the first days of the new regime, tools were developed to diminish the possibility of direct judicial challenge and to circumvent the regular courts. Renewal of the use of exceptional courts was the first measure of the regime to convict opponents and insure favorable results. The Civil Courts could not be trusted to secure the Revolution and deal with powerful opponents like Muslim Brotherhood (Brown, 1997: 77), the same argument presented for establishing the Revolutionary Courts in Iran after the Islamic Revolution.

Naser established four different kinds of exceptional courts in different times after 1952 to respond to different challenges. Court of Treason (*Mahkamat al-Ghadr*) was established five months after the Revolution to investigate and try former political officials to punish and discredit them. Special military courts, established in July 1953, were to prosecute communists. Court of the Revolution (*Mahkamat-al-Thawra*), established in Sep. 1953, was to try crimes against political order or the Revolution (with no appeal). People's Courts (*Mahkamat al-Sha'b*), established in November 1954 was to suppress Muslim Brotherhood. Like Iranian exceptional courts, these courts were not bound by regular judicial procedures or by the loosest procedural guidelines and their members were politically appointed with almost no judicial backgrounds; the accused was not guaranteed the right of counsel (Brown, 1997: 78–79).

Another section of the duality package in Iran was special court for the ruling caste. The Special Court for Clerics[59] that its establishment was totally against the Constitution of 1979 was based on considering special privileges for the clergy. In a few years, its nature changed to be an instrument to get rid of dissident clerics and send them out of polity. The Special Court for Clerics has not been a section of the Judiciary that is inconsistent with general authority of the Judiciary in judicial affairs. Khomeini established this court in June 1987 by appointment of a judge (*hākem-e shar'*) and public prosecutor for it (Zerang, Vol. II, 2002: 282). Its special Procedural law was signed by Khāmenei three years later (Zerang, Vol. II, 2002: 282). Even the Constitution of 1989 is totally silent about this court.

Another idea behind the revolutionary justice is cleaning the society by resort to any makeshift. Immediately after the victory of the Islamic Revolution, executions became the rule rather than the exception all over the country, and then for a quarter of a century in cities as well as small towns away from the itinerary of foreign visitors and media.[60] Executions did not stop in the pools of people who were high-ranking officials of the previous regime. Many people were executed because of writing a journal about the events with critical approach, saying that they do not like Khomeini during the prosecutions and interrogations, possessing some books and statements from dissident groups, and being a member of these groups (Montazeri, 2000: pp.25–26 of ch.8). Revolutionary judges had no obligation to issue verdicts that were well reasoned out and documented with reference to the articles and principles of the law in accordance with which they are delivered. In some verdicts related to important issues like capital punishment, the judge would only write "In the name of God, the merciful and compassionate, execution."(Montazeri, 2000: p. 25 of ch.8) Even the name of the accused was not mentioned in some of these verdicts.

Cleaning the judiciary logically comes before the cleaning of the society. Massive purges of the judiciary were to serve this logic. The mass mobilization and participation in Iranian politics, which led to the rapid elite change after the Revolution, alienated the Old Regime political caste. In revolutionary point of view, the judiciary high-ranking officials and top judges and lawyers were considered to be part of this caste that should be filtered by the new regime to be replaced by the clerics who had always claimed to be fair and expert staff for this job. The purge of the judiciary was based on the Reform of the Judicial Organization and Recruitment of the Judges Act of 1979, approved by the Revolution's Council (Zerang, 2002: 232). The cultural dependency schools,[61] pessimistic about all aspects of Western cultures coming to the society, obliged this filtration, although some judges and lawyers were protesting against the brutality of the old regime.[62] The followers of this school picked over-simplistic views of the modernization process among Pahalvi regime elite, i.e. a universalistic and linear transition from traditional to modern and replaced it with simplistic ideas on Islamicization.

Where purge was not a possibility, political interference was the choice. Disciplinary system for judges from the Old Regime compromised their independence, especially because they were themselves subject to abuse. Public admonishment, suspension, and removal as powerful sanctions were abused to coerce judges to act in a partial way. In this system that has been subjected to institutionalized political interference, judges viewed independence as an absolute value and thus dismissed the value of accountability or overvalue.

For total cleaning of the society, the end should come before and prior to procedure. For the revolutionary justice, the "end" of the verdicts is more important than the procedure. If someone is supposed to be killed as punishment, the way of killing is secondary. In a case in Malāyer, district attorney said: "it was snowing and it was hard to stone them." So the condemned was executed (Montazeri, 2000: p. 21 of Ch. 6).[63] Torturing and threatening people to confess can be easily justified when the "end" comes before the procedure. The speed of trial was also more important than justice. Some of the trials were also out of control, and even the leader of the Revolution could not bring them under control. Khomeini had to declare amnesty three times to pour water on fires of revolutionary revenge that were out of control. The first one was amnesty for all except individuals who have killed or tortured a person in Jul. 8 & 15, 1979 (Khomeini, 1991: Vol. V. 111–113, 179). The second was amnesty with the same provisions and conditions as the amnesty of 1979 in March 18, 1980 (Khomeini, 1991: Vol. VII, 131–132). The third one dates Feb. 8, 1983 (Khomeini, 1991: Vol. X, 20). The irregularities and injustices created by the Revolutionary Courts led to Khomeini's letter to Revolutions' Attorney General regarding limitation of executions to murderers (Khomeini, 1991: Vol. IV, 159).

This inclination toward cleaning up the society by resort to law and order institutions, plus the idea of reviving the tradition, brought back the accusatory approach back because in revolutionary situations everyone who is not with "us" is stranger and therapeutic or conciliatory approach that is supposed to work among intimates does not work anymore. The idea of stranger first was applied to high ranking officials of the old regime and was extended to oppositional leaders and dissidents and even drug addicts and alcoholic drink consumers and women who did not observe *sharī`ah* law in their private matters. There was a shift from the trend toward remedial law in Pahlavi era with some therapeutic or conciliatory consequences to obvious accusatory law of the Islamic Republic with harsh penal or retaliatory consequences. This shift could be considered a kind of return to tradition.

Hierarchical charisma was another idea behind revolutionary justice that has its roots in the concept of religious revolution. Immediately after the Revolution, this was the revolutionary leader who had the authority to appoint judges; it was only the charismatic leader who could give judicial authority to judges to issue their decrees. Khomeini, then, transferred his authority in this area to Montazeri and Meshkini (Montazeri, 2000: p. 32 of ch.7). In a letter to all attorneys and judges of the Revolutionary Courts, Montazeri and Meshkini issued a guideline (Feb. 23, 1979) for handling the cases related to these courts and their duties and responsibilities (Montazeri, 2000: pp. 33–34 of ch.7). The main concern of Montazeri and Meshkini, in this guideline, is execution of Islamic ordinances regarding judiciary and justice. The criterion for recruitment for Revolutionary Courts is revolutionary and pure Islamic background (Montazeri, 2000: p. 34 of ch.7, Article 8). This guideline gives the judges of Revolutionary Courts upper hand compared to Revolutionary Committees and the Revolutionary Guards (Montazeri, 2000: p. 33 of ch.7).

Post-revolutionary Islamicization as Judicial Reform

After 1981 and consolidation of the Islamic regime, judicial authority was constitutionally vested in the Supreme Judiciary Council; this was a group with responsibility for supervising the enforcement of all Islamic laws and for establishing judicial and legal policies. The judiciary was entrusted with duties like investigating and passing judgment on grievances, violations of rights, and complaints, resolving of litigation, and settling of disputes. Judiciary was responsible of taking all necessary decisions and measures in probate matters as the law may determine, restoring public rights and promoting justice and legitimate freedoms. This body of government was to supervise the proper enforcement of laws and taking suitable measures to prevent the occurrence of crime and to reform criminals, uncovering crimes, prosecuting, punishing, and chastising criminals, and enacting the penalties and provisions of the Islamic penal code (Article 156). In practice, the last duty has been the covering and governing one. Islamicization of judiciary for the new regime was the key measure to achieve all other goals.

According to the Ordinary Courts Establishment Law of 1979, these courts were divided to Legal, Penal and Reconciliation Courts (Zerang, Vol. II, 2002: 271). This law ended the long dated structure of the Primary Courts after the Constitutional Revolution, i.e. division to Regional, Township and Provincial Courts.

The new Islamic regime could not include *'orf* (custom) among the sources of law since the classical theory of *feqh* limits these sources to four, the Quran, Traditions of Muhammad and Shi'ite Imams (*hadith:* what they approved by word, or deed or tacit approval), consensus (*ejmā'-e 'ulamā* if it indicates the occulted Imam's opinion that is almost impossible to reach) and reason (*'aql,* harnessed by faith). Although the Islamic jurists could not completely ignore *'orf* in the formulation of their decrees, but the Islamic government totally ignored it in legislation and policy-making that were supposed to be on the basis of *shari`ah.* Actually there was no institutionalized way like public survey or polls to capture the *'orf* of the time. The Islamic regime reduced later the discussion about whether a new custom should be preferred to a text based on an old custom to expediency of the regime, not expediency of the society. Even those customs that were recurrent and well-known, of general application throughout the whole society and not contrary to the sources of *shari`ah* like pre-Islamic Iranian celebrations and intermixture of male and female were denied especially by the judiciary. The government in this case took the same traditional role that judges of the old *mazālem* (extraordinary jurisdiction) and administrators of *shurteh* (police) and *hesbeh* (police of the guilds) took in the Islamic era and tried to play the role of interlocutor between law, society and religion.

Throughout all of the Pahlavi era, *'orf* was an instrument of the executive to make inroads into fields where *shari`ah* was supposed theoretically to be supreme by the public. The identification of the administrations with *'orf* in this era resulted in calling government outside the *shari`ah* law "secular" (*'orfi*). After the Revolution of 1979, *maslahat,* instead of *'orf,* became the instrument of the Islamic administrations to make inroads into exceptional necessary fields whereas *shari`ah* should be theoretically and practically be supreme.

Iranian Revolutionaries of 1978–1979 who removed an authoritarian monarchic regime and introduced a theocratic, and later an authoritarian and sultanistic regime brought about a new order that the actual behavior of individuals were interpreted according to it. The social revolution changed some of the basic norms, though some of the new norms were very similar to the old ones, e.g. *obligatory* unveiling to obligatory veiling. Now the Islamic state was the personification of a legal order that was not a system of norms coordinated to each other but it was hierarchies of different levels of norms which lower ones were not necessarily determined by higher ones. The Constitution and *shari`ah,* both, were supposed to be the highest level within national law. This was led to contradictory statutory laws stemming from the Constitution and *shari`ah.* The status of customary law was decreased

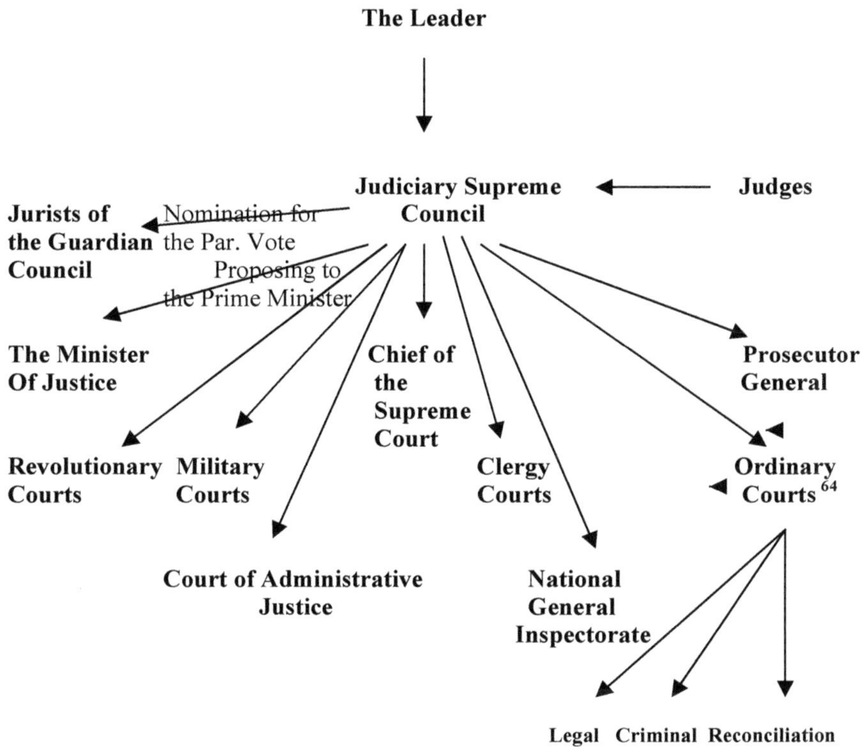

Fig. 5.1. The Chart of Iran's Judiciary, 1979–1988

* There is nothing about Revolutionary Court and Clergy Court in the Constitution of 1979

** Of the five members of the Supreme Judiciary Council, three were being elected by the judges and other two, i.e. the Head of the Supreme Court and the Attorney General, were being appointed by the Leader.

because of its relation to Old Regime. Custom, in post-revolutionary Iranian legal system, was not a constitutional institution. It is not a law-creating fact because it was believed that the law cannot be made but exists in the religious texts[64] and Islamic jurist are supposed to extract it (Khomeini, 1981: 69).[65] Therefore in post-revolutionary Iran, the Constitution is not the only source of statutes, statutes are not the source of the judicial decisions, and the judicial decisions are not the source of the duty they are supposed to impose upon the party. Theoretically, Islamic courts in post-revolutionary Iran do not and cannot create individual norms. The courts are not supposed to formulate already existing law but to enforce it. This is totally against the principles of jurist's law that is perceived to be the base of Islamic justice system. Shortage of jurists to fill the judgeship positions after the Revolution was crucial in implementing an Islamic civil law tradition while Islamic jurist's law has traditionally been more susceptible to implementation in a judicial system based on common law tradition. Immediately after the consolidation of Islamic regime, the ordinary courts were supposed to implement *shari`ah* law primarily, and only use statutory law by default. When the Constitution was approved and the process of Islamicization went on, the ordinary courts were supposed to implement statutory law primarily, and only Islamic jurisprudence by default in the absence of it.

The Minister of Justice was supposed to be the link between the executive and judiciary powers. With rendering all administrative, executive and judicial authorities of judiciary to the Supreme Judiciary Council (Article 157), the role of the Ministry of Justice decreased to a mailer who should deliver the message to the cabinet in administrative and budgetary issues and whose demands should never be rejected. After a quarter of century of I.RI.'s Constitution, there is still this need to clarify the responsibilities and missions on the Minister of Justice.[66]

Special courts have a different story. They do not follow the law of the country and do whatever they are asked to do, usually by the leader. Article 159 of the Constitution of 1979 prohibits the establishment of any court without legal permission. According to this Article the courts of justice are the official bodies to which all grievances and complaints are to be referred and the formation of courts and their jurisdiction is to be determined by law. IRI's peculiar dual system, i.e. coexistence of regular courts with Revolutionary, Military, and Clergy Courts and even different public attorney office for each and every one of them shapes a judiciary hierarchy which was not even abolished in the post-1989 period because its serves as an instrument of political control and repression. Here we have a clash between the need for legal rationalization (Weber) and the political need of the regime for survival that works in the opposite direction.

The revolutionary government changed the formulation of the rule of law from "If the competent organ has established in due order that a subject has committed a delict, then an organ shall direct a sanction against this subject" to "If a subject has committed a delict, an organ shall direct a sanction against the delinquent." Most of the statements of *shari`ah* law are organized in the latter way.

The new legal norm, i.e., declared as Islamic norm, was neither able to determine the law-applying organs and the procedure to be observed by them nor able to determine the judicial and administrative acts of these organs. The religious norm apparently lacked its own formal or adjective law to apply its substantive law in a concrete case. Hence, almost all the regulations and ordinances of the judiciary and executive branch of power stayed the same with some minor literal changes and the statutory laws were only amended.

To justify the transfer from monarchical to Islamic legal order, the Islamic revolutionaries claimed that Islamic legal order has no gap, while no legal order acknowledges that it has a gap (Kelsen, 1961: 146). It was assumed that the judge could find the relevant norm in the religious texts because it was believed that God is omniscient and knows every case that is to be brought in the court in advance and has provided the rules needed to take care of the case. Although the judges have historically created the whole Islamic legal system, Iranian revolutionaries believed that the judges are not authorized to act as legislators. They believed that the body of rules that the judges lay down is only the expression of preexisting law, not the law itself. The judges, in their perspective, are the discoverers of the law not the creators. This was only a fiction that the power of the judges who were supposed to be absolute Islamic jurist is absolute. The judges were but organs of the state; they had only such power as the organization of the state entitled them.

Iranian ruling clerics resorted to different types of administrative discretions which permit the sovereign to reform legal institutions in the interest of assuring public order and survival of the regime (*maslahat-e nezām*). The inadequacy of the 1979 Constitution forced Khomeini to set up a new organ, called Majma'-e Tashkhis-e Maslahat-e Nezām (the Council for Distinguishing Expediency of Establishment, shortly named the Expediency Council). The ongoing tension between the parliament and the Guardian Council in critical matters like property, labor, and trade laws was a deadlock for the legal system of the country. There were lot of cases that the Majlis and the Guardian Council couldn't decide on, and there was a need for a council to pass these cases up to for a final decision. There was no mechanism in the Constitution for giving an end to the disputes because of the inconsistent responsibilities of both sides: the Majles was to legislate based on the necessities of the time and the Guardian Council was to ensure the compatibility of approved laws with the criteria of Islam and the Constitution. These two had lots of frictions due to the readings of *foqahā* of Islam and reading of realities by MPs.

In spite of what was claimed, these discretions had nothing to do with the revival of administration of justice in pristine Islam. They are closely associated with the well-accepted rights of the rulers in Iranian absolutism to prescribe the way to deal with offences whose punishments are not specified in the main legal sources. Good examples are the punishments prescribed by the Expediency Council for drug trafficking and drug addicts. I.R.I has an established record of such administrative innovations. I.R.I. created a multi-tiered court system and provided a limited appellate mechanism, court of cassation and supreme judicial court. In the areas outside *shari`ah,* there is the Court of Administrative Justice which handles complaints of administrative injustices.

Constitutionally mandated primacy of Islamic law and doctrine, which are objectified in clerical lifestyle over all aspects of Iranian life, was institutionalized in post-revolutionary Iran. By resort to this mandate, clerics dominated all appointed and theoretically defined elected bodies of government.

In spite of the Islamicization approach, ruling clerics had to have a change in the legal educational outlook. They have implicitly accepted this idea that students of Islamic law need to have a grounding in Western approaches to law as well as in the humanities and they need to study sciences and humanities in addition to the more traditional Islamic subjects. Other Islamic nations had the same experience (Piscatori, 1986: 18).

Right after the Revolution, lawyers were literally pushed out of the judicial system. There was a desire for a legal system that was simple, non-technical and straightforward.[67] In revolutionary point of view, one of the objectives of Revolution was to make lawyers unnecessary.[68] In Shi'ite revolutionaries' utopia, cleric judges are supposed to be just and fair and hence there is no need for lawyers in the courts that are ruled by these just judges. They were brought back after several years but remained under the control of the clergy.

The statement that the post-revolutionary law was simple return to legal system of pristine Islam is open to four questions: 1) was Islamic law neatly separated from common and civil law families? 2) Are new Islamic models of legal system under the influence of modern ideologies that have their roots in the West? 3) Can we find new bases and foundations in Iran's state law that have nothing to do with *shari`ah?* and 4) Is it possible to transplant any kind of legal system, Islamic or Western, in any society? In general, the above statement ignores the phenomenon of law as part of a social and political process. Law, society and politics are analytically autonomous but in real world, they are under piecemeal alterations over time due to interactions of ideology and structure, changes in individual situations and culture, multiple sources of reglementation, mutual obligations of social and political forces and dynamic interpretations of legal and non-legal texts. This makes us to think about law as a process (Moore, 1978), and not merely a text, that can be explained by uncertainties in situations and indeterminacies in culture.

The idea of the judiciary police, presented by the first Supreme Judiciary Council, was directed to full independence of the judiciary from executive branch of power. The presenters knew that one of the most important obstacles of judiciary's independence was its lack of power to enforce the courts' judgments. Although this idea was lost among the harsh challenges between political factions and groups in the immediate post-revolutionary era, it was addressing a problem with a long history.[69]

5.5 CHALLENGES AND DILEMMAS: DYSFUNCTIONAL PERFORMANCE, PUBLIC RESISTANCE AGAINST ENFORCING SHARI'AH LAW, BACKLOGS AND UNACCOUNTABILITY

The Islamic regime after consolidation in 1981 was very serious about Islamicization especially the judiciary, and judicial reform as Islamicization of judiciary system was at the center. The reforms were implemented and produced an independent judiciary, but independent from executive and legislative powers, not the leader and his office. The ruling clerics expected to insert clerics to the judiciary as judges and execute Islamic ordinances in this process, and in this respect they succeeded. Considering the general goal of Islamic revolutionaries to clean the society and Islamicize all individuals through the judiciary and judicial decisions, the reforms failed.

The dilemmas and challenges to expected reforms in this period could be categorized into substantial, theoretical and procedural challenges. The most important substantial challenge to Islamicization as the judicial reform in this period was the dysfunctional performance of the national court system. It was believed that revolutionary national justice system might be able to navigate the maze of obstacles in front of Islamicization of the judiciary only through more collaborative, inside-out, and bottom-up conceptual perspectives and social processes. But the idea about bottom-up change was based on mobilizing mass society without any resort to civil society institutions and democracy activists. Revolutionary ruling caste tried to be less reliant on external (outside-in) perspectives and local (bottom-up) participation, with more emphasis on hierarchical (top-down) decision-making together with internal (inside-out) awareness to hold greater promise of achieving widely shared justice change aims. There was a growing gap between worldwide substantive legal commitments to the rule of law and the domestic dysfunctional performance of national court system.

The second substantial and essential obstacle for Islamicization of the judiciary was reluctance of the public against some of the sections of Islamic Penal Code like amputation, chopping the fingers, arms and legs, stoning and lashing. On the law of retribution, a large number of groups including lawyers and intellectuals voiced opposition, and wrote letters to various newspapers on the subject. Their letters, which were meant to help and adjust Islamic laws to the requirements of modern society, were met with hostility from the government. The clerics regarded lawyers' behavior as opposition to the state, rather than an action meant to serve the legal system of the country. As a result, the most activist Iranian lawyers and some of the legal associations later in the fourth period of judicial reform affected the consolidation of a non-violent reform movement which was loyal to rule of law in pursuing democracy and vindication of civil and constitutional rights of Iranian citizens.

The third substantial challenge was profound internal impediments to reform. Among the first steps toward judicial reform in an Islamist point of view were the reform of the clerical establishment and the method of religious instruction, the change of relationships between religious activity and personal gain and between the seminary and political power, and reform in the organization of Shi'ite seminary. The conservative, mostly non-politicized clergy was totally against these reforms.

The fourth substantial challenge was backlogs. Cases were often delayed for months and years, with the accused being held in jail without the possibility of bond. In cases were the opportunity of appeal was offered by the judiciary officials, it was so subject to influence by the original judges as well as the officials of the government that the convicted person rarely was able to present his case before she/he had served many years of her/his sentence. Due to the gap between morality and law, and between norms and law, there have been an increasing number of cases filed in the judiciary. This is also true about the fourth period of judicial reform in Iran.

The most important procedural challenge was lack of any mechanism to address judicial accountability. The main dilemma of judicial reform in this period was non-congruency of judicial independence and accountability (a code word for anti-corruption, anti-incompetence, or anti-delay). The judiciary in the Islamic Republic Constitution was completely independent from executive branch, not from the leader's office, but there was no mechanism for judicial accountability to any elected body. There was no limit on judicial independence through elections (except election for three members of the Supreme Judiciary Council), disciplinary systems, retraining certification requirements, or court management interventions. On the other hand, internal disciplinary system, life tenure regardless of ineffectiveness and inefficiency, and individual independence of the judge to manage a calendar or caseload badly undermined the quality of judicial performance. According to *shari`ah,* the verdicts were final. This situation brought up the dilemma between enhancing judicial independence (at the expense of accountability) and enhancing accountability (at the expense of independence).

The theoretical challenge of judicial reform in this period was the pretense of greater knowledge of *'ulamā*. Judicial reform in this period was based on the pretense of greater knowledge of *'ulamā* about how to fix the judicial problems. The belief in this knowledge that was not actually possessed did more harm than good. Even if such knowledge existed, the realization of whatever plan or design was heavily dependent on active participation and practices of the community at large. Islamic judicial system could not overcome its submerging conditions because it did not share and did not improve the limited navigational tools of its participants. These systems emerged through the many rocks and hard places of dysfunctional systems and their pathologies.

These dilemmas and challenges had some consequences like creation of a new ruling class of clergy, increasing the tension between modern and traditional, and deteriorating women's status in the society. Clerical judges as the high judges of the state and Islamic jurists in the Guardian Council, Expediency Council and Expert Council have had the final say in Iranian politics. They have recruited their loyalists in almost all governmental positions and had unaccountably benefited from these positions. The Islamic world has been struggling with the tension between modernity and Islamic tradition for more than two centuries. At the center of this ferment were three foundations of Islam, i.e. *sharī`ah* or the legal system based on the Quran and the teachings of the Prophet Muhammad, *ummah* or the Islamic community and *'ulamā* or the Islamic experts. The Islamic Republic annulled all the legal achievements of women during Pahlavi era. In issues like age of marriage, custody, right to work, dress code and social equality, *sharī`ah* replaced all laws based on European laws. For example, according to the law of the Islamic Republic a woman's life is worth only half that of the man and therefore we had to pay the family of the killer of my mother blood money if we wanted to ask for the death penalty for him. This is precisely the kind of law my parents were against.

Chapter Six

Fourth Period: Post Khomeini Era

The inherited hierocracy of the sultanistic regime of late Khomeini era facilitated the rise and consolidation of an authoritative sultanate regime, which could not stop securing political forces under his command and strengthening appointed bodies of government. In this situation, sidelined and weakened elected bodies had no role other than legitimizing the political regime among new strata. Above the law, unaccountable, and non-responsible leader of the country that is projected in the Constitution transgressed all the so-called legal limitations and challenges. Islamicization was continuously the legitimizing tool for the absolute rule of the ruling jurist addressing traditional strata.

Yazdi was committed to implement the unfinished task of Islamicization. His way of formal Islamicization, i.e. de-specialization, generalization and personalization of the courts, was totally fit to its judicial organizational equivalent of centralization of power in the hands of the Head of the Judiciary, implemented by the revisions of the Constitution in 1989 and its political equivalent of personalization of power by the jurist in the political society.

Systemic and systematic political interferences and politicization of the judiciary, crushing backlog and delay due to lack of accountability, discipline, versatility and finality, and ignorance with respect to technicality almost killed Yazdi's initiative of the General Court and Shāhrudi's initiative of judicial development in their first terms of service. Yazdi's General Courts replaced the complexities of the procedural laws with the complexities of the jurist-oriented procedure that led to total ignorance of due process. The show of judicial development accompanied with doubling or tripling the judiciary's budget in some years led to more interferences, corruption, and delays. Political reformers also failed to see the underlying dilemmas of the judiciary and did not pay enough attention to the basic challenges of rule of law.

6.1 BACK TO AUTHORITARIAN STATE BUILDING

The charismatic authority structure of the Islamic regime during the period of 1979–1981 could not remain stable, but did not became traditionalized or rationalized (as Weber expects (1968: 246)), at least in a quarter of a century. The Islamic regime in post-Khomeini era reinforced the Islamicizing trend, which had become more and more problematic after 1981 when it could not keep up with its promises and expectations. Confronting increasing resistance from Iranian people, especially in big cities, the regime had to become more authoritarian to enforce the provisions and ordinances of Islamic *shari`ah*. It kept its non-rational/non-pragmatic features except in cases where the survival of the regime or the interests of the ruling caste were at stake.[1] The Islamic charisma could not be traditionalized because on the basis of tradition there was no room for an Islamic modern state with its specific features and with a jurist on the top. It was also far from democratic direction, although there are some weak and pale aspects of it in the Constitution of 1979.[2]

The *'ulamā* believed only in people's recognition (*bai'ah*) of the leader selected by the Islamic jurists, qualified by the ruling clerics beforehand, not in their rights to elect their leaders. Due to authoritarian political culture and weak civil society, the recognition of the leader's decrees and judicial decisions did not shift to the belief that the society has a right to enact, recognize, or appeal laws and decisions, according to its own free will. The Revolution had no success to impersonalise the power of the state but intensified the personalization of this power. Iranian society as a whole has had little experience with civil discourse leading to peaceful rotation of leaders and change toward democracy.[3] The hierocratic[4] authoritarian and, later, hierocratic authoritarian sultanistic structure of the state did not let the establishment to depersonalize charisma and transfer it through blood, tribe or community ties, artificial magical means, or special events. Due to the lack of grass root organization and plural authority of *'ulamā* in religious schools and seminaries, the clergy could not establish the office charisma. Khāmenei, as the successor of Khomeini in the position of the guardian, lacked the traditional, charismatic, and later legal, authority of the founder of the Islamic Republic.[5] After being selected by the Expert Assembly, his clique tried to forcefully and artificially combine in him all those three kinds of authorities which Khomeini had in different stages of his political life, in spite of his low religious and political status and the existence of constitutional impediments and political and social groups who did not look at him as *marja'* or charismatic leader. His appointment as the leader by the Expert Assembly before the revision of the Constitution was also unconstitutional, since the Constitution of 1979 stipulated that the leader had to be a *marja'-e taqlid* (source of emulation in religious issues). He did not meet the required standards for the position of *marja'iyyah* (being the source of emulation), i.e. *a'lamiyyah* (superiority of learning in the field of religious law), having a vast group of disciples in post-doc seminary programs, and receiving enough money from a voluntarily paid religious tax (*khoms*[6]) to support seminary students and pay for their scholarship. Forcing Montazeri to step down as Khomeini's successor in 1989,[7] banning him even from teaching regular courses and putting him under house arrest for five years (1998–2003), the propaganda campaign for the selection of Khāmenei as a *marja'* by Iranian state controlled radio and television, nomination by the political collective bodies like the Militant Clergy Association of Tehran and Association of Qom Seminary Faculty Members[8] and pressures by political and even intelligence officials on *'ulamā*[9] to endorse him as a *marja'* had no example in the Shi'ite history of nomination for the position of *marja'iyyah*.[10] He lacked the charismatic feature in the eyes of majority of Iranian people, even traditional strata and revolutionaries, because of his minor religious rank and his total support of the brutal clique who have had the power in all appointed bodies of the government. He was given by his appointees in state-run TV and Radio different titles like the leader of revolution, *āyatollāh* (literally meaning sign of God, major Shi'te clergyman), grand *āyatollāh,* and supreme leader, to compensate his lack of charismatic, traditional and legal authority respectively.

His nomination by the authoritarian political groups as a *marja'* after the death of Mohammad Ali Araki, widely emulated by Iranian Shi'ites, in Dec. 1, 1994 was an attempt by the political caste to 1) safeguard the clerical establishment as the most essential obligation rather than safeguarding the primary ordinances of Islam or the nation-state, 2) bring the *marja'iyyah* under the state control and subordination that paved the way for sultanistic hierocracy,[11] 3) increase the legitimacy of the religious state and give it the same basis for its claim that it was an "Islamic" state, 4) increase state control over the clergy and seminaries, and 5) have control over the religious taxes and endowments. His nomination proved the deep legitimacy, authority and penetration crises of the guardianship theory with a lightweight cleric is in this position. These crises were good points for people who believed that *velāyat-e faqih* (guardianship of the Islamic jurist) and *marja'iyyah* should not be combined. Elimination of *marja'iyyah* from the requirements for the leadership in the revised Constitution of 1989 was a move to solve this legitimacy crisis, although it made the problem more acute in an Islamic state because of separation of religious and political authorities while the ideology of the state negates this separation.

Iranian Revolution of 1979 was a transition from neo-patrimonial authoritarianism to revolutionary charismatic authoritarianism and later hierocratic authoritarianism. With promulgation of the absolute guardianship of jurist in the late Khomeini period (1987), the nature of the regime gradually turned to be a sultanistic one. According to this idea, the jurist is the absolute ruler and has authority over any public matter including the primary and secondary ordinances of *sharī`ah* (Khomeini, Vol. 20, 1991: 170). By resort to military and security forces and lacking support in other section of the elite and society, Khāmenei consolidated his sultanistic regime during Rafsanjāni's administration. With the rise of civil rights movement, this partially sultanistic regime had to transfer to a total sultanistic and hierocratic regime to survive. Without governmentalization of the religious institutions, the high demands for democracy, rule of law and vindication of civil rights (President Khātami's declared mandate) could end to a colorful revolution.

The main characteristics of the state in this period of Iran's contemporary history, 1989–2006, are demobilization of the masses after the Iraq-Iran war, organizing the militia and para-military forces to suppress the dissidence in all provinces, gradual decrease of public participation except for the civil right movement era,[12] decreasingly ideologized and increasingly pragmatized political society, and continuity of double faction predominance to 2005.[13] The de-ideologization of religion (Soroush, 1994) pursued by religious intellectuals, what is known as Kiān Circle,[14] was not able to stop the marching of ruling clerics' ideologized *sharī`ah* toward capturing all media outlets and cultural institutions, mainly in the hands of government, after Khomeini. The paradox of this era is rising of an ideology that has no interest in mobilization of the masses, but organizing the loyalist and so-called true believers in quasi-state organizations.[15] The pervasiveness of power seeking, associated with different practices of modern states as increased surveillance and political control, plus the expansion of state activities, constituted a massive exercise in power enhancement by the ruling clergy.

The Islamic state did not want to have a hold on civil society; it wanted to not have it at all or see it null. The process of licensing and qualification to establish a non-governmental organization in any social, cultural and political domain was made so hard that people would quit in the first steps of the procedure. The other policy of the state was to make fake associations in every area of work and public life, where some independent groups had already established by political and social activists.[16] People who could get independently and randomly through the licensing funnel would confront the judicial and security interference on a daily basis. This was not limited to political parties and groups or dissident intellectuals; all the labor, cultural, scientific and professional associations have been under the pressure of the government's security or disciplinary bodies to quit their independence and to stop presenting alternative policies or criticizing the government.[17] The hold of the Islamic state on civil society and NGOs, especially religious ones, became more and more heavy, pervasive, imperious and damaging.

Fragile semi-pragmatist (in economy and foreign policy)/semi ideologized (in domestic politics, culture and social policies) regime of Khāmenei during Rafsanjāni's presidency turned to be a total sultanistic regime in Khātami's second term of presidency. By the beginning of Khātami's presidency in 1997, the consolidation of Khāmenei's control over the religious institutions was complete. This regime led to a situation that independent clergy and other religious institutions had no economic autonomy and independent administrative apparatus, and clerical acts and religious institutions were all supervised by the state and directly under the control of Khāmenei and his office. The judiciary, now including thousands of clerics as judges and public prosecutors, that is a total governmental body was not and could not be an exception.

The regime gradually seized all the independence from clerical institutions like Association of Qom Seminary Faculty Members, and the board of Qom Seminary Administration. This was done by pumping billions of Tomans, almost all of them public finds, to the seminaries. Only after a few years, all the members of the seminaries' boards and associations were directly or indirectly appointees of the leader. At the same time, the ideologized rule made available to the *'ulamā* the external means of enforcement for the maintenance of their ever declining authority, even in the years of Revolution and after, for appropriating lots of public and confiscated funds and properties, annihilation of heretics, decreasing the power of minorities in polity, or at least for the collection of religious taxes[18] and other contributions. In return, the *'ulamā* offered their religious sanctions in support of the IRI's legitimacy, the domestication of subjects by resort to ideologized *sharī`ah,* and most of the time total support of the establishment.

In this era, the democratic aspect of two branches of government, i.e. legislative and executive, were in decline due to approbation and disqualification power of the Guardian Council and the pressures from the leader's office. The Guardian Council rejected all the bills of the Sixth Majles related to people's rights and judicial, social and political reforms.[19] The executive power was close-handed and the president could not even pick his cabinet ministers; they were usually selected by the forces coming through the leader's office, the Expediency Council, the Expert Council and other appointed bodies of government like IRGC, the judiciary, and the intelligence services.

The inherited hierocracy of the sultanistic regime of late Khomeini era facilitated the rise and consolidation of an authoritative sultanate regime, which could not stop securing political forces under his command and strengthening appointed bodies of government. Due to the weak civil society, the independent religious and non-religious institutions could not impede the accumulation and monopolization of all human and physical resources by the appointed bodies and establishing and strengthening of loyal para-military to keep the authoritative jurist in power and suppress all dissidents.

The Iranian political regime in post-Khomeini era swung between partial sultanism and partial democracy during Rafsanjāni's tenure. As times passed by, it leaned more toward the latter one. From one hand, the domination operated on the basis of discretion (Weber, 1968: 232). On the other hand, it is exercised by virtue of the ruler's personal autonomy that implicitly connotes sultanism that was a stronger version of patrimonialism, i.e. the personal rule.[20] This personal rule is usually realized by jurists' passion for 1) directly or indirectly appointing everybody with official position, 2) minutiae and their tendency to want to make all decisions, large and small, and 3) being over the law. With respect to politics, culture, policy-making, security and military issues, the ruler was involved in hands-on operations, pulling levers, and pushing buttons. The revision of the Constitution in 1989 facilitated the transition from a mostly hierocratic to a mostly sultanistic state. The transition has been continuous, and authoritarian reaction to reform movement between 1996 and 2000 increased the speed. Hierocracy of late Khomeini era was restrained by the tradition while the sultanistic regime of Khāmenei after 1997 was only restrained by the democratic forces of real politics. The increase of the power of appointed bodies like the judiciary and the Guardian Council, and ever-decreasing role of Majles can be understood in this context. All the powers of government were divided between the leader and its governmental staff, mostly appointed. The ideological mechanisms like approbation and disqualifications worked toward making elected bodies null or quasi appointed.

The sultanistic regime of Khāmenei after 1997 like the pharaohs, popes, caliphs and the Protestant summi episcope (the highest bishops) attempted, mostly without success, to impose religious beliefs and norms of its own making not only to the political society and polity but also on each and every individual. He was also claimed to be deputy of Hidden Imam and embracing some remnant of supernatural linkage, although this idea could not be sold easily this time. It was even claimed that the hidden Imam has endorsed most of the MPs of the Seventh Majles, selected by the leader's clique.[21] Powerful but unsuccessful reform movement after 1997 expedited the rise of a personalistic regime and made it to reinvigorate its coercive bases. Between 1997 and 2003, a faction of the authoritarians rose that had strong military connections and are known as the "militarist faction."[22] Militarism was very week even in the years of Iran-Iraq war but Khāmenei had no choice other than resort to the forces that have a thirst to power and totally obey him. He has been totally supportive for the low level militias who sometimes wear uniforms and participate in daily actions against dissident activists and individuals who do not observe *sharī`ah* law in their daily life. He has also opened many windows for the military forces that use their power to put pressure on the different branches of government and try to direct certain factions of the political system to work for them.[23] The higher-level IRGC commanders are picked up in a way that they are completely loyalist to the Leader and are against any reform. Khāmenei raised the level of military intervention in polity to show his strength, to fear the opponents, and to compensate his lack of popular legitimacy and social base.[24] Khāmenei and his clique let the half of his handpicked MPs in the Seventh Majles to be former IRGC commanders or people with the Revolutionary Guard background. The majority of the authoritarian nominees for ninth presidential elections in 2005 have had Revolutionary Guard background.[25] About fifty percent of the Ahmadinejād's cabinet members have security or military background.[26] The theocratic elements of Iranian polity that tended to be present in every period of Iranian modern history developed to a point of total and monopolized thirst for total and personal power that led to a total sultanistic regime.

According to the official interpretation of guardianship of the jurist (*velāyat-e faqih*), the leader has absolute right to rule. Due to his prerogative rights, all laws, all jurisdictions and policies, and particularly all powers of exercising authority are personal privileges of the head of the state. In this case, the authority to rule, to judge, to call a person into any services or to require obedience in all aspects of life- public or private- are vested rights in exactly the same way as the authority to use a piece of land. It is a kind of political authority that is not essentially different from that of the head of the household or a landlord or a master of serfs.[27] Similar views can be found in Reza Shah Era regarding the power of the king. In both cases, judges are asked to issue verdict based on the will of the head of the state. The emphasis of elite on state building during Reza Shah led to the emergence of an instrumental approach to the law; this view extended to the Islamic Republic. The expansion of the role of government could not be stopped at the door of law. The judges should be appointed by the government to have no resistance when the law is supposed to be used as a political tool.[28]

The semi-totalitarian aspect of the state continued in post-Khomeini era and mandated all kinds of things related to daily life-even the names of children.[29] But the most dramatic changes after the Islamic Revolution of 1979 came within the courts. In their quest for a pristine Islamic state, Iran's clerics reached into all aspects of people lives. This interference expedited and intensified in Khāmenei era. For a quarter of a century, the clerics who control Iran's courts have insisted on an ultra-strict interpretation of *sharī`ah* law. But the totalitarians are being challenged by reformers-women, students, lawyers, journalists and moderate clerics-who say the laws should be open to modification.

The motivation for proper execution of the tasks of the government in this period is no longer the office-holder's awareness of and commitment to the objective requirements of tasks themselves, plus his or her expectation that such commitment will be recognized by superiors and rewarded by advancement but either the immediate pursuit of the holder's private interest or the sense that being the caste of ruling clerics oblige. The molecular institutional arrangement for the exercise of rule in its increasingly diverse and significant everyday aspects is not the cognitively oriented performance of the duties of properly appointed individuals but the exercise of the rights of privileged individuals and groups.

Iranian authoritarians have always tried to take over the elected bodies by placing stealth candidates on the ballot, huge ideological disqualifications, stealing slogans from other groups, declaring the number of potential voters less than the real numbers[30] and establishing new and fake political groups before every election.[31] This was driven by members of the appointed bodies of government; their tactics are underhanded -they usually do not declare their real issue positions to the public. They have hoped that low participation and confusion will allow them to stack the elected bodies.

Other than duality in the whole political structure, there was a duality in the intelligence [32] and law and order structure between 1997 and 2005. The judiciary totally recognizes this duality. This duality became more sophisticated, improving the organization, visibility, level of resources, planning, and coordination of parallel institutions after 1997. Judges who hear cases where defendants have been abducted by plainclothes agents and kept incommunicado in illegal detention centers[33] reinforce the perception among prisoners that these "parallel institutions" are supported by the government. The judiciary, is not merely ignoring violations of the law being committed in order to deliver those who criticize the government to the courtroom, it is directly sanctioning these violations. The parallel security forces (*nahādhā-ye ettelā'āti-ye movāzi),* referring to the various extralegal agents of state coercion that have grown in formality, organization, and capacity, reflect networks of Basij [militia], Ansar-e Hezbollāh [partisans of the party of God], various intelligence services outside of the Ministry of Intelligence (in IRGC, the Disciplinary Forces, and the judiciary itself), and the secret prisons and interrogation centers at their disposal working hand in hand with the judiciary. The main functions of these illegal detention centers are monitoring, intimidation, and detention of political targets.

Parallel military forces such as the Ansār-e Hizbollah and Basij shadow intelligence services such as Hefāzat-e Etelā'āt-e Sepāh (Intelligence) of the IRGC and Hefāzat-e Etelā'āt-e Qovveh-ye Ghazai'iyyeh (Intelligence of the judicial authority), and the secret detention centers they control, are sanctioned by forces within the government. The illegal prisons, which are outside the oversight of the National Prisons Office, allow political prisoners to be abused, intimidated, and tortured with impunity. Even the space of legal prisons is divided between different security forces.[34] The government has failed in its obligation to protect citizens from ill-treatment of this sort, to close down the illegal detention and interrogation centers, and bring the individuals responsible for these acts to justice.

The Army, security apparatus, Revolutionary Guards and the judiciary remained under the firm control of the *vali-ye faqih* (jurist) who answers to no one "but God." As a result, the independent press was shut down,[35] the prisons were filled with writers, students and the so-called loyal opposition who were all Khātami's backers and no one of the appointed bodies of government were accountable. Even the Sixth Parliament was not allowed to oversee the appointed bodies including the judiciary.[36] The judiciary ignored all the correspondence from the Board of Constitutional Watch established by President Khātami in 1997.[37] Khātami maintained that it is his duty as President to implement the Constitution, pursuant to its Article 113 (Tabari, 2003). There has been no Constitutional Court that breaches of the Constitution would be referred to by the President based on Board of Constitutional Watch's reports. The Board of Constitutional Watch, during Khātami administration, was only a watchdog without any power to pursue its cases in the courts.[38] Article 113 of the Constitution that considers the President as the highest official in the country after the office of Leadership and responsible for implementing the Constitution does not mention any apparatus for doing this job. The commission compiled over one hundred complaints it considered valid and reported them to the President. The commission's efforts did not go much further, as the President did not have adequate power to stop violations of the Constitution (Arjomand 2000b:288; Tabari, 2003; Mehrpour, 2005).

The government of men, not laws, in this period, is based more on the grounds of hegemonic foundations of Khāmenei's sultanistic regime and less on juridical conceptions of the contractual grounds of the political society in some other autocratic regimes with better performance in rule of law. There is absolutely no reference to the technical adequacy of judicial forms. For Khāmenei and his appointees, the understanding of constitutionalism and parliamentarianism did not go beyond the idea of consultation (*mashverat*), which is offered to the leader by his appointees. The disqualifications of the nominees by the Guardian council have gradually made the parliament a council that its members are indirectly chosen by the ruler for the duration of his will.

The Islamic republic of Iran has not confronted with a formidable institutional challenge because of non-fulfillment of a variety of commitments to the Constitution. The over-law, unaccountable, and non-responsible leader that is projected in the Constitution—Articles 5 and 110—transgresses all the so-called legal limitations and challenges, while political changes and increasing demands for participation and competence cannot be canalized. There is also no powerful advocacy group to pose these kinds of challenges for the state. While the formal realization of the right to vote, the right to contract and protect property, and the ability to trade with other societies without predatory tariffs or unfair treatment all require institutional adherence to the rule of law through impartial and effective adjudication systems, the state ignores and neglects the necessities of these rules through ideological allocation of the resources to clients of the state, treating majority of population as second order citizens, and inflicting institutionalized fear on the people through terror, torture and police raid.

The Iranian government is in a level of development that cannot digest the paradox of the rule of law that necessitates states to be simultaneously strong and self-limiting.[39] The only pill for this digestion is independent powerful judiciary to realize strong enforcement of law and self-limitation of the state. Focus on an independent, impartial, and efficient adjudicative or dispute resolution function is totally absent from the list of the government's priorities. Institutional vehicles for effectuating the rule of law that assume priority among the rules themselves are totally dysfunctional.

For about two centuries before the Islamic Revolution, the struggle between the state and the *'ulamā* was a principal feature of Iranian polity. When *'ulamā* took the power in 1979, the power struggle between two camps began: the camp of *'ulamā* and *bazaar* on one side, and the camp of intellectuals, technocrats, activist women, and university students on the other side. The society in this period, especially after the war, was not homogeneous, but the polity was not ready to digest this to be representative of the whole society. The bifurcated society includes two or more value systems that led to a multi-norm society. In this tiered society, individuals and groups that are affiliated to one sub-culture consider their actions as norm and other's as crime or tort or abnormal. To enforce one legal system in this society gets more and more difficult. For example in most of the political and press cases, individuals are charged with accusations like criticizing the leader or presenting different readings of Islam that are totally common sense among another sub-culture. In some periods and in some areas the polity is quasi-pluralistic, but the state as a whole could not tolerate pluralism.

Over seventy years after Reza Shah's modernization, these "other" voices usually coming from university students, women and intellectuals found themselves once again confronting authoritarian forces who claimed the monopoly of power with resort to Islamic political tradition, and struggling to reinterpret *shari`ah* law, to make it more compatible to modern times.[40] The Reformers in 1990's asked for legislation of democratic and humane laws by the parliament and their enforcing by the law and order organizations. They demanded independent judges, due process, and independent lawyers.[41] Many voices in Iran have been challenging the institution of the judiciary.

I.R.I. has been facing major economic crises in its life after 1979. Inflation, unemployment and poverty are among the causes of the deteriorating social condition of most Iranians. Iranians has been wrestling with problems like double-digit inflation and unemployment, slow growth, declining labor productivity, large external deficit and debt, harmful private monopolies, huge tax exempt corporations, excessive regulations, and heavy budgetary reliance on oil revenues, dwindling middle class, capital flight and brain drain.[42] Average inflation in the years after the Revolution has been at least twice as high as during the 1970s, unemployment has been three times higher, and economic growth is two-thirds lower. As a result, Iran's per capita income has declined by at least 30 percent since 1979. By official admission, more than 15 percent of the population now lives below the absolute poverty line, and private estimates run as high as 40 percent.[43] Although the alarming rate of population growth in the first decade after the Islamic Revolution has been brought under control, both per capita income and domestic income distribution lag behind official targets. The ailing economy has brought the regime's legitimacy further into question.

6.2 RELIGIOUS AND STATE JUDICIAL SYSTEMS: FORMAL ISLAMICIZATION

It is possible to look at the development of Islamic *shari`ah* as a part of state building process in Muslim societies, where Islamists as an important section of the polity have been trying to strengthen the theoretical foundations of Islamic state in new world of nation-states. Development of Islamic *shari`ah* to the important base of the Islamic state could happen when Muslim scholars found out that 1) Islamic law covers a very small portion of the spectrum of government, 2) the range of interpretation of *shari`ah* law is practically dependent on time and location and consequently on who does the interpreting, and finally 3) even the small specified set of Islamic laws incumbent on the family and personal conduct are already widely modified, creating ample precedent for any government, progressive or conservative, to interpret them.

In Islamicization of polity, Islam has been considered to be an all-encompassing plan for human life and has been converted into the state ideology. This predisposes even nominal Muslim practitioners to want this matter ensconced in their governmental laws.

Here there is a connection between governments' adoption of these ideologized Islam and major setbacks for rule of law, good governance, democracy and human rights; in this process Islam would not even be stipulated as the state religion.

There is nothing about Islam per se that prohibits the construction of a government that reflects liberal, progressive tendencies in the very few areas of public life where *shari`ah* law has legitimate sway. On the other than, there is nothing about Islam per se that prohibits the construction of a totalitarian or authoritarian government that reflects despotic and autocratic tendencies in the many, as claimed, areas of public life where *shari`ah* law has ordinances. Different political factions in the Islamic Republic of Iran have been using one side of this double edged argument.

When the regime-supporting coalition, i.e. Islamic right and left of the first decade, lost its cohesion in post-Khomeini era and demands for development, rule of law, democracy and civil and constitutional rights increased after the end of Iran-Iraq war, the new leader and ruling group who believed in authoritarian/totalitarian ideology and sultanistic governance had no choice other than resort to any appointed body including the judiciary to remove controversial issues like serial killings of political activists and intellectuals by the Ministry of Intelligence, corruption of the high ranking officials, and dissatisfactions and grievances of the public from the political agenda. These actions led to further polarization and accelerated the delegitimization of the government. The authoritarian camp had the majority in the Fifth Parliament but its constituency decreased after 1997 to between 10–15 percent in 2000[44] when the judiciary was actively involved in prosecuting political activists and closing down independent newspapers.[45] This shows that the majority of the people did not buy the neutrality of judiciary or the Guardian Council.

Islamicization and not democracy was on the agenda for the ruling clerics. Islamicization is emphasized in the appointing decree of Mohammad Yazdi, dated 1989/7/14(1368/5/24).[46] Khāmenei has also mentioned Islamicization as the main goal of judiciary in his yearly speeches for the judiciary officials.[47] Islamicization is the real goal and what has been happening, as compared with codification under Dāvar, is to go to the finish line of this process, something that secularizing forces could not accomplish. Other than political control and ensuring the Islamicization, the judiciary's functions in this period have been the regular tasks of judiciary in civil law tradition and authoritarian regimes, i.e. 1) ensuring that lower-ranking officials implement decisions made at the top (Brown, 1997: 241), 2) providing the authoritarian regime with some level of legitimacy (Tate, 1992) based on those functions of law that are related to conceptualizing and managing the social environment, and 3) compensation of the losing in the electoral and legislative processes in the authoritarian camp.

One of the formal judicial Islamicization in this period is negation of the idea of prison. The high-ranking officials do not believe in prison. They think that in pristine Islam there was not any prison or prisoner, although they eagerly put political activists in prison when political control was the issue. This negation was partly because of huge increase of inmates after the Revolution. While the population doubled in a quarter of a century, the number of inmates was tenfold.[48] Hence they usually ignore the situation and rights of prisoners. Prisons in Iran are closed institutions from which the press, human rights groups, members of the public, and even the MPs and ministers are typically excluded.[49] Independent expert inspections yielding public findings are rare, and usually occur only after the situation has become so bad that has led to a crisis.

Even after a quarter of a century, the Islamic regime was not successful in merging of the typically revolutionary structure of dual sovereignty into a single one. The and Revolutionary Courts and Special Court for Clerics still were working due to the regimes' uncertainty about the regular courts to help it out during political crises. The radicalization of the revolutionary government (Brinton, 1938) immediately after the revolution extended to the rest of regime's life and kept the duality and hence "reign of terror and virtue" alive. Religious believes, organizations, and affiliations kept being consuming concerns of political life to legitimize the duality and secure the destabilizing situations.

The judiciary officials have claimed that the judicial reforms (*towse'eh-ye qazāii*) they have been pursuing come from the heart of Islam (Zākeri, 2002: 21). The same claim has been made after representation of any new idea-like democracy, rule of law, civil society, human rights, freedom and separation of powers- to Iranian society by the clerics and their loyalists, from authoritarian or reformist camps, when the religious establishment could not resist or reject it. This claim usually helps them to manipulate the idea in the desired way.

Enforcing punitive policies of the Islamic Law was one of the main features of Islamicization process in Khomeini era continued in the post-Khomeini regime. Punishment in IRI is not an instrument for enforcing the law or implementing justice. Punishment for an Islamist authoritarian and sultanistic state is the main goal of judicial procedure *per se*. There is lots of evidence for this statement. First, there is no let-up in the abuse of persons in pre-trial detention. There are many examples of arbitrary arrest, prolonged detention prior to trial, often in solitary confinement, torture and denial of the elements of fair trial, all implemented to punish the critics. Second, the Islamic punishments in use like stoning (*sangsār*),[50] decapitation,[51] blinding[52] and execution in public or in prisons are good evidence for a punitive policy to get rid of crimes,[53] even what is called financial corruption by the government,[54] promote virtue and prevent vice. Whenever public pressure on the state to stop execution has been high, the executions have been carried out in prisons.[55] There have been continued reports of amputations and public floggings. The official position of the judiciary is to ban shooting or photographing the execution of these punishment "due to misuse of these events to show the violent face of Islam, and misleading people who do not have strong faith."[56]

The number of executions has continued to be high in post-revolutionary Iran. The majority of them were carried out in public[57] according to which punishment takes place principally in camera. These include the public hangings of women on March 2001 in Tehran and August 2004 in Nekā.[58] In the heydays of tensions between authoritarian and reformist camps, the state television began to broadcast scenes of public hangings in 2001.[59] The death penalty is applied for crimes committed by persons under 18.[60] The Revolutionary Court has a record of fast track trials even in cases that lead to execution.[61] The authoritarian Islamic ideologues and judiciary officials have persistently defended these open-to-public harsh punishments.[62] Without referring to the polls, the judiciary officials have always claimed that Iranian people have been satisfied and happy with these public punishments and have appreciated the judiciary for doing this task.[63]

There are reports of torture in the legal system, particularly in pre-trial detention centres.[64] In political cases the pre-trial enquiry stage is often the harshest. The public statements of released detainees speak of being confined to small cells, interrogated in blind-folds, subjected to various kinds of psychological and physical pressure (from black and grey[65] to white torture[66]) to cooperate and, according to different reports, probably subject to some form of drug treatment to induce passivity and cooperation in front of the interrogators. Several improbable "confessions" have been released by the judicial authorities including those of veteran journalist Ezzatollāh Sahābi and student leader Ali Afshāri and then by bloggers and student activists, all denied by the detainees when released. Almost all detainees have declared that those confessions are extracted by resort to torture.[67] Ramin Jahanbegloo's case is the only case that the judiciary talked about an agreement reached between the detainee and the authorities to air his Interview/confessions on state run TV. Regardless of the authenticity and legitimacy (or lack thereof) of the contents of such spectacles, they reveal the techniques of gathering evidence in the judiciary.[68] Once convicted, the conditions of some seem to improve substantially but not for others.[69] For those who are released on pre-trial bail, the problem is different. The bail is often set so high as to be inaccessible to activists, intellectuals and others living on modest means.[70]

By resort to traditionalism and Third World nationalism, the Islamic Republic has always challenged the universality of human rights (Afhsari, 2001: 3). The drive for Islamicization of culture became a significant smoke screen for state exclusionary strategy (Afhsari, 2001: 12). Using cultural relativist debate in human rights discourse, the regime has continued to add charges that had clear sexual dimensions and drug addiction to demonize its critiques. While claiming high moral ground and superior Islamic paradigm, the Islamic Republic has used all measures of authoritarian regimes to protect and advance the political system built in the image of the Islamic ideology as understood by the ruling clerics. Like any authoritarian regime, it cracks down mercilessly and in total disregard of due process of law, suppresses street demonstrations, levels the charge of espionage against anyone deemed to be the enemy of the regime, and kills intransigent writers who refuse to forfeit their conscience (Afhsari, 2001: 292). Other than human rights violation, the clerical rulers often disregarded their own Islamic constitutional provisions (Afhsari, 2001: 291).

6.3 CODIFICATION AND TRANSPLANTATION: CENTRALIZATION AND GENERAL COURTS

After a very long process of substantive Islamicization, there was almost nothing to do about the substance of the law in 1990's other than enforcement. In the eyes of Islamists who saw their regime stabilized and strengthened, the substantial Islamicization had reached its objectives. What was left was procedural Islamicization; the new wave of Islamicization was focused on this issue. Any revision could only focus on methods and procedures and not on principles and themes. The heart of formal Islamicization with respect to codification was the introduction of the idea of general courts. General Courts (*Dādgāhha-ye 'Āmm,* also called *Dādgāhha-ye 'Omumi*) were expected to be courts presided by a cleric (not necessarily a *mujtahed,* as it was believed immediately after the Islamic Revolution) without beforehand investigation and prosecution and without any limit on its jurisdiction. It was the judge who could order investigation if he considers it necessary. This institution would make the office of public prosecutor, district attorney and attorney general redundant.

The revision of the Constitution paved the way for the general courts. The heart of the matter for the 25 members group, all appointed by Khomeini, which was working on the revision, was to centralize and personalize all the powers and authority of the judiciary in one person who should be an Islamic jurist (Article 157 of the 1989 Constitution). The Revision Council abolished the five-member Supreme Judicial Council as the highest judicial authority in the country and replaced it with a single appointment made by the leader. The appointee, the Head of the Judiciary, is responsible for all judicial administrative and executive matters; he proposes the Minister of Justice to the President, appoints the Head of the Supreme Court and Public Prosecutor-General, and change s or removes judges after consultation with the Head of the Supreme Court (Articles 160–164 of the 1989 Constitution). Without having a centralized judiciary and its non-elected positions, it was almost impossible to dissolve the office of public prosecutor (district attorney) all over the country. The generalization of the courts could happen till the regime reached its goals in centralization of judicial system. While the Prosecutor General and three elected judges were members of the Supreme Judicial Council based on the Constitution of 1979, it was impossible for the judiciary to draft the General Courts Law[71] and enforce it. With concentration all judicial affairs in one position, i.e. the Head of Judiciary, executive, administrative and judicial, it was not hard for Islamists to think about a courtroom with one person at the top with no other important functions for other.

The general court was modeled out of the traditional and *shar'i* courts in the Islamic world from 7th to 19th centuries. The Islamists were thinking and working on the idea of an Islamic court from a formal aspect; this began just after the victory of the Revolution (Zerang, Vol. II, 2002: 306). The dissolution of an institution, i.e. DAs' and public prosecutors' office, with about a century lifelong (established in 1910) was not an easy task to do. The Articles 162 and 163 of the Constitution explicitly refer to the public prosecutor. In a poll of judges from 23 provinces by Jahād-e Dāneshgāhi, asked about the constitutionality of the dissolution of DAs' and public prosecutors' offices % 69.9 percent of the interviewees considered this action unconstitutional (Zerang, 200: 310).

The goal of the establishment of this kind of court was totally different in the first and second decades of Islamic regime. In the first decade, the goal was to merely Islamicise one of the institutions of the state, while the goal in the second decade was to expedite the judicial process and to get rid of the huge backlogs from judicial procedures under the umbrella of Islamicizartion. Some technical problems were crucial in promoting the idea of general courts, like confession before the DAs and prosecutors and rejection in front the court. The Guardian Council had also some reservations in rejection of the Penal Procedural Law of 1987 regarding conformity of the authority of public prosecutors and their assistants (*bāzporses* and *dādyārs*) with Islamic standards, and hearings of confessions and witnesses by them (Zerang, 2002: 306).

According to Article 1 of the General Courts Law of 1994, these courts are established to review and settle all claims and litigations, to send all disputes and cases directly to the judge and to create a single judicial reference. The jurisdiction of the court includes all civil and criminal, litigious and non-litigious cases. The law refers all political crimes and cases related to Article 49 of the Constitution,[72] espionage and national security, drugs, and conspiracy to Revolutionary Courts as distinguished from General Courts (Article 5). The judges of the General Courts are expected to judge on the basis of statutory and codified laws and Article 167 of the Constitution. This article adds *fatwas* to the codified laws as the sources of judgment and emphasizes on the former to take another step toward Islamicization. According to Article 167 of the Constitution, in case of the absence of codified law, the judge has to deliver his judgment on the basis of authoritative Islamic sources and authentic *fatāwā*. He, on the pretext of the silence of or deficiency of law in the matter, or its brevity or contradictory nature, cannot refrain from admitting and examining cases and delivering his judgment.

There is no difference between two step appeal procedure of these courts and the previous courts other than negation of the rights of appeal. The General Courts Law made appeal to the court a privilege that should be confirmed by the court: this is the court that mentions in its verdict that a decision is appeallable or non-appeallable (Amendment 1 of Article 28). The appeal procedure has only one step: it is up to the Appellate Court of the same province that the primary General Court has issued its verdict to hear and review the case; this court is located in the capitol of each province (Article 20). The head of the first branch of the provincial General Court can be the judge of the appellate court. If the case is related to execution, stoning, amputation, confiscation, imprisonment of more than ten years, endowment, and marriage and divorce, it should be appealed to the Supreme Court (Article 21).

The idea of general court was totally against specialization of the courts with regard to jurisdiction; it was to ignore a century of work by Iranian elite to have a functional division of labor in the judiciary. The basic idea behind generalization was the expectation of an Islamic jurist as someone omniscient who is familiar with every aspect of human life. Islamists believe that Islamic *feqh* includes everything that a person needs for this life and the next one, and the jurists have the ways and means to extract every element of this absolute knowledge from Islamic texts. The main difference between General Courts and the traditional one was recognition of appellate Courts, but the appeallable cases are limited (Article 19 and 20 of the General Courts Law).

6.4 JUDICIAL REFORM AND REORGANIZATION: JURIST JUSTICE AND POLITICIZATION

The structure and functions of the judiciary in post-revolutionary era are detailed in Articles 156–174 of the 1979 Constitution. According to Article 157, the highest judicial power was a council known as the Supreme Judicial Council, later abolished in revision of the Constitution in 1989. This council had five members, including the head of the Supreme Court, the Prosecutor General, and three judges possessing the degree of *ejtehād,* to be chosen by all the judges of the country. This democratic feature of this body was not functional in an authoritarian regime and was stopped by the revised edition of the Constitution of 1979, which put an appointed official in the office of head of the judiciary. The occupier of this position should be a *mujtahed* but previous judgeship is not a must. The Ministry of Justice has merely been an administrative body, which provides the logistics for the judiciary. The Minister of Justice is to be chosen by the President from among those proposed to him by the Head of Judiciary (Article 160 of 1989 Constitution). The function of the Minister of Justice is to be a liaison between the judiciary on one hand and the executive and legislative body in administrative matters from the other. Another change in the revised Constitution regarding the judiciary was to transfer all the responsibilities of the Supreme Council of the Judiciary and the Head of the Supreme Court (suggesting amnesty to the leader, membership in provisional council of leadership and presidency) to the head of the judiciary.

The Council for Revision of Constitution abolished the five members Judicial Supreme Council three of them elected by the judges, as the highest authority in the Islamic Republic and replaced it with a head of the judiciary that is appointed by the leader (Article 157). It destroyed the collective leadership of the judiciary (Milani, 1992: 151). Consequently the partially elective nature of the judicial authority was denied. The Minister of Justice is also to be chosen by the President from "among those proposed to the President by the Head of the Judiciary" (Article 160) and hence the Parliament and the President as elected bodies have almost no say in choosing the Minister of Justice. There is an inconsistency between the duties and power of this position in the Constitution. It is the head of the judiciary who appoints the head of the Supreme Court and the Public Prosecutor-General; in the Constitution of 1979, they were appointed by the Leader. According to Article 164, the head of judiciary can remove judges after consultation with the chief of the Supreme Court and the Prosecutor General.

The establishment of the office of the head of judiciary in post Khomeini era, considered in the revision of the Constitution in 1989, was partly modeled after the office of the *qāzi al-quzāt* which was created in latter part of the 8th century. The traditional view on the judicial organization could not tolerate to see a council to direct and manage the judiciary; for hundreds of years, Iranian judiciary had been headed by a person at the top. The holder of this office in the Constitution, like *qāzi al-quzāt,* is merely the highest judicial officer with important administrative functions. He is not an independent judicial professional. From a practical point of view, the idea was the modern one of centralization: one head for the Judiciary Power to match the one Head for the Executive Power, which resulted in the abolition of the office of Prime Minister. This development in the Constitution of 1989 centralized all powers of the judiciary in one person that is appointed by the leader.

Jurist Justice

The most important reform in Iranian judiciary during Yazdi's term was executing the General Courts Law of 1994.[73] This court structure was modeled after the court structure of Islamic lands during centuries of Islamic civilization. In these centuries, the judge who was supposed to be just (*ādel*) was the only actor in the court. What could guarantee the justice was not the procedure but a characteristic of the judge, i.e. his fairness. The judge would be considered just and fair unless contrary was proved, that was almost an impossible task to do. His verdict was final and there was no appeal jurisdiction. From an Islamist point of view, the revival of the jurist justice in the form of General Courts was a way to revive Islamic civilization and Islamic judiciary.

The General Courts Law was claimed to be the pill to relieve caseload pressures in the courts, lower court costs, and reduce delay in adjudicative process. Instead of regulating new aspects of the civil litigation process, this bill submitted the standards regarding process, pleading, law practice and prosecution, relationships between multiple parties, motions, trials and judgment to judges who frequently had no experience in jurisdiction. The judges were coming directly from seminaries (in the 1980's) and security and disciplinary forces (in the 1990's) lacking any knowledge about judicial process or from prosecution branches without any academic education. The judge of the General Court combined many of the functions performed in other legal systems by judges, juries, prosecutors, district attorney, and in some cases lawyers.[74] The accumulation of these functions in a single person to expedite the trial procedure accorded the *qāzi* a large measure of judicial discretion. It led to arbitrary justice in some cases.[75] While there is no judicial procedure, the idea of jurist justice as the ideological and theoretical base of General Court is actually arbitrary justice. This law also transferred the duties of prosecutor to the police. Relieving case work was the secondary justification; the primary one was Islamicization.

The new government tried to get rid of the complexities of the procedural laws and replace it with the complexities of the jurist-oriented procedure that had little to do with judicial procedures. The establishment of General Courts was primarily and basically intended to reduce backlogs. As a result, by dissolution of the office of prosecutor it increased the number of cases sent to the Appellate Courts. There was no appeal jurisdiction in the technical judicial sense except for some harsh and heavy verdicts like execution, stoning, amputation, confiscation and prison terms more than ten years, and some administrative review of judges' decisions (Article 21 of General Courts Law of 1994). The execution of the General Courts Law did not make the judicial process swifter, less costly, and more accessible and the judiciary was still unable to process the demands within the new framework of adjudication. In a lot of cases, the judge has stopped the trial procedure due to lack of professional opinion in the middle of trial.[76] The consequence of enforcing the General Courts Law and sending cases without investigation directly to the judge was to increase the number of appeals to 70 percent of the cases decreed in primary courts over a decade from 1994 to 2004 [77]. Of cases sent to the Supreme Court, 77% Of the verdicts were overturned.[78] In a survey poll conducted in 1991, 1) 95 % of the judicial officials believed that the General Courts would not be effective in increasing the accuracy of decisions, 2) 58 % of the respondents believed that merging different courts would lead to decrease accuracy and rightness of the verdicts, and 3) 67 % of the respondents believed that one judge cannot have enough knowledge about different sections of legal profession.[79] The survey done after the implementation of the General Court Law of 1994 shows that only 52.2 % of the respondents think if they file a case the justice will be accomplished. Of the respondents, 51.7 % were not sure if the law would be enforced equally for ordinary people and people who have power. 82.7 % of the respondent believed that everyone who does not have money or good connection his/her rights would be violated.[80]

In establishing General Courts, court reformers in the authoritarian camp focused only on traditional processes of court or case management, and did not think about the likely behavior of lawyers, law scholars, media, and the public in response to these retrospections and returns to the past. The neglect of taking public reactions to the courts in which one official is the judge, jury, prosecutor, and public attorney into account completely undermined judicial reform of Yazdi aimed at containing cost, delay and backlog. This reform did not take into account the relation of the courts to the executive and legislative branches of government, the dependence of the court system to the Leader's office, other appointed bodies of government and political factions, the ideological selection of judges, and the role of new clerical judges who were totally ignorant of due process.

Arrogance about having a better design or method in Yazdi era was nothing more than an unrealistic command approach doomed to failure. No judge or lawyer or other actor working in the system had or have a good picture or sense of the system as a whole; they experience it in a solipsistic way, guided by their own vantage point and motivations. Judiciary expected lawyers and judges to work in ways that they see as contrary to their own professional interest in order to meet the higher needs of the political system as a whole.

In critical cases, the courts have expedited the legal procedure but the consequences for fair trial have been enormous. In Pākdasht Serial Pedophile Sodomy and Killing case, in which 22 children and three adults were killed,[81] the whole trial took only three sessions in less than a month. In another case, a court in Tehran issued an execution verdict for a student, in only three minutes,[82] later changed to 15 years imprisonment.

Prisoners are not dealt with in a proper way; temporary jails sometimes last more than a year and clerics as prisoners are dealt with in a different way;[83] prisoners are not allowed to publish their writings;[84] the division of labor is ignored under the General Court Law; in some cases, the heads of the local judicial branches do this division on an arbitrary basis and hence there is no uniformity in division of courts; the consent of public is not even one of the criteria of success and efficiency of the judiciary; the consent and satisfaction of the Leader, his representatives and his loyalists (Hezbollāh) comes prior to the satisfaction of public; and the cases are usually being transferred back and fourth from the primary to appellate courts and vice versa (Shāhrudi, 2001b: 13, 15, 19, 31, 34 & 35); there is no evaluation system in the judiciary (Kāzem Zādeh, 2002: 27–28, 52–54, 58); there is no training system for high ranking judiciary officials who directly come from seminaries and are not familiar with the judiciary system (Kāzem Zādeh, 2002: 29); there is no internship process in the judiciary (Kāzem Zādeh, 2002: 45); and different levels of judiciary officialdom are not defined (Kāzem Zādeh, 2002: 42).

Significant reforms in post-Khomeini era would threaten the vested interests of stakeholders who benefit from the status quo. Those in support of rational reform might risk their careers and personal safety. Ample security for those working on sensitive reform initiatives was rarely available. Given these impediments and conditions, Islamic reforms frequently failed. Failure took at least three different forms. First, reforms rendered disappointing results. For example, case management reforms did not demonstrate any appreciable impact on savings of cost or time. Only 24 % of cases sent to the Supreme Court were confirmed and from the rest, either the verdicts have been rejected or the investigations have been incomplete.[85] The involvement of the Supreme Court in the first place is proof of the complete failure of the system. From medical cases, 99 % are sent to the appeal courts.[86] The General Courts aimed at improving judicial performance and expediting the judicial process appeared vulnerable to the same problems they were designed to address: political interference, corruption, and bureaucratic delay. The General Court Law could not offer disputants a less-expensive, less-intimidating, and potentially more-equitable way in which to resolve their competing claims.

Secondly, interventions for one purpose undermined other equally important objectives. Strong support of the Leader and multiplication of the judiciary budget by putting pressure on the Sixth Parliament led to more intervention of the Leader's office in the judiciary. Seemingly efficiency measures like dissolving attorneys' positions undermined due process (because prosecutions were in the hands of judges) and normativity (because no judgment was produced in a way to be applicable to others). The court's refusal to allow the executive and legislative branches to play any role in judicial procedure led to more interference from the Leader's office, were traditionally executive and legislative branches were supposed to interfere like oversight and inter-organizational issues. These disappointments resulted in part from the failure to understand the internal dynamics of the judicial process from the bottom-up.

The General Court structure led to ignoring the scientific methods of investigation. Iranian judges do not usually use scientific and social-science data to buttress the factual basis of their judicial decision-making. The use of social-science evidence has not found its way into a broader range of legal dispute. Instead of scientifically based evidence and investigation, they rely on old traditional way of reaching the truth like confession and administering oath (*qusāmeh*).[87] Even if the judges had incentives to use scientific method in the investigation procedure, the judiciary lacks the structure to meet this demand. In one decade, between 1992 and 2002 the references to Medical Examiner's Office have had 600 % increase while this organization has only 30 % of the facilities and human resources and only 20 % of the laboratory facilities to meet these demands.[88]

The declared charter of judicial reform in Iran in Shāhrudi's administration (Barāti Niā, 2002: 68–69) is directly copied from UNDP goals for the judicial reform.[89] This charter while echoing general international standards it recasts them in a guise of regional context. The main objectives of the judicial reform in both charters are impartiality, competency, efficiency, and effectiveness, staying only on paper in Iran's case. Iran's judiciary has added some other objectives to the above list like religious and national public security,[90] finality of verdicts, increase of the people's trust to the judiciary, protection of individuals' dignity, and expanding justice (Barāti Niā, 2002: 69). The emphasis on women's rights and their access to justice in UNDP literature on judicial reform[91] is totally ignored in Iranian version.

Shāhrudi's administration has been busy with responding to intervening interests in the judiciary. Reform interventions pursued with the strategy of gradual approach to mediation, uncoupled with a systemic approach to court management. Individual and collective interests in the judiciary covered different types of interests like pecuniary concern, reputation, justice and efficiency.

Keeping independence was on the top of the list of priorities, but from whom, for what, and by which particular mechanism. Judiciary in this period emphasizes on its independence from legislative and executive branch to the level that the parliament has no right to oversight the judiciary and institutions under its control, and executive branch does not even have the right to mark out judicial bills or change the suggested budget of the judiciary by its head; executive power is only the mailman and has to send the judiciary's bill to the parliament and parliament has to pass it; otherwise the Guardian Council would veto the bill and confirm what the judiciary officials ask for. The executive power is also banned from sending bills regarding punishments for violation of laws by the judiciary.[92] The Article 90 Committee members even did not have access to judicial institutions, and MPs have not been allowed to be present in the trials or visit the prisons. The Sixth Majles unsuccessfully tried to change the status of the Prisons Organization by moving it from under the judiciary to the portfolio of the minister of justice, where it would be subject to oversight by the Majles. While the judiciary is totally independent from the executive and legislative branches but it is totally dependent to leader's office and other appointed bodies of government like IRGC, the Guardian Council and the Disciplinary Forces.

When Iranian judiciary officials talk about independence, they do not distinguish decisional from administrative, and individual from collective or corporate independence. They do not also distinguish independence as a shield from political interference (through protections of salary and proscriptions against non-consensual transfers, and from each political faction) from independence as a sword to curb executive branch excesses (judicial review of a violation of civil rights).

Independence may be understood, theoretically in the power of judicial review or, more practically, secure terms of employment. We can view a judicial system or process on a scale or level above the actual local behaviors of each of the actors in the system: judges, registrars, administrators, lawyers, clients, the press, politicians, businesspeople, citizens, foreigners, NGOs, and so on. This perception renders a very abstract and formal approach to thinking about the system and its characteristics of independence, integrity, or efficiency.

It is not clear to what extent does a life-tenure system enhance independence in Iran's judiciary system. Judges with tenure may not lose their jobs, but they may be deprived of resources (such as salary or one's administrative budget), subject to discipline, removal and downgrading,[93] or vulnerable to political pressure through the Leader's office or other appointed bodies of government. A life-tenure system does not in itself guarantee full, or even sufficient, judicial independence. It is not also clear to what extent does an external disciplinary system enhance accountability of this branch of government. External systems suffer from unsatisfactory resources, blocked access to information, or limited protection from corruption of their own processes. In other words, an external disciplinary system by itself is no guarantee for establishing full or even partial accountability. The net result of any reform measure is an empirical question (about which we know much too little) that (if we knew more) would render answers in quantifiably relative, rather than absolute terms. There may be reforms that advance independence much more than they detract from accountability and measures that advance accountability much more than they detract from independence, while basically independence measures and accountability are not necessarily mutually exclusive. It also stands to reason that some may detract from independence more than they advance accountability and detract from accountability more than they advance independence.

Where independence and accountability measures were necessarily mutually destructive, the officials simply made a choice toward independence.

Therefore the judiciary has a high corruption rate as a result of strong independence protections with the lack of effective accountability measures, or political interference with judicial decision-making due to weak accountability measures in front of elective bodies that compromise judicial independence protections.

Shāhrudi's administration kept working on formal Islamicization with regard to prisons. While closing the prisons in modern world was impossible, the judiciary officials tried to decrease the number of prisoners. Two of the most pressing issues with regard to prisons in the Islamic Republic during Shāhrudi's two terms have been overcrowding[94] (for judiciary officials) and the existence of detention centres outside the control of the National Prisons Organization [95](for reformers[96]). The policy of the judiciary has been implementing alternative ways of punishment[97] while it could not do anything about illegal detention centres. In early 2000's the Head of the Judiciary and the Head of the National Prisons Organization repeatedly noted that the high number of prisoners was the result of social circumstances outside the prisons, and that the judiciary and the organization was unable to settle all prison problems. They have said that the prison population had increased by 40 per cent over 2000 and that two thirds of the inmates were there for drug-related offences. Most of the inmates were between 22 and 30, and less that 3 per cent of them are women in the same year.

In light of the huge growth in the number of persons incarcerated for drug-related offences, one proposal has been to segregate such persons into new purpose-built institutions in the countryside. With regard to imprisonments related to economic crimes, the judiciary tried to change the banking check regulations. The judiciary officials believed that there is no imprisonment for economic crimes in Islam.[98] Other steps discussed have been reducing the number of inmates by reducing the number of offences calling for incarceration and making greater use of probation, particularly for women and children. A further proposal for reducing the prison population was to eliminate the holding of certain inmates beyond the term of their sentence when they are unable to pay off their civil debts.[99] To decrease the number of prisoners, the judiciary changed the procedure of registering the marriage with respect to dowry that based payment of the dowry on the wife's demand. The judiciary ordered Marriage and Divorce Registering Offices to change the term "*'end al-motālebeh*" (required by demand) to "*'end al-estetā'ah*" (required by ability).[100] The previous procedure considered women's dowry indispensable at any time after the establishment of marriage. According to the new procedure, a woman can demand their dowry if the husband is able to pay it. The new procedure will not let women to ask the judge to imprison their husbands if they refuse to pay for any reason. The judiciary sacrificed one of the basic and scarce rights of women in *shari`ah* law to decrease the number of prisoners. The social justification is the high amount of dowries in recent decades even among lower class families. The new procedure deprives women from one of their leverages in the family, makes the sanction of dowry almost void and leaves it inapplicable. Based on the new procedure, men can always escape paying their wives' dowry by hiding their property and disclosing wrong information about their wealth in the courts.

The situation of prisons in Iran is part of the ignorance of judiciary when it comes to the rights of human beings. Mental disorders, venereal diseases and tuberculosis in Iranian prisons were respectively three, two, and 8–10 times more than the average numbers of the whole society in this period.[101] Iran's judiciary does not recognize any rights for the prisoners: lengthy solitary confinements, deprivation of visitors, deprivation of having access to media, deprivation of walking and exercising, withholding the whereabouts of prisoners from their families, even deprivation of buying from prison's grocery[102] are only some examples of violations of prisoners' rights that are mentioned in Iran's Civil Laws.

As for the non-official detention centres where much of the prisoner abuse takes place, there were as many secret detention centres as there were secret service and military establishments combined with even non-military and non-secret service establishments, while no military or security establishment had the right to its own prison. The Head of the National Prisons Organization declared in 2001 that all non-official detention centres have now been brought under the control of his organization,[103] while 25 bloggers and web news editors were detained in these facilities in 2004.[104]

Iranian judiciary especially during Shāhrudi administration had this mission to support the counter-reform movement and stop reformers in any area. In seven steps almost all the reformers have been prosecuted and tried between 1999–2004 to break down any social, political and cultural movement and their representatives in the government.: first the most active journalists and editors, then university students, and then MPs, survey researchers, governmental officials,[105] artists, bloggers, and NGO activists.

The task of making courts as efficient as possible with respect to decreasing the weight of delay has been an urgent one. The judiciary officials in four terms of the judiciary headship in this period have tried to find substitutes for court actions in commercial arbitration, administrative boards and commissions, and justice of the peace system,[106] all remained on paper or did not go further from press conferences. Structural negation of localism and breaching the independence of the dispute settlement system from establishment to having function were the main reasons of this failure. The judiciary officials in Shāhrudi headship called this measure de-judicialization (*qazā zodāii*) of the dispute settlement.[107]

Most of the policies mentioned in the judiciary's charter for judicial reform in this period, i.e. fighting corruption in the judiciary, reform in the publicizing policies of the judiciary, and merging para-judiciary organizations in the judiciary[108]are responding to the illegitimacy crisis of the government. The judiciary has completely served the authoritarian camp in covering their corruption while they have cried for anti-corruption policies and actions. Anti-corruption campaign has been used to profile and blackmail private sector and to transfer resources to the authoritarian camp's political and propaganda machines.[109]

The judiciary officials kept supporting alternative justice. This is totally different from alternative dispute resolution. The authoritarian/traditionalist clerics who have the key roles in the judiciary do not believe in monopoly of judicial decisions and violence in the hands of the state. They have been supportive in cases which people with religious beliefs and sensations killed prostitutes[110] and individuals who committed vice,[111] although they have publicly denied this idea.[112] In their belief, the blood of dissidents who speak out and people who commit vice would be shed and God appreciate the killers.

Politicization, 1997–2006

The judiciary in this period does act as a politically motivated decision-maker and activist through which the unelected leader can exercise some degree of control over the actions of the elected bodies of government and independent groups; it is part of a congruent and collective effort of the appointed bodies to crush every independent effort directed to political and social reform, punish reform oriented officials,[113] and to make void all democratic features of elected bodies of government.[114] The judiciary has been one of the crucial instruments of the ruling clerics to limit the independent voices in the polity, helping the other factors of governmental forces like security system, police, para-military and military. Although the judiciary's direct involvement in the political arena increased tensions and decreased the level of legitimacy of the clerical rule, it contributed to the survival of the appointed bodies when the waves of democratic demands were high. This was not judicialization of the politics but the politicization of the judiciary.[115] Judicialization of politics means increase of social and political significance of the judiciary, and can only happen with highly institutionalized judiciary systems as contemporary democracies (Guarnieri & Pederzoli, 2002: 1). Judicialization does not happen in a society like Iran where judges have traditionally been subservient to the executive power and the king's court (jurist's *bait* after the Revolution). In this society the province of the courts or the judges could not expand at the expense of the politicians and the administrators and the judicial decision making methods could not spread outside the judicial power.[116]

The brutality of the para-military and militia when intelligence system could not act easily in suppressing activists was used to overcome the tensions produced by behind closed doors trials,[117] attacking the university dorms, closing the independent press, and public confessions of political activists in front of state-run TV camera. These brutal actions were based on the culture of hatred. Authoritarians have always been spreading hatred against outsiders, called secularists and liberals. They do it by demonizing and dehumanizing critics of the state and political activists. The ideological core of the state suggests that the Islamists which are simply good are at war with people who do not believe in the hegemony of *'ulamā* and are simply evil. Torture of the political activists, writers and journalists has not been an isolated incident but manifestation of hate rooted in the authoritarian reading of *shari`ah*. Hatred in Iranian prisons, formal or informal, is extricably linked with hatred increasingly fostered by almost all elements of appointed bodies of government, state-run Radio and TV channels, and major religious institutions, including rentier *marja'iyyah* and Friday prayer leaders. The judiciary officials even avoid using the word "torture" that is forbidden by the Constitution of 1979; instead, they use the word "*ta'zir*" that is a punishment in *shari`ah* framework. The nature of policies prosecuted by the Islamic state and the hierarchies deployed to carry them out makes such acts, whether called torture or *ta'zir*, likely. Torture of the prisoners and detainees in Iranian prisons by the judiciary staff or their disciplinary agents (*zābetin*) is a direct consequence of the "insider"/ "outsider" doctrine with which Khāmenei has sought to strengthen the foundation of his power. The justification for the so-called *ta'zir* with the permission of *shari`ah* arbiter is preparing prisoners to talk and confess in front of the TV camera, to softening them up. These interrogations have produced no information, other than the private aspects of prisoners' life.

Judiciary has been one of the key arbiters and manipulators, and sometimes harvesters, of this culture of hatred. Iranian judges in this era have rarely been a progressive force on the side of the individuals against the abuse of power by the ruler. All of the individual's cases against the Guardian Council, the judiciary and IRGC, for example, have been kept on file and no legal action was conducted.

Judicialization of politics happens where there is an independent judiciary, and judges try to give priority to their political cause when confronted with high politically profiled cases, and substitute their own view for those of policymakers and legislators. Politicization of judiciary, on the other hand, assumes that the judiciary does not enjoy some levels of independence from some branches of power, neither the high level of independence nor independence from the highest level of power. Where judiciary is politicized, the ruling class expands the judiciary's political role to the level of manipulating the structure of polity and sending out or bringing in some element of the polity.[118] It does not necessarily means that the courts are totally dependent on political actors. Even in authoritarian regimes, the judiciary can enjoy some form of autonomy but judicial independence, i.e. institutional guarantee and autonomy of judges in front of political branches, has to be considered a unique and peculiar feature of democracies (Guarnieri & Pederzoli, 2002: 5). The influence of political actors in the judicial arena not only happens in the political systems engaged with politicization of judiciary or judicialization of politics, but some levels of it can be found in any polity.

What has been going on Iran in this era is the use of judiciary by the Leader and his loyalists, similar to Reza Shah and his loyalists, to oppress independent institutions and groups and to make them null in the processes of decision-makings and elections. The divided sovereignty of the state does not explain politicization of judiciary whereas it usually increases the political tensions and delegitimizes the state, and does not fix the problems coming out of the duality; there was a stalemate between the elected and unelected branches of government over important policies and legislative decisions concerning survival and reform of the regime between 1997 to 2001. What explains the politicization of judiciary to oppress dissident is the ideology and strategies of the Reform Movement especially between 1997 and 2001. The Reform Movement was a non-violent movement that focused on promoting democracy, rule of law and civil society. It did not use mass mobilization to put pressure on the government. The key forces of this movement were intellectuals, journalists and lawyers. The judiciary is the best for oppressing this kind of movement. On the other hand there have been many cases of judicialization of politics in number of countries with non-divided executive systems (Shambayati, 2004: 253). The courts were not equipped to perform all the expected functions. They did not have the manpower, the tools, and the authority to be dispute settlers; they are expected to be solvers of the establishment's political problems.

Arjomand made an analytical distinction between "politicization of the judiciary" and the "judicialization of politics" (Arjomand 2003a) with the help of comparisons between the attempts by judicial organs to safeguard the political regime (e.g. sultanistic regime of Khāmenei and Kemalist regime of Turkey) and to safeguard Islamic ideological bases of the constitutional order in Turkey and Iran respectively. Brown's interesting finding (2002: p. 106) of "unexpected pockets of constitutionalist practice" within the judiciaries of the Arab world can be taken as an instance of judicialization of politics in sharp contrast to the politicization of the judiciary in the Islamic Republic of Iran in particular.

The result of politicization of the judiciary has been the clear, consistent and open violations of the Constitution. None of the journalists arrested and detained during the first wave of the press crackdown in 2000–2001 were promptly charged with a crime. Iran's Constitution requires that the authorities submit provisional charges to the competent judicial authorities within 24 hours. All political prisoners were cut off from communications for several long stretches, in some cases to six months. While in prison in early 2000 and 2001, a group of political prisoners provided secret interviews over prison telephones, passed letters to the press and international organizations through their families, and were able to pass messages to their families about the condition of other political prisoners or about their most recent encounters with their judges.[119] These testimonies, which document the invasion of privacy, threats of false prosecutions, and intimidation of writers and journalists critical of the government are typical of the experiences of the other individuals.

All trials in Iran are required to be public. According to Article 165 of the Constitution "trials are to be held openly and members of the public may attend without any restriction; unless the court determines that an open trial would be detrimental to public morality or discipline, or if in case of private disputes, both the parties request not to hold open hearing." Political and press-related cases must have a jury but the appointed bodies of government appoint the jury members for these trials from a pool of high ranking authoritarian officials. According to Article 168 of the Constitution "political and press offenses will be tried openly and in the presence of a jury, in courts of justice" but tens of newspapers are banned without any trial or in presence of a jury. The political and press cases usually involve informal sessions in chambers between judges and prisoners in which the judge urges the prisoner to "cooperate" or "confess." The prisoners are often brought into a courtroom in which they were faced with judge and complainant. In most of the press-related cases, the complainants are government officials or members of the militia. These "trials" not only violate basic due process rights but also raise the risk of the use of coerced confessions in closed sessions.[120]

Iran's judiciary has been at the core of the systematic crackdown on those who express views critical of the government. A handful of judges appointed by and accountable to the Leader define and enforce the law. The judicial system in practice violates basic due process rights at every level. These include the rights to be promptly charged with a criminal offense; have access to legal counsel; have adequate time and facilities for preparation of a defense; to be tried before a competent, independent and impartial court in a public hearing; to be able to examine the evidence and produce evidence on one's behalf; and, to have a conviction reviewed by a higher court. The violations are flagrant and systematic, and they undermine any capacity to seek remedy or justice. Responsibility for the systematic violations of due process extended to the highest levels of the judiciary. Judges in political cases often "visit" the accused in interrogation rooms and secret detention centers. There is no formal and real separation between interrogator, prosecutor, and judge.

Totally against Article 35 of the Constitution, those held for expressing their political views have been regularly denied the right to counsel. Many are told that any decision to retain counsel will reflect unfavorably on their cases. For those who did obtain counsel, many were never allowed to meet privately with their attorneys, and their attorneys were not given access to their files. During the early stages of the press crackdown, several well-known attorneys who acted as defense counsel in cases relating to journalists or editors were arrested and detained themselves. Many attorneys are now afraid to take on the cases of those held for political reasons. Defense lawyers could not carry out the most basic tasks required to act on their client's behalf. Attorneys brave enough to take freedom of expression related cases are constantly at risk of being arrested and detained, often on the charge of "disseminating lies."[121]

Although Article 164 states "a judge cannot be removed, whether temporarily or permanently, from the post he occupies except by trial and proof of his guilt, or in consequence of a violation entailing his dismissal, [and] a judge cannot be transferred or re-designated without his consent, except in cases when the interest of society necessitates it, that too, with the decision of the head of the judiciary branch after consultation with the chief of the Supreme Court and the Prosecutor General," lots of judges who has issued verdicts unpleasant for the Leader and the Head of Judiciary have been removed, transferred, and re-designated without their consent.[122]

The Guardian Council put its decisions over any oversight and litigation of individuals referred to the judiciary.[123] The judiciary negates the oversight of the parliament,[124] and considers itself only accountable to the Leader.[125] The Guardian council believes that its decisions, especially disqualification of people who want to run for public offices, are final and no one can question and investigate them.

Politicization of the judiciary has rendered it a very high level of unpredictability. The Iranian legal system, especially in political cases, is totally unpredictable. Political activists can be accused of conversion, sentenced to death, and then freed in a couple of years (Āghājari's and Eshkevari's cases[126]). The basis for predictability in judicial systems is respect for the principle of innocence until proven guilty. This is totally absent in judicial and legal culture of Iranian ruling caste and clerics.

The context of politicization is the organic links between the judiciary and the authoritarian camp. In many cases, the verdicts of the judges are reported in the authoritarian newspapers weeks before the official announcement of the verdicts.[127] This is, according to reformers, a proof of guiding the judiciary and trials from outside of this body. This organic links has provided judicial immunity for the authoritarian camp. Almost all the cases filed by the reformers against individuals in the authoritarian camp never prosecuted or tried in the courts.[128] Even in the non-political cases where one side was affiliated with the unelected bodies and their staff, the accused were acquitted or received very mild sentences.[129] The cases brought to the court under the public pressure led to acquitting people who had ties with authoritarian camp.[130] A few people from this camp, indicted and imprisoned, were treated differently in prison.[131] The judges in political cases have issued different verdicts for the same crimes.[132] The authoritarian and reformist press have been totally treated differently in each step of their trial procedures.[133] The judiciary has had two different approaches to investigating and prosecuting MPs when the majority of Majles was reformist or authoritarian.[134] The police and judiciary almost never investigated and prosecuted cases of assault, attack and aggression against dissident individuals and groups' properties and locations like newspaper buildings, NGOs' sites, and students' associations.[135] The authoritarian groups and appointed bodies of government have been above the law.[136] In politically oriented cases, only some sections of the files have been leaked to the press.[137]

The judiciary lacked a unified procedure to deal with different political and press cases. University students were tried and imprisoned for the similar actions, like demonstration, committed by teachers and workers without any judicial implications.[138] Members of religious minorities, including Sunni Muslims, are prevented from serving in the judiciary and security services. They are even deprived of having mosques in Iran's big cities.[139] In April 2004 Sunni Majles representatives sent a letter to the Leader, Khāmenei, decrying the lack of Sunni presence in the executive and judiciary branch of government, especially in higher-ranking positions in embassies, universities, and other institutions. The discriminations are supposed to facilitate politicization of different branches of government in favor of the authoritarian camp.

The politicization of judiciary has led to a systematic denial of the last remaining mechanisms for accountability in front of those individuals who were imprisoned for their political expression or opinions. Where there has been a case against dissidents, the judiciary has always been on the side of the Leader and his loyalists. The judiciary has always refused to consider cases against the Leader's loyalists or its verdict has been in their favor. Under Iranian law, those convicted of a crime, if allowed, have to appeal to a higher court within ten days of notice of their conviction, though they do not have the right to appeal.[140] In practice, however, many political prisoners have never had the chance to appeal their convictions. They are told that if they appeal, they will be sent back to prison or additional charges will be brought against them.

The reason of resort to the judiciary to silence other voices and using it as an effective force in counter-movement after 1997 is ineffectiveness of negotiation and bargain between reformists who were not in the government and the ruling authoritarians, the impossibility of wiping out dissidents while the executive power was not totally under the control of authoritarians,[141] difficulties of oppressing all young people who were engaged in a reform movement only by police, para-military and militia in a dual sovereign state, and the non-violent strategy of the reformists. The authoritarian leadership selected politicization of the judiciary as a tactic when other forms of conflict resolution, i.e. negotiation, administered rule and fighting to the scale of civil war were not possible or desirable.

The goals of politicization of judiciary in Iran is not achieved through "judicial review" that is the most effective way for judicialization of politics and it could be one of the tasks of the constitutional court; that goals are achieved through ideological profiling, prosecution and trial of the political parties,[142] political activists, writers, artists, intellectuals and journalist, torturing and pushing people to confess in front of the state-run TV cameras,[143] and active involvement in policy-making via the Expediency Council. All of these actions are directed toward undermining the partially democratic process that is based on the Constitution of 1979.

The evolution of religious authoritarianism, from charismatic to hierocratic authoritarianism and then to sultanistic authoritarianism, accentuated the intrinsic political nature of judicial decision-making. To understand the specific reasons why political intervention in judiciary occurred at different speeds and intensities in this period, as in Reza Shah era, a comparative analysis of a range of authoritarian regimes can help to identify general trends as well as the particular features of specific periods. There are four sets of elements that may directly affect the growth of political intervention in judiciary: the politicians (how they are recruited and their levels of legitimacy, authority and influence; in case of Iran, nepotism and cronism), the political system in which they operate (its structure, the means of gaining access to power, and the powers it renders to politicians; in case of Iran, upper hands of appointed bodies of government), how the political system reacts to crisis (in case of Iran, suppression and closing the public sphere), and the characteristics of the judicial system (in case of Iran, stretching the procedure, under-educated judges, instability of law, and overwhelmed by case-load).

The judges are called upon to make decisions that do no harm to what is called "establishment" (*nezām*[144]). They are usually faced a complex network of expectations and interests of the ruling class. Whenever a case has some friction with these expectations and interests it has no way to go to the courts, and it goes, the outcome is clear beforehand.

Politicization of judiciary in Iran, in both Khāmenei and Reza Shah periods, was not designed to fight poverty or crime, or improve health or education but to preserve absolute power of the leader, shah or jurist, to stop free flow of information, to interfere in the process of expansion of public sphere, and to oppress dissidence. In spite of show off for fighting against crimes and corruption, the judiciary has done almost nothing to do the job in both periods. Politicization of the judiciary guarantees that there is no way to check the way political power is exercised, there is enough control over dissidents and there in no control over the misuse of power. While the potential province of courts has been inevitably expanding as a result of the growth of both public functions and public agencies, the courts have been harnessed not to participate in the formulation, elaboration and implementation of public policies. Where judicial intervention was invoked in matters related to public health, at the end there has been a deadlock.[145] Courts are politicized but they have no way to be in the center of political debate and act as important channels for the articulation of political demands: they have almost no role in monitoring the operation of the state and the distribution of powers between the different branches and levels of government. While the political culture and social context paves the way for politicization of the judiciary, the specific context in which courts operate, the specific characteristics of the legal and social systems, the low rates of economic development and social mobility and instability of legislation and of judicial decisions do not let the courts intervene in public policy issues. The weakness of the judiciary reflects a general consent within the political and administrative classes.

After 1997, the judiciary was the heart and the backbone of the rule of the authoritarian clergy, by intimidating intellectuals,[146] political activists[147] and MPs[148] and giving cover and support to some kind of air of terror[149] into the country that was thirsty for reform. The judiciary has been closing the independent media, political parties and NGOs that reformists were trying to establish, while the demand to establish these institutions has always been increasing.[150]

The courts' anti-civil reform campaign became even more overtly hostile to the reformists after 1997. Tens of newspapers were closed and hundreds of political activists and journalists were tried—mostly behind closed door courts[151]—and imprisoned by the courts between 1997 and 2002. This process of prosecution of every political activist, intellectual and journalist were expedited after 2000.[152] In the meantime, the Islamic regime has always denied having political prisoners.[153] Over the years, thousands of reformists and other political opponents, even loyalists,[154] have passed through the jails, usually without trial or charge; even if they are charged, the charges have been repeatedly changed during the trials.[155] According to detainees' family members, Iranian civil-rights groups and international organizations like Human Rights Watch, torture is "widespread and systematic": beatings, obligatory confessions in front of state run TV, and long term solitary confinements in official prisons as well as illegal detention centers[156] staffed by various intelligence and security agencies and the Disciplinary Forces.[157] Many detainees have suffered permanent physical and psychological injuries while in detention.[158] Khāmenei has always proved himself as ready to employ maximum force to quell protest or unrest. Almost all Iranian intellectuals and political activists have been physically assaulted or harangued into fear and silence by the leader, appointed bodies like the judiciary or groups that are directly related to the leader's office.

The courts appeared to be policy-makers in political and cultural issues in this period. By closing more than 100 newspapers in only less than four years between 2000–2004 in a country that getting license for founding a press is a privilege for the insiders, arresting editors, writers and book publishers, banning movies and dramas, the judiciary has been making media policies: drawing red lines for the editors, implicitly making clear who is over critique and over the law, and declaring who can work in the media and who cannot. Iranian courts also make policies when they apply the law to new institutions like Internet cafes or financial companies.

The judiciary high-ranking officials have been very interested in having a role in all political decision-making and policy-making even in low-level matters. They have been trying to have a say in foreign and domestic policy and decision-making. The judiciary established a special committee to oversight the implementation of the Leader's policies in foreign relations[159] and to prosecute individuals who criticize National Security Council's decisions.

Some lawyers and the reformists declared this decision against the law.[160] A branch of the Revolutionary Court was given responsibility to prosecute the violators.[161] The judiciary even declared any discussion about negotiation and talks with Americans illegal.[162]

The consequences of these dilemmas are intellectual interest in law, public distrust and dissatisfaction, increase of the power of organized violent militia coming from lower classes and public disappointment. The pressure of judiciary on political activists[163] and intellectuals and their non-violent approach to politics and their belief in rule of law increased intellectual and scholarly interest in law. The Guardian Council rejected all the reformists' bills regarding due process and rule of law[164]; this process showed the Islamic reformists the challenge they have to present an interpretation of Islam consistent with human rights, democracy, and rule of law.

When Iranians in 1999 were asked "if someone's right is violated, can she/he vindicate her/his right through legal procedure," 84.9 percent of the respondents believed that the probability is low or relatively low. Among the respondents, 80.6 percent also believed that people who do not have enough money or connection, their right would be violated.[165] This militia is totally supported by the Leader's office and hence is under the protection umbrella of the judiciary. According to a survey by the Management and Planning Organization, the judiciary is the least popular public institution in Iran.[166]

Four groups are important social actors in this period. The politicization of judiciary can be seen in the way these groups are treated in the courts. Women were one of the important ones. Their activism is based on fighting for equal rights. Immediately after the Islamic Revolution the principle of equality that Iranian state insured by joining different international treaties and conventions was rejected. In ruling *'ulamā'*s view, this principle like many other democratic principles could not be applicable in a system formed by Islam, i.e. *'ulamā'*s interpretation of this religion. According to them, there is no equality between man and woman in the *sharī`ah*. In judicial affairs, the *zemmi*'s and female witness is not of an equal effect as the witness of a male Muslim.[167]

There were hundreds of female journalists and publishers active in this period. The women advocates were also instrumental in bringing back the Family Court that was disbanded after the revolution. In 1990's, eighty percent of those going to Family Court to dispute divorce and custody cases were women. There has been a big woman's lobby in Iran. There were more female members in the Sixth Parliament then there were in the US Senate at the time. Women were very active in spreading information, saying what women should know about marriage, what they should know about dowry, how the judge is giving the dowry to women and how women can try to negotiate their situation in the court. The women's movement has been instrumental is raising the age of marriage from nine to 13 years for girls and passing new laws that give divorced women better custody rights.

The Government enforces gender segregation in most public spaces and prohibits women from interacting openly with unmarried men or men not related to them; however, as a practical matter these prohibitions have loosened after 1997. Women should ride in a reserved section on public buses and enter public buildings, universities, and airports through separate entrances. Violators of these restrictions would face punishments such as flogging or monetary fines. Women were prohibited from attending male sporting events, although this restriction did not appear to be enforced universally. Women were not free to choose what they wear in public, although enforcement of rules for conservative Islamic dress eased after 1997. Women were subject to harassment by the authorities if their dress or behavior was considered inappropriate, and were sentenced to flogging or imprisonment for such violations. The law prohibited the publication of pictures of uncovered women in the print media, including pictures of foreign women. There were penalties, including flogging and monetary fines, for failure to observe norms of Islamic dress at work. The law also provided for segregation of the sexes in medical care.

Legally, the testimony of a woman has been worth only half that of a man in court. A married woman must obtain the written consent of her husband before she may travel outside the country. The law provided for stoning for adultery; however, in 2002 the Government suspended this practice. Women have the right to divorce, and regulations promulgated in 1984 substantially broadened the grounds on which a woman may seek a divorce. However, a husband was not required to cite a reason for divorcing his wife. In 1986 the Government issued a 12-point "contract" to serve as a model for marriage and divorce, which limited the privileges accorded to men by custom and traditional interpretations of Islamic law. The model contract also recognized a divorced woman's right to a share in the property that couples acquire during their marriage and to increased alimony rights. Women who remarry were forced to give up custody of children from earlier marriages to the child's father. The law allowed for the granting of custody of minor children to the mother in certain divorce cases in which the father was proven unfit to care for the child.

The legal system also discriminated against religious minorities who receive lower awards than Muslims in injury and death lawsuits and incurred heavier punishments. In 2002 the Sixth Majles approved a bill that would make the amount of "blood money" (*diyeh*) paid by a perpetrator for killing or wounding a Christian, Jew, or Zoroastrian man the same as it would be for killing or wounding a Muslim; the bill ultimately was passed by the Expediency Council in Dec. 27, 2003.[168] All women and other religious minority members, however, were excluded from the equalization provisions of the bill.

Iranian journalists, in this period, attributed a diversity of meanings to political discourse. They were active in establishing the culture and extending the literature of due process. In a country that has historically established a poor civil society, and a state that has been developing faster than market and civil society, it has been very hard for the journalists to be relatively autonomous of the state. The country has experienced with authoritarian politics, but not with cataclysms and reversals, revolution and war, reform and counter-reform, advance and retreat. These experiments span more than one century up to the turn of the millennium.

The heart of the problem for journalists remained in the political sphere: How it was possible to create a protection umbrella for journalists who were in the position of accused, defendant and prisoner in any stage of the judicial process in an authoritarian regime? Where does the Constitution and rights confine the state? How can political activists, political parties, and lawyers facilitate political transformation to this situation? Iranian journalists were more successful than ever to publicize these questions and some of their answers during the reform movement, 1997–2001. Although journalists' political orientations were more visible or less visible from one time to another, they were always relevant in one way or another. Considering this relevancy, the judiciary tried to totally crack down the independent press,[169] and control other sections of the press, even by checking the correspondents for each newspaper.[170] Governmentalization of the whole media profession was the policy of the appointed bodies of government. Iranian lawyers in press trials supported the journalists' cause.

Iranian lawyers engaged in a variety of forms in liberalizing politics.[171] Although the Iranian Bar Association has been very weak and passive, even when its members were jailed and tried by the judiciary because of doing their jobs,[172] individual lawyers became the springboard for liberalizing political sentiments in Khātami era. Although in spite of Old Regime barristers in France, they were not the architects of civil society (Halliday and Karpik, 1997: 6), they helped the reformists to canalize their grievances and demands into critical non-violent actions.[173] After the 1990's, the process of making judicial procedure more open and transparent met its limit, i.e. rule of law while interpretation of law was totally in the hands of authoritarians.

Shāhrudi's [174] team in the judiciary used their position to break down any civil society institution and eliminate intermediate associations especially institutions in the area of press, law and legal profession. But these institutions did not directly engage in politics and carried less peril for their survival. Viable civil society institutions had no protection from and against the government. The judiciary licensed 4,500 lawyers who haven't taken bar exams from the Bar Association from 2001 to 2004.[175] The judiciary's explanation was that the country needs more lawyers and the association is too elitist. Therefore, lawyers could get their license to practice from the same body that appoints judges.

Iranian lawyers never acted as collective actors who could fashion the state as well as society over a long period of time. They could not help craft a civil society and a moderate state because the state was not ready to hear that citizens had rights and that individual freedoms could exist within a moderate state, and citizens had no power to push the state to recognize these rights. They never constituted themselves as spokesmen for the public.

Campus political activism grew after June 1997 presidential election. Different governmental and pseudo-governmental institutions suppressed this activism that showed to be reflected in demonstrations and meetings. The students' tone increasingly one of anger and despondency led to rallies protesting the banning of independent press and treatment of detained students, support for dissident clerics such as Montezari, and open criticism of the political establishment, including the Leader, his appointees and the President. Groups of hooligans, including, in particular, the Ansār-e Hezbollāh, often confronted such student rallies and meetings.

Most of the leading dissident student leaders have been held in solitary confinement for months, tortured to confess being involved in what was described as activities "to overthrow the system by peaceful means." A number of them were convicted for their participation in the student demonstrations in July 1999. The perpetrators of the raid on the University of Tehran dorms, which triggered the student protests, have apparently been released, without conviction, after secret hearings because, in the words of the judge, "there were no private plaintiffs involved." In April 2001, a provincial court in Khorramābād convicted 121 persons, mainly students, but including a deputy governor of the province, of participating in "riots" there in August 2000. The unrest grew out of attacks by hooligans on a national meeting of Iranian students and the blockading of the meeting's invited speakers. As seems to be the pattern in such cases, the hooligans themselves were not charged, let alone convicted. A number of university students were detained for articles in their student newspapers deemed to be blasphemous, an offence that could draw the death penalty.[176]

Authoritarians transformed law from a *framework of* into *an instrument for* rule as a political category. The administration of law in sultanistic authoritarian regime is not held to consist in the application of rules to particular cases but to politically control the masses and secure the personal order and obedience of the subjects.[177] The tendency of the authoritarian regime in administration of justice has been to act "in accordance with substantive ideas of justice, with utilitarian [and pragmatic] considerations and in terms of reasons of state" (Weber, 1968: 268).

In Iranian judicial and legal systems not only high-level decisions are made by the political power but low level decisions and actions, if sensitive for the establishment, are also heavily and directly influenced by immediate needs of the establishment to silence any critical voice and empty the polity from any potential or active alternative. The characteristics of this system can be summarized as weak courts, chaotic decision making,[178] high level of political involvement in the activity of the judiciary, high levels of police coercion, continuous attempts at major legal reform from outside the judiciary, though unsuccessful, a legal culture heavily influenced by ideological models mixing Islamic history and the Eastern Bloc experiences, scarcity of legal literature, limited distribution of judicial opinions, interference of different courts even in the same case,[179] and scarcity of legally trained personnel. This system is very similar to Eastern Europe in late Communism and early post-Communist era. In this system, institutional decisions tend to be centralized driven by the ruling clergy.

The degree of development of special courts, like Military and Revolutionary Courts and Special Court for Clerics, is a measure of the mutual power relationship of the imperium to the strata with which it must reckon as supports of the power. Khāmenei was more concerned about the clerical dissent and increased pressure on religious opposition. Religious dissident figures and even non-clerics were usually brought before the Special Court for Clerics during Khāmenei's leadership.[180] Due to the crucial role of Revolutionary and Clerical Courts, the Military Courts have less important role in silencing the dissent compared to the Pahlavi era. It was only used for high critical cases like serial killings.[181]

The courts and supporting public institutions were increasingly considered critical to the realization of reform objectives. Judicial institutions did not hold the least promise of providing an effective check on political, economic, and cultural threats to the foundations of Iranian society. High-ranking officials of post-revolutionary Iranian judiciary have always been worried about emergence of a democratic and law-based national society. No branch of government is designed to hold political and economic actors accountable to law, or to ensure commercial and property rights and obligations. All these laws are supposed to be enforced through impartial judgment, while all the judges are appointed on the basis of being partial and loyal to the establishment and to the Leader. The policy of the judiciary has been to get rid of the non-loyal judges and recruit individuals loyal to the Leader. In 2000, 30 high-ranking judges of the Supreme Court resigned because of the policies and actions of the judiciary officials and then resignation of all of them accepted immediately.[182] Iranian courts are not independent from undue political interference; they do not maintain integrity in the face of private financial pressures, and do not operate at a high level of efficiency, especially given frequently inadequate allocations of human and financial resources.

Shari`ah mainly defines obligations and rarely deals with benefits (welfare provisions) and rights (constitutional, civil and human) while modern civil law makes a balance between obligations and duties from one hand and benefits and rights from the other. In the frame work of modern states, the emphasis has moved from the duties incumbent on a subject to the rights a citizen can demand (Bobbio, 1996: ix). *Shari`ah,* even in the age of revolutions and nation-states and even among its diverse and well educated carriers, views politics primarily from the sovereign point of view. During the transfer from one generation and one age of rights to the other,[183] the carriers of *shari`ah* has totally been away from theoretical challenges of positive and natural rights, and their societies were rarely disposed to relevant developments. These benefits and rights are historically associated with the rise of modern nation-states and *shari`ah* is usually considered over-the-state or a pre-modern state phenomenon. It channels behavior (criminal law but not environmental law), and provides background rules (contract, and commercial law, but not corporate law). Modern civil law usually considers the public aspects of behaviors and contracts that extend to what is not usually considered in contractual relationships from a private law consideration. *Shari`ah* does not define the scope, powers and limitations of such elements of governance as the obligatory institutions of public agencies. *Shari`ah* is not established in a way to include the complex of constitutional provisions, like judicial review and constitutional court (Ackerman, 1997), bodies of legislative enactments, such as codes and statutes, and the continually developing body of judicial doctrine. *Shari`ah,* as it is represented by its conservative and reformist believers, rejects the concept of natural or inherent rights, unless we say every right that *shari`ah* considers for individuals is natural and the other rights are not. While some aspects of state positivism, like this idea that the ultimate lawmaking power lay in the state and state monopoly on lawmaking and exerting violence (Merryman, 1969: 19, 22) are agreed upon by the jurists who believe in the

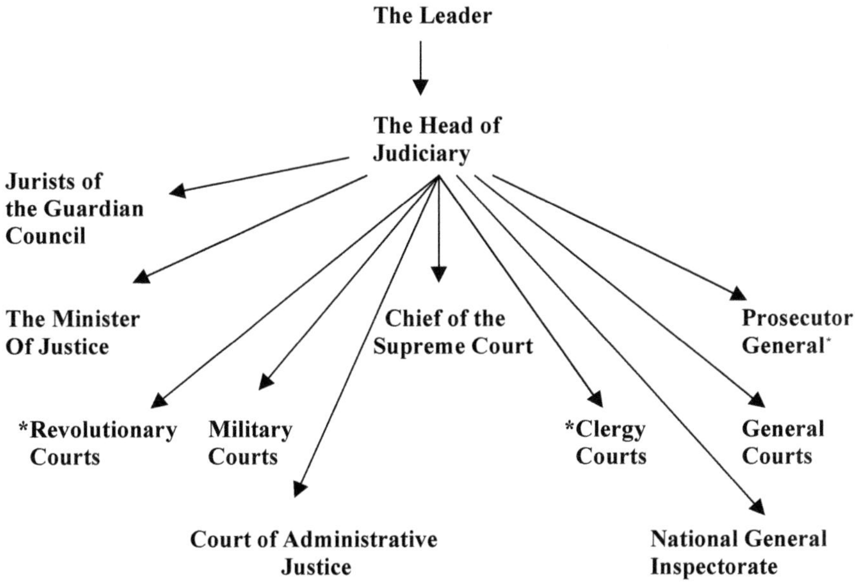

Fig. 6.1. The Chart of Iran's Judiciary, 1989–2006

* There is nothing about Revolutionary Court and Clergy Court in the constitution

theory of guardianship of jurist, the idea that law is of divine origin did not lose its vitality among them.

As it can be seen in the chart (Fig. 6.1), every power in the judiciary in this period is concentrated in the Head of Judiciary and through him, in the hands of Leader. This judiciary that lacks any elected officials with judges who can be transferred or removed at any time by the Head of the Judiciary and other high ranking officials of the judiciary (Article 164 of the Constitution) cannot be independent.

Iranian judiciary is formally independent (Article 156 of the 1989 Constitution) but merely from the elected bodies of government. All the high-ranking officials of the judiciary including its head are directly and indirectly appointed by the leader (Article 157 of the 1989 Constitution) without any formal input from the elected President or Parliament; the minister of justice is chosen by the President from among candidates nominated by the head of the judiciary (Article 160 of the 1989 Constitution); the parliament cannot draft judicial laws (Article 158 of the 1989 Constitution); the Parliament has really no power of oversight over the judiciary and all the judicial policies are dictated by the leader; and judges are regularly removed from the post they occupy, transferred or re-designated without their consent when their decrees in political files are not satisfying for the establishment.[185] This non-elected body of government has a number of political functions like representing on the Council for the Revision of the Constitution (Article 177), membership of its head in the country's national Security Council, and membership of its representatives in the Press Monitoring and Political Parties Commissions. The judiciary that is seen as the enforcer of the ideological cause of the Islamic regime in the preamble of the Constitution cannot be neutral in political tensions, and has never been neutral.

There was a gulf between the judiciary officials and judges that most powerful ones were clerics on one side, and the society's secular elite on the other. Law students, lawyers, and even some subordinate judges were mostly progressive in their political orientation and have mostly studied the European laws that form the framework, but not the content, of most sections of Iran's legal system. The presiding judge, on the other hand, was mostly a cleric with expertise in the Shi'ite version of Islamic law or an ex-prosecutor or ex-law enforcement staff with which the legal system has been sprinkled since the Revolution. In spite of recruiting thousands of clerics graduated from seminaries, the judiciary had no program to train these people according to the needs of judiciary. There is a major for legal studies in Qom Seminary[186] but legal education is not a requirement in recruiting judges.

The judgments, rendered in Iran's Criminal Courts, illustrate the clerics' perspective and lifestyle. Boys and girls are usually arrested and fined for allegedly making flirtatious faces at each other or taking hands while walking along the street. In many judgments, the clerical magistrates have found defendant guilty based not on any particular law, but on their own discretions.

Law applying organs like the judiciary and the executive power have had four approaches to the Constitution and other regulations:

1) To ignore some of the articles with this justification that the time for enforcing those articles has not arrived; this means that enforcing the law is up to the government.
2) To declare that a general rule does not apply in a given case; this means that the administrative or judicial organ is authorized to invalidate a general rule for a concrete case, though the rule remains valid and can be applied in other cases.
3) To pick or prioritize some of the articles over others when there is contradiction between different articles of the Constitution; this means that different law-applying organs may have different

opinions with regard to the constitutionality of an article of the constitution or a statute.

4) To pass on or reject the legality of ordinances.

The Constitution only recognizes the Guardian Council to review conformity of the parliament's bill with Islam and the *shari`ah,* to interpret the Constitution and to review the constitutionality and legality of statutes,[187] and the Parliament to interpret the ordinary laws (Arts. 98 & 73). The Guardian Council has often reviewed or interpreted statutory and ordinary laws and even ordinances and ratifications of the cabinet and governmental councils.[188] The Constitution itself does not grant to every citizen the right to make an application to a constitutional court. The General Prosecutor is neither in charge of the protection of the Constitution. Dissolving the office of general attorney and district attorney, centralizing all powers of the judiciary in one appointed official and making all the highest offices of the judiciary appointed positions, the revision of the Constitution in 1989 facilitated the rise of a constitutional system in which political expediency trumps law, rather than the other way around.

The Guardian Council and the Expediency Council did not confine in the realm of negative legislation[189] and settling disputes between the Parliament and the Guardian Council (Article 112).[190] The Expediency Council has passed many bills that were not included in the disputes.

In Iran, there were other courts besides the ordinary courts, especially administrative courts which had to apply executive circulars. Hence there was a contradiction between administrative and ordinary courts. The Iranian courts, even the higher ones, never were in the position to annul a statute or invalidate an act as unconstitutional. There was no judicial control over the legislative power. The control of the Guardian Council is ideological and juridical, not judicial. The Guardian Council does not usually interfere with the judicial affairs because the judiciary like the Council is directly under the control of the Leader. The inclusion of six lawyers in the Council does not change its ideological and juridical nature to a court-like institution because 1) the Islamic jurists have upper say in reviewing the statutes, and 2) they are indirectly appointees of the head of the judiciary and the Leader, and they are not there because of their professional career as judges, and 3) the most important one, determination of conformity with Islam and the Shari'a is a prerogative of the religious jurists.

Although there was no special jurisdiction for high status groups like the burghers of a city, the nobles or the commoners in Muslim judicial system, the Islamic regime established a special jurisdiction for clergy,[191] although unconstitutional. In this system, no distinct social class did theoretically enjoy any judicial privileges. In this era, *qāzi* was not the sole judicial authority to which any and all litigations were submitted: the violations of law in business world like hoarding, overcharging, and swindling are tried in executive courts that are not part of the judiciary; the prosecutions in political and press cases are not under the control of judiciary officials; the leaders' office controls all the procedure.

The most important development in the judicial system in this era is the rise of "arbitrary justice" (*'edālat-e khodsarāneh*) and its recognition by the judiciary. That was, in a sense, the continuation of revolutionary justice of early 1980's.This kind of justice is based on one of the ordinances of Shi'ite *feqh* where it says that true believers can kill people who deserve to be murdered if they have license from a *mujtahed*.[192] Mohamamd Taqi Mesbāh Yazdi[193] is the most famous supporter of this ordinance.[194] The perpetrator should only pay the blood money to the family of the slain. According to supporters of this ordinance, the monopoly of violence does not belong to the state and each and every believer can enforce *shari`ah* laws.[195] The para-military loyalists of the regime are the judge, prosecutor and executioner of these underground courts at the same time. They have always been supported by the leader[196] and judiciary and, never punished for their crimes.[197] This is totally different from 'politicization" or political use of courts; political use of the courts is to use the judiciary to suppress the dissidents by long term prisons or making them to confess in TV programs to public support, while obstinate justice has basically nothing to do with the judiciary and if discovered, judiciary has to play with it to the point of acquitting the perpetrators. When the regime cannot publicly prosecute its dissidents due to duality in the polity or fear of public uprising, obstinate justice is the solution. In latter case, the judiciary has to confirm the suppression of the dissidents and non-conformists by para-military forces and to protect the violators of the law by resort to *shari`ah* ordinances, while in the former one, it is the judiciary itself that violates the law to protect powerful politicians.

Three famous cases are the serial killings of intellectuals and political activists, serial killings of prostitutes in Mash-had,[198] and serial killings of people who are not considered obedient to Islamic rules in Kerman, all by hooligans and thugs related to clerics. In each case, the argument of the killers, all "true-believers" in clerical establishment, was one of the *shari`ah*'s ordinances that true-believers can kill the sinners and delinquents whose blood may be shed with immunity. The killers are responsible to prove this characteristic in the killed after committing the action (crime) (Article 295, section 2 & Article 226, Islamic Punishment Act of 1991). The regime uses this kind of justice to get rid of its dissidents and non-conformists and increase its legitimacy among its loyalists- in short, political and social control, while it is in total contradiction with Articles 32, 36 and 156 of the Constitution and Article 217 of the Criminal Procedural Law. This justice denies the total authority of the state in enforcing the law and violence over its citizens. This act belongs to the pre nation-state era.

There are a variety of values underlying the discourse of law and society in this period. Authoritarians have been explicit about the values they pursue and how they determine which to privilege when they conflicted with one another. They do so not to maintain their own accountability, but to enable people who are benefited from the Islamic regime to consider adoption of these tools to determine whether they share authoritarian judgments balancing these values. The tool set they have designed is not flexible and cannot be implemented in any number of ways that does not permit organizations to make their own determinations of priorities and balance suited to their particular philosophies and needs.

Legal resolution of value conflicts permits the dominant social group to articulate a vision of the political community's collective identity and value. The emphasis on a community's construction of identity suggests that regulations may nevertheless prove beneficial in creating social stability and facilitating the formation of group values and interests. The institutional structures, consisting not only of the organization of the courts and alternative disputing forums but also of the infrastructure surrounding courts, merely represent official value system and ignore alternative value systems.

The development of legal theory in the second decade of the Islamic Republic was dominated by the old struggle between the common doctrine of the society, and articulate doctrine of the ruling clerics, claimed to be the Islamic tradition and *shari`ah*. Enforcing almost all *shari`ah* laws in spite of public disagreement is for strengthening the social bonds between authoritarian constituency and preventing their collapse under public pressure.

In 2000's the regime increased cases of public hangings and public floggings after the re-election of President Khātami, and then backed away from enforcing the harshest manifestations of *shari`ah* law like stoning and public flogging.[199] The ruling clerics didn't change the laws because they thought they were outdated or ineffective; they stopped enforcing them because of all the international pressures regarding the judiciary. All the laws the clergy threw out of the window immediately after the Revolution made a come back in a way or another, although mangled and disfigured; where there are procedures governing civil and penal codes, they are usually replicas of pre-1979 legal system.

In the Law of Retribution of 1982, as the core principle of *shari`ah* law and its symbol for Iranians, the decision to punish is left to the victim, rather than a court, which represents society as a whole. The Reformers believe that these ancient ideas of vengeance and harsh physical punishments don't belong in a modern state. Basically an eye for an eye and a tooth for a tooth policy gives victims of serious crimes or their relatives, the right to demand punishment or restitution in the form of blood money, where government has no other institutions of punishment. In this system, the punishments are often fixed but can vary regarding the status or gender of the victim and perpetrator. The case of a father killing his son is an example of this legal system. According to one interpretation of the Islamic law, the father is immune from the death penalty because he has killed his own flesh and blood, or in other words the father has ultimate authority over his children and he can do whatever he wants. Here we can pose the very unconventional question as to whether or not the government should play a role in bringing justice by treating the father like any other criminal. In other words, what is the role of the public or society in this particular case? When there is no nation state to protect individuals' rights and father has ultimate authority, father killing can be a norm.

In Iran's courts in this period and other period discussed in this study there is no role for the public. According to the Constitution, jury can have presence only in press and political trials. The second case has never executed and the Guardian Council rejected a bill regarding the presence of jury in political trials passed in the Sixth Majles. The press court in this period even did not care about the jury[200] that is basically appointed by the appointed bodies of government.[201] There is no way for the ordinary people to be a member of the jury in courts that review press cases.[202] After every thing published in the reformist newspapers that authoritarian did not like, the judiciary expected the editors in chief to write a public letter of confession[203]; the judiciary in this period has a derogatory policy toward activists to belittle those who criticize the establishment, especially the rule of the Guardian.

It has been very difficult for Iranian reformers to frame an argument for their cause based on alternative value systems. Iranian campaigns for freedom and democracy use an Iranian vernacular -civil liberties, civil rights, constitutional rights- not the international language of human rights. There is no such thing as the entrenched individualism of human rights in the Iranian and Islamic law and culture; its focus on protecting individual human beings is not in the Iranian grain. Even the Iranian reformers have preferred the limited language of civil or constitutional rights to avoid the inclusion of the human rights literature.

Iranian system of judicial administration has been becoming increasingly litigious-"i.e. individuals and groups are choosing more often than ever to resolve their differences within formal processes and structures rather than through informal and personal bargaining and compromise" (Dubois, 1982: 3). The increased caseloads of the courts, especially in the area of economic transaction, partially testify this phenomenon.[204] The judiciary had no method to divert these cases away from the courts by the availability and attractiveness of several non-adjudicative methods and forums for dispute resolution. Alternative dispute resolutions have been introduced to overcome the pressure of this phenomenon. This litigious society and failure of the judiciary to confront with it in a way or another, both, are telling us about how society is transferred to a new phase of social structure and how the state is incompetent to understand that and react to it. Both institutional structure and the perception about the law affected the huge flow of disputes to the courts.

Promised Unimplemented Reforms

There is a general unfitness of state judicial organizations to the needs of the times in an age of tremendous social and cultural forces. Even the authoritarian[205] camp felt the need for a competent judiciary. The development in the judiciary, in response to backlogs, lengthy trials and delays,[206] has not been effective due to the discrepancy between the public idea of justice and current practice. According to the public job satisfaction surveys (not by the judiciary), the judiciary is at the bottom of the list[207] in the eye of public opinions.[208] The judiciary closed down all the independent survey centers and has published the results of surveys run by itself that all are in favor of the judiciary.[209] The leader and his appointed bodies never wanted to accept popular dissatisfaction with administration of justice. There was no endeavor from authoritarian faction to convince the society that the judiciary is effective; there was also no endeavor, other than political rhetoric, from the reformers to convince the society that existing legal system was archaic. The judiciary did not even have the capacity to draft judicial bills (Shāhrudi, 2001b: 11). The Head of the Judiciary declared the judiciary as a ruined institution in his first speech in the judiciary.[210] The reformers did not present any policy or plan to carry courts and procedure from obscure, wasteful, and non-intrinsic methods to a system that stands as a model of administrative efficiency and responsibility in the region.

Iranian judiciary during Shāhrudi's term, starting 1999, offered a list of legal reforms that most of them had never been implemented. The function of these declared reforms was window dressing for foreigners when they contacted the judiciary for making reports. The first and long-promised one was re-establishment of the public prosecutor office (*dādsetāni*) which could reduce the absolute discretion that judges have had in the court room, including in most cases being judge and prosecutor and, in some cases, jury and defence counsel as well. That draft legislation was approved by the cabinet and Majles Judicial Affairs Commission in March 2000 and late June 2000 respectively and was introduced on the floor of the Majles in early July 2000.[211] It was passed in Oct. 20, 2002.[212] In a sense, this could be considered as Shāhrudi's direct response to the failure of Yazdi's Islamicization. Even after the passing of Amendment to Revolutionary and General Courts Establishment Law of 2002 to re-establish public prosecutor office, the judiciary could not establish these offices even after three years in all provinces[213] due to shortage of personnel and budgetary problems.[214]

The second promised reform was the amendment of the punishment provisions concerning defaulted loans (approved in Sep. 20, 1998).[215] Many individuals convicted based on Article 13 of Financial Conviction Law of 1993 remain in jail after having served their conviction, being unable to pay back the underlying debt. This practice has apparently been so widespread [216] that the group has become the second largest category of prison inmates.[217]

The third and only fully implemented reform was licensing the lawyers by the judiciary, totally against the will of Iran's Bar Association who wanted to protect its independence and issue the license for lawyers.[218] According to Amendment 187 of the Third Economic Development Program Bill (approved on April 6, 2001 in the parliament), the judiciary may license the law school graduate to establish legal consultancy institutions. This judiciary interpreted this amendment as the green light to do the traditional job of bar associations, i.e. giving bar exam to law school graduates and, if successful, qualify them as lawyers. According to Seyyed Hussein Mar'ashi, the Deputy of the Head of Judiciary, "undertaking the law practice affairs in general is the policy of the judiciary"[219] and hence the Sixth Majles bill to nullify this amendment[220] was rejected by the Guardian Council.[221] The judiciary administrations in post-Revolutionary Iran did not trust any independent legal organization and always declared that these organizations are not I.R.I-friendly.[222] The judiciary has always wanted to be the only source that issues the license of lawyers in both Pahlavi and I.R.I. regimes. This development follows on the other encroachments that have occurred on the autonomy of the Bar, including control over who stands for election to the Bar Association Council, the disciplining of members of the Bar and indeed the "suitability" of all applicants for admission to the Bar.

The fourth reform that was persistently pursued by the judiciary officials and had almost no result with respect to decreasing backlogs was the introduction of what is known in some other cultures as alternative dispute resolution (ADR), i.e. the provision of reconciliation/mediation facilities to remove certain types of cases from the court and expedite their settlement.[223] This reform was approved by the Parliament as the Article 189 of Third Developmental Plan Law of 2001.[224] It was supposed to reduce the backlog in court logs that exists in this period, decrease the number of inmates and expedite dispute resolution (2001).[225]

The fifth project was the establishment, with the cooperation of UNICEF, of a system of juvenile courts. In spite of allocating a very small section of Procedural Law of General and Revolutionary Courts of 1999 to the juvenile delinquency cases and designating some branches of General Courts to these cases, the judicial system and judges have been ignoring the provisions that take these cases into special consideration.[226] The structure of General Courts leaves no place for Juvenile Courts. The main issue here is the definition of the term "juvenile": the judges usually consider the *shar'i* definition of this term while most of the lawyers and legal communities in Iran and abroad take the legal definition into consideration. The Article 49 of Islamic Penal Law exempts children of penal liabilities and leaves the definition of childhood to *shari`ah*. The Article 1 of the Amendment to Article 1210 of Civil Code of 1991 considers 15 and 9 as the ages of *shar'i* maturity for males and females respectively while the age of legal maturity in most of the national and international laws-including the UN Convention on the Rights of Child that Iran is also a signatory to it- is 18. This is based on most famous interpretations of *shari`ah* in Shi'ite schools of law.

A sixth project concerned the disciplining of judges, i.e. to treat more seriously any infringement by judges of the provisions of the law.[227] This project did not consider the apparent blatant disregard by at least a few judges of the instructions set out in the matter of pre-trial treatment of suspects. The processing of complaints by the families of political and intellectual detainees against Judge Sa'id Mortazavi and Judge Hasan Ahmadi Moqaddas[228] never went before the Tribunal. Mahmoud Hāshemi Shāhrudi reported that 40 judges, clerks and middle-men had been suspended in 2000[229]; in 2003, he reported that 300 judges have been removed between 1999 and 2004[230]; no one related to political and press trials. Iranian judiciary has always grappled with restoring confidence.

Other reforms mentioned by the judiciary were the re-introduction of *res judicata*,[231] a concept that had been abandoned at the time of the Revolution as "having lost its value," and the reduction of the cases being referred back by the Supreme Court for a new hearing.[232] Another promised reform, only to foreigners, was legislation to narrow the definition of *mohāreb* (waging war on God) to those acts involving the use of firearm.[233]

This never happened. This concept is a very dangerous weapon in the hands of the judicial officials that, while only occasionally invoked, has hung over the heads of all those advocating change.

Prohibition of execution of individuals under 18 years old[234] passed by the parliament in July 2004 (later vetoed by the Guardian Council), and banning stoning women in January 26th 2003[235] were other reforms that the judiciary promised to follow under the pressure of Europeans, most of them never accomplished.[236] Even after the prohibition of execution of individuals under 18, the Judiciary has executed individuals under 18.[237] Other than execution, individuals under 18 years old that are convicted for other crimes have been amputated.[238]

Development of the judiciary was more important than reform for Shāhrudi's administration. The Head of the Judiciary and other officials usually talked about judicial development and not judicial reform. What the judiciary officials mean by development is authority (Shāhrudi, 2001a: 22). The main agenda of the judiciary in Shāhrudi's term is to extend the authority of the judiciary by including judicial review to the list of responsibilities of the judiciary, expansion of its supervising and inspecting authority, having its own enforcing and prosecuting organization (judicial police) (Shāhrudi, 2001a: 28–29), and claiming more independence for the judiciary in general and for the judges in particular (Shāhrudi, 2001a: 28). For including judicial review, Shāhrudi points out to Article 167 of the Constitution where it says "in case of the absence of any such [codified] law, he has to deliver his judgment on the basis of authoritative Islamic sources and authentic *fatāva;* he, on the pretext of the silence of or deficiency of law in the matter, or its brevity or contradictory nature, cannot refrain from admitting and examining cases and delivering his judgment." There are always some spaces for the judges to interpret the law since gaps remain despite and perhaps because of the growing number of laws especially in civil law tradition. As Kelson has pointed, judicial decisions are not and can never be purely declaratory of the law (Guarnieri & Pederzoli, 2002: 5). Another Article of the Constitution that is referred to for justification of judicial review by the judiciary is Article 161 where it says "the Supreme Court is to be formed for the purpose of supervising the correct implementation of the laws by the courts, ensuring uniformity of judicial procedure, and fulfilling any other responsibilities assigned to it by law, on the basis of regulations to be established by the head of the judicial branch.." For ensuring the conformity of judicial procedures, the Supreme Court sometimes has to undertake the same function as judicial review. According to Shāhrudi, the decisions of the Supreme Court regarding unified procedures are as reliable as law. He also believes that the jurisdictions of Administrative Justice

Court and General Inspection Organization should be increased to include substantial matters other than formal ones (Shāhrudi, 2001a: 40).

The causes for mentioned reforms were high level of public grievances, more concentration and centralization of power, and ideological control. Legal experts evaluate integrity by reference to disciplinary systems, codes of ethics, or the number of complaints launched. Iranian judiciary official figures reduced judicial reform to efficiency; in their view, judicial reform is understood as annual rates of disposition (how many cases in; how many out), and the operational systems utilized (court and case management for event tracking and not accountability).

The new leader's team in the judiciary tried to get rid of backlogs with destroying the institution of due process and general attorney, while keeping the title. They drafted a new bill for civil procedure, and the fourth Majles that was shaped by vast disqualifications of Islamic left nominees passed it. This resolution called for restructuring of the courts so that they might reliably defend the interests of the state. They viewed case-by-case prosecution and adjudication as a process that is too rigid, inflexible, insular, incremental, and limited to rely on in designing and implementing public policies. In this wave of reform, there was nothing about legal reform, ensuring supremacy of law, and protection of citizens' rights. Ideas like increased training for judges, attorneys, and law student, internship, more assistance for judges in the form of court-appointed experts, special social-science masters, or specially trained law clerks, and formal structures to provide the courts with reliable syntheses and analyses of contemporary social-science findings were absent.

The judiciary was unable to adjust the competing interests that emerged during periods of rapid social change. They were also unable to think about and implement alternative processes like mediation and arbitration to divert and resolve some of the disputes that would otherwise end up in court. Mediation and arbitration have proved to be of some value as alternatives to courts (Sander, 1979).

Lawyers could not do anything to decrease the backlogs by, for example, directing clients toward negotiated settlements rather than to force resolution of disputes in the adversarial setting of the courts. They were not considered as colleagues in the judicial process by the judiciary to expect their help. According to Amendment 128 of the Criminal Procedural Regulation of 1999, lawyers can be present in primary investigations if permitted by the judge. Judges in the judicial procedure had become agents of conciliation and compromise in millions of cases, especially on economic and commercial disputes, rather than neutral arbiters of disputes between theoretically irreconcilable adversaries. This volume of cases had made the judicial process too slow, expensive, and in some areas inaccessible to large numbers of people.

The other reason for case overload has been the multi-functionality of courts in Iranian social and political structure, intensified in post-revolutionary era. Iranian courts have been being asked to perform a number of functions other than dispute resolution, including extensive public policymaking, involvement in resolving broad political, economic and cultural issues, political campaigning and administration.

The judiciary in this era is part of an institutional package to socially control the society and individuals in a totalitarian way. The judicial reform, authoritarian/totalitarian style, is headed to totally control any individual in any personal and private matter. The strategy for totalitarian control can be seen in 1) the circular of the vice police regarding sexual segregation, dress code, having pets, and broadcasting music in public[239] totally supported by the judiciary, 2) the use of Basij forces by the judiciary as its authorized executive agents and overseers[240] and then establishment of Social Intelligence Organization (Sāzmān-e Hefazat-e Ejtemā'i) whose mission is to gather information in neighborhoods, factories, universities, schools, seminaries and any other public spheres on people's personal and private behaviors to help judiciary to fight against vice in the society,[241] 3) checkpoints all around the country for illegal checking of cars and individuals[242]- usually looking for music and video cassettes, CDs, DVDs, alcoholic drinks, and non-authorized intimate relationships- that are parts of the ideological machine of control, and 4) transfer of authority to regulate licensing of NGOs from the executive power (the Supreme Administrative Council) to the judiciary.[243]

6.5 CHALLENGES AND DILEMMAS: INTERFERENCE, CORRUPTION, AND DELAY

Although both Yazdi and Shāhrudi headships in the judiciary accompanied with serious efforts to make the judiciary more effective, while making advantage of independence from elected bodies of government, i.e. executive and legislative branches, they totally failed in implementation of the promised reforms. They both had every support from the leader as his appointees and had no problem in increasing their budgets or passing their bills in the parliament but it could not produce an effective judiciary.

There was no commitment to a sustained and all-embracing reform. Iranian judicial system from 1989 has made no commitment to different areas of substantive political and economic reforms that are the bases for a full-fledged reform in Iranian society. Clerical authoritarian political regime sought to consolidate the power of appointed bodies of government and eliminate the electoral aspects of elected bodies through disqualifications, vetting progressive bills, and profiling for activists to deprive them from active participation. The authoritarian regime is totally against popular elections, more accountable and transparent public service, and the effectuation of domestic human rights protections. The reform movement in late 1990's was totally unsuccessful in pursuing its democratic and accountability causes. The rentier system of allocating resources based on ideological-kinship bonds have led to an economy in service of actors who have access to powerful agents in the polity. Different administrations have not loosened their grips on economic systems, have not embraced a freer marketplace, and have not recognized a broader range of real and intellectual property rights. In pursuit of these hostilities toward democracy, human rights, judicial accountability, rule of law, and free knowledge-based economies, the clerical-authoritarian regime has generated an enormous amount of grievances and suffering in the public. The Guardian Council vetoed all new substantive law regarding civil and constitutional rights, political justice reform, joining international treaties like Women's Rights Conventions, and press law reform, passed by the Sixth Parliament. The judiciary has always supported the authoritarians with regard to these issues. The judiciary emphasized on executing *shari`ah* law and in executing the ordinances of Islam did not even take the conditions into accounts (Shāhrudi, 2001b: 12).

This context of consolidation of political regime and standing against any legal reform led to persistent failures in institutional performance. The judiciary during the rule of Khāmenei developed to be one of the most dangerous branches of government; it was intertwined with the politico-military structure based on mafiacracy to do the missions ordered to it. Iranian courts have been fragile political institutions. The more resilient political, economic, and cultural forces easily undermine the effectiveness of these courts. Iranian judiciary is well-funded, supported, and overprotected compared to other branches of the government, but it is under-trained, politically motivated and directed from outside in each and every critical verdict.

The judiciary was totally incapable to answer new demands of the population in post-war situation. As courts became more important in political control[244] beside social control that is the persistent function of the judiciary, the incentives to influence them also grew, and illegal interference persisted. In Iran, every court of the judiciary that is not already occupied by the loyal agents of the Iranian ruling caste, even the Supreme Court, remains vulnerable to political intimidation, acts and threats of violence, replacement and enticingly large bribes. Bribes are considered necessary to advance or defend claims successfully. Iranian style political control not only resort to existing norms to distinguish permitted behavior from the forbidden but also based on building new norm for the society to privilege some segments of the society over others.[245] As far as the Islamic regime cannot govern long by brute force alone, courts and law are supposed to affect the regime legitimation and consolidate the clerical rule.[246]

There is no survey conducted on the issues related to the judiciary. Two leading survey institutions which usually conducted surveys on political and governmental issues, one public and the other one private, were charged for selling information to foreigners and closed by the judiciary in 2002. In some interviews conducted by the author, the majority of respondents indicated that they had bribed judicial officials and all of them said that it was almost impossible to get a quick and fair judgment without monetary influence. In sum, the law that proscribes corruption has profoundly limited effects on the market incentives for bribery.

There is almost no implemented law regarding the rights of Iranian citizens to impose new burdens on courts. The Guardian Council vetoed all the new bills of the Sixth Parliament, which were supposed to create new rights and new forms of legally cognizable claims and disputes.

Case filings have been on the rise because of no security in financial and monetary markets and lack of alternative ways of settling disputes; the number of bounced bank checks in a period between 1994 and 2000 have been 11.5 millions. This number was only 200 thousands in 1993.[247] The judiciary has been following the policy of de-criminalizing bounced checks[248] and transferring the responsibility of bouncing to the banks.[249] The judiciary has also been trying to de-judicialize dispute settling to get rid of around 4–5 millions cases filed every year.[250]

In spite of establishment of General Court with the mission to decrease caseloads, courts are falling still further behind. The number of cases filed has been increasing between 11 to 13 percent every year,[251] while the population increase rate has been around 1.8 percent in the 1990's and 2000's. The number of cases has been increasing at a rate of 100 thousands every year. When courts receive cases, and cannot resolve them, leave the remainder for subsequent years of court work or eventual abandonment by the parties. In September 2000, the Civil Court with fourteen judges assigned to civil matters (beyond small causes) for the entire city were hearing cases filed between 1986 and 1990. In Iran, disposition times increased from 1981 to 1993 by 85% in part because of changes in the economy. Between 1987 and 1997, the number of civil cases in the courts doubled from over 1.8 million to over 3.9 million, then to 5 million in 2003[252] and 7 million in 2005.[253] The judiciary has been overwhelmed by the new demand for its services.

The failure to satisfy minimum human rights standards in the administration of criminal justice has been common. Pretrial detention and the use of torture have been extremely widespread. Zero tolerance for criticizing the leader and his appointed bodies, strong security measures, limited representation for the poor, weak forensic tools, prolonged detention without an early hearing by a judicial officer, kidnapping political activists in the streets, unofficial prisons, and the ease with which common people become insensitive to inflicting pain on others each contribute to the continued use of physical and psychological coercion.

The causes of this common failure are deeply systemic. The interference in the judiciary by the social and political forces is attributable to three major factors: strong incentives, weak disincentives, and ample opportunity. The incentives in support of illegal influence of judicial behavior are strong. Weak terms of judicial employment, including low salaries, politicized appointment, transfer, or promotion systems, insecure terms of office or tenure, and limited forms of economic and personal security have increased the need to seek illegal monetary payments and to avoid political affronts. Frequently the disincentives are equally weak. Vague ethical norms, the gap between ethics and law in Shi'ite legal tradition, a poorly regulated and fragmented body of legal professionals, weak monitoring capacity, corrupted review systems, and ineffectual prosecution and enforcement substantially sustain systemic impunity for illicit practices. Opportunities for corruption remain unchecked by an opaque procedural system of limited joint communication, reason-giving, or publicity, a slow and fragmented process with multiple steps and appeals, and a state monopoly on the resolution of legal disputes that puts too much discretion in too few hands.

Backlog and delay derive from a lack of accountability, discipline, versatility, and finality. Court administration system usually lose track of matters, events, records, and evidence.[254] Case processing is discontinuous, fragmented, protracted, and excessively permissive of adjournments, provisional ex parte procedures, and appeals. Settlements are rare, and few alternatives to trial are available or well developed. Litigation is still viewed as the primary means of dispute settlement (not to mention dispute escalation). Finality is elusive. Appellate rights are not permissive, but usually allowed by negotiations. According to Marvi, Deputy of the Head of Judiciary between 1999 and 2004,[255] in 70 percent of the appealed cases, the verdicts are changed.[256] Cases linger beyond the life span of the original parties, thus triggering additional hearings to satisfy notice and process requirements for new rights-holders directly affected by the judgment. Provisional and post-judgment remedies for failure to comply with final judgments are additionally inadequate to deter non-compliance.

In this case, there is a significant difference between the expectations and actual performance of judicial institutions and the gap may be growing as a result of quick normative, and slow institutional, change.

The legal commitments of reformist camp in the executive and legislative branches of power during 1997–2004 did not set in motion a process of democratization, vindication of civil, constitutional and human rights, and rationalization, due to inadequate investments in institutional development. As law took on greater importance in this period, legally cognizable claims in the public sphere increased, but less people come to the courts expecting justice. The only phenomenon that flattens this higher demand of justice is the negative feedback of continued failure of the judicial system: if litigants distrust the system or find it ineffective, they will pursue private, extralegal strategies or simply abandon their cases or lump their legal injuries.

The Reform Movement could not push the judiciary to achieve substantive commitments; commitment to institutional reforms seemed impossible to achieve. Even uniform imperfections in enforcement were in the horizon of long-term judicial change, taking into account the importance of primary agents in the judicial and legal process. Individual incentives and practices of law and order enforcement were in conflict with those of the reformers.

Political reformers failed to see the functional justifications for the phenomena they were criticizing. For example, control of judicial appointments in the hands of the Leader (anti-independence) established in post-Khomeini Iran restructured an entirely venal and politically motivated judiciary. The independence of judiciary from the executive branch was only a cover to give the whole control of this branch to the office of the Leader. Corruption in the judiciary flourished as 1) a response to the inefficiencies of tenured under-trained and ideologically selected judges, and 2) invasive, mafiacratic, and extortionist office of the Leader.

Delay, in this system, was not a sign of working hard to get it right without cutting corners. Adjournment culture developed in the early 20th century because it was really hard to get to court on time when one had to travel great distances and notification systems were poor. Delays as a reality of the judicial system in this period[257] can also be attributed to incompetence, the economic conditions of rural and urban life, technical complexities in judicial process,[258] and incompetence of judges due to ideological and political selection of judiciary officials and judges.

Problems persist because they serve the interests of powerful politicians, monopolists, and professional elites including some lawyers. Iranian politicians did not appreciate the benefits of limits on their own power. Rich families and corporations may prefer to purchase justice than to subject them to impartial decision-making. Lawyers paid by court appearance have had strong incentives to protract litigation into a series of fragmented, discontinuous proceedings. Therefore, reforms pursued by both judiciary officials and reformist camp met substantial resistance from those who benefit from the status quo. Shortsighted analyses of the political nature of judicial reform, coupled with optimism to affect change, resulted in deep disappointment.

In this situation, we are confronting with mutual reinforcement of problems. Interference, corruption, and delay reinforced one another. Poor terms of employment and recruiting judges from the pool of prosecutors and even torturers made judges more vulnerable to corruption and less likely to combat interference and delay with sufficient commitment. Political interference and delay were also conducive to corruption because these conditions gave judicial administrators, from the different offices of the judiciary power to the court registrar, the ability to extract rents for altering outcomes or pushing matters forward or back. Because of the corruption of judges, the legitimacy and trust necessary from the public's perception to support their independence was lacking, and the incentives to preserve or even create delay increased.

The judicial system in this period has no substantive commitment to democracy, free market, and détente demanded by the majority of the population. Political and economic interference with impartiality and delay in the administration of justice currently undermines even the achievement of core objectives of the judiciary in the eyes of authoritarians. An excessively partial or slow process of this branch of government renders fundamental public legal principles ineffectual, eviscerates private legal rights and obligations, cultivates the conditions for corruption, and favors the powerful over the weak. Institutional dysfunction thus undermines equality under the law and corrodes the incentives critical to legal compliance.

What are the chances that within, say, a short period the Iranian judicial system will become independent from political interference, rid itself of systemic and systematic manifestations of political interferences, and bring under control a crushing backlog? Most observers and participants in the system would respond that the chances are practically nil, and the situation "desperate"—if not entirely hopeless. Thus, the first aspect of the analogy is the apparent impossibility of effective justice reform.

Of the many impediments to reform, one of the most frequently identified is the lack of political will or leadership. This complaint echoes from common jabber in the corridors of authoritarian political cultures where people defer to the most senior authority for his signal before taking action. Many people within the Iranian courts believe that judicial reform in Iran will not progress even slightly without an explicit commitment from the judiciary officials and the Guardian Council, but experts from outside the polity believe in the power of civil society institutions and their power to negotiate with the state.

The Supreme Court in Iran is not in the position to have any impact on the reform process. There is also no constitutional court to be the last resort for reformists. The choice of the Guardian Council in 2000–04 in vetting all the Sixth Parliament's moves to pass laws in favor of vindication of people's civil and constitutional rights was considered absolutely blow up to the prospects of judicial reform in reformists' eyes, and the delays or ignorance in reviewing these bills in the Expediency Council suspended any progress toward important judicial and legal reform initiatives. In thinking about reform, people are in constant search for a leader as the key to success. Reformist camp has continued to look for a pacesetter in the high ranks of the government or judiciary itself to inspire and command effective justice reform.

The Iranian judiciary has been engaging with meta-dilemma in this period, i.e. a dilemma over how to deal with dilemmas. The judiciary has suppressed any voice in the press dealing with judicial dilemmas. The judiciary officials did not want to hear about the judiciary, thinking that explication of dilemmas may 1) open a much wider range of potential problems and necessary strategies that should be designed to avoid either paralysis or catastrophe, 2) expose expected strategies for critical evaluation, and 3) help to bolster both the theory and practice of different approaches to judicial reform.

The judiciary officials' option has been to ignore that a dilemma exists. They have always dismissed the competing values, trivialized the values advanced by the less preferred options, and ignored the risk of failure of an incremental or systemic approach. When faced with unsatisfactory choices, they did not sweeten one of the alternatives.

Reform proposals in post Islamic revolutionary era were based on inaccurate assessments and did not have a positive impact in addressing critically important problems. This is particularly important in Iranian judiciary where there has been a large deviation between law and practice, law and ethics, and law and custom. Awareness toward the problem was totally absent because of lack of candor, quantitative empirical tools, and qualitative assessments. Powerful interests of new political caste repressed candid assessments, and very few reforming communities had an adequate set of empirical tools. Even where both were available, most quantitative analysis has often been deficient in qualitative assessment of what value the judicial system should produce and at what cost of time or money. Authoritarian reformists did not expose to other models to think beyond overly simplistic models of alternative judicial institutions and processes. In-depth exposure to other systems could provide legal reformers with a comprehensive checklist of detailed considerations to be addressed in a sustainable reform initiative. Legal communities were severely isolated and had little awareness of other models. They were closed to the idea of drawing on the experience of other nations; they could not identify with any nation. The common isolation or narrow focus of legal communities produced a parochial perspective that limited the range of conceivable remedies.

There has been no open debate in the arena of judicial reform over the best way to select judges, how to overcome the tensions among judicial quality, accountability and independence, problems of judicial misconduct and disability, evaluation of judicial performance, judicial activism, how to speed the pace of litigation, reduce the court costs, and improve the utilization of scarce resources. No survey and polls has been done on these issues.

Chapter Seven
Overviews and Comparisons

Judicial reforms are very complex social and political phenomena and are affected by various social, economic and historical forces. By comparing different periods of judicial reform and the forces behind them, this research attempts to develop a model of the judicial reform in a developing country by linking social revolution and state building process. Secularizing and Islamicizing forces released after social revolutions have been the pushing forces of judicial reform in 20th century Iran. Secularization and Islamicization aspects of the reforms have come along together to shape the political and social structure of the society. Each aspect in different periods contributes to our understanding of the very complex processes that culminated in large scale reorganization of the state institutions including the judiciary.

By looking at the politico-legal systems and component groups of the political society and polity in each period, we can see the changes in the political system and its equivalent in the legal system. The ups and downs of the judicial reforms can be related to the ups and downs of the interactions between religious and state judicial systems. Each of the political regimes also necessitated and called for its own judicial reform to fit the judiciary with the demands and needs of the political regime. The success and failures of the judicial reforms may be explained by the practicality of the principles adopted, the relative strength of the competing social forces, and problems each phase of the reform was confronted to. Judicial reformists were pursuing different agendas by codification and transplantation in each period that led to different and even contradicting results.

7.1 STATE BUILDING: OVERVIEW

Iranian state formation and the dynamics of her social institutions from the medieval through the early modern and modern periods has already been a topic of discussion among specialists in Iranian institutional history (Mahbubi Ardekāni, 1999; Rāvandi, 1977). This is the main political process in Iranian polity in the 20th century. The nature and form of the state has been changing in the whole century and each and every administration tried to change it or have a share in this process to put its own stamp on it in this transitional period for political institutions.

Iranian political regime was totally non-democratic in the whole 20th century except four periods, i.e. 1906–1911 immediately after the Constitutional Revolution, 1941–1953 after the demise of Reza Shah till the American supported coup, 1979–1981 immediately after the Islamic Revolution, and 1997–2001, during civil rights movement. Other than these short periods, parliaments and other elected bodies of government were reduced to almost cypher, and there was no free formulation of political preferences, through the use of basic freedoms of association, information and communication, for the purpose of free political competition.

For classifying different non-democratic regimes of Iran during the period of my study, I used terms like authoritarian, patrimonial, neo-patrimonial, sultanistic, hierocratic, and charismatic in this study. Authoritarian regimes are deliberate and careful attempts by non-elected rulers to deal with a crisis of legitimacy either by invoking a carefully crafted, selective, and often inaccurate past or by offering promises, perhaps willfully false, of future material gain—an appeal to developmentalism—in order to fragment the opposition (Crystal, 1994). They incorporate a limited, not responsible, political pluralism with political demobilization and depoliticization of the population (Linz, 1975: 179, 264 & 269).[1] In my point of view, Iranian political regimes in 20th century have been authoritarian with different attributes. In spite of some totalitarian factions in Iranian polity after the Islamic Revolution, the political regime kept its authoritarian feature. As my study shows, the range of non-democratic regimes, even in one country in a century, as well as democratic ones is enormous.

Qājārs appealed to tradition to consolidate their *patrimonial authoritarian* regime while their legitimacy was under question by new demands of new strata of urban bourgeoisie, intelligentsia and *'ulamā*. The Constitutional Revolution, instigated by intrusion of the West into the country in the 19th century and disastrous wars with Russia (Lambton, 1965: 649), put pressure on Qājārs to accept the parliamentary regime and the constitution but it did not take so long for them to demolish it. The bombardment of the parliament by Mohammad Ali Shah on June 24, 1908, and the setback of constitutionalism in 1908–1909 was almost the end of the beginning of a constitutional regime. Like the first

Ottoman constitutional period, 1876–1878, "the torch of the constitutional government had been lit, allowed to flicker briefly, and was then extinguished (Devereux, 1963: 251).

When the social movement agitating for reform and opposing the absolutism demised, and intraelite rivalries in the Majles (parliament) and among the anjomans (councils) distracted and divided the intelligentsia's attention (Bayat, 1991), eventually draining the Constitutional Revolution of its initiative, energy, and vision, the small group of foreign-educated elite could not have a stable position in the polity. The constitutional period of 1906–1909 and its institutions were ephemeral and resulted in little that was substantial or lasting. The necessary and sufficient conditions for monarchical democracy were absent due to economic (the low level of development), social-structural (the tribal nature of communal divisions), institutional (the lack of historical background for representative institutions), and ideological (orientation of regime and opposition toward violence as the first resort that takes the presence of state violence as its point of departure) context of the time.

Due to very slow process of consolidation of the political regime after the shocks of the Constitutional Revolution, overthrow of Mohammad Ali Shah and a rise of Ahmad Shah as a constitutional monarch with no desire to be absolute but ineffective, weak and incompetent, some sections of elite could pursue their own reform projects after 1909. An example is the reform pursued by Mirzā Hasan Khan Moshir ul-Dowleh in the judiciary after 1909, including the 1911 LJO that I discussed in chapter 3 of this work.

Arjomand characterizes Pahlavi regime as "neo-patrimonial" in preference to "sultanistic"[2] or "authoritarian" (Arjomand 1988).[3] As I have used the term, neo-patrimonial is only one kind of the "authoritarian" type due to its traditional features of the political structure (patrimonial), modern features of bureaucracy (neo), and legitimacy crisis (authoritarian). Pahlavis appealed to Iranian nationalism/progress to legitimize the kingship of a new dynasty and to justify state authority and violence in the framework of a *neo-patrimonial authoritarian* regime. Although Iranian elites were successful in centralization of power and state building during Pahlavis, the society had a painful experience of failure at democratization. The end of the WWII, the demise of Reza Shah, and the inexperienced young king brought about an opportunity for constitutionalists to make a pause in the neo-patrimonial authoritarianism of Pahlavis between 1941 and 1953. This period of constitutional monarchy came to an end by the U.S. supported coup and overthrowing of Mosaddeq administration.

After the Islamic Revolution of 1979 five factors led the country towards greater centralization. First, the revolutionaries and clerics' agenda to dispossess higher classes of society during Pahlavi from private sector industry and land led the new government to nationalize many sectors of the economy. Second, the power struggle immediately after the Revolution especially in provinces on the borders which inhibit ethnic groups and religious minorities forced the government to centralize all administrative functions to safeguard the new Islamic state. Third, the desire to enforce all Islamic law in the land and to homogenize the society based on the new ideologized religion and clerics' lifestyle gave prominence to the need for greater centralized authority in all spheres of life. Fourth, eight-year long war with Iraq from 1980 to 1988 postponed or stopped enforcement of some chapters of the Constitution including the third and seventh chapters, on people's rights and on city and village councils respectively. And fifth, the need to politically control so-called anti-Islamic or anti-establishment forces led the clerics to monopolize the power and to close all the ways and means to decentralization.

Khomeini's revolutionary charisma objectified in a *revolutionary populist* regime; this regime replaced the developmentalist/nationalist regime of Pahlavis. Going back to Juan Linz's earlier studies of "authoritarian" and "totalitarian" regimes and typological subdivision of authoritarianism on the basis of the disaggregation of its various dimensions (1975), the mobilizational subdivision (Linz, 2000: 175–84) is useful to explain early phases of the Islamic regime. Only in the small period of 1979–1981, the regime is legitimate and we cannot call it authoritarian, although it is a partial and tutelary democracy. The Islamic regime transferred from a populist to hierocracy/theocracy, i.e. an Islamic regime with a jurist on the top who had all characteristics of the king (unaccountable, over-the-law, lifelong tenure, with only one exception: non-hereditary character), and then to a sultanistic authoritarian regime during Khāmenei leadership. There are some strong totalitarian tendencies in the Islamic state, very similar to Safavid state (Savory, 1987), but the political regime as a whole has not been a totalitarian one (Chehabi, 2001). Khomeini's regime between 1981 to1989 with a high cleric as a king enforced its order through psychic coercion by sanctioning religious benefits. The administrative staff of this regime claimed a monopoly of the legitimate use of hierocratic coercion. Hierocratic regime of Khomeini tried to prevent the rise of the secular powers through ideological recruitment, injection of clerics into any public institutions to check on the development of universities, military, judiciary and parliament and to make the founding of any independent group almost impossible, while sultanist authority of Khāmenei put its effort on religious institutions to assimilate religious affairs into political administration. Hierocratic regime of Khomeini claimed an autonomous charisma and law of its own, secured obedience and firmly restrained the polity. With its claimed charisma, hierocratic regime protected its loyalists. The hierocratic power gradually extended its control over the individuals.

Shi'ite *'ulamā* who were rejecting the absolute rule of caliphs for centuries embraced the absolute rule when they gained the chance. This showed that their eschatological hope in the second coming of Mahdi, the prophet's legitimate successor, was a total worldly desire for absolute power and not an ethical or merely theological desire for justice. The leader of the Islamic regime holds all powers and, in particular, the power of jurisdiction. Although the Constitution of the Islamic Republic makes a compromise between the otherworldly and this-worldly powers, this is the so-called otherworldly who has the upper hands.

Khāmenei's authority did not have its root in people's or even *'ulamā*'s content; he was selected by an assembly, i.e. Expert Assembly, whose representatives were qualified by the Guardian Council, all its members appointed by the previous leader. The sultanistic regime of Khāmenei between 1989 to1997 was operating primarily on the basis of discretion.[4] The increase of the power of Expediency Council and increase of its members is an evidence for this characteristic. The nontraditional elements of the Khomeini regime ware not rationalized in impersonal terms even in a regime without his charisma. The lack of traditional Islamic authority (*marja'iyyah*) facilitated the rise of a sultanate regime with more secular features. Due his early leave from seminaries, Khāmenei could not inherit the religious aura in the eyes of religious constituency. His authority was mostly derived in its actual organization from nonreligious models. During Khāmenei's regime, the line between regime and state was blurred, personalistic nature of the rule became more clear,[5] regime was characterized by personal rule unchecked by restraints, norms, or ideology; the Constitution, in spite of the revisions of 1989 in favor of the leader, was mostly ignored; the social bases of the political regime was narrowed down; and the corruption of the political system negatively affected economic development.[6] The limitation of pluralism was de facto, implemented more or less effectively, confined to strictly political groups totally loyal to the foundations of I.R.I., i.e. guardianship of the Islamic jurist.

Most of the political groups were created by or dependent on the state. This regime did not base its rule on any class and leaned on the loyalty of high-ranking military officers, judiciary, police and intelligence service officials, ex-patriots returned from Iraq, and rentier clerics, all appointed by Khāmenei.

Khāmenei and his associates and loyalists did not represent any class or corporate interests. The trend of Khāmenei's regime between 1989–2001 is directed towards personal rule, but loyalty to the ruler is motivated neither by his embodying or articulating an ideology, like Khomeini's regime, nor by a unique personal mission that was objectified in Khomeini during the Revolution, nor by charismatic qualities of Khomeini, but by a mixture of fear and rewards to his collaborators.[7] The binding political norms and bureaucratic rules and regulations were constantly violated by the arbitrary personal decisions of the leader. The definition of absolute guardianship of the Islamic jurist, i.e. a person, not an office, who is over-the-law, unaccountable, and over-the-oversight-of-any-elected or appointed-body, in the last years of Khomeini era was totally helpful for the rise of a clerical sultan. The personalist state fashioned by Khāmenei and his loyalists and characterized by clientalism, nepotism, cronyism, and corruption was completely unrestrained by legal or rational norms. There has been a pronounced cult of personality around the leader and he has tried to crave charisma and surround himself with the trappings of charismatic leadership precisely because he knows he lacks it. He invented new titles for himself like the Supreme Leader (*maqām-e mo'azzam-e rahbari*, Imām Khāmenei).

Ideology in this period is mere window dressing and has no functions like giving people a sense of mission, legitimation, guiding regime's policy formulation, and commitment to some holistic conception of man and society. There was no pro-regime intellectual to articulate this ideology. Khāmenei even did not pay lip service to the Constitution. He has been always against multi-party system.[8] All enforcing powers of the state are personal property of the Leader. Nevertheless, elements of a legal-rational order were not totally absent. These elements that could be seen in the Constitution and public sphere lose their strength when confronted with strong sultanistic tendencies in the Constitution and the government as legal and real regimes.

The sultanistic regime of post-Khomeini era with some openings for partial democracy transformed to a total sultanistic and hierocratic regime in response to Civil Rights Movement; this transformation completed the subordination of priestly to this-worldly power and exercised supreme authority in religious beside secular matters by virtue of its autonomous legitimacy. The hierocratic regime treated religious affairs simply as a branch of political administration. In this regime, God and Imams have been properties of the state, complying with religious rules has been a state affair, and dogmas and rituals are accepted, rejected, modified, and reconstructed at the ruler's discretion. The sultanistic regime of Khāmenei rose to power when in the post charismatic era the importance of individual action was going to diminish even as an atom in a mass society by resort to the intelligence, the militia, IRGC, and the police. In this regime, a single and centralized hierarchy with an unambiguous apex monopolized all important decisions. Autonomy of the formal segments, consultation and elections were mostly theatre, and known to be such. The endeavors of groups with authoritarian ideology to explain the stratification of status group by loyalty to the leader[9] totally failed, showing the end of charismatic discipline. Only the various types of coercive forces could take care of this out of date phenomenon.

The priestly charisma that gradually merged into the routinized power during Khomeini reached to its perigee point in the end of his era. From Khomeini to Khāmenei, there is a transfer from revolutionary charismatic authoritarianism, mainly established between 1978 and 1981, and hierocratic authoritarianism between 1981–1989, to hierocratic authoritarian sultanism in the periods of 1989–1997 and 2001–2005. There are two periods in which some signs of democracy are visible: 1979–1981 and 1997–2001. The democratic forces in these periods pushed for more free and fair elections but at the end authoritarian forces smashed these forces through suppression of independent press, suppression of independent activists and tougher disqualifications.

The nature of the Constitution of 1979 and its revision contributed to the rise of a hierocratic authoritarian sultanistic regime. This type denotes the IRI as a "mixed type." Hierocratic authoritarian sultanism is a more personalistic subtype of hierocratic authoritarianism that would be applied to the latter part of Khāmanei. In this type, the religious legitimacy of the ruler is primary, and his political authority is based on it. *Velayat-e faqih* is the religious principle of legitimacy. It was impossible for the parliament, as the main obstacle for absolute rule of the leader, to play the role envisaged for it by the democrats. Even if the leader and his appointed bodies of government had complied with the exact letter of the Constitution of 1979 and its revisions, they still had it in their power to render the parliament impotent. Even it is hard to talk about the democratic or anti-authoritarian spirit of the Constitution while it gives priority to Islamic beliefs and ordinances-interpreted by its carriers, i.e. *'ulamā-* in each and every disputable matter. Even if the parliament was potent on the basis of the Constitution, the *'ulamā* who accepted the Constitution were not prepared to respect it; they had no alternative at the time.

Table 7.1. Political and Legal Systems in Twentieth Century Iran

Period	Political Regime	Legal System	Politico-legal System	Component Groups of Polity
-1907	Patrimonial Monarchy	Dual Judicial System	Customary Law *Shari'ah*	Clerics, Princes Guilds, State-land Conditional Holders[10]
1907–1909	Constitutional Monarchy	"	"	Clerics, Princes, Intellectuals, Guilds, Land Holders
1909–1925	Patrimonial Monarchy	"	"	"
1925–1941	Neo-patrimonial Authoritarian Monarchy	State Law System	Administrative or Public Law	Clerics, Military, Intellectuals, Bāzār Technocrats, White Collars, Landlords, Univ. Students,
1941–1953	Constitutional Monarchy	"	"	"
1953–1979	Neo-patrimonial Authoritarian Monarchy	"	"	"
1979–1981	Revolutionary Charismatic Authoritarianism /Partial Democracy	Ideologized Jurist's Law	Dual Law (Administrative/ Islamic)	Clerics, *Āqā-zādehs*[11] Bāzār, White Collars-Univ. Students, Intellectuals
1981–1989	Hierocratic Authoritarianism	"	Islamicized Law	"
1989–1997	Hierocratic Authoritarian Sultanism	Formal Jurist Law	Islamicized Administrative or Public Law	Clerics, *Āqā-zadehs,* Bāzār, Technocrats, White Collars, Workers, Military, Univ. Students, Intellectuals
1997–2001	Hierocratic Authoritarian Sultanism/ Partial Democracy	"	"	" + Women and Lawyers
2001–2006	Hierocratic Authoritarian Sultanism	"	"	"

These are the common characteristics of the state in four periods of Iran's contemporary history:

1) Typically close and highly personal relationships between near-peers in political sphere—patrimonial or neo-patrimonial—mostly limited to governmental officials. This has been an institutional component of the Iranian state.
2) Expansion of the state's power in Iran rarely accompanied by a process of autonomization of civil society, as a realm where 1) different and diverse forms of not necessarily political power become established or remain, 2) new forms of relations between individuals and between groups are discovered and institutionalized, and then 3) a network of associations and unions are tied together to limit the state power and make it accountable. State building in Iran meant just that the ruling center claims for itself all political business. Islamic state, in post-revolutionary era, added direct involvement in all religious concerns to the previous concerns of state pertaining to the production and distribution of status, power and wealth.
3) Lack of ability to build up through taxes a treasury from which to finance an apparatus of rule from the center. The percentage of tax in the composition of the revenue of the Iranian government decreased from 83% to 23% (Arjomand, 1988: 215) when the *khāleseh* (state lands) were transferred to new class of rulers. The oil revenues in the hands of government have made tax revenues almost irrelevant.
4) The Iranian state during the 20th century was neither ready to recognize the autonomy of different businesses of civil society, nor to discipline its own activities. New forms of law and new institutions were mostly intended to extend the state's operations not to rationalize and moderate them.
5) The state's power even in the second period did not become lodged within a new set of purposefully designed, expressly coordinated offices, with distinct tasks, faculties and facilities of rule. The state offices usually manned by personnel selected for their kinship or friendly relationship with the ruling caste, not for their ability to perform the related abilities efficiently, competently and responsibly. The power was based mostly on brute force and/or justified through *shahanshāhi* (monarchical) or Islamic ideology, incongruous to discursive articulation and to rational argumentation. Neither the constitutional machinery,

including its eventually semi-democratic approach, nor the cultural preferences and social practices of the people in question could help to change the direction. There was never a constitutional arrangement like judicial review of legislative or leader's power to secure public and private rights of the individuals. Iranian courts have never asserted the right to be authoritative interpreters of the Constitutions of 1906 and 1979. The Constitution is not what the courts say it is; the ruler and the circle of his loyalists (the Guardian Council) say what the Constitution is. Since Iranian courts have never been in the position to interpret the Constitutions of 1906 and 1979, no fundamental issues of governmental structure and political procedures come before them. Courts do not usually concern themselves with issues of civil liberties and civil rights. The details of how Iranians may not enjoy freedom of press, assembly, and religion have never been the object of litigation and court rulings.[12] Legal institutions do not usually affect the processing of constitutional issues and they have more impact on policymaking. The public sphere colonized by the state, and state-controlled media did not have ability to mandate, monitor or sanction public policies.

6) The state, except for very short periods of time, i.e. 1907–1909 and 1979–1981, was instituted in order to provide security and assistance to certain social strata, and to maintain and extend the privilege and leverage of special groups. Each individual was never practically defined as the citizen of the state with equal rights under the law.
7) Even in the framework of the Iranian Constitutions of 1906 and 1979, most of the critical decision sites are almost expressively constituted according to patrimonial rather than bureaucratic criteria. Clientalism, specially after the increase of oil revenue percentage in the national income, has been alive; informal ties of mutual or asymmetrical obligation and networks of personal associates and cliques have constituted the actual carrying structures of all significant processes of information-sharing, resource allocation, task assignment, and career progression in public and governmental offices. All manner of state activities have been initiated and conducted only by means of these structures, hidden behind the official ones, and often cross-purposes with them.
8) Under all political regimes and all constitutions and their revisions, the people were incapable of deciding for themselves. The right to legislate has been certainly reserved only for the mainly

non-elected political caste. The laws enacted by the Majles were always subject to approval by a non-elected body, be it the king, the senate, the leader of IRI, or the Guardian Council. It has been the appointed body who determines whether or not the proposed legislation conforms to monarchic, Islamic, or expedient principles of the ruling class. The Islamic Republic did not create a situation of a penumbra of Iran's Constitution of 1979. Even the *Hadith* and the Quran were not literally at the center; the interpretation of these texts by the ruling class and the cultural negotiation of different approaches to the meaning of those texts in the context of Islamic Republic have been more important than the texts themselves. In this system, legislation was not subject to review by the Judiciary; it is subject to the will of the political caste which has the power. The "penumbra" of the Iranian Constitutions has tended to reside not in case history, in *shari`ah* and in traditions even older than that, but in the day to day expediency of the ruling caste justified by the ideologized religion or *shahanshāhi* ideology. The Constitutional review in Iran has been totally in the hands of the leader, king or jurist (Supplemental Article to the Supplement of the 1906 Constitution,[13] Article 177 of 1989 Constitution[14]), and his appointed bodies. Both half of the Guardian Council's members are directly or indirectly appointed by the leader; the Majles has actually no say in the selection of the lawyer members. The judiciary appoints the nominees, and there is no cap on the number of MPs who have to vote for a nominee to be selected for the Council (Art. 91, Sec. 2).

9) Second and fourth periods are comparable with respect to neutralization of democratic institutionalization. Both Reza Shah and Khāmenei administrations tried to consolidate the power of the head of the state and all appointed bodies of government, and weakened the power of independent legislative and judiciary branches of power. Mohammad Reza Shah finished the job of his father by establishing Senate that was mentioned in the constitution of 1906 but was not realized then till 1940's. Khāmenei also finished the job of Khomeini in giving total upper hands to the Guardian Council and the Expediency Council with respect to the parliament.

10) In the whole 20th century, the state has limited local and independent autonomies, replaced home-grown leadership with appointed officials, leveled out traditional differences in the management of public affairs, created new burdens for the populace (conscription,

imposts, fees for administrative and judicial acts), imposed linguistic, religious and cultural practices on local populations, and limited the individuals from having access to information and data. It has also refused to produce or distribute accurate and up-to-date fundamental information on the trends of economy, society, culture and politics, and violated numbers of the individuals' rights, civil, constitutional and human. Homogenization and unification have been different umbrellas for consolidation of the power and rule of the government, and political control.

11) Even at the end of 20th century, the terms liberty and security did not become synonymous. Self-regulated governments did not secure the individuals as the essential atomic elements of its mechanics. The freedom of individuals to pursue their private interests was not necessary to security of the public. Liberty was not a technical requirement of governing the natural processes of social life. In the whole 20th century, the security of laws and individual liberty did not presuppose each other. The individuals were institutionally deprived of their negative (determined as what is not prohibited by law or by reference to imprescriptibly natural rights[15]) and positive (determined as what is secured by the government to guarantee the proper use of freedom and optimal functioning of natural processes) liberties. The governmental reason has always been identified with the rationality of the sovereign. The limiting of political power never was part of the state-building process. The mutual adjustment of the antinomic principles of law and order was never on the agenda of the government of men, not of laws.
12) The role of ideological appeals in sustaining authoritarianism has been prominent in the whole 20th century, from nationalism to populism, and from developmentalism to Islamism. All these ideologies have served the interests of the ruling caste: nationalism for Europe educated intelligentsia, populism for revolutionaries, developmentalism for technocrats and Islamism for clerics.

The issue of law and social agency in Iran's politico-social history has to be examined in the context of three different types of politico-social structures, i.e. *amir* (ruler) *-a'yān* (notables) and "military-patronage" regimes in Qājār era, king-court and bureaucracy-clients regimes in Pahlavi era, and jurist-bait and clerics-clients regime in IRI. A'yān, court and bait are the links between the highest authority and second order political powers; military, bureaucracy and clerics in different periods are the social bases of the political power and the ones who guarantee the survival of the regime.

The affinity between *bāzār* and religious power in pre- and post revolutionary era, that is typical of Iran's social and political structure in the 20th century, grew into a formal alliance against the white and blue-collar strata. This changed to the alliance of *bāzār,* revolutionary corps and clergy against technocrats, bureaucrats and workers after the Islamic Revolution. The charismatic figure of Khomeini and hierocratic sultanistic figure of Khāmenei used hierocracy and its heritage respectively to domesticate a subject population in charismatic and post charismatic eras. The integration of so-called royal and priestly power into the jurist/king (*velayat-e faqih*) that was supposed to erase the duality of religion/politics led to absolute power of the guardians. Ethics and salvation that were not dominant in Shi'ite thought were abandoned again in the theory of Islamic state. Very similar to caesaropapism, the predomination of hierocratic sultanism changed the substance of religion in public sphere. As Weber instructs us, "whenever caesaropapist predominates . . . it is inevitable that the substance of religion is stereotyped in terms of the purely technical, ritualist manipulation of supernatural powers, and any development toward a religion of salvation is impeded" (Weber, 1968: 1163). It seems that the Islamic governance has had the same function in post-revolutionary Iran.

Basic to the failure of the democratic experience intended during the Constitutional and Islamic Revolution was the absence of the foundations upon which any constitutional regime must rest: national unity, common objectives, respect for the law by both the rulers and the ruled, independent groups and institutions, venues to survey, publish and broadcast public opinion, and understanding and acceptance of their duties as well as their rights by all citizens, irrespective of rank, position, religion, ethnicity, gender, age, ideology, and social or economic status. Acquiring a constitution and parliament have not been enough. Although an articulate public opinion existed in the capital and, later, big cities and sporadically presented in the media, it was neither articulate nor aroused in a national framework. After two years of work, all the public survey research centers were closed and the effective directors of these centers were imprisoned by Khāmenei's regime.

The masses, mostly poor, uneducated or undereducated, and disenfranchised, lived in the provinces and were concerned primarily with the struggle to stay alive. Nothing in their experience has prepared them to act as citizens as distinct from subjects (*ra'iyyah*). The king, and later, the leader have always been the source of authority, not the people.

7.2 RELIGIOUS AND STATE JUDICIAL SYSTEMS: OVERVIEW

Although Iran adopted a written Constitution ratified by popularly elected conventions in 1906–7 and 1979, many of their framers and ratifiers continued to believe that Islamic jurists should enforce their monopolized religious rights-rights that are not mentioned but implied in the sacred texts and also implied in the Constitutions-against laws enacted by popularly elected legislatures. The tension between modern and traditional, secular and religious, and democracy and patrimonialism was echoed in the realm of law and judiciary. Rationalization and centralization for reformers meant reducing the judicial prerogatives of the clerics while insisting on reconcilability of modern judiciary and *sharī`ah* law. Although the idea of man-made law was challenging the anti-secularists' view on the sufficiency and completeness of *sharī`ah*'s provision and captured the formal aspect of law, perceived God's law always came back in the substance of law. The reformers' reinterpretation of religious texts and presenting a secular religious-based value system was a threat to 'ulamā's social power and authority over religious matters. By orienting Iranians' loyalty toward the nation rather than the monarch or a traditional religious-based value system by rebuking *'ulamā* for having failed to lead the country in the direction of process, reformers usurped the moral and cultural authority of the traditional elites and effectively questioned the foundations of the clerics' authority (Ringer, 2004: 46).

Principles. In each of these four periods, there are implicit or explicit principles that agents of change have had in their minds or have been acting based on the. From each period to another one, these principles are basically changed (Table 7.2). These principles reveal the basic differences in politico-legal cultures and different judicial policies of each period under study. For example, unity of judge or multiplicity of judges in a judicial system establishes two different judicial processes. The other important differences are the educational requirements of the judiciary officials and judges, hierarchy, relationship between law and *sharī`ah* in each period.

Transformation

This study on Iranian judiciary system focused on four different transformations from one set of judicial reform and reorganization to the other in 20th century Iran based on a general theory of judicial reform depicted in figure 7.1. These transformations are parallel to different transformations of political system in Iran, and their stages reflect the four mentioned social and political processes. The first transformation is based on the transition from a patrimonial state law and a jurists' law to a dualistic legal system i.e. the establishment of a state law and court in the modernization process beside *shari`ah* law and court at both local and national levels after the Constitutional Revolution. *Shari`ah* in the Islamic world was believed to be beyond the power of human enactment and codification by almost all clerics and was identified as the basic law of the traditional system of life (Berkes, 1964: 94). In this transition, the remote causal factors are the change in norms and values and reconfiguration of social institution, and the near cause is the restructuring the power. The change of the legal culture dictates how the legal change occurs.

In this period, the scope of the functions and jurisdiction of *shari`ah* courts is severely contracted. The influence of the *qāzi* (judge) as an independent power that had been diminishing for several centuries under and after the Seljuqs, reached its critical point under the Safavids. Although the *shari`ah* courts in this period were made subordinate to the temporal patrimonial powers as represented by the *'orfi* (customary) courts and the semi-military hierarchy under the *divānbigi* (Lambton, 1953: 121), these courts never totally lost their power until the judicial reform of Dāvar under the neo-patrimonial authoritarian power of Pahlavi dynasty. The members of the judiciary in this model are admitted, and not appointed, by the Shah who as a religiously non-legitimate ruler, was compelled to pay the greatest regard to the wishes of the local *honoratoires* (Weber, 1978: 822–23). The long and persistent absence of rational and strong central authorities did produce autonomous local communities and a dual judicial system, which were recognized in practice by the state.

The second transformation in the judiciary and change of the model of judicial reform is based on centralization of the judiciary, assimilation of adjudication to administration (Weber, 1978: 645) and overcoming the duality of the traditional legal system that had been recognized and endorsed in the Supplementary Fundamental Law of 1907 and the first Civil Code of 1911 (Arjomand, 1988: 66). The Civil and Penal Codes of 1939 and 1940 finally omitted all references to *shari`ah* and to religious courts. So the dual system was replaced by a unified system of state law on the Civil Law model (See Appendix III) in the framework of state-building process.[16] All of these developments are the results of institutionalization of political power, now in the hands of Pahlavis.

Judicial reform in the first decade of Islamic revolutionary regime can be characterized as the transformation of the Shi'ite jurist law into the law of the state (Arjomand, 1993: 100) on the one hand and ideologization of the unified Civil Law system, on the other. This was the third transformation. The impact of the takeover of the constitutional state by the Shi'ite legal tradition was involvement of Shi'ite jurists in drafting

Table 7.2. Principles of Judicial Reform in Each of the Four Periods of Reform: 1906–2006

1911-	- Multiplicity of judges in the courts (except for the Reconciliation Court) (Mansur ul-Saltaneh, Mirzā Mostafā, 1911: 373) - Dual structure of courts: secular and religious (state courts and courts of *mujtaheds*). This was established by the Constitution of 1906 (Browne, 1966: 376, Article 27; 381, Article 71) - Centralization of the judiciary (unaccomplished)
1927-	- Unity of Judge in the court ('Āqeli, 142–144) - Administration of the judiciary by the personnel who received European education - Monopolizing the issue of judicial provisions to the state (Āqeli, 143) and appointing *mujtahids* as judges by the government (Āqeli, 167). This is the state that in some categories gives over the power of judgeship to courts of *mujtaheds* or assembly of *mujtaheds* (as the appeal court of the courts of *mujtaheds*). In this framework, *shari'ah* courts are considered as special courts (approved by Majles, 1931) "and no cases may be referred to a Shari'ah Court without authorization from state courts and the office of the Attorney General" (Banani, 78). "The civil and Penal Code of 1939 and 1940 finally left no room for *shari'ah* law at all" (Banani, 79). - At no time may the laws be contradictory to the *shari'ah* in principle - Uniformity of judicial procedure
1979-	- Conformity of laws with *shari'ah* (not to be contradictory is not enough) - Enforcing all Islamic laws in public and private spheres (unaccomplished) - Reversing uniformity of judicial procedure, although against the Article 161 of the Constitution: "The Supreme Court is to be formed for the purpose of supervising the correct implementation of the laws by the courts, ensuring uniformity of judicial procedure, and fulfilling any other responsibilities assigned to it by law, on the basis of regulations to be established by the head of the judicial branch."
1994-	- No hierarchy in the judicial organization other than the Head of judiciary and staff - Legal procedures are enforced on the basis of discretion of judiciary officials (unaccomplished) - Annulment of professionalism in the court system - Generalization of the courts

legal documents, advising in procedural matters and responding to questions of law to implement Islamicization. The Islamic Revolution is the near causal factor of judicial reform in the post-revolutionary Iran that restructures the state and pushes for the first phase of judicial reform based on Islamic ideology.

In the second decade after the Revolution and mainly after the death of Khomeini, low ranking clerics and laymen were added to the active agents in Islamicization process, and the ideologized jurist law of the third period transformed to the lay-judge law of the clerical authoritarian regime to institutionalize the power of clerics. The generalization of the courts was to give more power to these lay judges. This was the fourth transformation. In this transformation, adjudication changes to be a way of direct control of the opposition and defiance. In this system, the judiciary pursues an anti-rationalization process, and arbitrariness and political discretion are the rules. The goals of judicial system in this period are not to apply and enforce laws and regulations impartially, predictably and efficiently-as it was demanded by the people during the Revolution- but to enforce Islamic law–as read by clerical authoritarians- and the will of clerical ruling elite. The centrality of the judge in judicial process and floating character of the laws make all verdicts unpredictable. The politicization of judiciary is the main strategy of the ruling elite to survive in a partial democracy/partial authoritarinism political society during the Civil Rights Movement established by resort to the constitution of 1979. The main causal factor for judicial reform in this model is the change in political structure.

Judicial reform in Iran begins with formal secularization to avoid harsh reaction from *'ulamā* and then secularization extends to substance of the judiciary, i.e. laws, when the state is enough powerful to exert its authority on judicial institution. The Islamic Revolution of 1979 is a big shift; it did not reverse the process by formal Islamicization but focuses on substantial Islamicization to suitably react to substantial secularization as the last development. When the Islamic regime is relieved with Islamity of substance, then it is turn for formal Islamicization in the fourth period of Iran's judicial reforms in the 20th century.

The conflict between state and religious authorities all over the 20th century, the increase of literacy rates and enrollment in institutions of higher education, increase of internal migration, and the rise of urban centers especially during Mohammad Reza Shah (Appendix VII) did not lead the country from traditional and then charismatic authority to legal-rational authority. Formal and substantive secularization of 1910's to 1970's ended up with substantive and formal Islamicization of 1980's and 1990's. These developments may be understood in terms of lacking the intermediate institutions (Chehabi, 1990: 15), the weakness of emerging middle class, the weak alliance of the *'ulamā* and the intellectuals, and the opposition of *'ulamā* toward a governmental body which could legislate. The function of representative assembly, even right after the Constitutional Revolution and the Islamic Revolution was not to legislate but to ensure that the old laws not to be broken by the monarch (before the Islamic Revolution) and to enforce Islamic rules (after the Revolution).

7.3 CODIFICATIONS AND TRANSPLANTATIONS: OVERVIEW

An important issue in the development of Iranian society from the early modern period has been the importation of ideas from the West that changes the ideology and worldview of certain social groups and manipulates the norms and values of the whole society. Changes in the norms and values do not solely explain the internalized need of judicial reform in 20th century. Reconfiguration of social institutions went hand in hand with the changes in norms and values and led together to two important social revolutions, i.e. the Constitutional Revolution of 1906 and Islamic Revolution of 1979. The first phase of judicial reform was accomplished immediately after the social revolutions while the political regime tried to restructure in accordance with the new demands, expectations and necessities. The institutionalization of judicial change, i.e. building new judicial institutions and implementing new judicial procedures is the main subject of second phase of judicial reform that happened during Dāvar's and Yazdi's judicial reforms as aftershocks of revolutionary quakes.

Iran became a large-scale borrower of Western models in the 20th century, even in post-revolutionary era, despite declamations on the "originality and purity of Islamic law." This time the Communist Bloc was the role model. Western models were formally borrowed in economic, social, cultural, and political spheres, even if a careful jurisprudence has disguised them in the Islamic substance or some judges have been unaware of their origin. But compared to the period between the Constitutional and Islamic Revolutions, the scale was lighter.[17] This light transplantation can be explained in terms of putting the state at the center of any legislation that has no precedent in the Islamic *sharī`ah*. Another way of explaining this phenomenon is looking at the interaction of legal and judicial systems on the one side and social and political systems on the other. Offer and demand of legal and judicial models is ruled not only by the necessities of ideological doctrines and techniques of legal experts but also by the political and economical obligations and decisions that govern the polity in domestic and international arenas.

In the first and second periods of judicial and legal reform, the European laws were added to the sources of law, while in the third and fourth periods there was a conscious endeavor to get rid of this source and purify the law and make it pure Islamic. *Shari`ah* was the substantial source of the legal system but the model of East Bloc provided the forms. The real jurisprudence was totally under the influence of the modern authoritarian/totalitarian states' judiciaries. This is totally against Watson's argument about the exchangeability of sources of law during legal reform, when he says, "even in a time of conscious legal reform, the sources of law are often not considered candidates for reform" (Watson, 1983: 1156).

Structural Changes

The judicial structure varies from period to period, but instead of reviewing those differences in detail, the focus here is on the structural reforms. If we compare those four different charts of judiciary, brought up in previous chapters, these remarks could be made:

1) Because of the type of the regime in almost all of these periods, i.e. authoritarian with different versions and colors, the administration of justice is controlled by the leader of the country (shah or *vali-ye faqih*) and/or the executive power. They are at the top of the chart and the shape of the structure looks like a pyramid. There is no democratic process in the judiciary; the only exception is the selection of three members of the Supreme Council of the Judiciary by judges between 1979 an 1989.
2) The regime, *shāhanshāhi* or Islamic, has had a fragmentation strategy to control the judiciary. This two-folded strategy includes de-politicization of judges, usually enforced through the recruitment policies, and creation of a special tribunal in charge of political cases.[18] This strategy removes the ordinary courts from direct involvement in the repression of political crimes and guarantees the verdict that the regime expects from a court. The Military Court during Pahlavi and the Revolutionary Courts during the Islamic regime do this job other than their other responsibilities. In some sections, these courts are not enough for repression and one of the ordinary courts is picked to do the job. This court in both Reza Shah and Khāmenei regimes is called the Special Court for Governmental Officials.[19] Due to this strategy and creation of several special judicial tribunals, even the ordinary courts did not enjoy true institutional independence they were able to maintain a certain degree of autonomy.

3) The organization of the judiciary extends in the first period to the level that includes Supreme Court of Cassation and Appellate Courts. Regular courts are also more specialized.
4) During second period oversight institutions, i.e. Disciplinary Courts for Judges, National General Inspectorate, and Court of Administrative Justice, are established. There is also more specialization in the primary courts structure, i.e. Property Court, Itinerant Court, Reconciliation Court, and Juvenile Delinquency Court. Shari`ah Courts are part of the courts of Justice in this period, while they were put in different section in the first period.
5) The Islamic Revolution added three aspects to the previous chart. First, it led to the founding of Supreme Judiciary Council that substituted individual decision making with a collective one. Judges could also elect some of the members of this council and this was a move toward making the judiciary an elected body of government. The second development was the total separation of executive and judiciary powers, while making judiciary more dependent on the Leader. The minister of justice has almost no power in making decisions, policy making and structural changes. The third development was the establishment of more special tribunal other than the Military Tribunals that had precedent in Pahlavi regime. Clergy and Revolutionary Courts have been indispensable parts of the Islamic regime.
6) Leaders of the post-Khomeini era got rid of the collective headship of the judiciary and its elected member. They also de-specialized the Primary Courts and dissolved the office of district attorneys in all districts. Instead, they established General Courts that resided by judges who performed the roles of prosecutor, jury, investigator, DA and the judge, even the lawyer, at the same time.

Judicial reform is at the heart of Western legal culture because it represents the intersection of reason and will, "which are thought to be the twin sources of a legitimate legal order" (Kahn, 1999: 7), but this concept has always met with strong resistance in Iranian socio-political structures and legal and political culture, culture although a lot of people have been fighting for it in different social movements all over the 20th century. There has always been the will-based on national modernization and then to Islamicization- to reform but judicial reforms have rarely been beneficial for critical actors of different political regimes in Iranian contemporary history. Iranian society at the verge of its Enlightenment project in the 20th century and high demand for reason and enforcement of its will has been striving to experience judicial reform as the application of reason to will and absolute power of the state, and establishing rule of law, while the political structure has been consolidating its foundations on the basis of real power and not the legal-legitimate one.

The modern Iranian legal system in different periods of 20th century was mostly based on what was described as civil law in the nineteenth and early 20th centuries in European history.[20] This legal system is primarily designed to be a seamless body of legal prescriptions based on simple principles. Scholars and politicians in this system are principal drafters of law and the judiciary has little authority over codification. "Judges were to apply the law but their decisions were not given authority as precedents" (Jacobs, 1996: 4). Lawyers in this system remain overshadowed by magistrates and judges in the conduct of trials. Courts in civil law system are state institutions rather than a battle ground for attorneys sponsored by private interests. The logic of change and development in Iran's judiciary system follows the logic of change and development in any legal system based on civil law. The main difference between legal development in Iran's legal system and legal systems in developed countries is that there is no longer distinction between civil and common types of law in developed countries (Jacobs, 1996: 4) while this difference is still important in Iran's legal system. Iranian legal system has always escaped any element of common law tradition due to the politicians' fear of more independency for judges in reaching to their verdict and establishment of the precedence as one of the sources of law. It is still the state that can change the law and legal procedure not the judicial decision making process *per se,* although norms and customs in Iranian society change and develop like norms and customs in any other society. Iranian courts usually do not make policies when they apply the law to new situations. They usually do not interpret the law in novel ways. They also do not have the habit to cite their previous decisions or those higher courts to justify their interpretation. There has always been a cleavage between social norms and norms that courts' decisions are based on. The provisions of the codes and the ritual of courts do not usually dramatize the dominant norms of the society; they usually reflect the norms of political elite who exert the norms to socially control the whole society.

7.4 JUDICIAL REFORMS AND REORGANIZATIONS: OVERVIEW

Each of the political regimes of 20th century Iran required its own judicial system; each of them also necessitated and called for its own judicial reform to fit the judiciary with the demands and needs of the political regime. In short periods of constitutional monarchy and populism, the judiciary could not pursue any reform program. Judicial reforms came after the consolidation of each political regime. Neo-patrimonialism of Pahlavis required an administrative law that should be shaped by transplantation and codification. Hierocratic authoritarian regime of post-revolutionary era had to Islamicize the judiciary to make it compatible with clerical rule. Hierocratic sultanistic regime of Khāmenei needed a judiciary totally under the control of the leader and had no choice other than destruction of any formal procedure in the judiciary.

As it was already discussed in the introduction, the contemporary history of Iran can be categorized in four different periods. This categorization is based on social movements, social processes and critical events (as shown in Table 7.3). The four periods of judicial reform in Iran (summed up in Table 7.3) were totally influenced by the different kinds of judicial reform in international arena with respect to the shape of adoption or reaction to different developments. Table 7.3 is intended to show "types" of judicial reforms in the context of a socio-political regime for each period. Each of these periods begins and ends with an important event: the victory of Constitutional Movement (1906–1907), transition from Qājār to Pahlavi Dynasty (1925), the victory of Islamic revolution (1979) and the death of Khomeini (1989). Iran's judiciary system endures concurrent developments in Iranian polity, society and culture in those periods.

Every period of judicial reform in 20th century Iran is interlocked with a special kind of state. The judicial system and the judicial reform that is pursued cannot be understood without grasping the core of the state structure. For example, in the Islamic revolutionary period, with the emergence of bureaucratized hierocracy, the state's relationship to law underwent a radical change. The personal authority of the sovereign *faqih* (Islamic jurist) became the source of all laws. The authority of law was grounded not on its content but on the will of the unaccountable political commander-in-chief, charisma or non-charisma. This places the ruled at the mercy of the ruler. Although the judicial, the legislative, and even the executive power of the state were not subject to various customary limitations and these powers did what they have ability to do, lack of political organization and intellectual abortiveness did not let the political regime to be an actual totalitarian one, even through enforcing the power of the true-believers of totalitarianism. Absolute monarchy of the *faqih* did not stand for lawless government but for authoritarian government by public law.

Table 7.3. Four Periods of Judicial Reform in Iran: Characteristics and Specifications, 1906–2006

Period	1911-	1927-	1979-	1994-
Main Agendas of Society	Rule of Law/ Justice	Nationality/Centralized State/ Progress	Islamic Ideology/ Islamic State	Authority & Legitimacy/ Civil and Constitutional Rights
The Answer	Constitution	Authoritative Development	Islamization	Clerical Autocracy/ Democracy
Crucial Political Event	Constitutional Movement	Change of Dynasty	Islamic Revolution, Rise of Charisma	Death of Charismatic Leader
The Model of Judiciary System taken from	France, Belgium, Switzerland	France, Belgium, Switzerland, Italy	Revolutionary Regimes, modifies as theocratic	Authoritarian Regimes, modified as theocratic
Overall Goal	Establishment of House of and Justice and Access to Justice	Westernization and Secularization of the Judiciary System	Islamization of the Judiciary System	Reduction of Backlog in the Courts, Response to Illegitimacy Crisis
Main Causes Guiding the Course of Judicial Reform	Pressures of a Social Movement and Campaign for Justice	Centralization and State- Building	Pressures of a Social Revolution	Consolidation/ Political & Social Control
Consequences for Social Structure	Increase of the Power of Intellectuals Coming from New Educ. System	Creation of a New Social Class of Landlords, Decrease of 'Ulamā's Power	Creation of a New Ruling Class of Clergy	Militarization of Middle Level Power / Increase of the Organized Militia Power coming from Lower Class
System of Law	Mixed (Jurist + State law)	State Law	Mixed (Jurist Law + Revol. Law)	Mixed (State Law+ Jurist Law)
Ideal Type of Law	European Law	Internally Consistent Body of Rules	Ideologized *Shari`ah*	Ideologized *Shari`ah*
Judges	More than a Judge Figure (Magistrate)	Judge Figure	Jurist/Judge/ Activist	Judge/Activist
Agents of Change	Foreign Educated Officials	Foreign Educated Officials	Islamists/ Clerics	New Generation of Judge/Prosecutor/ Executioner(s)

The level of success and failure of the judicial reform is partially dependent on the stability of the political regime during these four periods. When the instability is high, e.g. in the first period that the average lifetime of ministers of justice is five months, ignoring the reshuffles (Appendix V), the judiciary officials cannot pursue any program, though well planned. The secret of Dāvar's success in his judicial reform was the stability of the Mehdi Qoli Khan Mokhber ul-Saltaneh administration (1927–1933), which was an exception during Reza Shah's reign. Hoveydā's administration, 1964–1977, was the only stable administration during Mohammad Reza Shah's reign (Appendix V) but Hoveydā had no reform agenda on the table. Islamicization of judiciary during the 1981–1989 and generalization of the courts during Yazdi's headship, 1989–1999, are also due to political stability in those periods, although both of them were failure with respect to their claimed goals, i.e. bringing about justice, expediting the judicial process and getting rid of backlogs.

In the whole 20th century, civil society institutions were not considered as central elements of the legal regime. Family and state are the most important units of the social structure, when legislation and jurisdiction is considered. The arrangement for the exercise of rule, if any, in its diverse and significant everyday aspects was always the rights of privileged individuals not the cognitively oriented performance of the duties and responsibilities of officials. The dominant trend in state/society relations in the 20th century was the expansion of rule and not the expansion of rule of law. This expansion, even to the bedroom and living room of the individuals, was more visible and explicitly thematized and justified in post-Islamic Revolutionary era.

The typical judicial system in the whole 20th century, as it can be seen in the figures of previous chapters, can be presented as a pyramid, while the typical civil law system that Iranian judicial system was based on is usually visualized as a set of two or more distinct structures. The dualities inside the judiciary, especially after the Constitutional and Islamic Revolutions, were not in the level to make the judiciary be visualized as a set of two or more distinct structures. The king or the leader had the power to interfere in the judiciary and they did not share their power with any independent or dependent institution. Iran's judiciary was never an independent branch of power in the 20th century, i.e. independent from other branches of government while letting them to do their mission, freedom of judges to evaluate the facts of the disputes before them and to construe the applicable law without any direct or indirect pressure being imposed upon them by others, securing independence of judges as to one another, dealing with all issues of a judicial nature by the judiciary alone, secure judicial tenure, or the right of judges to defend their independence with the constitutionally protected right of assembly.

There have been a variety of distinct professional careers in legal professions in Iranian society but most of them are governmental positions. The lawyers as the only non-governmental legal workers have always been under pressure to follow the legal directions dictated by the state; Iranian lawyers in all of these four periods seem tame compared to the interventionist French lawyers in pre- and post revolutionary France who challenged the state directly (Halliday & Karpik, 1997: 9). Iranian lawyers, like German lawyers of 18th and 19th centuries, were more creatures of the state in post-Constitutional and post-Islamic Revolution eras. In both periods of early emergence of strong state during Reza Shah and Islamicization of the state, Iranian lawyers could not transfer from quasi-civil servants and second order judicial profession, compared to judges, to private legal professionals. In both periods, the bar was under heavy pressure of the state to be organizationally dependent, and Iranian lawyers could not press for a free bar, self-employment, and self-regulation, creation of their own voluntary association and engaging in political activities. The historical precedence of a strong state, the complications of state-building, and the residue of civil service orientation, all confounded the profession's procedural and liberal inclinations that had been stimulated by the European example. The Islamic Revolution that was firstly supposed to facilitate this orientation further suppressed proceduralism in disputes and prosecutions, open admission to the bar, and profession-wide consensus. More internal conflicts compelled lawyers to turn more to the state as an arbiter.

The courts in the whole 20th century have not been the arena for power struggles between individuals and government agencies, especially security, disciplinary and military forces. The judicial reforms in all of these four periods squeezed the different and ad hoc tribunals which could settle lots of cases before sending them to the official courts.

Court Scheme

I considered political structure changes, reflected in social movements and regime changes, as the causes and judicial reform as the effect, for these reasons: 1) the courts as part of the general government have not played the role of guarantors of the political structure; 2) courts depend on the same political processes that sustain legislative and executive institutions; 3) many components of the judicial process including judicial reform are the product of political and social conflicts. Conflicts not only surges around judicial structure and procedures but also surrounds questions of staffing and resources; 4) judiciary hardly could have a reciprocal effect on social structures as an independent branch of government due to instability in the political structure; 5) Iranian courts have not any role in distributing values; the ideology of the state, whether nationalism, or Islamism, has been the source of values enforced by naked coerce; and 6) courts have never been an important actor in stigmatizing or legitimizing the power of government. Iranian judiciary could not have a life of its own. These points justify the structure of the study, i.e. discussion of political regime, and social setting prior to judicial reform and its goals, causes, dilemmas and consequences.

Judicial reform is indispensable from any social revolution and state building process. What makes a set of judicial reforms different from others are underlying legal systems, political forces, ideologies and the special relationship of state and social structure. Adoption of, for example, dual court structure during first period of judicial reform or general courts during fourth period was the result of the gap between social and political structures in post-Constitutional Revolution era and mass society in post-Islamic Revolution era respectively. Although conjugation of the socio-political

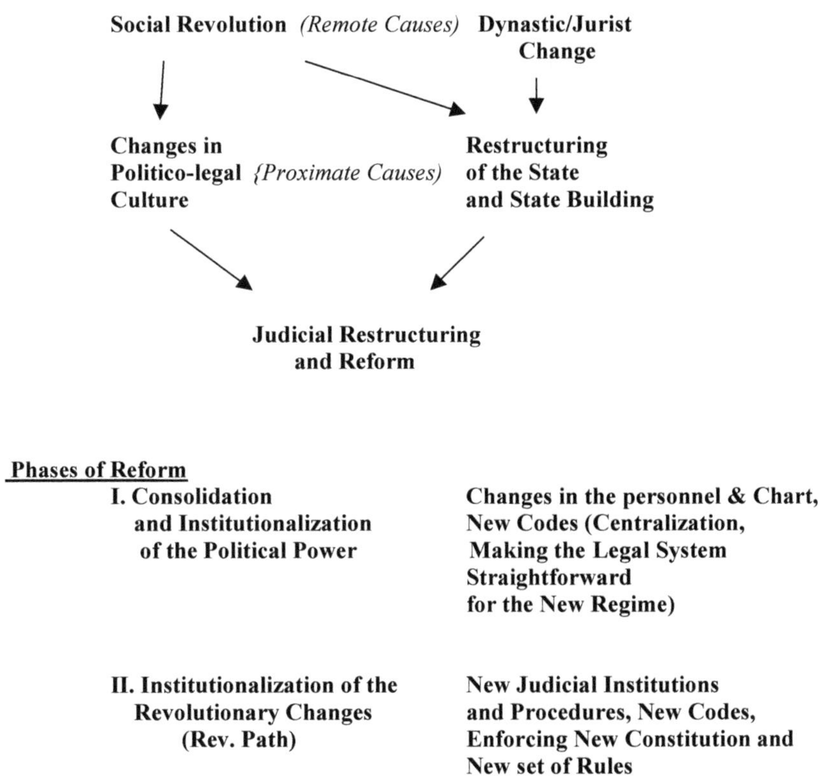

Fig. 7.1. General Causal Model of Judicial Reform in 20th Century Iran

forces and structures could be considered as the cause of judicial reform, centralization of the state or politicization of the masses was only "*a*" cause of judicial reform among others.

There are some challenging ideas in this scheme: 1) judicial reforms are directly or indirectly caused by social revolution, not by the consciously made decision of the governments to increase their effectiveness or legitimacy of the regime; 2) judicial reform happens when the consolidation of power is over; 3) other than purging, judiciary is centralized during judicial reforms caused by social revolution; and 4) judicial reform is not motivated by immediate need of new regimes to be consolidated but is pursued as part of the administrative reconstruction. This is true that the politicians make the decisions about the reforms in the judiciary but their decisions are the last chains of a whole process and the root causes are critical in shaping the trends and ways of implementing the reforms.

State building and social revolutions are the causes of judicial reform not because they occurred before the judicial reforms or they are usually associated with judicial reform but because there are sufficient evidence to warrant that judicial reforms are caused by these developments in Iran. There is also no known common cause for all these developments.

Constitutional Basis for Judicial Regimes

If we compare two different constitutions of 1906–7 and 1979 (revisions could not change the basic structure of these texts) with respect to judicial regimes that came out of them, these may be the results:

1) Both constitutions obliges the courts to reason well their verdicts out and document them with reference to the articles and principles of the law in accordance with which they are delivered (Art. 78, 1906; Art. 166, 1979). This is not part of what courts usually do in a daily basis, especially in political and press courts.
2) Both constitutions require the courts to try political and press offenses openly and in the presence of a jury (Art. 79, 1906; Art. 168, 1979). Courts have always violated this principle.
3) The head of the judiciary branch that is directly appointed by the Leader and the minister of justice that was indirectly appointed by king are responsible for the employment of judiciary officials and judges, their dismissal, appointment, transfer, assignment to particular duties, promotions, and carrying out similar administrative duties in 1979 and 1906 constitutions respectively (Art. 80, 1906; Sec. 3, Art. 158, 1979). This is one of the articles that have always been totally executed in the whole 20th century.

4) According to both constitutions, judges cannot be removed, transferred, re-designated, and dismissed except in special conditions (Art. 81 & 82, 1906; Art. 164, 1979). Both Pahlavi regime and IRI have violated these articles.
5) There is no procedure for electing judiciary officials in both constitutions. In 1906 Constitution, the general attorney is appointed by the king with the suggestion of the Chief Justice (Art. 83); in 1979 constitution, this was the judiciary council and then the head of the judiciary who appoints all the judiciary officials (Arts.158 and 162). People had no say in the judiciary.
6) The only exception for the regular courts of law in both constitutions is Military Court. Military Courts, in both, are to be established by law to investigate crimes committed in connection with military or security duties by members of the armed forces (Art. 87, 1906; Art. 172, 1979). They will be tried in public courts, however, for common crimes or crimes committed while serving the department of justice in executive capacity. The office of military prosecutor and the military courts form part of the judiciary and are subject to the same principles that regulate the judiciary. Both regimes violated these articles by trying non-military staff.
7) Only the 1906 Constitution approved Courts of Appeal (Arts. 86 & 87, 1906). The 1979 constitution negated the appeal court and only considered the Supreme Court as the court that is to be formed for the purpose of supervising the correct implementation of the laws by the courts, ensuring uniformity of judicial procedure, and fulfilling any other responsibilities assigned to it by law (Art. 161). The Constitution of 1979 has given this power to the judiciary to form different courts including appellate courts (Art. 159) or to refer a case to that court. This is not the right of the people to appeal to higher courts but it is a privilege that the judiciary officials bestow Iranian people. This statement that "the formation of courts and their jurisdiction is to be determined by law" (Art. 159) gives this right to the judiciary to establish any courts including appellate courts if it requires.
8) Administrative Justice Court in the 1979 Constitution and Cassation Court in the 1906 Constitution have the same function, i.e. to investigate the complaints, grievances, and objections of the people with respect to government officials, organs, and statutes (Art. 173, 1979; Art. 88, 1906).
9) On the basis of 1979 Constitution "no one may be arrested except by the order and in accordance with the procedure laid down by

law. In case of arrest, charges with the reasons for accusation must, without delay, be communicated and explained to the accused in writing, and a provisional dossier must be forwarded to the competent judicial authorities within a maximum of twenty-four hours so that the preliminaries to the trial can be completed as swiftly as possible. The violation of this article will be liable to punishment in accordance with the law Art. 32). The 1906 Constitution mentions the same thing (Art. 10 of the Amendment). This has never been enforced, especially in political and press cases.

10) Both constitutions declare that courts are only established on the basis of law. The courts of justice are the official bodies to which all grievances and complaints are to be referred (Arts. 73 & 74, 1906; Art. 159, 1979). Revolutionary and Clergy courts are explicit violations of the relevant article in post-Islamic Revolutionary Iran.
11) Both constitutions require trials to be held openly and members of the public may attend without any restriction unless the court determines that an open trial would be detrimental to public morality or discipline, or if in case of private disputes, both the parties request not to hold open hearing (Art. 76, 1906; Art. 165, 1979). This exception has turned to be a rule, especially in political and press cases.
12) The IRI Constitution like the 1906 Constitution is the product of a number of compromises at several stages among different social forces. The different drafts and revisions show clear influences from the Islamic authoritarians, Islamic traditionalists, Islamic nationalists, and Islamic democrats with different attitudes about the judiciary and law.All the main articles supporting human rights and freedoms such as Articles 21–28 of 1979 Constitution are qualified with the condition of agreement with the "Islamic principles" that make the Constitution dysfunctional in these areas, and clerics can always supercede it.Law abiding and respect for the Constitution became a rallying point for the reformists after 1997, while the religious establishment, especially with respect to judicial affairs, totally ignored it. Professions including the bar came to occupy no heralded position in the both constitutions of 1906 and 1979.
13) There is no mechanism for judicial review in both constitutions of 1906 and 1979. Judicial review has been totally absent in Iranian legal culture and is considered in total contradiction with the *shari`ah* courts' procedures and absolute power of the government.

As it can be seen, rule of law has never been one of agendas of the Iranian state in the whole 20th century. Only the articles regarding the rights and privileges of the state are fully enforced. The focus on constitutional politics should not make us to ignore the distinction between routine politics and the constitutional politics (Elster, 1995), on the one hand, and between the kind of politics involved in the making of the 1906 and 1979 constitutions and the social and political requirements for making it work (Frerejohn, Rakove & Riley, 2000: 27).

Iran's first Constitution remained basically unchanged till 1979 from the one granted in 1906, after the Constitutional Revolution had put an end to autocratic rule on paper. There was a supplement in 1907 and amendments in 1925, 1949, 1957 and 1967. The 1979 Constitution was revised in 1989.

Comparisons

My theoretical point of view on the political system, politico-legal system and polity's component groups and comparisons are summarized in Table 7.1. What do these periods have in common?

1) Freedom of government in the rotation and removal of judges on the basis of ideology, expediency and considerations of ruling class;
2) Legal reforms have always been done through violating the existing law and against the supervision of the majority of parliament and ignoring the legal procedure (Āqeli, 153 & 160);
3) Almost no power for the civil society institutions in the area of judiciary;
4) Dependence of judges on political authority (Āqeli, 157 & 200–203; Bozorg, 2000: 185–190) and continuing violation of judges' independence;
5) Dependence of law practice on political authority (Āqeli, 159 & 189);
6) Non-democratic central government who do not recognize the independence of powers and due process;
7) Non-deference of powerful people to the verdicts of the court (Āqeli, 325);
8) Unpredictability of injunctions, sentences and writs due to speedy change of rules and regulations, corruption of law enforcement personnel, and lack of uniformity of judicial procedure in some periods;
9) Corruption like venality of judicial offices;
10) Nullification of previous administrations' procedures by the later ones and instability in judicial affairs;

11) Negation of some of the judiciary's authorities by rejection of judiciary's duty to oversight the enforcement of laws and regulations and revival of capitulation in different periods (Bozorg, 2000: 194 -223).

Beside the above similarities, each period of judicial reform has its basic challenges and problems, summarized in Table 7.4.

Table 7.4. Main Problems of the Four Periods of Judicial Reform: 1906–2006

-1911	- Power of the Clerics opposed to the state courts (Eqbāl, 1976: Ch. 5) - Getting refuge in the house of clerics by felonies (Eqbāl, 1976: 172) - Giving trivial verdicts to people by clerics (Eqbāl, 1976: 172)
1911-	- Lack of familiarity of the judges with the procedures of the new courts - Shortage of personnel with adequate legal training - Exemption of aliens from the reach of Iranian law by the system of capitulation - Partial effect of the judiciary in the capital
1927	- No optimization between the speed of trials and the settling of disputes on one hand and meeting justice from the other (Āqeli, 131) - Shortage of personnel with adequate legal training - Legitimacy crisis (Āqeli, 324) - Opposition of clergy against the measures while commercial middle class and intelligentsia gave Reza Shah wavering support (Ghani, 326). Intelligentsia backed his nationalist creed. - Legal system was expensive, cumbersome, and complicated for Iranian individuals at this stage - Gap between local and informal mechanisms and dispute solution on one side and the formal and state-sponsored system on the other
1979-	- Insufficient number of *mujtaheds* for recruitment in the judiciary - Public resistance against execution of some Islamic laws like stoning and amputation
1994	- Public opinion totally against judicialization of politics pursued by authoritarians who rule the judiciary - Unaccountability of the judiciary to any elected bodies of government

Reform Advocates

As a result of high growth rate of the government's size and its authoritarian policies, advocates of judicial reform in the four periods under discussion are mostly found in the government. Due to different composition of governmental officials, we can observe different groups of people as agents of change in the judiciary.

In the first and second periods, the agents of change are foreign educated officials of the judiciary who push for reform. In the third period, Islamist revolutionaries and clerics who are injected to the judiciary as judges are the pioneers of Islamicization. In the fourth period, the sultanistic regime's loyalists were upgraded to judgeship to be the agents of the reform. These agents have different backgrounds in law and order positions, from prosecutor to executioner, and from security operational agent to military staff.

The judiciary officials in different sections of Iran's contemporary history have pressed for greater judicial autonomy, centralization and, in some periods, professionalization. Judges have usually had an insignificant role in reforms and reorganizations due to their inability to articulate an independent political vision, domination by the executive power and leader's baits or king's courts, and corruption. Iranian judges have never been able to speak collectively in support of judicial reform.

The bar associations, mostly non-independent and lowly politicized, were not often able to focus on legal and judicial reform. Until recently, civil society institutions, reformist parties and human rights and democracy advocate organizations remained focused on effecting at the political society level and rarely directed their attention to strengthening the rule of law and correction of judicial procedures. Even after 1997, reformists did not expect the judiciary to be on their side and were suspicious about any kind of up-down judicial reform. When captured the majority of the Sixth Majles, reformists' hopes focused on legal changes rather than on court structures and internal judicial trends. Reformers gave particular attention to revising the legislative framework for manipulating judicial procedures directed to due process that all failed due to vetting of the Guardian Council. Judicial decisions had a sustained impact on Iranian polity, where the administrative courts made use of the autonomy granted them to strike out boldly against the executive branch.

The non-governmental advocates of judicial reform became outspoken after 1997 when judicialization of Iranian politics was taken as a policy by the authoritarian faction to hamper reform agendas. The reformists could not think about judicial activism because they had no hope to effect change through court decisions. Even after 1997, Iranian political reformists and advocates for democracy and civil rights have not presented any reform charter or agenda other than legal change. Although a well-formed agenda has not begun to emerge out of reformists' discussions on judicial issues, reading the various declarations, statements, manifestos and pronouncements of reformists between 1997 and 2006 reveals several common reform demands:

1) Judiciary needs far more autonomy to reduce the powerful influence exerted by appointed bodies of government and the office of the Leader;
2) Budgeting, oversight of investigations, and annulling judicial decisions, when they are inconsistent with the Constitution, should all be transferred to the legislative branch and the president as the person who has the responsibility to implement the Constitution (Article 113);
3) Special and exceptional courts, i.e. revolutionary and clerical, must be abolished. Civilians should not be tried before military and clerical courts;
4) All solitary confinements should be declared illegal; lawyers should be allowed to be present at all trial procedures; all courts should be open; temporary detentions should be decreased to one month and be enforced in only security and spy cases; the correction facilities should be transferred from the judiciary to the municipalities; the General Courts should be abolished; the Civil Procedural Law, the Islamic Punishment Law, and the Prison Regulations should be changed.

These recommendations are considered deeply destructive by the ruling clergy and judiciary officials because they go to the core issues of rule of guardian and relationship of different branches of the government. The issues on which reformists tend to focus have almost nothing to do with caseload management and alternative dispute resolution. Despite the consensus on the end-goals of judicial reform, there is often discord between many reform-minded and civil society-based activists over the means to achieve it. The party leaders and religious intellectuals tend to be more cautious and base their agenda on the Constitution while secular intellectuals tend to take a far more confrontational and uncompromising approach.

7.5 CHALLENGES AND DILEMMAS: OVERVIEW

The debate over religion and modernity and modernizing Islam in the Muslim world will continue for decades to come. Iraq and Afghanistan created their new legal system after Sep. 11, 2001 events and their aftermath, making the Iranian experience even more important. Iran's Islamic Revolution gave birth to Statism-Islamism and then prepared to deliver an Islamic reformation.

Judicial reforms in the first and second periods discussed in this study mixed Western and Islamic Law. The ideas relating transition from traditional judiciary to a modern one could be useful today when Muslim societies are trying to figure out how to reconcile Islam and the Western achievements in social management, ideas like democracy, rule of law, civil society, human rights, and due process.

The puzzle-ordeal is a useful metaphor for the expected judicial reform in Iran because there is no straightforward route or algorithm for achieving multiple and sometimes conflicting objectives beside dangerous routes in front of reformers. Indeed, each route seems to offer the likelihood of failure, significant costs, or unintended consequences. During the whole 20th century, Iran did not feature an independent judiciary, a well-educated bar, and a modern procedural code. Judicial reform in Iran neither advanced independence nor accountability. The judiciary system produced a quality of systemic behavior that falls far below the positive characteristics of intelligent actors and well-designed codes. The parameters under which reformers in every period could tune with were very limited. The bottom-up perspective, both in judiciary and the public, would have incalculable value in generating new perspectives on age-old issues.

Indeed, the ordeal of judicial reform contains multiple exits for those attempting to attain specific, sometimes conflicting, and almost elusive justice objectives. Navigating the path toward one goal may distance reformers from still another. We are presented with a series of undesirable choices or dilemmas, including determinations of reform design and method, as well as the most profound obstacle of all: the social dilemma of individuals whose short-term self-interest is inconsistent with the articulated values of the collective.

Can this ostensibly impossible puzzle be solved through the self-organization of simple participants? Can we take full advantage of pursuing bottom-up perspectives in our diagnosis of the pathologies and our possible prescriptions of the cures? Can reformers start from a presumption of relative ignorance and work more collaboratively and with greater humility to create better systems? Can the collective actions of reformers get them through the puzzle-ordeal of dilemmas they confront in judicial reform? Going through the ordeal is arduous and uncertain, requiring appraisals of the roadblocks and the ingenuity to get around them.

Ignoring the complexities of this puzzle-ordeal, Iranian judicial reformers have always picked executive and then guardian appointment that is weak on judicial independence rather than election, legislative appointment and court appointment that are strong on independence. Executive and guardian appointment of judges in Iran has never been strong on accountability, what judiciary with this kind of appointment of judges is supposed to be. Legislative appointment that is stronger on independence than executive and guardian appointment, and stronger on accountability than judicial self-appointment has never been on the table in Iranian judicial reform agenda. There has never been a procedure for appointment of judges in Iran. Promotions to high ranking positions are usually based on political ties and loyalty to the leader, shah or jurist.

Other than external factors, judicial guarantees of independence in Iran's bureaucratic judiciary is weak because 1) advancement up the career ladder, like any other civil law country, is competitive and promotions are granted according to formal criteria combining seniority and merit that is determined by hierarchical superiors, and 2) judges are supposed to be capable of performing all organizational roles associated to their rank and are recruited not for a specific position but for a wide set of roles.

In all of the periods discussed, judges are subordinate to the executive power or the guardian and his appointees (Table 7.5). The independence of a judiciary can be analyzed and understood based on how the judges are recruited, promoted, transferred, and removed. These elements can be used to assess the extent of both internal and external judicial independence, the relationship between the judiciary and other branches of government and protection of judges from undue pressures from within the judiciary (Guarnieri & Pederzoli, 2002: 45).

Human resource deficiencies have always been critical. Lawyers in Iran have been at a relatively low rung of professional rankings, and legal educators have struggled to attract talented students. The talented students have always been attracted to medicine and engineering. Judicial positions are far less desirable than one would presume. Only loyalists to the regimes, kings and leaders could conceive the role of the judge and general attorney in 20th century Iran. High status and psychic income have always been unavailable to regular graduates of law schools. Talented students have not wanted to be judges in a system that gives them weaker civil service roles.

Even if one could solve these recruitment problems, limited financial resources posed an additional impediment. Experts have always bemoaned the low level of public financing in the courts; however, beyond intentional neglect, Iranian political institutions have been reluctant to invest in institutions that do not function sympathetically and partially in their interests.

Table 7.5. Recruitment, Promotion, Transfer, and Removal of Judges in Four Periods of Iran's Judiciary

	1910–1927	1927–1979	1979–1989	1989–2006
Recruitment	Appointment by Executive Branch and Shah	Appointment by Executive Branch and Shah	Appointment by the Supreme Council of Judiciary	Appointment by the Head of Judiciary
Institution in Charge of Promotion and Transfer	Ministry of Justice	Ministry of Justice	Supreme Councilof Judiciary	Head of Judiciary
Removal	Supreme Administrative Council Minister of Justice +	Disciplinary Court + Minister of Justice*	Disciplinary Court + Supreme Council of Judiciary	Disciplinary Court + Head of Judiciary**

Sources: Article 159 and 181 of the Judiciary Organization and Shari'ah Courts and Reconciliation Magistrates Law of 1910, Article 20 of the Recruitment of Judges Act of 1927, Article 157 of the Constitution of 1979, and Article 158 of the Constitution of 1989

* Between 1936 and 1943 The Supreme Council of the Ministry of Justice had to hear and review some cases against the judges (Zerang, Vol. I, 2002: 318, 347, 446; Zerang, Vol. II, 2002: 47). These cases include administrative violations, behaviors incompatible with judicial prestige, and enforcement of personal opinions.

** In this period and other periods, the disciplinary Court (or the Supreme Administrative Court in the first period) reviews the case and issues the verdict; the verdict should be enforced by the Minister of Justice, the Head of the Judiciary or the Supreme Council of the Judiciary in different periods.

Lawyers have always complained about the way they struggle to make a living, and uncorrupted judges justifiably complained about their salaries as substantially less than the back street grocers. It was unlikely that a legislature or clientele reward a judiciary or bar when there was very little perceived social value to be rendered by their services. Thus, in a vicious cycle, solving one problem seemed to require solving them all simultaneously.

Due to fundamental problems in the law schools and ideological recruitment of the judges, they as the most important human resources of the judiciary were not equally capable of the range of skills required by trial-court work, i.e. adjudication, administration, community relations, legal research, and negotiation. Judicial quality was always defined in terms of judges' political compatibility with the preferences of political power.

The conditions of the legal community were frequently inhospitable to reform. The improved performance of a judicial system ultimately was a matter for the reformers from different political factions. Reform depended heavily on the participation of local legal opinion leaders and practitioners. External pressure and assistance through occupation and micro-management by a foreign power or international institution that could only function as a push never happened in Iran. However, the society most in need of effective reform tended to have the lowest levels of participation in the reform process. Without widespread participation in reform by primary participants in the operation of the system, the risks of non-implementation or unintended consequences substantially increased. In most periods of judicial reform, secular or religious, the primary participant could not participate in the reform process because the authoritative reforms did not cover their concerns.

Political change is only the necessary condition for judicial reform. After any political change, different Iranian administrations believed that judicial reform has automatically happened or could happen. They ignored this fact that judicial reform depends on a political-social-legal strategy that can overcome the powerful forces in support of the status quo. Few experts in the judicial system had the sophistication to develop a political strategy, and reformers thus had difficulty aligning political leadership at the top and the social forces' demand for change at the bottom with necessities and potentialities of the judiciary.

There has been no recognition for social and scientific procedures in all periods of judicial reform in Iran. Judicial concepts as trial by jury, respect for the rights of individuals, the application of scientific methods in establishing evidence, and a formalized trial procedure have always been in embryonic form during the whole 20th century. Court proceedings have rarely been recorded in special registers; defendants, even not accused of murder or grand robbery, were not usually set free on bail; and victims of crimes like rape, beating or murder were not always examined by a qualified physician.[21] Most of the procedures were not designed to ensure better protection for the citizens. Creation of the courts were not usually a move in this direction and the passage of the laws could not achieve this end because of governments' view on judicial procedure, i.e. as an instrument for consolidation of power and survival. The arbitrariness of proceedings and the accompanying extortion practiced by officials always de-institutionalized every effort to vindicate individual rights and establishing the stable institutions of justice.

There has not been a learning process involved in the rise and decline of Islamic ideological judicial reform. Some of the premises of the earlier generations of political modernizers and legal reformers are taken for granted by the contemporary advocates of Islamicization of the judiciary, i.e. authoritative development and focusing on state instead of civil society. The process of internship has also been totally ignored in the post-revolutionary judiciary. What does this mean for the dynamics of the process of Islamicization? This means up-down, non-participatory, and unwanted reform that has always failed.

One of the leading assumptions of the judicial reformers in the whole 20th century has been that the only effective administrative organization of a court system is one that is unified, with vertical lines of authority featuring centralized management, budgeting, and rule making vested in a central government under the control of the king or leader. Having the old model of continental nation-state in mind, the court reformers did not want to consider a variety of organizational models. They ignored elements that might be appropriate in a particular court system, depending upon the available sources of court funding, the need for local flexibility and discretion, the pressure for standardization, and strength of forces resistant to change.

There are four tensions in the whole story of judicial reform in 20th century Iran. The first tension has been between national, political unity and effective government mostly in first and second periods; the second has been the tension between ethnic and local judicial diversity and centralized judicial system, mostly in the second period; this is related to the adaptations of centralism and power sharing devices within the branches of government, and power sharing devices between central government and the provinces. The third one has been between the collective and individual rights in all those four periods. The fourth tension has been between authoritarian and democratic readings of Islam in the third and fourth periods.

As a result, the judiciary has failed in dedication to the fundamental goals of judicial reform, i.e. peaceful resolution of private civil conflicts, enforcement of criminal laws, restraint upon governmental intrusions, efficient operation and to be safety valve for the amelioration of repressive laws.

Conclusion

As a very brief statement of my argument, I demonstrated that despite the various changes in the judiciary there has never been rule of law in Iranian society. My first argument is about continuity. I have shown this descriptively. My second argument is in two parts: (1) there were moments when the system might have changed, but (2) reforms mostly failed. My third argument is that the form of the judicial system varied from one period to another. (Table 7.3) This is established both descriptively, and by demonstrating the causes of the reforms. In chapters 3 to 7, I tried to demonstrate that my argument is the most plausible of various contending explanations.

As opposed to justice oriented approach, where a state claims reform to bring justice for all people within its territorial boundaries regardless of their religious and ethnic backgrounds, state-building/social revolution orientation refers to a reform framework in which a state claims to implement due process and/or rule of law (religious or secular) to consolidate its authority over its subjects with accumulated grievances and revolutionary agenda. Around the early and late 20th century, a total of four comprehensive judicial reform projects were followed by different administrations to formally and substantially rationalize, secularize and later Islamicize judicial procedures and practices. What explains the sequence of dissolution and purging and then restructuring and recruitment processes in Iranian judiciary during 20th century? Why did different states restructure the judiciary and almost completely changed the judges after their short term consolidation? What factors account for the variation in the timing of the dissolution and purging processes? Answering these questions, I clarify how a non-Western state like Iran integrated into the Western state system in late 19th and early 20th century and tried to depart from it in the late 20th century. This would provide clues about the development and the future evolution of Iran's state system and its judiciary and generally the upcoming developments in the Middle East.

My research contributes to our understanding of modern state-building and codification/transplantation in non-Western states and provides insight into the dynamic relationship between domestic institutions and international practices from one hand and the dynamic between traditionalist and modernist forces in a polity on the other. The dynamic between these forces are projected in reform and social revolutions' agendas. Therefore my study advances a state-building/social revolution explanation regarding the judicial reform in non-Western countries. Providing a social/polity-based explanation, i.e. the weak and loose mirror/weak isolation/transitional transplantation theory, links the judicial reforms to the expansion and centralization of the state on one hand and social revolutions on the other. After the state system evolved into a secular one based on a common Western civilization, it demanded that government centralize and secularize as a precondition for the integration to the modern world and ending the capitulation. The state-building/social revolution approach argues that Iranian state pursued the way toward judicial reform when the elite perceived that the host countries of Western civilization have to modernize and secularize, or as a reaction to Islamicize, including their judicial system. I claim that the establishment of state-based legal institutions and demands of social revolutions in non-Western countries best explains different waves of judicial reform, if any.

In contrast, international power relations, efficiency, and economy based approaches offer their own hypotheses to explain the different waves of judicial reforms. According to international power relations theory, Western states were sufficiently powerful to impose their expected reforms on increasingly resistant non-Western countries. Traditional explanations for the judicial reform which rely on power relations do not account for non-Western states' decisions to begin and accomplish judicial reform. On the basis of efficiency theory, non-Western domestic interest groups were merely interested in administrative manipulation of a bureaucratic system including the judiciary; and based on Marxist theory, law and judiciary as sections of superstructure have not been the main priority of the state and social movements, both, and judicial reforms are only a show for putting people in sleep; the emphasis should be on economic development and the change in class structure.

I tested my state-building/social revolution argument and the alternative explanations, i.e. dictates from the West, administrative manipulation, and economic development and justice oriented reforms in comparative case studies of four periods of judicial reform in Iran. I follow two research strategies. First, I relied upon Mills' methods of difference and agreement to establish correlations between the judicial reform and the competing explanatory factors. I have two examples of total failure to reform (reforms after 1911 by Moshir ul-Dowleh, and the General Courts of Yazdi administration), one partly success and partly failure story (reforms immediately after the Islamic Revolution; failure because of failing to deliver justice as was promised, and success because of enforcing some of the shari`ah laws and more formalizing shari`ah laws already on the books) and one example of mostly successful efforts to reform (Davar's reform of 1927). Failure and success in these cases are defined according to the goals and objectives of reform put forward by the regimes in each period. These observations offer variation on the explanatory factors, i.e. social revolution that involves changes in ideology and politico-legal culture and state building process. Change of the ideology includes the change of perception of non-Western countries' legal system from the Islamist ideology point of view. Using both qualitative and quantitative data, correlations of the explanatory factors with the way of decision-making to reform the judiciary reveal that while none of the observations falsified the social revolution/state-building hypothesis, four observations contradicted the West dictated reform approach (unless we believe in a very thick version of conspiracy theory that fighting against capitulation was itself led by the Western countries), three observations contradicted the administrative manipulation approach, one observation contradicted the economic development approach and two observations contradicted justice orientation approach.

Four observations contradict the power relations theory, i.e. West dictated reform approach: 1) constitutional and Islamic Revolutions of 1906 and 1979 were internally instigated and the revolutionaries in both movements had clear agendas for judicial reform; 2) at least some of these agendas have been projected in both constitutions of 1906 and 1979, drafted after social movements. Constitutional bases for judicial reform are not dependent to the eyes of beholder; 3) Western governments were explicitly or implicitly against the third and the fourth rounds of judicial reform and Islamic revolutionaries had anti-Western agenda; and 4) capitulation was supported by the Western countries till the beginning of second period of judicial reform. One of the goals of second period of reform was to abolish capitulation. This goal totally falsifies this idea that different administrations during Reza Shah were puppets of the imperial powers.

Three observations contradict the administrative manipulation approach: 1) The main approach to judicial reform during the Constitutional Revolution was based on populist approach to judicial reform. The demand for justice was popular and could be traced in intelligentsia's literature; 2) judicial reform in the third period was ideologically instigated and was part of the Islamists' mission to build a new society based on Islamic doctrines; and 3) Dāvar's Centralizing agenda was way more than administrative manipulation; he wanted to have a centralized judiciary that is part of the state's machine to enforce law and order all over the land. His reforms' practical implications were particularly apparent for the educated elite and for the growing ranks of government and local and traditional authorities.

One observation contradicts the economic development approach; judicial reform of the third and fourth periods were to enforce shari`ah laws and establish a just and later powerful government. At last, two observations contradict justice orientation approach: 1) Reforms during second period did not have justice as the main agenda; and 2) the most powerful Islamists who led the second period of judicial reform did not believe that justice comes first; in their belief, Islam comes first.

In a second stage, I used process-tracing to eliminate spurious correlations by uncovering the chain of events leading to Iranian rulers' motivations to dissolve the existing judiciary and build a new one. I focused on the ten observations that I used for Mills' tests of agreement and difference. In order to trace the process leading reform, I relied upon intra-governmental debates, parliamentary discussions and proceedings, exchanges between administrations and their opponents, and reports of the Iranian newspapers to test which of the specified explanations motivated rulers' decisions to reform the judiciary. My research, using both published primary and secondary sources, suggests that Iranian rulers' decisions reflected their perception of how a non-Western country had to confront the necessities and implications of a modern state or a state in the modern world and its state-based legal system that could clarify and enforce state control over its subjects. They also reacted, in a way, to the demands of the social movements and their aftermath.

I shaped the appropriate ideal-types for politico-legal regimes in each period in this study on the basis of what has been happening in the judiciary and the strategies and policies selected for judicial reform and reorganization. I tackled the basic misunderstanding implicit in this idea that modern judicial system replaced the Islamic law or the *shari'a* in Pahlavi era and Islamic judicial system replaced the modern one after the Revolution of 1979 and showed that modern formal judicial system replaced not the *shari`ah* courts but the dual "'orfi or state + *shari`ah*" court system.

FAILURE OR SUCCESS

I have been trying to do three distinct tasks in this study. First, I wanted to explain this fact that throughout the twentieth century there has never been rule of law in Iran and in the situation of lawlessness it was very difficult for any administration to pursue a successful judicial reform, regardless of its goals and causes in different periods. No judicial reform by the judicial officials could establish an independent and effective judiciary as it was delineated in the preliminary objectives. The lack of an independent and effective judiciary could have been in turn one of the reasons for a "failure of the democratic experience." Other than short periods and short-lived governments like Mosaddeq's and fist term of Khatami's presidency, Iranians could not even experience partial democracy. This has been explained in each section on state building process in the beginning of each chapter.

Second, judicial reform was a real possibility but it mostly failed. During the twentieth century there was a real chance that judicial reform would "succeed" in the sense of producing an independent and effective judiciary due to opportunities brought about by social and political movements, the regime changes, and changes in the social settings. If not independent, effective judiciary was a reasonable expectation for twentieth-century Iran but it never succeeded because of five common reasons (and lots of uncommon reasons): 1) the social revolutions of 1906 and 1979 ended up with change of administrations and not the way of administration and the relationship between state, civil society and individuals, 2) institutional dualities in the area of political structures, political elites and judiciary, 3) resort to illegitimate means even for legitimate causes, 4) political instabilities, and 5) institutional political interferences. Due to dilemmas of each period, the political elite could not reach to its defined goals, whatever they were. This was not due to the inability of revolutionary regimes to carry through on their promises but structural problems and obstacles that are mentioned in each period.

After periodizing Iranian judicial reform history in terms of attempts at judicial reform, I established for each effort at judicial reform (1) how serious it was (2) whether, if implemented, it would have produced an effective and independent judiciary and how feasible it was, and (3) why it failed.

Since I have been trying to explain judicial reform in each period and change between each of those four periods, I clearly defined each period in terms of variation in the judicial system and then proceeded to explain the variation by reference to what I thought the main causes were. This came after explaining the politico-social background of each period.

This is the main argument of my study: judicial reform in each period of 20th century Iran had different causes, goals and dilemmas. What these reforms have in common is their up—down, power concentration, and authoritarian characteristic. In the first period, judicial reform is a response to one of the demands of the Constitutional Revolution of 1906 to establish foundations of justice in the country. In the second period of judicial reform, administration and process of justice are more important that justice per se. The Islamic Revolutionaries of the late 1970's wanted reform in the judiciary to consolidate the new regime and Islamicize the society from above. In the fourth period, judicial reform was intended to put an end to modern procedural justice and consolidate the personal power of the jurist. The causes of changes in the scheme of judicial reform from one period to the next are mainly explained with regard to change in the social setting and political structures.

Most of the time attempted judicial reform failed to produce an independent and effective judiciary (and not rule of law) as understood by different elites. Despite the apparently dramatic changes in the political and judicial system from one period to another, in all periods the state was responsive to elites rather than masses and weak civil society institutions and consequently there was no effective and independent judiciary and rule of law.

I am not writing a history of the Iranian judicial system. What distinguishes my account from others is 1) to go further from presenting a calendar of events, 2) to explain the social and political contexts of the reforms, 3) looking at legal and judicial systems as structures in interaction with other structures in the society, and 4) trying to understand the mechanisms and processes of change. This study is not an explanation of the causes of change from one type of judicial system to another in the 20th century Iran but an explanation of why, on each of several occasions, there were attempts at judicial reform and why they mostly failed.

EPILOGUE

1. Should reformers in each period stress judicial independence or accountability, enforcing law and order, peace or justice, efficiency, human, civil and constitutional rights or national security? How much should judicial reformers understand (through qualitative and quantitative empirical research and survey) about the target system before they make recommendations in order to limit these failures? Is research too slow and inconclusive to justify further delay in tending to press needs? To what extent should reformers supply resources in support of judicial reform (without sufficient levels of demand) at the risk of waste? Or should they wait for demand to bubble up? Should judicial reformers draw on foreign or local expertise and resources? Should judicial reform be more of a supply- or a demand-side approach? Should political strategies work from the top-down or the bottom-up?

The Iranian legal literature on reform appears to be silent on these issues. Political activists and lawyers explain judicial reform failure as a function of the interests of powerful actors who take advantage of the political process. Dilemmas, especially the double sovereignty and modern/traditional problematic, are noted frequently in discussions diversely ranging from due process, to execution of *sharī`ah* decrees, but it seems that, even when the dilemmas of judicial reform are central to the discussion, the subject attracts no serious or formal consideration.

2. Iranian judicial reformers in the future will confront the dilemma of incremental vs. systemic reform. Mediation pilots cannot touch upon the common lack of finality in the litigation process, and as a result where incentives for settlement are consequently weak, mediation may be unlikely to succeed. Ethics training for judges in the corrupt system will do little to reverse the underlying motivations for the receipt, if not solicitation, of bribes. The appointment of outsiders will do little to alter the corporatist culture of a career judiciary.

3. Why does reform still seem so impossible? One reason is the Iranian legal system's distance from legal and judicial developments in global arena. Iranian judiciary is far behind the ideas of technical standardization, professional rule production, human rights, intra-organizational regulation in multinational enterprises, contracting, arbitration and other institutions of *lex mercatoria* and other forms of legal pluralism. These legal frameworks claim worldwide validity independently of the law of the nation-states and in relative distance to the rules of international public law (Tuebner, 1997: xiii). Iranian judiciary has ignored the consequences of globalization process in the legal and judicial arenas.

4. Judicial reform mostly failed because it has been in fact unfamiliar and threatening. However, if those eventually subject to the judicial reforms had a voice in their design and could articulate their concerns in advance of reform determinations, defensive behavior could be substantially mitigated. Inside-out (rather than outside-in) and bottom-up (rather than top-down) reform processes foster a greater familiarity with the actual conditions of the host system and its many participants, are more likely to supply a respectable theory of agent behavior, reduce immunity (enjoyed by outsiders in particular and even high-level officials on the brink of retirement) from the consequences of reform, and minimize the harmful projection of foreign attitudes and ideas.

5. Different Iranian judicial administrations during the past century have added agencies, have merged organizations and courts, and have changed responsibilities of the judiciary's different sections and their relationships. These changes have been produced by law, by executive fiat, by legislature committee mandate, by appointed bodies of government like the Guardian Council or the Expediency Council, and internal transformation

like social movements. They have often involved considerable investment of money, time, social capital and political efforts. These organizational changes had not increased the efficiency, accountability and independency of the judiciary.

FURTHER STUDIES

There are still some questions regarding the context and consequences of judicial reform in Iran to answer. Some of them relate to the interaction of judicial reforms and other aspects of reform like economic, political, social and cultural reform. Here we can ask about the interactions between judicial institutions on the one hand and economic, religious and cultural institutions on the other and specifically the consequences of politico-judicial interaction and intersection of courts with politics for other processes like economic development and state building. Some others relate to the organizations and institutions inside the judicial domain and how their internal structures and functions impact probable judicial reforms in the future. In this regard someone can ask about the organization of legal institutions like bar and legal NGOs, local, national, regional and international, and legal professions and positions and different functions of these professions including judgeship, law practice, paralegal, notary, and public attorney positions. Each of these professions can be studied independently with respect to their impact on judicial reform and reorganization. A critical area of study will be the development of Iranian legal culture and its impact on judicial reform and vice versa. In this regard we can ask where is the place of judicial reform in Iranian legal culture and how can the dual legal culture[1] and legal order be influenced by change in the norms and values on the one hand and dual political culture and political order on the other.

Another area of work will be comparative studies on judicial reform in the Middle East. In my study I could only cover 20th century Iran and its four periods of judicial reform with some references to Turkey, Egypt and Saudi Arabia and I miss the opportunity for detailed comparative analysis, especially with Egypt and the Ottoman Empire and also new Afghan and Iraqi regimes in the aftermath of Sep. 11, 2001 event. Cases with similar pace of modernization in the Middle East like Egypt (Brown, 1997 & 2002; Horowitz, 1994; Cannon, 1988) and Turkey (Berkes, 1964), with dissimilar paces like Saudi Arabia and Yemen, and some revolutionary cases like France (Carey, 1981; Mousnier, 1979) and Russia (Quigley, 1990) that agree with Iran in displaying both the cause and effect are suitable cases to build a causal model. In selecting the cases for comparison,

I will select cases that have most cultural, social, economic and political similarities with Iran in those four periods of judicial reform. I will only consider the Middle Eastern and revolutionary societies' judiciary systems to build my own models for explaining judicial reform in Iran. There are some passing comments and footnotes that allude to the comparison, but nothing systematic in this study.

Appendix I
Chronological Outline

Judicial reform has always been in the minds of Iranian reformers and intellectuals in the twentieth century. This reform has been described as one of the pillars of the nation-state building (Mansur ul-Saltaneh, 1911: 369). In this chronological outline, I will present most of the important ideological, legal, judicial and organizational developments and reforms in the area of judiciary and jurisdiction.[1]

1. CHANGES IN LEGAL-POLITICAL CULTURE: IMPORTATION OF IDEAS CONCERNING JUDICIAL REFORM

- Rule of law in general (Ādamiyyat, 1970: 139; Ādamiyyat, 1976/1990) and in judicial procedure and equality in front of law (1861) (Ādamiyyat, 1970: 157; Ādamiyyat, 1961: 136)
- *Sharī`ah* is not the fountain of justice (Ādamiyyat, 1970: 158)
- Constitutional rights of individuals (1884) (Ādamiyyat, 1961: 214)
- Legal equality of individuals, in front of law and courts (1906) (Foroughi, 1906: 153–159; Mansur ul-Saltaneh, 1911: 98, 100). Aiming gun towards Ayatollah Nuri's head to not dissent the equality of individuals in front of the law (Mokhber ul-Saltaneh Hedāyat, *Memoirs and Occurrences* (*Khāterāt va Khatarāt*))
- Court of Ministers (Mansur ul-Saltaneh, 1911: 340)
- Independence of judiciary power (Mansur ul-Saltaneh, 1911: 362) and monopoly of judiciary power as a branch of government over investigating and issuing the verdict of a litigation (Mansur ul-Saltaneh, Mirzā Mostafā, 1911: 362–3); any other court like military one can only be created by law (Mansur ul-Saltaneh, 1911: 365)

- Open and free trial for all (Mansur ul-Saltaneh, 1911: 367–8)
- Professionalization of the courts and dividing them first into executive, criminal and civil courts and then civil courts into Peace courts, Commercial courts, Primary courts, Courts of appeal, and the Supreme Court (Mansur ul-Saltaneh, 1911: 370–79).
- The rule of law as a necessary condition for market economy and economic development (reformers, 1990's)
- Civil society institutions insure vindication of individuals' rights and rule of law (reformers, 1990's)

2. JUDICIAL REFORMS BEFORE THE CONSTITUTIONAL MOVEMENT: THE CREATION OF JUDICIAL SYSTEM

- Mirzā Āqāsi's decree for prohibition of torture in judicial procedure (1846) (Ādamiayyat, 1969: 302–3)
- Amir Kabir's decree for prohibition of torture in judicial procedures (1850) (Ādamiayyat, 1969: 302–3)
- Establishment of the Department of Justice competent to settle disputes between the state and individuals, between foreign citizens who were working for Iranian government and also between foreigners and Iranians, and customary (*'orfi*) disputes between Iranian citizens (Divān Khāneh-ye 'Adlieh) (1850) (Ādamiyyat, 1969: 302–3)
- Creation of Ministry of Justice (only in name) (1858) (Nashat, 1982: 44)
- Issuance of a decree by Nāser ul-Din Shah that everybody could personally his or their petition(s) for his judgment (1860) (Floor, 1983: 121)
- Reestablishment of the Divān Khāneh-ye 'Edālat (1861) (Floor, 1983: 121)
- Establishment of justice boxes (*sanduq-e 'edālat*) (1864) (Floor, 1983: 122)
- Relegation of the trial of foreign subjects to the Ministry of Foreign Affairs (1868) (Nashat, 1982: 44)
- Publishing *Vaqāy'-e 'Adliyeh* (*Judicial Chronicle* or *Judiciary News*) founded by the Ministry of Justice (1871) to report on administrative reforms and new regulations decreed by the Ministry of Justice
- Creation of six courts and offices i.e. Criminal Court (*Majles-e Jenāyat*), Executive Office (*Majles-e Ejrā'*), Antiquated Land

Court (*Majles-e Arāzi ye Atiqeh*), Commercial Court (Majles-e Tejārat), Investigative Court (Majles-e Tahqiq), and the Office for Drafting Bills (Majles-e Tanzim-e Qānun) by Mirzā Hosein Khan Sepah Sālār (1871) (Amin, 2003: 427)

- Introduction of stamp duties for documents and deeds (1871) (Lambton, 1987: 291)
- Promulgation of Department of Judiciary Code including separation of powers, regulation regarding due process, scientific investigation and prison reform (1872) (Mahbubi Ardekāni, 1999, Vol.2: 5)
- Creation of the Attorney General Office (1872) (Ādamiyyat, 1972: Ch. 7)
- Dismissal of Mostashār ul-Dowleh, the Minister of Justice (1872)
- Introduction of a police force along European lines in Tehran (Sep. 1873) (E'temād ul-Saltaneh, 1877–1880: Vol. III, 141).
- Promulgation of the Code of Tanzimāt-e Hasāneh (beneficent reorganization) (1875) (*Ketābcheh-ye Tanzimāt-e Hasāneh-ye dowlat-e 'Āliyeh va Mahruseh-ye Iran),* if enforced, could remove the judicial authority remaining to the governors by transferring control of the jurisdiction of the *'orfi* and partially shar'i courts to the Majles-e Tanzimāt. This Majles specified that the *shar'i* court had to be approved by both sides, and Majles-e Tanzimāt had to be notified of the choice, and only the ruling of that court would be binding (Nashat, 1982: 53).
- Box of Justice (*sanduq-'edalat*) (1875) (Nezam-Mafi, 1989: 52)
- Nāser ul-Din Shah established a committee which was charged with the codification of the provisions of *shari`ah* (1877) that produced no result (Amin al-Dowleh, 1962: 94)
- Council for the Investigation of Grievances (Majles-s Tahqiq-e Mazālem) (1882) (Nezam-Mafi, 1989: 52)
- Abolition of the *jezyeh* (poll tax) on the Zoroastrian minority in Iran (1884). The tax, paid only by non-Muslims in Islamic lands, was removed by pressure on the Qājār government asserted by the Persian Zoroastrian Amelioration Fund founded in Bombay in 1854 (http://www.bartleby.com/67/1351.html).
- Mirzā Malkum Khan (1833–1908), a leading proponent of constitutional reform, published in London his newspaper *Qānun (Law),* in which he advocated reform and criticized the tyranny and corruption of the Qajar regime (1890–98). He was one of several advocates of reform, among them Fat'h Ali Ākhundzādeh

(1812–78), Mirzā Āqā Khan Kermāni (d. 1896), and Abd ul-Rahim Tālebov (1834–1911)

- (http://www.bartleby.com/67/1351.html).
- Abd ul-Husein Mirzā translated into Persian Montesquieu's *On the Spirit of the Law* and Adam Smith's *The Wealth of Nations* (1905)
- (http://www.bartleby.com/67/1352.html).
- Publication of the first book on the constitutional law in Persian (1906) introducing new ideas like sovereignty of the people (*hākemiyyat-e melli,* at the time called *saltanat-e melli*) individuals' rights and legal equality in the framework of constitution (Forughi, Mirzā Mohammad Ali Khan-ebn-e Zokā' ul-Molk, *Hoquq-e Asāsi i.e 'Ādāb-e Mashrutiyyat-e Doval*, 1906: 9, 15, 129–153)
- Mozaffar ul-Din Shah's order for recreation of an 'Edālat Khāneh (House of Justice) to insure justice (1905) (McDaniel, 1974: 57; Kasravi, Vol. I, 1977: 60ff)

3. MEASURES AND EVENTS DURING THE FOUR PERIODS OF JUDICIAL REFORM IN IRAN'S JUDICIARY SYSTEM: 1906–2005

1906–25: Continuation of Creation

- Recognition of rights of Iranian individuals in the first constitution of the nation-state (based on the Belgian constitution of 1831) (Articles 8–25) (1906) (Browne, 1966: 374–375; http://www.bartleby.com/67/1352.html)
- Separation of powers (1906) (Browne, 1966: 376, Article 28) and defining judicial power as "the determining of rights" in the constitution of 1907 (Browne, 1966: 376 Article 27)
- Creation of the court of cassation for civil cases by the Constitution of 1906 (Browne, 1966: 381, Article 75)
- Signing of the Supplement of the Constitution by Mozaffar ul-Din Shah which the judiciary as one of the three powers of the government (Kasravi, Vol. I, 1977: 285ff)
- Creation or revival of four skeleton civil courts: the Court of Property and Financial Claims, the Criminal Court, the Court of Appeals, and the Supreme Court of Appeals (Divān-e Tamyiz) (1907) (Banani, 1969: 69)

- A move to end the rights of *bast* (refuge) in a *mujtahed*'s house by the Parliament (unsuccessful) (1907)
- Creation of regulations regarding due process
- Centralization of the judiciary system by the Minister of Justice, Mokhber ul-Saltaneh (1908) (Arjomand, 1988: 47)
- Establishment of the Office of Drafting Laws (1908) with the missions of translating laws, providing the regulations for the Office of Attorney General, setting fourth the attributes and levels of heads and members of the courts and judiciary staff, establishing the reconciliation courts, and answering the judicial questions of the courts (www.iranbar.com/pe191.php)
- Creation of a court to settle differences of opinion between *shar'i* and *'orfi* courts (1908) (Banani, 1969: 69)
- Allocation of a specific budget for the judiciary (1909) (*Surat-e Mashruh-e Mozākerāt-e Majles (Parliamentary Proceedings),* Second Parliament, 146*)*
- Recreation of the office of Public Prosecutor (*modda'i al-'omum*) in the Cassation Court (1910) (Mobārakiān, 1998: 363)
- Dissolving the old judiciary system and formation of a new one (1911) (Amin, 2003: 497)
- Setting up a temporary judiciary by the Majles which with the assistance of the French jurist Adolphe Perni drew the new civil code (Banani, 1969: 69–70)
- Approval of the Judiciary Organization and Shari`ah Courts and Reconciliation Magistrates Law (1911) including 325 articles and dividing the courts to three levels of primary, appellate and cassation courts (Amin, 2003: 497)
- Enactment of the Law of Registration of Deeds passed by the Majles on May, 1911 (1911) (Arjomand, 1988: 47)
- Reorganization of the judiciary (1911) (Zerang, Vol. I, 2002: 142; Amin, 2003: 497)
- Establishment of a judiciary committee in the Majles (1911)
- Formulation of a civil code under the guidance of a French jurist, Adolph Perni (1911) (Banani, 1961: 69)
- Issuing the decree for law practice exam as a condition for getting license for this profession by the Minister of Justice, Forughi (1914) (www.iranbar.com/pe191.php)
- Promulgation of commercial code (1915)
- New regulations for law practice and law practice exam (1917) (www.iranbar.com/pe191.php)

- Establishment of law school (1921) (Mahbubi Ardekāni, 1999, Vol.1: 404)
- Dissolution of the judiciary by Seyyed Ziā (1921) (Amin, 2003: 529)
- The first election for Iranian Bar Association, Majma'-e Vokalā (1921) (www.iranbar.com/pe191.php)
- Approval of the registration of documents and property by the Majles and its amendments (1921, 1923 and 1925) (Mahbubi Ardekāni, 1999, Vol.2: 170; *Official Magazine of Justice Department,* Vol. 1, No. 10, 1928, p.6)

1925–1979: Reconstruction and Modernization

1925–1941 Reza Shah

- Introduction of experimental commercial and penal code (1924 and 1926)
- Amendments to the Properties and Documents Registration Act (1926) (*Official Magazine of Justice Department,* Vol. 1, No. 10, 1928, p.6)
- Total dissolution of the old Ministry of Justice (Tehran's section, Feb. 9, 1927; other provinces, March 7, 1927) and opening of the new one (April, 25, 1927) by Dāvar, the Minister of Justice ('Āqeli, 1990: 7, 106, 141)
- Passing of General Properties and Documents Registration Act (1927) (*Official Magazine of Justice Department,* Vol. 1, No. 10, 1928, p.6) and creation of Properties and Documents Registration Office as one of the judiciary's sections (Amin, 2003: 542)
- The abolition of Capitulation on May 1928 (Amin, 2003: 547)
- Ratification of Regulations for Properties Registration Act (1928) (*Official Magazine of Justice Department,* Vol. 1, No. 10, 1928, p.6)
- Passing of the settlement between the State and Individuals Act by the Parliament (1928) (*Official Magazine of Properties and Documents Registration,* Vol. 1, No. 6, 1928, p. 3)
- Promulgation of laws regulating trust funds, damages, methods of testimony in court, individual claims against the state, the trial costs of aliens, the jurisdiction of *shari`ah* courts and their limitations, inheritance, and use of court injunctions as supplements to the Civil Code (1928–1930)

- Appointing first Public Attorney and establishment of Public Attorney Organization (Amin, 2003: 545)
- The Organizational Principles Law (1928) ('Āqeli, 1990: 188)
- Creation of Court of Administrative Justice (1928) (Amin, 2003: 546)
- Creation of the National General Inspectorate (1929) (Amin, 2003: 546)
- Abolition of capitulation (1928) ('Aqeli, 191)
- Passing of Trial Principles Law (1928)
- Codification, simplification and unification of *shari`ah* law in the area of public sphere in the framework of the Civil Code (1928)
- Opening of the New Qasr prison as a modern penitentiary facility (1929) (Amin, 2003: 546)
- Establishment of New Bar Association, Kānun-e Vokalā, with the recommendation of the Minister of Justice, Dāvar (1930) (www.iranbar.com/pe192.php)
- Creation of Marriage and Divorce Registration Offices and leaving them mostly to clerics (1931) ('Āqeli, 1990: 185–6)
- Establishing legal ages for marriage and enhancing the divorce and property rights of women (1931 and 1935)
- Making Western clothing and headgear compulsory (1928 and 1935)
- Provision of a jury for trials concerning political and press offences (on paper) (1931)
- Passing of the Patent Law (1931) (Khal'atbarry, 1933: 45)
- Passing of the Companies Registration Act (1931) (Khal'atbarry, 1933: 45)
- Permission for enforcing the Justice Department's Bills after ratification in Justice Committee of the Parliament (1932) (*Parliamentary Proceedings*, Session 81, 1932)
- Registration of documents and property (1932) (Arjomand, 1988: 66: Banani, 1961: 72) requiring that the registration of legal documents, of ownership, and of other transactions concerning property be carried out in secular state courts only.
- Ratification of new Commercial Code (1932) (Khal'atbarry, 1933: 10)
- New Due Process Act including 505 articles (1934) (Amin, 2003: 543)
- Abolishing the use of honorary titles (1935)
- New Law Practice Regulations (1935)

- Approval of the second and third volumes of the Civil Code by the Parliament (1935)
- Passing a law concerning the employment of judges by the Parliament requiring all of them to hold a degree from the Tehran Faculty of Law or a foreign university (1936)
- New Law Practice Regulations (1937), recognizing the independence of the Bar Association with respect to revenues, funds and expending (financial independence)
- Enacting laws regulating the practice of attorneys and legal experts (1939)
- Establishment of military tribunals based on "Military Criminal and Procedural Law" (1939) (Amin, 2003: 487)
- Promulgation of a law concerning bankruptcy (1939)
- Inviting French and Italian law professors (eight French and two Italian professors) to teach in the Faculty of Law of the Tehran University (1922–39) (Banani, 1961: 75)
- Passing the version of Civil Code with 789 articles by the Majles (1939)
- Passing of new Civil Procedural Law (1939)
- New Civil Law Code (1939)
- Changing the laws concerning marriage, divorce and family relations four times from 1926 to 1940, each constituting a further departure from the strict *shari`ah* principles (Banani, 80)
- Adding 378 articles to the Civil Code defining the rights of the state in matters like inheritance and the probating of wills (1940)
- Penal Code of 1940 (Arjomand, 1988: 66; Banani, 1961: 74))

1941–1951 Mohammad Reza Shah I

- Decrease of the jurisdictions of special courts by Foroughi (1941) (*Parliamentary Proceedings,* Vol. 13, No. 1, session 7: 46)
- Using the judiciary as the legitimizing force for the new king (Bozorg, 2002: 21–39) through trials of the second level officials of the last king administration (1941–42)
- Dissolution or putting some limits on the functions of some special courts like Governmental Staff Court (Divan-e Jazā-ye 'Ommāl-e Dowlat), Treasury Trial Court and Military Court (Divān-e Dādresi-ye Dārāyi) (Bozorg, 2002: 41–44) (1941, 1942, 1943 & 1949)
- Sending the bill of judge independence to the parliament by the judiciary department (1941) (Bozorg, 2002: 44–48)

- Dissolution of the Supreme Council of the Judiciary as the special court for trial of judges (1943) (Zerang, Vol. II, 2002; 42; Bozorg, 2002: 47)
- Election of the board of directors by the members for the first time (1946)
- Transferring the trial of political crimes to the military tribunals under the title of "Committing Crime against Security and Independence of the Country" (1949) (Amin, 2003: 638)
- Decrease of the jurisdiction of the Governmental Officials' Penal Court (1949) (Zerang, Vol. II, 2002; 42)
- The Bar Independence Bill was ratified and enforced during the Mosaddeq administration (1952)
- Instability in the administration (16 cabinets and 19 ministers of judiciary department in only 10 years) (Bozorg, 2002: 59)
- Continuing violation of laws related to press trials
- Violation of the separation of powers and convictions of some kinds of crimes by the Interior Department and increase of Military Courts' domain of action (especially after 1948, after attempt against the Shah's life) (Bozorg, 2002: 73; Zerang, Vol. II, 2002; 74)

1951–1953 Mohammad Mosaddeq

- Judicial reorganization and filtration (1952) (Bozorg, 2002: 82–86)
- Revision of the law pertaining to employment of judges (Sep. 1952) (Ladjevardi, 1988: 85)
- Abolishment of the Department of Supervision of the Ministry of Justice, and creation of the Office of the Disciplinary Prosecutor of Judges (1952) (Ladjevardi, 1988: 85–6)
- Annulling the interpretation of Article 82 of the Constitution (1952) (Law Collection of 1952)
- Empowering the Minister of Justice to replace the presiding officers of the judicial branches of the Court of Cassation and the Disciplinary Courts (Divān-e Kishvar va Dādgāh-e Entezāmi) (1952) (Ladjevardi, 1988: 86)
- Limiting the jurisdiction of the special courts (*mahākem-e ekhtesāsi*) and then their dissolution (1952) (Zerang, Vol. II, 2002; 83)
- Passing of the Judiciary Organization Bill (1952) shutting down or merging some of the primary courts of provinces to others

- Creation of the Judicial Supreme Council (1952) (Bozorg, 2000: 184)
- Reform in the legal procedure (1952) (Bozorg, 2002: 86–87)
- Giving independence to the Iranian Bar Association (1952) (http://www.iranbar.com/pe193.php)
- Firing of more than 200 judges (1952) (Zerang, Vol. II, 2002; 97)
- Ratification of the Press Law and arrangement of press courts with the presence of jury (1952) (Amin, 2003: 643)
- Ratification of the Office of Public Attorney for the Disciplinary Court for Judges (1953) (Amin, 2003: 644)
- Passing the Local Dispute Settling Board Bill (1953) never established due to the 1953 coup (Amin, 2003: 644–5)

1953–1979 Mohammad Reza Shah II

- Nullification of what Mosaddeq administration did in the area of judiciary (1953–56) (Bozorg, 2002: 116–124; Zerang, Vol. II, 2002; 116–120)
- Passing the Independent Bar Association Law by the joint commission of the Parliament and Senate (1955) (www.iranbar.com/pe191.php)
- Dissolution of the Supreme Court by the Ministry of Justice, 'Abbāsqoli Golshai'iān (1956)
- Increase of the number of Primary Courts (1956) (Zerang, Vol. II, 2002; 128)
- Judicial reorganization in the area of special courts like establishment of "young criminal court" (1959), "governmental staff court" (1955 and 1960), "moving court" similar to Rove Court in the U.S. during the revolution (1956), "nomad court" (1956), "Houses of Equity" (1963), "Arbitration Councils" (1956) (Bozorg, 2000: 132–146; Zerang, Vol. II, 2002; 142)
- Expedition of legal procedure by geographical and quantitative development of the courts and manipulation of the legal procedure code (1954—71) (Bozorg, 2000: 128–31 & 155–62)
- Establishment of a governmental council in the judiciary (1960)
- Granting of capitulatory rights to the U.S. citizens (1964)
- Establishment of the Family Protection Court (1967) (Zerang, Vol. II, 2002: 135)
- Approval of new Family Laws (1967 &1975) (Bozorg, 2000: 168–170)
- Signing the ICCPR and ICESCR in 1968 and ratification of both Covenants in 1975 without reservations.

- Enlargement of the competence of Arbitration Councils-staffed by the government-selected personnel-to try cases involving sums up to Rs 200,000 (1976) (Graham, 1978: 137)
- The letter of fifty-three lawyers to the imperial court demanding an independent judiciary (1977) (Bakhash, 1984: 14)
- Establishment of a watch-dog committee by sixty four lawyers to defend the Constitutional laws and independence of judiciary (1977) (Bakhash, 1984: 14)
- Forming of the Association of Iranian Jurists to look after the interests of prisoners (1977) (Bakhash, 1984: 14)
- Dissolution of Dependent Local Courts (1977)
- Joining to the International Criminology Institution by the Iranian government (Bozorg, 2000: 171)
- Vast violations of human, civil and constitutional rights of Iranian citizens (1953–1979)

1979–89: Popular Islamicization

Establishment of IRI, 1979–1981

- Appointment of Sādeq Khakhāli by Khomeini as the chief *shar'i* judge to try so-called anti-revolutionaries and high-ranking officials of the Old Regime (Feb. 23, 1979) (Khomeini, 1991: Vol. III, 326)
- Approve of the Reform of the Judicial Organization and Recruitment of the Judges Act by the Revolution's Council (March 8, 1979) (Zerang, Vol. II, 2002: 232)
- Dissolution of the Supreme Court and its public prosecutors' office, also the Judges' Disciplinary Courts and its public prosecutor's office (March, 14, 1979) (Zerang, Vol. II, 2002: 233)
- Release of Khomeini's statement about confining the jurisdiction of Revolutionary Courts to trial of people who were involved in anti-revolutionary activities before and after the victory of the Islamic Revolution (March 15, 1979) (Khomeini, 1991: Vol. III, 427)
- Opening of the Supreme Court with new members (April 4, 1979) (Zerang, Vol. II, 2002: 233)
- Broadcasting of Khomeini's letter to the Attorney General regarding the limitations of executions to only two areas: 1) where it is proved that the accused has killed someone, and 2) when someone has committed genocide or torture leading to death (May 12, 1979) (Khomeini, 1991: Vol. IV, 159)

- The Annulment of capitulation (May 13, 1979)
- Approval of the Extraordinary Courts for Anti-revolutionary Crimes Law by the Revolution's Council in June 17, 1979, (Zerang, Vol. II, 2002: 226–277)
- Declaring amnesty for all except individuals who have killed or tortured a person by Khomeini (Jul. 8 & 15, 1979) (Khomeini, 1991: Vol. V. 111–113, 179)
- Transfer of Prisons Administration Organization from the Police to the Judiciary (Sep. 4, 1979) (Zerang, Vol. II, 2002: 234–5)
- Supreme Judicial Council issued proclamation to direct courts to suspend all un-Islamic legislation (1979)
- Filtration of the judiciary (1979)
- Transfer of the Military Courts from the Military to the Judiciary based on Article 172 of the Constitution (1979)
- Suspension of the Family Protection laws of 1967 and 1975 by the Revolution's Council (1979) (Omid, 1994: 75)
- Ratification of new family laws, giving men the exclusive right of divorce, unless women demanded and obtained the right on marriage and stipulated in their marriage contract, lowering the age of marriage from 18 to 13, legalizing polygamy, giving men automatic right of custody over their children, for daughters after the age of 7 and for sons after the age of 2, and empowering husbands to bar their spouses from taking employment (Omid, 1994: 76)
- Sacking all women judges (1979)
- The Special Civil Courts were established to adjudicate over matters relating to family law, succession and *awqāf* (1979)
- Closing down the Lawyers' Association (Kānun-e Vokalā) (1979)
- Annulment of capitulation for the U.S. citizens (1979)
- Shutting down the Bar Association (Kāshāni, 1992: 3) (1979)
- Creation of the Supreme Council of the Judiciary by approval of the new constitution in a national election (1979)
- Stopping women's admission to judicial positions and law schools (1982) (http://www.iranbar.com/ph112.php)
- Creation of a dual judiciary, regular and revolutionary (1979)
- Regularizing of the Revolutionary Courts (1979)
- Injection of a mass number of clerics to the judiciary system by the Islamic regime (1979–1981) to Islamicize the judiciary
- Replacing the secular law by the decrees of the ruling jurist (1979)
- Crying for independent judiciary through legal provisions, elected judges, and budgetary autonomy in the upcoming constitution by the Iranian Bar Association (1979) (Bakhash, 1984: 77)

- Set up of the Special Civil Courts (*dādgāhha-ye madani-ye khās*) replacing Mohammad Reza Shah's Family Protection Courts (1979) (http://www.dadgostary-tehran.ir/farsi/gozaresh/index.asp)
- Establishment of a clerical board in each city to investigate cases and settle disputes on clerics (1979) (Khomeini, 1991: Vol. VI, 253)
- Closing the Iranian Bar Association by the government (1980) (Kāshāni, 1992)
- Amnesty with the same provisions and conditions as the amnesty of 1979 (March 18, 1980) (Khomeini, 1991: Vol. VII, 131–132)
- Creation of judicial police (1980) (Bozorg, 2000: 286)
- The Bar Filtration Act of June 1980 ratified by the Revolutionary Council (Kāshāni, 1992: 4)
- Election of three members of the Supreme Judiciary Councils by the judges (July 13, 1980) (Zerang, Vol. II, 2002: 249)
- Incorporation of Army Judicial Organization to the Judiciary (1981) (Daryābāri, 2004: 34)
- Appointment of Montazeri by Khomeini as the qualifier for the judges who were nominated for membership in the Supreme Judiciary Council (June 9, 1981) and appointment of Abdullāh Nuri as the leader's representative in the supervisory board for the election of three members of the Supreme Judiciary Council (May 17, 1981) (Khomeini, 1991: Vol. VII, 233, 311).

Hierocracy Established, 1982–1989

- Khomeini's statement in 8 articles regarding the Islamicization of judiciary and enforcing the laws (Jan. 24, 1982) (Khomeini, 1991: Vol. IX, 644–647)
- Establishment of a commission to follow Khomeini's Eight Articles Commandment that included Abd ul-Karim Musavi Ardebili (the Head of the Supreme Court), Hussein Mousavi (the Prime Minister), Akbar Nāteq Nouri (the Interior Minister), Mohammad Emami Kashani (the Head of the Court of Administrative Justice), and Mohaqqeq Dāmād (the Head of the National General Inspectorate) (1982) (Khomeini, 1991: Vol. IX, 662)
- Approval of Hodud (Penal) and Qesās (Retributive Justice) Law (Aug. 25, 1982), Islamic Punishment Law (Oct. 13, 1982), Blood Money Law (*diāt*) (Dec. 15, 1982), and *Ta'zirāt* Law (Aug. 9, 1983) (Zerang, Vol. II, 2002: 296)
- Revolutionary legislation in the areas of labor and land reform (1982)

- Qesās Bill (Islamic Penal Code) was passed by the Majles, and approved by the Guardian Council (Aug. 1982) (Milani, 1988: 310)
- Approval of the "Law on the Conditions for the Selection of Judges," that rescued judgeship to the *mujtaheds* (seminary trained experts on Islamic law) (1982) (Bakhash, 1984: 227).
- Appointment of Seyyed Ja'far Karimi as the first head of the Disciplinary Court for Judges and Public Attorneys by Khomeini (Dec. 29, 1982) (Khomeini, 1991: Vol. X, 20)
- Amnesty for the third time after the Islamic Revolution (Feb. 8, 1983) (Khomeini, 1991: Vol. X, 20)
- Integration of the Revolutionary Courts into the Ministry of Justice (1983) (*Ettelā'āt Daily,* July 8, 1983)
- All so-called un-Islamic codes adopted since 1907 were declared null by the Supreme Judiciary Council (August 1982) (Milani, 1988: 309)-Disbarring 57 lawyers by the Islamic Revolutionary Public Attorney and verdict of the *shari`ah* judge (June 1983)/Disbarring 32 lawyers by the same office (August 1983)/Disbarring 52 lawyers by the same office (December, 1983) (Kāshāni, 1992: 5)
- Transfer of the mission and organization of the 8 Articles Commandment Commission to the judiciary (1983) (Khomeini, 1991: Vol. X, 179)
- Appointment of the acting chair of the Bar Association by the Judiciary (1984) (Kāshāni, 1992: 5)
- Integration of the Ministry of Justice and the Revolutionary Courts in 1984 (Arjomand, 1988: 167)
- Creation of the National Correction Measures and Prisons Organization (1985) (Bozorg, 2000: 287–8)
- Dissolution of the clerical boards that were functioning as special courts for clergy under the auspices of Revolutionary Courts (Rayshahri, 1990: 251).
- Creation of itinerant court (1987)
- Establishment of the Special Court for the Clergy (Dādgāh-e Vizhe-ye Rowhāniyat) on the basis of a letter from Khomeini dated 25 Khordād 1366 (15 June 1987) (Daryābari, 2004: 18)
- Appointment of Ali Fallāhiān and Ali Rāzini by Khomeini for Attorney and the Shar'i Judge of the Special Court of Clergy respectively (Khomeini, 1991: Vol. XI, 329, 330)
- Killing thousands of political prisoners (mostly Mojāhedin Khalq members) while they have already convicted to years of imprisonment (Aug. 1988)

1989–2005: Authoritarian and formal Islamicization/Politicization of the Judiciary

1989–1997 Authoritative Economic Development

- Establishment of the Unit of Enforcement of Judgments for the purpose of enforcement of the judgments delivered by the common courts; civil and penal
- Dissolution of Supreme Judiciary Council in the revised constitution (1989)
- Dissolution of the judicial police (1990) (Zerang, Vol. II, 2002: 287)
- Passing of the Special Court for Clergy's Establishment Law and its circular (1990) (Daryābari, 2004: 18 & 279)
- Signing the CRC in 1991 and ratification of it in 1994 with a general declaration and reservation to the effect that the Islamic Republic makes reservation to the articles and provisions that might be contradictory to the Islamic *shari`ah,* reserving the right not to apply any provisions incompatible with Islamic Laws and the international legislation in effect.
- Stopping the election of the Bar Association by the Parliament on Oct. 1991 while the ad for the election was published on Sep. 1991 (Kāshāni, 1992: 3)
- Passing of the General and Revolutionary Courts Establishment Law (1994) (*Kayhān* Daily, July 5, 1994)
- Abolition of public attorney offices and abolition of hierarchy
- Mass appointment of prosecutors and interrogators as judges

1997–2005 Reform Movement vs. Politicization of Judiciary

- Appointment of the Board of Constitutional Watch by the President Khātami (1997)
- The new Civil Procedural Law was passed by the Parliament (2000) (*Iran* Daily, April 12, 2000)
- The judiciary tried all Iranian participants in a conference held in Berlin and convicted them to years of imprisonment and fines (2000). They were charged with activism against national security and disseminating propaganda against the Islamic Republic (Chicago Tribune, Dec. 19, 2001). The appeal court decreased some of the punishments (Iran Daily, Dec. 27, 2001)
- The trial of some of Ministry of Intelligence staff who killed numbers of political activists and writers between 1997 and 1998 led

to short term imprisonments in Primary Court (2001). These members were acquitted in the Appeal Court (http://64.233.161.104/search?q=cache:Ts60rAHC8KgJ:www.emrooz.org/pages/date/81–11/10/report.htm; http://64.233.161.104/search?q=cache:3E351m5Xze8J:asre-nou.net/1381/dey/14/m-khabar.html). The defendants were free on bail (Iran Daily, Feb. 4, 2002).

- The judiciary established a special committee to oversight the implementation of the Leader's policies in foreign relations and to prosecute individuals who criticize National Security Council's decisions (*Hayāt-e Nou* daily, Oct. 30, 2001).
- After the Khorramābād Turmoil, only the students who were attacked by Ansār-e Hezbullah were tried. Out of 130 students who were convicted to imprisonment in Primary Courts, only 40 students were acquitted in the Appeal Court (2000) (*Nou Rouz* Daily, Oct. 8, 2001)
- Sixty MPs were summoned (between 1–4 times), tried and some put in jail (2001) (*Āftāb* Daily, Dec. 17, 2001). The accusations were based on what these MPs said about appointed bodies of government.
- President Khātami's constitutional reminder to the judiciary on prosecution of vast number of MPs (2001) (*Nou Rouz* Daily, Oct. 10, 2001)
- The Revolutionary Court of Tehran put 44 of the members of National Religious Forces under trial that led to verdicts of between 4 months to 10 years imprisonment of 33 members and dissolution of this organization (2002) (iran-emrooz.de/khabar/nehzat810506.html). They were accused of adopting an approach to change the Constitution and overthrowing the Islamic regime (Alizādeh's letter to the Majles Speaker, Mehdi Karrubi, *Resālat* Daily, April 19, 2001). Tehran's Revolutionary Court announced different set of accusation in its statement: insulting the Leader, communication with anti-revolutionary groups and having relationship with foreign countries, insulting religion, sacred matters and values (kayhannews.com/800201/0ther15.htm). In a press conference, Alizādeh added spying for foreigners to the mentioned list of accusations (*Nou Rouz* Daily, Feb. 6, 2002)
- Establishment of the intelligence service of the judiciary (*Hayāt-e Nou* Daily, Sep. 25, 2002)
- Zahrā Kāzemi was killed while under arrest (June 25, 2003). In the trial of this case, the judiciary accused one of the Ministry of Intelligence staff that was acquitted in the end. No one was

considered responsible for her death (http://akhbar.gooya.com/politics/archives/014044.php)

- Creation of National Bar Association (2003) (*Yās Nou* Daily, May 19, 2003)
- The closure of two survey research institutes, the Āyandeh Research Group and the National Institute for the Study of Public Opinion, and detention of their directors in connection with an opinion poll on US-Iranian relations[2] Those arrested were accused of not reflecting public opinion but of attempting to shape it. They were also accused of, but not yet charged with, "spying for the USA" and "selling national security information to foreign intelligence services." They were kept in prison, under harsh conditions and extended solitary confinement (2002). Abbās Abdi and Hussein Qāziān were adjudicated to 8 and 9 years of imprisonment in Primary Court respectively (*Āftāb* Daily, Feb. 4, 2003) and 4.5 years of imprisonment in Appeal Court (http://64.233.161.104/search?q=cache:DxKN5gISkJwJ:www.nimrooz.com/html/783/132744.htm)
- Formation of the Association for Defending Prisoners' Rights (2004) (http://khabarnameh.gooya.com/politics/archives/009158.php)
- Death sentence for Prof. Āghājari on the charge of apostasy (2003), later changed to 5 years of imprisonment (three years irrevocable, and two years suspending) and deprivation of social rights for 5 years (http://akhbar.gooya.com/politics/archives/014271.php; khabarnameh.gooya.com/politics/archives/013915.php)
- The order of Shāhroudi for establishment of another intelligence service in the judiciary called Social Intelligence Organization (Sāzmān-e Hefāzat-e Ejtemā'i). The mission of this organization is to gather information in neighborhoods, factories, universities, schools, seminaries and any other public spheres on people's personal and private behaviors to help judiciary to fight against vice in the society (2004) (http://www.bbc.co.uk/persian/iran/story/2004/11/041107_a_iran_judiciary.shtml; http://www.farsnews.com/NewsVm.asp?ID=111350)
- Arrest of 25 bloggers and online journalists (2004) (http://akhbar.gooya.com/politics/archives/018671.php)
- Dissolution of the Board of Constitutional Watch by Ahmadinejād administration (http://www.sharghnewspaper.ir/841111/html/iran.htm#s364683)

Appendix II

Comparing Four Sociological Theories of Legal Change

	Maine	Durkheim	Marx	Weber
Nature of law	Free Agreement of Individuals	Objective Form of Collective Conscience; Law as indicator of the Deep Moral Core, Visible Symbol of Social Solidarity, and product of Changing Morality Driven by Division of Labor	Instrument of Economic Control	Expression of Political Domination and Norms
State and Law	State as Arbiter of Conflicting Contractual Claims	State as the symbol of Coercive Potential of Legal System	Coercive Function of Law in protecting property and Suppressing dissent Function of Proletaria	Rise of centralized states based on legal rational authority
Society and Law	Social Mechanisms of Legal Change (Status to Contract)	Society symbolizes solidarity in the form of law; Legal system represents a set of believes and values that are shared by the members of society	Law as a Response to Economic Conflict between Social Classes;Law as a Part of Institutional Superstructure	Rise of Capitalism as reason of the Growth of Legal Rationality
Theory	Evolutionism	Functional Evolutionism	Historical Materialism (Monistic)	Historicism, i.e. All Historical Events are Unique, Ideal Types of Structures
Stages Of Legal Development	3: No Law, Customary Era of Codes	2: Repressive Law to Restitutive Law	5: Communism, Serfdom Feudalism, Bourgeoisie, Socialism (Implicit)	No Stage: Tension Between Formally Irrational, Substantively Irrational, Substantively Rational, Formally Rational[3]

Appendix III

Main Characteristics of Three Legal Traditions: Civil, Common and Socialist Law

	Civil Law	Common Law	Socialist Law
Beginning	450 B.C. Publication of Publication of XII Table in Rome	1066 A.D. Normans conquered England	1917 A.D. October Revolution
Domain of Action	Most Part of the World	Former British Empire	Former Socialist Bloc
Components	Roman Law, Canon Law, Commercial Law	Precedents, Customs, Statutes Opinions of Experts, Principles of Morality	All Components of Civil Law
It is a product of	Rise of Nation-States	Disintegration of Holy Roman Empire, Rise of British Empire	Rise of a Social Movement
Basic Intellectual Forces	Secularism, Separation of Powers, Rationalism, Natural rights	Natural Rights, Ancient Constitutions Guild of Lawyers	Socialism, Historical Materialism
Law-making Power	State Legislatures	Individuals, Groups, Judges, Professionals	Class State Bureaucracy
Sourcesof Law	Constitutions, Statutes, Regulations, Custom (descending order)	Judicial Decisions, Books and Articles by Legal Scholars, Unsystemic Accretion of Statutes, Regulations, Customary Practices	National and Local Councils' Decisions
What is law-making?	Abolish All Prior Laws	Codes are not rejection of the past.	Abolish All Prior Law
Characteristicsof Law	Complete, Coherent, Clear, Gapless	No Pretense of Completeness	Complete, Coherent, Clear, Gapless

(continued)

(Continued)

	Civil Law	Common Law	Socialist Law
Legal System	Simple, Non-technical, Straightforward	Technical	Simple, Non-technical, Straightforward
Role of Judiciary	Emphasis on Certainty, Contempt Power	Judicial Discretion, Contempt Power	Endorsing Ruling Class Interest
What is Law?	What the aw school professionals say	What the judges say	What the state says
Mostly Considers	principles that it presupposes	consequences that it involves	principles that it presupposes
Judicial System	Pyramid	Two or More Distinct Structure	Pyramid
Legal Profession	Variety of Distinct Professional Careers	A Single Entity	No Entity (Theoretically)

- A legal tradition is a set of deeply rooted, historically conditioned attitudes about the nature of law, about the role of law in the society and the polity, about the proper organization and operation of a legal system and about the way law is or should be made, applied, studied, perfected, and taught (Merryman, 1969: 2).
- There are many different legal systems within each of these three families of legal systems.
- Legal traditions are not internally homogenous

Appendix IV

Taxonomy of World's Legal Systems (Mattei, 1997)

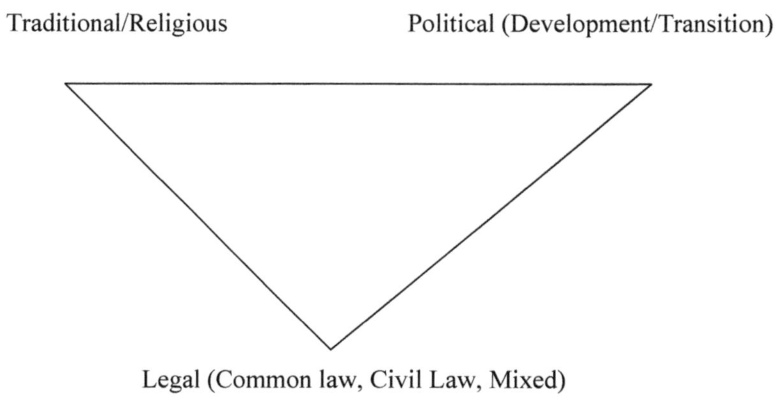

T: Chinese, Islamic, Japanese, Hindu

P: Socialist, Post-socialist, Africa, Latin America

L: English, American (Common Law), Scandinavian (Mixed), French and German Inspired (Civil Law)

Appendix V

Iranian Highest Judiciary Officials, Ministers of Justice, Members of the Supreme Judicial Councils, and Heads of the Judiciary, 1906–2006

Prime Ministers or Presidents	Ministers of Justice
Presidents	
Mahmood Ahmadinejād, Aug. 2005	Jamāl Karimi Rād
Mohammad Khatami, Aug. 1997–Aug. 2005	Esmā'il Shushtari
Akbar Hāshemi Rafsanjāni, Aug. 1989–Aug. 1997	Esmā'il Shushtari
Prime Ministers	**Ministers of Justice**
Hussein Musavi, Oct. 1981–Aug. 1989	Mohammad Asghari, Hasan Habibi
Mohammad Reza Mahdavi Kani, Aug.–Oct. 1981	Mohammad Asghari
Mohammad Javād Bāhonar, Aug. 1981	Mohammad Asghari
Mohammad Ali Rajā'i, Aug. 1980–Aug.1981	Ebrāhim Ahadi
Mehdi Bāzargān, Feb.–Nov. 1979	Ahmad Sadr Hāj Seyyed Javādi
Shāpur Bakhtiār, Jan.–Feb. 1979	Yahyā Sādeq Vaziri
Gholāmreza Azhāri, Nov. 1978–Jan. 1979	Husein Najafi
Ja'far Sharif Emāmi, Aug.—Nov. 1978	Mohammad Bāheri

(continued)

Prime Ministers (continued)	**Ministers of Justice**
Jamshid Amuzegār, Aug. 1977–Aug. 1978	Sādeq Ahmadi, Gholāmreza Kiānpoor
Amir Abbās Hoveydā, Jan. 1965–Aug. 1976	Bāqer 'Āmeli, Javād Sadr, Manuchehr Partou, Sādeq Ahmadi, Gholāmreza Kiānpoor
Hasan Ali Mansour, Mar. 1964–Jan.1965	Bāqer 'Āmeli
Amir Asadullah 'Alam, Jul. 1962–Mar.1964	Mohammad Bāheri, Gholāmhusein Khoshbin
Ali Amini, May 1961–Jul. 1962	Nour ul-Din Alamuti
Ja'far Sharif Emāmi, Aug. 1960–May 1961	Mohammad Ali Hedāyati, Mohammad 'Ali Momtaz, Husein Najafi
Manuchehr Eqbāl, Apr. 1957–Aug. 1960	Mohammad Ali Hedāyati
Hussein 'Alā, Mar. 1955–Apr. 1957	Abbas Quli Golshaian, Ali Amini
Fazlullah Zāhedi, July 1953–Mar. 1955	Jamāl Akhavi, Fakhr ul-Din Shādmān
Mohammad Mosaddeq, July 1952–Aug 1953	Abdul'ali Lotfi
Qavām, July 1952	Mostafā 'Adl
Mohammad Mosaddeq, May 1951–July 1952	'Ali Hey'at, Shams ul-Din Amir 'Alā'i
Hussein 'Alā, March–May 1951	Shams ul-Din Amir 'Alā'i, Jamāl Akhavi
Hajiali Razmārā, June 1950-March 1951	Mohammad 'Ali Buzari
Ali Mansur, March–June 1950	
Mohammad Sā'ed, Nov. 1948-March 1950	Sajjādi
Abdulhusein Hajeer, June-Nov. 1948	Nezām ul-Saltaneh, Abbās Qoli Golshāiān
Ebrāhim Hakimi, Dec. 1947–June 1948	Mohammad Soruri
Qavām ul-Saltaneh, Jan. 1946–Dec. 1947	Ali Akbar Musavi Zādeh
Ebrāhim Hakimi, Oct. 1945–Jan. 1946	

(continued)

Prime Ministers (continued)	**Ministers of Justice**
Mohsen Sadr, June–October 1945	Amānollah Ardalān, Hasan'ali Kamāl Hedāyat
Ebrāhim Hakimi, May–June 1945	Allahyār Sāleh, Amānollah Ardalān
Mortezā Qoli Khan Bayāt, Nov. 1944–April 1945	Mostafā 'Adl
Mohammad Sā'ed, March–Nov. 1944	Allāhyār Sāleh
Ali Suhaili, Feb. 1943–March 1944	Allāhyār Sāleh
Mohammad Sa'ed, July 1942–Feb. 1943	Asadullah Mameqāni, Mohsen sadr
Ali Suhaili, March–July 1942	Majid Āhi, Mohsen Sadr, 'Ali Asghar Hekmat
Mohammad Ali Forughi, Aug. 1941–March 1942	Majid Āhi, Abbās Qoli Golshāiān
Ali Mansur, June 1940–Aug. 1941	Majid Āhi, Mohammad Soruri, 'Ali Hey'at
Ahmad Matin Daftari, Oct. 1939–June 1940	Ahmad Matin Daftari
Mahmood Jam, Nov. 1935–Oct. 1939	Ahmad Matin Daftari, Mohsen Sadr
Mohammad Ali Foruqi, Aug.1933–Nov. 1935	Mohsen Sadr
Mokhber ul-Saltaneh Hedāyat, June 1927–Aug. 1933	Ali Akbar Dāvar, Ahmad Matin Daftari
Mostowfi al-Mamālek, June 1926–June 1927	Mostafā 'Adl, Hasan Vosuq, Ali Akbar Dāvar
Mostowfi al-Mamālek, June 1926–June 1927	Mostafā 'Adl, Hasan Vosuq, Ali Akbar Dāvar
Mohammad Ali Forughi, Oct. 1925–June 1926	'Emād ul-Saltaneh Fātemi, Mohsen Sadr
Sardār Sepah, Oct. 1923–Oct. 1925	Mo'āzed ul-Saltaneh
Moshir ul-Dowleh,June–Oct. 1923	Ebrāhim Khan Hakim ul-Molk

(continued)

Prime Ministers (continued)	**Ministers of Justice**
Mostowfi al-Mamālek, Feb.–June 1923	Momtāz ul-Molk, 'Amid ul-Saltaneh
Ahmad Qavām, May 1922–Feb. 1923	Moshār ul-Saltaneh
Moshir ul-Dowleh, Jan.–May 1922	Sardār Mo'azzam Khorāsāni
Ahmad Qavām, May 1921–Jan. 1922	Ebrāhim 'Amid, Moshār ul-Saltaneh
Seyyed Ziā Tabātabā'i, Nov.–May 1921	Mostafā 'Adl
Sepahdār Rashti, Oct. 1920–Nov. 1921	Soleimān Khan, Sālār Lashkar
Mirzā Hasan Khan Moshir ul-Dowleh (Pirniā), March–Oct. 1920	Mosaddeq ul-Saltaneh
Mirzā Hasan Khan Vosuq ul-Dowleh, Aug. 1918- March 1920	Nosrat ul-Dowleh Firuz
Najaf Qoli Khan Samsām ul-Saltaneh Bakhtiāri, May–Aug. 1918	Nasr ul-Molk,
Mirza Hasan Khan Mostowfi ul-Mamālek, Feb.–May 1918	Mokhber ul-Saltaneh, Nasr ul-Molk
'Ain ul-Dowleh, Dec. 1917–Feb. 1918	Mokhber ul-Saltaneh
Mohammad Ali Khan 'Ala' ul-Saltaneh, May–Dec. 1917	Momtāz ul-Dowleh, Nasr ul-Molk
Reza Qoli Khan Nezām Māfi, Oct. 1916 (shadow government)	Seyyed Hasan Modarres
Mirzā Hasan Khan Vosuq ul-Dowleh, Sep. 1916- May 1917	Firuz Mirzā Nosrat ul-Dowleh
Mohammad Vali Khan Sepahdār 'Azam Tanekāboni, April 1916	Mahmood Khan 'Alā' ul-Molk
Abd ul-Husein Farmānfarmā, Feb.–April 1916	Mohammad Ali Khan 'Alā' ul-Saltaneh
Mirza Hasan Khan Mostowfi ul-Mamālek, Aug. 1915–Feb. 1916	Mohammad Ali Khan 'Alā' ul-Saltaneh
'Abdolmajid Mirzā 'Ain ul-Dowleh, May–Aug. 1915	Fat'hollah Khan Sardār Mansur

(continued)

Prime Ministers (continued)	**Ministers of Justice**
Mirzā Javād Sa'd ul-Dowleh, May 1915	
Mirzā Hasan Khan Moshir ul-Dowleh (Pirniā), March-May 1915	Zakā' ul-Molk, Hakim ul-Molk, Abd ul-Husein Taymurtāsh, Mosaddeq
Mirza Hasan Khan Mostowfi ul-Mamālek, Aug. 1914–March 1915	Mokhber ul-Saltaneh
Mohammad Ali Khan 'Alā' ul-Saltaneh, Dec. 1913–Aug. 1914	Esmā'il Khan Momtāz ul-Dowleh
Najaf Qoli Khan Samsām ul-Saltaneh Bakhtiāri, June 1912–Dec. 1913	Mirzā Hasan Khan Moshir ul-Dowleh, Esmā'il Khan Momtāz ul-Dowleh
Mohammad Vali Khan Sepahdār 'Azam Tanekāboni, Feb. 1911–June 1912	Moshir ul-Dowleh
Mirza Hasan Khan Mostowfi ul-Mamālek, July 1910–Feb. 1911	Dabir ul-Molk, Mohtasham ul-Saltaneh
Mohammad Vali Khan Sepahdār 'Azam Tanekāboni, June 1909–July 1910	Vosooq ul-Dowleh, Moshir ul-Dowleh
Mirzā Javād Sa'd ul-Dowleh, March –June 1909	Mirzā Hasan Khan Moshir ul-Dowleh
Kāmrān Mirzā Nā'eb ul-Saltaneh, March 1909	Mirzā Hasan Khan Moshir ul-Dowleh
Moshir ul-Saltaneh, June 1908–March 1909	Moh'tasham ul-Saltaneh
Nezām ul-Saltaneh, Nov. 1907–June 1908	Mehdi Qoli Khan Mokhber ul-Saltaneh, Mokhber ul-Saltaneh, Mo'ayed ul-Saltaneh
Nāser ul-Molk, Oct.-Nov. 1907	Mehdi Qoli Khan Mokhber ul-Saltaneh
Mirza Ahmad Khan Moshir-ul-Saltaneh, Aug. 1907-Oct. 1907	Mirzā Hasan Khan Pirniā (Moshir–ul-Dowleh), Nezām ul-Molk, Mohtasham ul-Saltaneh, Moshir ul-Molk
Mirzā Ali Asghar Khan Amin ul-Soltān (Atābak A'zam), Apr. 1907–Aug. 1907	Mirzā Mohammad Ali Khan 'Alā' ul-Saltaneh, Seyyed Mahmood Khan 'Alā' ul-Molk
Soltanali Vazir Afkham (Baqāyā), Mar.–Apr. 1907	Abdolhusein Mirzā Farmānfarmā

(continued)

Prime Ministers (continued)	**Ministers of Justice**
Mirzā Nasrullāh Khan Moshir ul-Dowlah, Aug. 1906-March 1907	Mirza Ahmad Khan Moshir ul-Saltaneh

Sources: Shajii, Zahrā, *Nokhbegān-e Siāsi-ye Iran* (*Iranian Elite*), Tehran: *Sokhan*, 4 Vols; Zerang, Vol. I & II, 2002; Azimi, 1989; Alamuti, 1995: 'Aqeli, 1995

THE MEMBERS OF THE SUPREME JUDICIAL COUNCILS AND HEADS OF THE JUDICIARY IN POST-REVOLUTIONARY IRAN

Mahmoud Shāhrudi 1999–2006

Mohammad Yazdi 1989–1999

Mortezā Moqtadaii, Mohammad Musavi Boujnurdi, Hasan Mar'shi, elected Members of the Supreme Judicial Council, 1988–

Mohammad Musavi Khoiinihā, Attorney General, July 9, 1985–1989

Yusef Sāne'i, Attorney General, Jan. 8, 1983–July 9, 1985

Rabbāni Amlashi, Attorney General, June 27, 1980–Jan. 8, 1983

Abd ul-Karim Musavi Ardebili, Head of the Supreme Court, June 27, 1980–Aug. 14, 1989

Mohammad Huseini Beheshti, Head of the Supreme Court, Feb. 22, 1979– June 27, 1980

Abd ul-Karim Musavi Ardebili, Attorney General, Feb. 21, 1979–June 27, 1980

Hussein Musavi Tabrizi, Sep. 15, 1981–Jan. 27, 1984

Ali Quddusi, Revolution's Attorney General, Aug. 5, 1979–Sep. 15, 1981

Mehdi Hādavi, Revolution's Attorney General, Feb. 27, 1979-Aug. 5, 1979

Sources: Khomeini, 1991, Vol. III; V, 275; VII. 105, 107; XI, 71, 215

Appendix VI

Historical Documents and Photos

1. DĀVAR, YAZDI, SHĀHRUDI

Ali Akbar Dāvar (1886–1937) (Aqeli, 12)

Mohammad Yazdi (1931–)

Mahmud Shāhrudi (1948–)

2. KHOMEINI'S VERDICT REGARDING KILLING THOUSANDS OF POLITICAL PRISONERS WHILE THEY HAVE ALREADY BEEN CONVICTED TO YEARS OF IMPRISONMENT

متن حكم اعدام مجاهدين خلق در شهريور 67 توسط خميني، انقلاب اسلامي

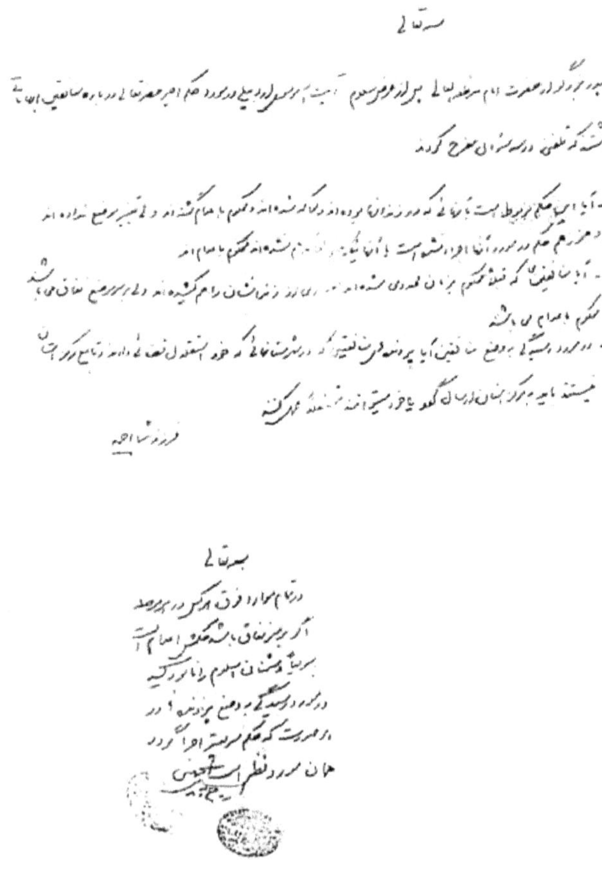

بسم‌الله‌الرحمن‌الرحيم

از آنجا که منافقین خائن به هیچ وجه به اسلام معتقد نبوده و هر چه می‌گویند از روی حیله و نفاق آنهاست و به اقرار سران آنها از اسلام ارتداد پیدا کرده‌اند، و با توجه به محارب‌بودن آنها و جنگهای کلاسیك آنها در شمال و غرب و جنوب کشور با همکاریهای حزب بعث عراق و نیز جاسوسی آنان برای صدام علیه ملت مسلمان ما، و با توجه به ارتباط آنان با استکبار جهانی و ضربات ناجوانمردانه آنان از ابتدای تشکیل نظام جمهوری اسلامی تاکنون، کسانی که در زندانهای سراسر کشور بر سرموضع نفاق خود پافشاری کرده و می‌کنند محارب و محکوم به اعدام می‌باشند و تشخیص موضوع نیز در تهران با رای اکثریت آقایان حجه‌الاسلام نیری دامت‌افاضاته (قاضی شرع) و جناب آقای اشراقی (دادستان تهران) و نماینده‌ای از وزارت اطلاعات می‌باشد، اگر چه احتیاط در اجماع است، و همین طور در زندانهای مراکز استان کشور رای اکثریت آقایان قاضی شرع، دادستان انقلاب و یا دادیار و نماینده وزارت اطلاعات لازم‌الاتباع می‌باشد، رحم بر محاربین ساده‌اندیشی است، قاطعیت اسلام در برابر دشمنان خدا از اصول تردیدناپذیر نظام اسلامی است، امیدوارم با خشم و کینه انقلابی خود نسبت به دشمنان اسلام رضایت خداوند متعال را جلب نمائید، آقایانی که تشخیص موضوع به عهده آنان است وسوسه و شك و تردید نکنند و سعی کنند [اشداء علی الکفار] باشند. تردید در مسائل قضائی اسلام انقلابی نادیده‌گرفتن خون پاك و مطهر شهدا می‌باشد. والسلام.

روح‌الله الموسوی الخمینی

این نامه تاریخ هم ندارد اما در پشت آن آقای حاج احمدآقا نوشته است:

پدر بزرگوار حضرت امام مدظله‌العالی

پس از عرض سلام، آیت‌الله موسوی‌اردبیلی در مورد حکم اخیر حضرتعالی درباره منافقین ابهاماتی داشته‌اند که تلفنی در سه سئوال مطرح کردند:

1- آیا این حکم مربوط به آنهاست که در زندانها بوده‌اند و محاکمه شده‌اند و محکوم به اعدام گشته‌اند ولی تغییر موضع نداده‌اند و هنوز هم حکم در مورد آنها اجرا نشده است، یا آنهایی که حتی محاکمه هم نشده‌اند محکوم به اعدامند؟

2- آیا منافقین که محکوم به زندان محدود شده‌اند و مقداری از زندانشان را هم کشیده‌اند ولی بر سرموضع نفاق می‌باشند محکوم به اعدام می‌باشند؟

3- در مورد رسیدگی به وضع منافقین آیا پرونده‌های منافقینی که در شهرستانهائی که خود استقلال قضائی دارند و تابع مرکز استان نیستند باید به مرکز استان ارسال گردد یا خود می‌توانند مستقلا عمل کنند؟

فرزند شما، احمد

زیر این نامه نوشته شده:

بسمه‌تعالی

در تمام موارد فوق هر کس در هر مرحله اگر بر سر نفاق باشد حکمش اعدام است، سریعا دشمنان اسلام را نابود کنید، در مورد رسیدگی به وضع پرونده‌ها در هر صورت که حکم سریعتر انجام گردد همان مورد نظر است.

روح‌الله الموسوی

3. OPEN EXECUTION

Appendix VII

Trend of Urban Population, Literacy, Enrollment in Institutions of Higher Education, Internal Migration and the Court Structure in 1927, 1968, and 1984 in Iran

Trend of Urban Population of Iran

Year	Urb. Pop (in thousands)	Population(m)	% of Urban Pop.
1956 (1335)	5,954	31.4	19
1966 (1345)	9,794	38.0	26
1971 (1350)	12,398	41.3	30
1976 (1355)	15,854	47.0	34
1986 (1365)	26, 845	54.3	49
1991 (1370)	31,837	57.0	56
1996 (1375)	36,818	61.3	60

Sources: The Iranian national censuses of 1956, 1966, 1976, 1986, 1991, and 1996, *Salnameh-ye Amari-ye Keshvar,* 1355/1976 & 1375/1996

Trend of Literacy Rate in Iran

Year	Literate (in thousands)	Population(m)	Literacy Rate
1956 (1335)	1,911	10.1	% 19
1966 (1345)	5,556	25.5	% 22
1976 (1355)	12,877	38.2	% 38
1986 (1365)	23,913	48.4	% 49
1996 (1375)	41,582	69.2	% 60
2006 (1385)	54,273	68.7	% 79

Sources: The Iranian national censuses of 1956, 1966, 1976, 1986, and 1996, *Salnameh-ye Amari-ye Keshvar,* 1375/1996, CIA World Factbook (https://www.cia.gov/cia/publications/factbook/geos/ir.html)

Enrollment in Institutions of Higher Education	
Academic Year	Number of Students
1971–71	74,708
1975–76	151,905
1978–79	175,675
1986–1987	167,971
1991–1992	344,045
1996–1997	1,192,738*

Sources: *Salnameh-ye Amari-ye Keshvar (Iran's Statistical Yearbook),* 1361/1982–83: 117; *Salnameh-ye Amari-ye Keshvar,* 1375/1996–7: 649–652

* This number includes students at public and private universities and higher education centers (public=579070; private (Azad University)=613468).

Internal Migration in Iran			
Year	Pop. (in thousands)	Migrants	% Total Population
1956 (1335)	18,955	2,081	11.0
1966 (1345)	25,079	3,224	12.9
1972 (1351)	29,526	4,275	14.5
1976 (1355)	33,709	5,056	15.0
1996 (1375)	60,055	8,840	14.1

Sources; Bill, 1972; 63–65; *Salnameh-ye Amari-ye Keshvar,* 1353: 69; *Salnameh-ye Amari-ye Keshvar,* 1363: 89; *Salnameh-ye Amari-ye Keshvar,* 1375: 73–74; *National Census of Population and Housing,* 1956, and 1976, vol. 186

THE COURT STRUCTURE IN DĀVAR'S ERA, 1927

Cassation Court (4 branches)

Appellate Court (10 branches)

Reconciliation Court (17 branches)

Primary courts (in provinces other than the capital, 35 branches)

* Āqeli, 1990: 141–143

THE COURT STRUCTURE IN POST-MOSADDEQ ERA, 1968

Regional Courts (194 branches)

Township Courts (168 branches, later increased to 319 branches)

Provincial Courts (66 branches, later in 1974 increased to 69 branches)
Shar'i Court (1 branch)
Itinerant Court (9 branches)
Houses of Equity (*khāneh ensāf*, 10280, in 1977)
Arbitration Councils (*shurā-ye dāvari*, 274 in 1977)
*Zerang, Vol. II, 2002: 126–137

THE COURT STRUCTURE IN THE POST-REVOLUTIONARY ERA, 1984

Revolutionary Courts (70 branches)
Courts of Justice: Civil Courts (205 branches)
Special Civil Courts (99 branches)
1st Class Criminal Courts (86 branches)
2nd Class Criminal Courts (156 branches)
Courts of Peace: Ordinary Courts of Peace (124 branches)
Independent Courts of Peace (125 branches)
Supreme Court of Cassation (22 branches)

THE COURT STRUCTURE, 1996 & 2004

Primary Courts (2123, 3064 branches)
Appellate Courts (283, 315 branches)
Revolutionary Courts (218, 285 branches)

Notes

NOTES TO CHAPTER ONE

1. I will use Arthur Schiller's definitions of this term in this study. Jurists' law, as opposed to state's law, in Schiller's definition is the law developed by experts that are concerned with the law, and their activities can be classified in three categories: to aid in drafting documents, to advise in procedural matters, and to respond to questions of law (1958: 1226). I will consider law as "the complex of constitutional provisions, bodies of legislative enactment, such as codes and statutes, and the continually developing body of judicial doctrine (s), explicit or implicit." Today barely anyone defines law as the mere aggregate of rules that govern society (Mattei, 1997: 5).
2. This is my definition of the term: "political systems with a) limited political pluralism, b) irresponsible, unaccountable and mostly unelected leaders c) without neither extensive nor intensive political mobilization, d) in which a leader or a small group exercises power within formally ill-defined limits." This is my manipulation of Linz's definition of this term (2000). I do not agree with Chehabi's view on rule of law being of the key components of consolidated authoritarian regime (2001). How irresponsible, unaccountable and mostly unelected leaders in most of the authoritarian regimes can advocate and enforce rule of law while the civil society mechanisms are so weak to pursue and push for this agenda? If rule of law is one of the fundamental elements of democracy "without which the unpredictability of public life renders the implementation of governmental decisions and policies uncertain" (Chehabi, 2001) how a non-democratic system could advocate rule of law? What kind of law is enforced in authoritarian regimes? How rule of law could be enforced when the independent publication and broadcasting is almost nil? If the will of the leader is considered to be the law, that is the case in the Islamic Republic of Iran, how this personal rule could be considered rule of law as it is understood in democratic context?
3. In this study, *shari`ah* (the straight way or discipline of human activity (Arnold, 1931: 290), path or track by which men may achieve salvation (Vesey-Fitzgerald, 1955: 86)) or, in a narrow definition of this term, Islamic

law) is not a holdover from the past, a framework for returning to ancient roots, or "a complex, multi-stranded set of ideas and practices that Islamic people molded and modified as they resisted and accommodated Euro-American imperialist ventures" (Collier, 1996: 2), but a complex, diverse and multi-faceted set of ideas and practices that Muslims have molded and modified as part of their cultures and lifestyles as they confronted the realities and challenges of life throughout the centuries of rise and demise of Islamic civilization and the interaction of sacred texts with local, regional and global cultures. Muslims believe that *shari`ah* is God's plan for their individual and communal life, public and private, local, national, and global. *Shari`ah* is "the whole duty of man . . . . high spiritual aspiration and the detailed ritualistic and formal observance which to some minds is a vehicle for such aspiration and to others a substitute for it; all aspects of law . . . and even courtesy and good manners are part and parcel of the *shari`ah,* a system which sometimes appear to be rigid and inflexible; at others to be imbued with that dislike of extremes" (Vesey-Fitzgerald, 1955: 85–86).

4. Oliver Wendell Holmes believes that "the law embodies the story of a nation's development through many centuries (1963: 5).
5. http://www.britannica.com/eb/print?tocId=68933&fullArticle=true
6. The latest motivation of judicial reform in other parts of the world is to make the legal system more market friendly (Messick, 1999) that has nothing to do with Iran.
7. By independence of the judiciary I mean "a set of institutional guarantees aimed at assuring judicial impartiality" (Guarnieri & Pederzoli, 2002: 4–5).
8. For the definition and social and political bases of judicialization of politics and judicial activism see Sousa Santos, 1999; Vallinder's definition of the first term refer to "the process by which courts and judges come to make or increasingly to dominate the making of public policies that had previously made by other governmental agencies (1995). Judicial activism refers to breaching the legal limits of the judiciary and going far from judicial restraints.
9. By ideologization, I mean making an ideology out of something that is not essentially an ideology like a religion, a tradition or science. Ideologization of science is to preface scientific ideas from philosophy or religion. Ideologization of religion is to turn religion to an instrument for gaining power or to overcome legitimacy crises of the establishment. Ideologization of religion transforms it into the realm of 'ism's (www.unesco-heute.de/1202/discussion.htm—43k).
10. Iranian activists and politicians who have talked about judicial independence have not presented a clear set of guidelines for this characteristic. In Iranian political literature, it is not clear if judicial independence means freedom of judges to evaluate the facts of the disputes before them and to construe the applicable law without any direct or indirect pressure being imposed upon them by others, independence vis-à-vis the executive and legislative branches of government, independence of judges as to one another, dealing with all issues of a judicial nature by the judiciary alone, secure

judicial tenure, or the right of judges to defend their independence with the constitutionally protected right of assembly. I borrowed these guidelines from Sherif (1999).

11. In some texts, the term "source of law" is used as an exact synonym for "method of lawmaking" (Watson, 1998: 112); Kelsen as a positivist thinks that all areas traditionally mentioned as sources of law i.e. statutes, judicial precedents, opinions of experts, customs and the principles of morality are themselves law (Kelsen, 1961: 132).
12. The change of a principle public legal institution that is recognized by the law (Bozeman, 1971: 67) is a good example of this kind of reform.
13. Islamicization is a social and political process in which all aspects of life will be based on doctrines and teachings of Islam. The propelling forces of this process are people and groups who believe in Islam as a complete system which provides divine instruction on everything from daily rituals, law, and politics to matters of the spirit, and to which all other forms of thought and social organization are alien.

    Islamicization in general can be defined as firmly grounding all aspects of life and affairs of the society—economy, culture, politics and social relationships—in Islamic practices and principles through devising and enforcing *shari`ah* as the all-embracing sacred law of the Islamic community. Practice of *shari`ah* in this special reading of it includes how human beings should relate to one another in their daily social intercourse; how the expanded functions of the state are to be organized; how people should deal with the details of marriage, intercourse, inheritance, divorce, diet, economic practice and the like; how norms and values, policies and regulations are to be established, imposed, manipulated and revised, how human knowledge and science should be developed; and in short how all human activities are to be regulated. Islamicization is accomplished by empowering Muslim jurists to assess the legality of the actions of individuals on the basis of their compliance with God's commands and requires the conversion of the system of jurist law to the system of public law of the state.
14. A recent example of law reform through the state is law reform in the Soviet Union before the collapse in 1988 whose goal was to strengthen political, economic and social rights and freedoms of Soviet people and ensuring the supremacy of law (Quigley, 1990: 59).
15. http://www4.worldbank.org/legal/leglr/judicialreform.html
16. In this study, I will be indifferent to the intentions, dispositions and purposes of the individuals whose lives made up the historical processes in which I am interested. My attention is centered on structural conditions and functional effects, and on the institutional background and institutional consequences of judicial reforms. What I am concerned about is successful mediation of history and theory.
17. This tripartite categorization is mentioned in Skocpol and Somers's piece on comparative study (1980).
18. http://ghest.com/news_view.asp?news_id=11712; http://ghest.com/news_view.asp?news_id=11712

19. Watson points to these factors as three tests of satisfactory source of law (Watson, 1998: 112).
20. These waves have their own distinctive features and are distinguished from each other by relations of power between the state elite and the rest of the population, sequence of social development, state capacities, the level of state centralization, penetration and extraction, the level of political mobilization and legitimacy, and the strength of civil society (Wimmer, 2002; 79). Chazan et. al argue that there have been four great waves of state building, each following the collapse of empires: South America in the 19th century (the Spanish Empire); Europe after World War I (Russia, Austria-Hungary, Ottoman Turkey); Asia and Africa after World II (Belgium, Holland, France, Britain and Portugal) and Central Asia and Eastern Europe in the late 1980s (the Soviet Union).
21. The important models are German (imposition from above), the U.S. (conquest from below), Swiss (fully nationalized maintaining a considerable degree of ethnic heterogeneity), French (learning and politicization), and early Balkan states of 1878–1914 period or most of the former colonial states after WWII (external forces) (Wimmer, 2002; 80–81; Franzinetti, 2005).
22. In Britain (http://www.ukconstitution.net/politics/issues/Judicial_reform.html), Chile (http://ergosum.uaemex.mx/noviembre98/gallegui.html) and Latin America (www.oas.org/legal/english/osla/judicial_reform.doc)
23. Starr (1992) and Messick (1993) explain changes in legal systems of Turkey and Yemen by focusing on the role of nineteenth-century imperialist powers in transformation of these societies' status codes to codes based on separation of religious from secular law; for the influence of colonialism on legal system see Merry's article on cultural power of law in colonized society (2000).
24. In Dāvar's terms, when proposing the reforms to the parliament, "expediting the judicial process and securing justice," Āqeli, 1990: 131; in Yazdi's term, when justifying the 1989 changes of the Constitution regarding the judiciary, "centralization in the managements of the judicial branch of the government to speed up the investigation of judicial matters" (*Kayhān,* Oct. 30, 1990, quoted in Moslem, 2002: 81); in Khomeini's term, when criticizing the judiciary of the previous regime, "the bureaucratic organization of the Ministry of Justice has attained unimaginable proportions and, in addition, quite incapable of producing results. It is things like these that make our country needy and produce nothing but expense and delay" (Khomeini, 1981: 58–59). This criticism is to make the case for the alternative : "When the juridical methods of Islam were applied, the *shari`ah* judge in each town, assisted only by two bailiffs and only a pen and inkpot at his disposal, would swiftly resolve disputes among people and send them about their business" (Khomeini, 1981: 58). This view is exactly what was going to be the General Court and could not send people about their business as it was promised.
25. Weber, *Wirtschaft und Gesellschaft* (*Economy and Society*), 368, taken from Kelsen, 1961: 175

NOTES TO CHAPTER TWO

1. As opposed to *shar'* that is administered by clerics and is mostly based upon Quran and *sunnah, 'orf* is administered by secular judges who decide cases and settle disputes according to common sense, traditions, or precedents and was usually orally handed down. The *'orf* usually took cognizance of criminal cases, and *shar'* of civil cases (Benjamin, 1887: 439).
2. Tyan has explained this point in the following statement: "Since the *qāzi* was the delegate-representative of the governor, he had to be one, just as the governor was" (Tyan, 1955: 241).
3. Mullah-ye Najafi in Isfahān, Seyyed Zain ul-'Ābedin in Khorāsān, Mullah 'Abdollāh Brujerdi in Hamedān, Mullah Esma'il 'Aqda'i in Yazd, Hāji Mullah Mohammad-e Khumami and Hāj Seyyed Mohammad Bāqer Rashti in Rasht and Āqā Mohammad Ali Behbahāni in Kermānshāh are some examples of 'ulamā who were administering justice in their provinces, ignoring the secular courts of their region (E'temād ul-Saltaneh, 1966: 684; Amin ul-Dowleh, 1962: 167; Nafisi. 1965: 68; Rāvandi, 1977: 496 & 529).
4. Frye, Richard, Hires of the Achaemenids Emperor Ardeshir and the Cycle of History, http://www.cais-soas.com/CAIS/ardeshir_and_cycle_of_history.htm
5. Hamid Algar had already exposed his thesis in his *Religion and State in Iran, 1785–1906* (1969).
6. Severe punishment has always been a characteristic of Iranian legal system. For interrogation purposes, beating and torturing have always practiced, from Achaemenids to the Islamic Republic. Crucifixion, chopping off feet and hands, gouging out eyes were common practices (Dandamaev & Lukonin, 1989: 120).
7. This rule was called "*e'tebār qazieh mahkum behā*" or "the validity of a case which is adjudged for." This rule is based on the idea that settlement of the disputes is the main goal of judiciary not reaching to the heart of the matter and discovering the realities related to the case (Ja'fari Langroudi, 193).
8. Land granted by the state to high provincial authorities to levy their salaries or pensions against the taxes of a particular district. It was usually given for life. Since the holders of the *toyul*s paid no tax, large part of the country were outside of the direct control of the central government (Minorsky, 1965: 799–801; Lambton, 1953: 155). Granting toyuls was not a norm in pristine Islam and during Ummayyids and Abbasids. It became a norm after the Mogul invasion (Ja'fari Langrudi, 1278–279).
9. The *shar'i* courts did not have imprisonment in their verdicts.
10. The source of law for *shar'iah* courts was Islamic *shari`ah,* while *'orfi* judges relied on the *shari`ah,* oral tradition, precedent, local customs, and reason (Floor, 1983; 115).
11. Some examples are Mirzā Reza Khan-e Grānmāyeh, Mirzā Abdollāh Sādiq ul-Molk, Mirzā Zain al-'Ābedin Kāshāni, Mirzā Nasrullāh Khan Nā'ini, later Prime Minister of Muzaffar ul-din Shah, and Moshir ul-Dowleh-ye Pirniā.
12. Gerber has evidence that in the Ottoman empire the majority of the rulings were in favor of the poor and against the powerful (Gerber, 1994: 40–1)

13. Nezām ul-Molk laid down this rule that the *qāzi*s should be allocated a monthly salary by the national or local officials (Lambton, 1988: 74) to prevent direct payment to judges by plaintiffs and defendants.

NOTES TO CHAPTER THREE

1. In years immediately after the Constitutional Revolution, laws regarding judiciary were not passed in the parliament but in the judicial committee (Zerang, Vol. I, 2002: 187).
2. Medieval *'iqtā* had been transformed to the system of land grants called *toyul* in the Qājār period (and *timār* in the Ottoman empire). Land granted to army officials for limited periods in lieu of a regular wage (Lambton, 1967; http://www.britannica.com/eb/article?tocId=9042736). In this system, parts of the country are parceled out to various important officials, nobles, or generals entrusted to collect revenue. The *iqtā'* system was established in the 9th century AD to relieve the state treasury when insufficient tax revenue and little booty from campaigns made it difficult for the government to balance its budget.
3. Moslem, Mehdi, "The Making of a Weak State: The Iranian Constitutional Revolution of 1905–1906," Centre for the Study of Democracy , University of Westminster , May, 1995 Research Papers, Number 6 (http://www.ciaonet.org/wps/mom01).
4. Ibid
5. The urban population of Iran was less than 20 percent in the whole 19th century (Issawi, 1971: 26–28: Amir Ahmadi, 1982: 91)
6. This Moshir ul-Dowleh is different from Nasrullah Khan Moshir ul-Dowleh who was PM at the time of the *farmān* (order) of 1906/1324 A.H.
7. This was Regent Mirza Abolqāsem Khan Nāser ul-Molk's idea (Zerang, Vol. I, 2002: 192; due to minority of Ahmad Shah, first 'Azed ul-Dowleh and then Nāser ul-Molk took the position of regency after the death of Mohammad Ali Shah. He was regent from 1910 to 1918: http://www.iransoc.dircon.co.uk/WebPage952.html). This idea does not only belong to Iranians. Legal distinctions between urban residents and peasants in 11 provinces extended from Mao's era to 21st century (http://www.nytimes.com/2005/11/03/international/asia/03china.html).
8. *Surat-e Mashruh-e Mozākerāt-e Majles* (*Parliamentary Proceedings*), First Parliament, 585.
9. On the Parliament floor, Amin ul-Shari`ah said: "Jurisdiction is the task of *mujtaheds*; 'Adliyyeh (the judiciary) is not the place of jurisdiction" (*Parliamentary Proceedings,* Vol. 4, No. 2, 1910: 31–32).
10. In Ottoman Empire, in spite of dual system of courts, provincial administrative councils did the same thing: "they were allowed to hear appeals from Seriat [*shari`ah*] court decisions involving large amount of money, thus extending their powers into judicial area" (Shaw & Shaw, 1977: 87, 218).
11. Ali Akbar Dehkhodā was tried in the Parliament for writing against Islam, requested by Seyyed 'Abdollāh Behbahāni. He was acquitted from the charges (Amin, 2003: 492).

12. The same thing can be said about all Muslim countries in the Middle East, especially Turkey (Starr, 1992), Sudan (Fluehr-Lobban, C, 1986) and Egypt (Brown, 1997).
13. A woman charged with adultery, was put in the hole and was given the chance of escape while she was stoned; if God was on the side of the charged woman, she could save her life. The Islamic Republic, later, revived this Godly-worldly punitive approach.
14. Articles 145 of JOSCRML and circulation of Mirza Hasan Khan Moshir ul-Dowleh (2, Zel-Hajjeh 1327 A.Q./Dec. 15, 1909) made the jurisdictions of these two courts more clear (Zerang, Vol. I, 2002: 204–206).
15. This aspect of the legal system is true for a period of about four millennia, from Hammurabi (1795 B.C.) to the Iranian Constitutional Revolution (1906).
16. *Loghat Nāmeh-ye Dehkhodā* (*Dehkhodā Dictionary*)
17. Muhammad B. 'Ali al-Shawkani had the same role in modernizing Yemeni judiciary in the 19th century (Haykel, 1994: 53; Haykel, 2001 & 2002). By insistence on *ejtehād* (independent judgment of a scholar) and negating the validity of *ejmā'* (consensus) and *qiyās* (analogical deduction), he opened the way for new understanding of Quran and *Sunna* (the normative custom of the Prophet). He gave the Sunni *hadith* collections an exclusive authoritative value and generally used them to bolster already established Zaydi doctrine (Haykel, 1994: 54).
18. The Ottomans merged the Supreme Religious Court and Supreme Judicial Council as part of the secular judiciary to a new body, i.e. Supreme Council of Judicial Ordinances to get rid of the difficulties of the dual system (Shaw & Shaw, 1977: 79). The Supreme Religious Court was carrying out *shaikhulislam*'s (jurisconsult and the last resort of appeal from the lower religious courts) judicial and legal function. The Ottoman Shaikhulislam was the Head of the Ottoman Judiciary, sometimes referred to as the Chief Mufti of Istanbul. This Council was divided into three departments: 1) the Department of Laws and Regulations, which assumed the legislative function of both old councils, 2) the Department of Administration and finance, charged with administrative investigation, and 3) the Department of Judicial Cases, which acted as a court of appeals. The first department found a counterpart in Iran during Sepah Sālār's judicial reform (Drafting Bill Office (Dāyereh-ye Tanzim-e Qavānin)) but the second and third departments could not find any counterparts until the Constitutional Movement.
19. During Tanzimāt era, 1876–1909, there were four court systems in the Ottoman Empire: secular civil and commercial courts, consular courts, mixed trade courts, and religious courts (Shaw & Shaw, 1977: 246–7)
20. Nā'ini believes that all judicial affairs are to be handled by the *mujtaheds* (Nā'ini, 1955: 71).
21. Originally mentioned in Marling to Grey, no. 231, 10 October 1907, Foreign Office Archives, FO 416 Confidential Print.
22. Hasan Modarres, one of most influent clerics in the parliament agrees with this idea that "[we can] adopt statutory laws from our religious regulations

and adopt the way to enforce them from laws of other nations" (*Parliamentary Proceeding,* the Second Parliament, Vol. III, 1289).

23. Turkamān, www.iranbar.com/pe191.php
24. This constitution that was called "the Fundamental Law" (Nezām-Nāmeh ye Asāsi) was drafted by a group of political elite, including Mirzā Hasan Khan Moshir ul-Dowleh and Mirzā Hosein Khan Mo'tamen ul-Molk. It was translated from the European constitutions (Kasravi, Vol. I, 1977: 58)
25. Ottomans separated legislative and judicial functions in 1868, when the Divān-e Ahkām-e 'Adliyyeh (Ministry of Justice) was established. This ministry served as the legitimate context for considering civil and secular courts (Nadolski, 1977).
26. The Supplement was drafted by a commission including Sa'd ul-Dowleh, Seyyed Hasan Taqi-Zadeh, Hāj Hosein Amin ul-Zarb, Mostashār ul-Dowleh, Moshāver ul-Molk, Mokhber ul-Molk, and Hāji Seyyed Nasrullāh Taqavi (Kasravi, Vol. I, 1977: 285 ff)
27. According to Article 81, judges cannot be temporarily or permanently dismissed without trial. According to Article 82, judges cannot be transferred without their consent.
28. Ottomans had the same problem during the Tanzimāt era, when the Charter of this reform did not recognize the independence of the judiciary (Berkes, 1964: 146).
29. The movement to put Islam as "the" source of law in constitutions in most countries is more recent. Governments might have referred to Islam in their constitutions, and used elements of Islamic law in family law, but "the source of law" phrase in constitutions is recent and goes with Islamist movements. In Egypt and Pakistan it has had a conservative effect with respect to advances for women.
30. When the power of secularists increased in the Reza Khan government, this law was passed in1925 (Zerang, Vol. I, 2002: 269).
31. Egyptians and Ottomans had another system of courts in the late nineteenth century that is called mixed courts (Cannon, 1988: 65–88; Berkes, 1964: 165: Shaw & Shaw, 1977: 74–74, 145). The mixed courts are very different from the dual, *shari`ah-* state courts. They were commercial courts (really for arbitration between foreign or *zemmi* and Muslim merchants) set up in the Ottoman Empire, including Egypt and Tunisia, and had no counterpart in Iran. The commercial court Mansur ul-Saltaneh 'Adl mentions (1911: 373) was in imitation of these courts. The idea of mixed court is totally different from the idea of mixed jurisdiction, as it is different from legal pluralism. Mixed jurisdiction is a combination of two or more systems of law like Civil and Common, or Civil and Socialist law (Orucu, 1996: 336) that include two or more doctrines, individual rules in similar areas, legal procedures and institutions, while the idea of mixed court is about two or more judicial institutions or a mixture of them for settling the disputes. The Commercial Courts after 1840 (reorganized in 1862) in Ottoman Empire were mixed courts and composed of three judges appointed by the government and four assessors representing the merchants, Ottoman and European alike (Shaw & Shaw, 1977: 118). Mixed jurisdictions reflect different

legal families and legal traditions, while mixed court systems do not necessarily reflect those traditions or families.

32. In the Persian political and judicial literature, it was not hard to find these kinds of argument: for example look at Jalal al-Din Davāni's treatise on *Divan-e Daf"-e Mazālem* (This treatise has never been published). Ottomans used this treatise to justify the establishment of secular courts in their territories (Berkes, 1964: 165). Jevdet Pasha, like everyone else in the 19th century, read manuscripts.
33. They were given this power too in the 1930s (Banani, 1961: 72).
34. The people who drafted Iran's Commercial Code were careful about the bordering between Civil and Commercial Codes; they drafted the Commercial Code in a way that it was silent about matters that were already considered in the Civil Code, mostly based on *shari`ah* (Khal'at Barry, 1933: 11). The Iranian Commercial Code was mainly based on local commercial customs, while had International Commercial Codes in its perspective.
35. "Complete History of Law Practice in Iran" (Tārikhche-ye Kāmel-e Vekālat dar Iran) in official website of Iran's Bar Association (http://www.iranbar.com/pe191.php); In 1914, Zakā' ul-Molk Foroughi as the Minister of Justice issued an order obligating the lawyers to do the exam for getting license. According to this order, lawyers should be ranked to three degree: degree one for law practice in reconciliation courts, degree two for primary and appellate courts, and degree three for the higher and Supreme Court. In this way, the legal profession was totally in the hands of the state.
36. "Complete History of Law Practice in Iran" (*Tārikhche-ye Kāmel-e Vekālat dar Iran*) in official website of Iran's Bar Association (http://www.iranbar.com/pe191.php)
37. www.iranbar.com/pe191.php
38. *Ruznāmeh-ye Majles (Majles Chronicle),* No. 54, 1908
39. Moshir ul-Dowleh was forerunner in the grand task of clearing the jurisdictions of *'orfi* and *shar'i* courts. Before this law there was no border between *'orfi* and *shar'i* courts and the people were confused in referring their cases to these courts.
40. This Article is also brought up, with somehow different translation, in Banani, 77
41. The Ministry of Justice and three-stage judicial procedure in the Ottoman Empire were established in 1870, half a century before Iran. The Ministry of Justice was the expansion of hierarchical secular court system in the framework of the Ministry of Judicial Pleas (Nezārat-i Divāni) created by Mahmut II. "By the end of the century the Ministry of Justice included a Supreme Judicial Council, a Court of Cassation, and an Appeals Court" (Shaw & Shaw, 1977: 75). This was a big jump from Mahmud II who died in 1839. The end of century Ministry of Justice was the result of the 1868 split of Divān-i Ahkām-i 'Adliya. (See Berkes, 165)
42. www.iranbar.com/pe191.php
43. *Surat-e Mashruh-e Mozākerāt-e Majles* (*Parliamentary Proceedings),* Second Parliament, 146.
44. *Rouznāmeh-ye Majles (Majles Chronicle*), No. 55, 1908: 2.

45. www.iranbar.com/pe191.php
46. The members of this commission were Seyyed Mostafā Mansur ul-Saltaneh 'Adl, Mohammad Ali Zakā' ul-Molk Forughi, Hāj Seyyed Nasrollāh Taqavi, Āqā Seyyed Mohammad Qomi, Shaikh Mohammad 'Abdoh Brujerdi, Seyyed Ali Qomi, and Shari'atzādeh (Amin, 2003: 511).
47. This 'third wave' seems to be totally inconsistent with 'Āqeli and Banani, who attribute the Civil Code and Law of Civil Procedure entirely to the drafting commission under Dāvar. During the third wave, in my view, these laws were drafted but did not have a chance to be passed. When Dāvar got the position of Ministry of Justice, these laws were re-drafted and passed in the parliament.
48. Other than this, the judiciary was dissolved twice: during the incumbency of Minister of Justice, Mirzā Hasan Khan Moshir ul-Dowleh in 1920 (Zerang, Vol. I, 2002: 289) and immediately after the selection of Dāvar as the Minister of Justice in 1926 (Zerang, Vol. I, 2002: 290).
49. *Sourat-e Mashrouh-e Mozākerāt-e Majles (Parliamentary Proceedings)*, Third Parliament, 197.
50. "Complete History of Law Practice in Iran" (*Tārikhche-ye Kāmel-e Vekālat dar Iran*) in official website of Iran's Bar Association (www.iranbar.com/pe191.php)
51. This was annulled in 1909, and afterwards, only the convicted should pay 10 percent of the claim.

NOTES TO CHAPTER FOUR

1. By 24, he was Tehran's Prosecutor General. He later studied law in Switzerland. In 1927, he shut down Iran's Justice Ministry to completely revamp it. In less than three months, a new system was born. It combined European legal code with Islamic jurisprudence. The new system had local courts, regional ones and a Supreme Court. Judges decided which cases should be handled by the clerics.
2. .The non-European countries category includes- but is not limited to- Turkey, China, and even Afghanistan (Zerang, Vol. I, 2002: 216).
3. See Parsa, 1989: chap. 1.
4. Military tribunals acquired a growing importance from 1950s on. Most of the dissidents were tried by the Military Courts. Military Courts were also used to try some of the offences in the anti-profiteering campaign of August 1975 (Binder, 1978: 137).
5. These tribunals served the executive power and partially staffed by qualified legal personnel. They had unlimited power to fine and sentence, powers that cannot be challenged by appeal within the normal law courts (Binder, 1978: 137). One example is the Tax Court administered by the Ministry of Finance.
6. "Pressure on family or friends, or the threat of charges which a person is powerless to disapprove, are the standard methods of obtaining collaboration . . . . there have been instances of prosecution of military defiance council . . . . A more direct form of intimidation has been lengthy detention without trial. This has been applied to recalcitrant writers as well

as politicians." (Graham, 1978: 147) Khāmenei has been doing the same thing from the beginning of his rule.

7. http://www.sedona.net/pahlavi/gvt.html
8. Watson thinks that "borrowing from another system is the most common form of legal change" (1983: 1125).
9. http://home.att.net/~aturpat/tabrizie.htm
10. As Kelsen explains, essentially a separation of the judicial from the so-called executive power is possible only in a comparatively limited measure. A strict separation of the two powers is impossible, since the two types of activity usually designated by these terms are not essentially distinct functions. The judicial function consists in the execution of general norms (Kelsen, 1961: 273).
11. The case of interpretation of Article 82, doing away with the independence of judges, known as the Dr. Mahmoud Afshār case; when Dr. Afshār who was one of the judges of the Cassation Court could not be influenced, Dāvar interpreted Article 82 by resort to the parliament, adding this phrase to the article that "change of the location of a judge without changing his position is not against this article" (Ā'qeli, 1990: 201–203).
12. A very good example is Ali Mansur's case. When Mansur, the Minister of Transportation, was acquitted by the Cassation Court, totally against the will of Reza Shah, Nayyer ul-Molk, the head of Supreme Court and Seyyed Mohsen Sadr, the Minister of Justice were ousted from their positions (Ā'qeli, 1990: 294–295). The trials of high ranking officials and members of elite, like 'Abd ul-Hossein Taymurtash and Nosrat ul-Dowleh Firuz whom Reza Shah was suspicious about them was totally ordered by him and the judiciary had no independence in those trials ('Āqeli, 1990: 244–260).
13. Thinking of the scale of violence and violation of rights, this list is fairly exhaustive, and consists entirely of members of the elite who posed a political threat to Reza Shah. Under Mohammad Reza, the elite members are fewer, as named here right after the list of killings by Reza Shah. Baqi counts some 350 Savak victims, mostly students and a few clerics between 1971 and 1979 (http://www.emadbaghi.com/en/archives/000592.php). The numbers under the IRI are massive in comparison; between Feb. 1979 and June 1981, 497 political figures were killed by the Islamic Republic (Abrahamian, 1999: 125).
14. http://itsa.ucsf.edu/~ico/history/1historicalsetting.html
15. In this year, the state courts were given partial appellate jurisdiction over the Shari`ah Courts (*Record of Parliamentary Legislation, First Parliament*, 116–118; Banani, 1961: 78).
16. Sangelaji (1890–1944) was one of the critiques of traditional Shi'ites beliefs who denied the raj'at (return) and the occultation of the 12th Imam. He wanted to modernize Shi'ite Islam to adjust with the demands of new epoch. His main strategy for religious reform, similar to Seyyed Qutb, Mohammad 'Abdoh, Rashid Reza, Mehdi Bāzargān, Ali Shari'ati and Mahmud Taleqāni, was return to Quran. His main agenda was to clear Quran from superstitions built around it (*Mahv al-Muhum* (*Obliteration of Fictitious*), 1944,

Tehran, Taban: www.quranian.net/ modules.php?name=Downloads&d_op=viewdownload&cid=1).

17. The *shari`ah* compilations utilized for drafting of this code were Sharh-e Lom'eh, Sharāye,' and Makāseb. This code was modeled on European civil codes (Shāyegān, 1945: 35–39).
18. Kelsen invented the constitutional court in 1920, but judicial review was not really institutionalized in civil law systems until after WWII.
19. John M. Mathews report this trend of state administrative reorganization in the U.S. (1922).
20. *Parliamentary Proceeding,* Sixth Legislative Period Volume
21. 'Ali Hey'at and Abdul'ali Lotfi served as ministers of justice during Mohammad Mosaddeq administrations (March-April 1951, July 1952-Aug 1953).
22. An exception was annulment of removal of judges by the Amendment of the Justice Department Act of September 1957.
23. The number of judges in Appellate Courts was decreased from 4 to 3 (Zerang, Vol. I, 2002: 329).
24. http://www.iranbar.com/pe192.php
25. Mehdi Hādavi, the first Revolutionary Attorney General after 1979, says, "I, myself, ruled against the previous king [Mohammad Reza Shah] regarding the lands confiscated by his father. Some other judges like Judge Sajjādiān who was appointed as the Chief Justice of the Supreme Court after the [Islamic] Revolution issued such verdicts. Mahmud Samsāmi Mohājer adjudged the king's sister and the Supreme Court confirmed his adjudication" (*Payām-e Hājar,* Sep. 15, 1999).
26. These courts were the Governmental Officials Penal Court, Procedural Court of Ministry of Finance, and Special Court for Lawyers (Zerang, Vol. II, 2002: 41–42).
27. The jurisdiction of Military Courts increased after 1948 (Zerang, Vol. II, 2002: 74).
28. http://www.iranbar.com/pe193.php.
29. The proceedings of the Judiciary Committee have never been published (Zerang, Vol. I, 2002: 287).
30. Two hundred judges were fired by Mosaddeq administration (Zerang, Vol. II, 2002: 95).
31. Zerang, 2002: 400–407; During Dāvar's Ministry of Justice, a law on public gatherings required that permits be obtained to hold any public gathering, indicating time and place, the subjects to be discussed, and the names of the sponsors, so that they would be available for punishment if the law was violated or the events went in the way that the government dislike (Shaw & Shaw, 1977: 286).
32. Arthur Millspaugh, an American employee of the Iranian government as the Administer General of the Finance of Persia from 1922 to 1927 and from 1943 to 1945, refers to this problem in his personal report: "Our inspection service sent scores of accused officials and employees to the Ministry of Justice for prosecution and trial; but they were acquitted or *nolle prossed* with discouragingly monotonous consistency" (Millspaugh, 1946: 132).
33. I copied this categorization of dilemmas from Chodosh, 2003: 589.

NOTES TO CHAPTER FIVE

1. The killings began five days after Khomeini's return on Feb. 16, 1979: by March 14, seventy people have been executed; by November the death toll had risen to 550 (Bakhash, 1984: 60).
2. Maududi believes that the function of the state, other than transcending the bounds of Islam, establishing a political order on the moral principles of Islam, and facing the problems of secular ideologies, is the execution of the *shari`ah:* "The Quran lays down that Allah is the sovereign and the Law-giver and His revealed law must be adopted as the law of the land." (1960: 2–11, 5) Khomeini presented this thesis in Najaf during his exile after 1962. This line of argument appears in one of his most influential books, a collection of his addresses at Najaf entitled, *Hokoumat-e Eslāmi or Islamic State* (Khomeini, 1981).
3. Although the idea of *maslahat* has been foreign to Shi'ism, it has been common to all traditional Muslim monarchies, Shi'ite or Sunni, that allows the discretionary powers of the ruler—sultan, imam or caliph, and *valiy-e faqih* in the Islamic Republic—on grounds of public interest (*maslaha*). For the Sunnis, it has always been part of the *siyasa al-shar'iya,* and refers to extra-*shar'i* or often anti-*shar'i* norms, punishments and other measures of policy and statecraft. The big difference is that it is in practice above the *shari'a* norms and can trump them, whereas *'orf* or custom is below the *shari'a* and can never trump it. This could be the reason of being *'orf* as a default category of valid law both in the *shari'a* and in the Constitution of 1979. In the Qājār period this sort of thing could be referred to as *hokumat-e 'orfi,* but even there the emphasis was on *hokumat* and not on *'orf.* This is precisely what Khomeini meant when he introduced it in the context of *velayat-e motlaqeh ye faqih*—it is super-*shar'i* and not sub-*shar'i* norm.
4. The say, "our religion is Islam, our law is heavenly book of Quran and the Prophet's *Sunnah.* Legislation of another law in Muslim land is heresy, and opening a venue in front of the owner of *shari`ah,* and its obligation is also another heresy due to no obligation from *shari`ah,* and considering people liable to it is the third heresy" (Nā'ini, 1955: 74).
5. It was also called *feqh-e istā* (static jurisprudence)
6. It was also called dynamic jurisprudence.
7. One "school of thought" claims that Shi'ite people have espoused "*ekhtiār*" or "choice," whereas other school has adopted a school of thought known as Jabrieh or cosmological determinism which emphasizes compulsion or predestination over choice. The Ekhtiār School nurtures logic and reasoning, and condones *ejma'* (consensus), *qiyās* (analogical human reasoning), and *ejtehād* (exercise of opinion in questions of Islamic law). The Jabrieh school discounts these qualities and treats them as mere *beda'* (fabrication). Twelver Shi'ite theology agrees on most points with the Mu'tazilite school of theology, which stressed free will, among other things, while Ash'ari school rejected Mu'tazilism and free will. However, theology has not been of great importance to most Muslims. Iranian Shi'ism in the past few centuries developed a practice that limited freedom of choice in major questions;

according to this tradition the rest of the population must emulate their chosen *mujtahed*(s) on all questions they ruled on. This dominant Usuli school had been challenged by the Akhbāri school which said all Shi'ites could interpret traditions themselves, but this school virtually died out in Iran and Iraq. Later. Usuli school leaned gradually more towards the Akhbāri school through its nominalistic views on the sacred texts, something that could be called nominalistic Akhbārism. Recent attempts to revive pro-choice ideas have some background in Iranian Shi'i thought. Iranian ruling clerics have recently embraced religious authoritarianism and have attempted to force the whole population into a single belief and practice.

8. On the basis of Article 4 of the Constitution of 1979, "All civil, penal financial, economic, administrative, cultural, military, political, and other laws and regulations must be based on Islamic criteria. This principle applies absolutely and generally to all articles of the Constitution as well as to all other laws and regulations, and the *fuqahā'* (jurists) of the Guardian Council are judges in this matter."
9. The violations are typically related to the process of legislation. Khomeini issued a governmental order during the third parliamentary election in 1988 to order the Guardian Council to confirm the result of the election in Tehran (http://www.sharghnewspaper.com/830122/parlim.htm). Almost all of the confiscations were justified on Khomeini's governmental order (http://www.irica.com/Asp/News/207151.asp). When the Shi'ite seminaries ran out of qualified religious jurists to occupy judgeship positions, Khomeini opened the way for unqualified ones by a governmental order (*hokm-e hokumati*) (Khomeini, 1991: Vol. 19, 245). Khāmenei used this power to ask the Guardian Council to confirm the result of sixth parliamentary election in Tehran. He asked the Sixth Parliament to stop working on an amendment to the Press Code that could give more freedom to the press and limit the judiciary in banning and closing the press (*Parliamentary Proceedings*, Aug. 7, 2000; http://www.jomhourieslami.com/j-eslami/About/b1.htm). He justified the results of rigged parliamentary election in 2004 by resort to this power of the jurist (*Parliamentary Proceedings*, April 20, 2004; http://www.sharghnewspaper.com/830122/parlim.htm). In another move, he ordered the Guardian Council to confirm two reformist candidates for ninth presidential election (Mostafā Mo'in and Mohsen Mehr Alizādeh); the Guardian Council (http://mag.gooya.com/president84/archives/029713.php) and some sections of the political society, mostly authoritarians interpreted this move as a governmental order issued by the leader; reformists did not agree (www.ilna.ir/print.asp?code=200006;eqbal.ir/political/othernews/last/8434100912.php; www.baztab.com/news/24660.php).
10. Dualities like the Islamic Revolutionary Courts and common courts, Revolutionary Corps and the Army, the President and the Prime Minister, the Revolutionary Committees and the police, the social security and the Imam's Committee for Relief, etc.
11. http://www.aviny.com/Article/Azghadi/DinDarHasheyeh2.aspx.

12. Islamic law and legal system(s) is (are) based on widespread adoption of the legal and administrative institutions and practices of the conquered territories (Schacht, 1964: 19) and the teaching of Quran and prophet Mohammad
13. While emphasizing on Islam as an ideology, Shari'ati and Bāzargān had differences in reading Islam and Islamic scriptures as ideological texts. Islam for Shari'ati was an engine for revolution and a blueprint for a radical transformation of the social order (Mirsepassi 2000, 59–60) while for Bāzargān, it was an important part of everyday life, a general program for social and political life and an spiritual medium to delightful life (*hayāt-e tayebeh*) (Bāzargān, 1998)
14. Proceedings of the Expert Council for Drafting the Constitution of IRI, Session 15 (http://hoqooq.com/article.php3?id_article=144)
15. This is Mohammad Ali Araki's theory on the legitimate state (Kadivar, 1998: 12).
16. In Persian, this politicized community is usually and inadvertently called *mo'menin* or *motadayyenin*. From the official point of view, the members of this community are first order citizens and the remainder of are second order citizens.
17. A lot of scholars believe in the passage of Iran from a secular to an Islamic state during the Islamic Revolution (Bakhash, 1984: 7).
18. Wood alludes to this in the context of American Revolution (1991, 5–8).
19. "From Constitutional Monarchy to Juristic Republic," 2002, in http://www.kadivar.com/Htm/Farsi/Speeches/Speech810518.htm, and *Theories of State in Shi'ite Jurisprudence,* 1998 (Tehran: Nai) quoted from http://www.kadivar.com/Htm/Farsi/Books/Book01/Sec054.htm
20. http://www.iran-press-service.com/articles/nouri_challenges_khameneh'i_201299.htm
21. http://r0ozonline.com/01newsstory/016600.shtml
22. raha.gooya.name/politics/archives/000513.php; khabar.gooya.com/politics/archives/004060.php
23. Beeman, William O., *Cultural Impediments to U.S.- Iran Understanding,* 2003, p.7, quoted from http://www.brown.edu/Departments/Anthropology/publications/DOUBLE_DEMONS-12–03–2.pdf.
24. Absolutist clerical rule resembles more to the Qājār style of leadership than that of the Pahlavis.
25. Peter Berger argues about the secularizing influence of some religious ideas like a strict monotheism, disenchantment of the world and historization (Berger, 1973: 123).
26. Other views are Islam as an overall value system and base for culture, and Islam as a system of spiritual experience as it is presented in Islamic mysticism.
27. http://www.irib.ir/occasions/tashkhise%20maslahat%5Ctashkhise%20maslahat.htm
28. There are lots of cases in *shari`ah* where a new *'orf* superseded an old rules (Kritzeck, 1960: 63).

29. This was changed later due to the shortage of *mujtaheds* to fill all the judgeship positions.
30. These *shar'i* judges were directly appointed by Khomeini: Malek Huseini (Jul. 16, 1979), Mohammad Taqi Shāhrokhi (Jul. 22, 1979), Abd ul-Javād Jabal 'Āmeli (Jul. 23, 1979), Mohammad Hasan Amr ul-Lāhi (Sep. 7, 1979), Seyyed Mohammad Huseini Kāshāni (Oct. 1979), and Esmā'il Ferdowsi (Nov. 27, 1979) (Khomeini: 1991: Vol. V, 195, 249, 261, 563, & Vol. VI, 7).
31. Collegial adjudication was still under way till 1980 in Criminal Court.
32. In Islamic tradition, only one judge has the position of authority in the court. (http://lankarani.com/Arabic/books/jm1/j24.html). In shi'ite tradition, this is based on the so-called authentic *hadith* of 'Omar-ebn-e Hanzaleh on the necessity of choosing the most just judge when there are many. Later in post-Khomeini era, limited collegial adjudication was accepted. In 2003, the judiciary declared that the verdicts of the press court would be issued by three judges (*Hamshahri* Daily, Oct. 14, 2003). This was never happened. Section 3 of the General Judicial Policies passed in the Expediency Council (May 2004) confirms the multiplicity of judges in important cases (http://www.sharghnewspaper.com/830306/gover.htm). This approval does not present any measure for importance. The judiciary approved the multiplicity of judges in some of the cases in criminal courts.
33. "In the course of studying Islamic law in its everyday practice, I have been increasingly struck with its similarities to the common law form" (Rosen, 2000: 39). This is mostly true about the Sunni tradition that accepts reasoning by analogy *(qiās)* as one of its sources of law. When Islamic law gives priority to Quranic prescriptions and Prophets' *Sunnah* and considers any case totally different from other cases, it increases its distance from common law system.
34. Khomeini always believed that Muslims are to do their religious duties and to accomplish their obligations; they are not supposed to think about consequences (Khomeini, 1991: Vol. 20, 99).
35. This theoretical tension produced lots of confusion and inaction in the judicial system.
36. A ruling on a point of Islamic law that is given by a recognized authority (http://wordnet.princeton.edu/perl/webwn)
37. Dastghaib, Abd ul-Hussein, *Proceeding of the Assembly to Draft IRI Constitution,* Session No. 4, Aug. 19, 1979 (http://www.irisn.com/ketabkhaneh/mashroh/01/MATN_MASHROH_MOZARAKERAT_04.HTM)
38. Immediately after the Islamic Revolution, the leader's delegation was institutionalized in universities, military and IRGC, the Construction Jihad, and every other revolutionary organization. Nothing can be done in these institutions and organizations if these delegates disagreed.
39. The disqualifications and cheatings during the seventh parliamentary election in 2004 were mostly directed to accomplish this goal in Khāmenei's era.
40. In Weber's view, legitimacy may be ascribed to an order in the four mentioned ways (1964: 130).
41. These judges were permitted to hear cases if they only were proficient in Islamic law and only as long as there were insufficient *mujtaheds* to occupy

the positions (Law on the Conditions for the Selection of Judges, 1982). Most of the eliminated judges and lawyers were active against the Pahlavi regime. They launched protests and participated in demonstrations. In some provinces, all the judges resigned collectively to protest the "killings of defenseless people' in their province or government repression and violence. In some other provinces, the judges and lawyers held sit-ins to protest hooligans and thugs attacks and burning of the public buildings. In some areas, they filed suits against hooligans and those police and military officers who either organized them or failed to prevent their actions (Parsa, 1989: 152).

42. *The Free Man and the Freedom of the Man* (http://www.shariati.com); *Where Shall We Begin?* (http://www.shariati.com)
43. http://www.irna.ir/occasion/ertehal/english/will/lmnew2.htm
44. This term, beginning with the French Revolution, usually evokes images of rigged judgments handed down by pitiless regimes whose moralistic severity is usually attributed to some form of millenarian or eschatological ideology (Shapiro, 1992: 656).
45. "In the positive position, the burden of legal transformation was thought properly to fall on the legislature, while natural law position assumed a transformative role for adjudication" (Teitel, 2000: 24).
46. Sāzmān-e Ettelā'āt va Amniyyat-e Keshvar (Intelligence and Security Organization of the Country)
47. http://persepolis.free.fr/iran/revolution/revolution.html
48. This is a report to Montazeri as one of the top revolutionary clerics of the country: "Inside the cell, it was so dark that no one could tell if it was day or night; there were ten people in the cell; we saw a girl in a cell who was eating her own excrement" (Montazeri, 2000: p. 27 of ch.8). In another report to the leader, dated 1986, there are indications about different kinds of torture: breaking teeth, ripping hairs, breaking legs, abortion because of being beaten, lashing by cable, kicking, burning by lighter, burning by kerosene and diesel fuels, burning the genitals with a piece of wood, etc (Montazeri, 2000: p. 28 of ch.8). Rafsanjani also talks about the rumors of torture in his memoirs of 1981(Rafsanjani, 1999: 440). These tortures were mostly inflicted on people for profession and confession in front of the TV cameras. In an act of ideological cleansing, between three to four thousand prisoners-claimed to have eclectic taste in religiosity and eclectic method in understanding religion—who were already convicted to five years to life in prison were executed in some weeks in 1988 (Montazeri, 2000: pp. 18–27 of ch.10; Appendix IV-1). When the regime failed to impose, under a controlled environment impossible to create in larger society, a strict regime in the prisons that demanded religious conformity (Afshari, 2001: 293), it massacred thousands of prisoners who refused to acquiesce to the Inquisition's demands.
49. In 1980's Iranian individuals were imprisoned for the non-violent expression of their political, religious or other conscientiously beliefs. There were frequent arbitrary arrest and detention of political suspects and/or their families. Torture, inhumane or degrading treatment or punishment of prisoners

was the rule not an exception. Incommunicado detention and solitary confinement were frequently conductive to torture. Administrative Regulations Governing Revolutionary Courts and Public Prosecutors Offices contained inadequate provisions to ensure fair trial. Summary trials (five minute court appearance), arresting individuals without charging or trying them, and keeping people in prison after acquaintance were norms. (*Iran: Violations of Human Rights, Document Sent by the Amnesty International to the Government of the Islamic Republic of Iran,* London: 1987,48–55, 70,79 ,85).

50. Khalkhāli stated in an interview "If we hadn't executed them, they would have executed us the next day" (http://www.library.cornell.edu/colldev/mideast/khalkl.htm).
51. As Hussein Ali Montazeri, Khomeini's principle deputy, describes the massacre and vast violations of human, civil and constitutional rights of individuals in his memoirs when he was under house arrest in Iran (Montazeri, 2000: pp. 33–34 of ch.7).
52. Investigations for the following offenses fall under the jurisdiction of the Revolutionary Courts: 1) All of the offenses against the internal and external security of the Country, combating and behaving in a corruptly manner on the earth; 2) Uttering slander against the Founder of the Islamic Republic of Iran and the Honorable Leader; 3) Conspiracy against the Islamic Republic of Iran or carrying arms, use of terrorism, and destruction of building against the IRI's system; 4) Engaging in espionage for aliens; 5) All crimes involving smugglings and narcotic items; 6) The cases pertinent to Article 49 of the Constitution. The definition of jurisdiction of the Revolutionary Court is totally ambiguous to make it easy to refer any case to these courts, if necessary: "Investigations of all civil, criminal, non litigious cases are within the jurisdiction of the common courts. The extent of the jurisdiction of such courts is comprehensive and general, except for the cases which fall under the jurisdiction of the Revolutionary Courts." On the basis of offences number one and three, as defined here, every case can be tried in the Revolutionary Court.
53. For example, in jurisdiction, district, and division of labor
54. 'Qanun-e Tashkil-e Dādgāhha-ye 'Omumi va Enqelāb' (the Law for Establishing General and Revolutionary Courts), July 1994.
55. http://www.iranjudiciary.org/english/courts/rev-courts.htm
56. http://www.dadgostary-tehran.ir/farsi/moror/3.htm#b15
57. http://www.dadgostary-tehran.ir/main.asp
58. http://www.dadgostary-tehran.ir/farsi/moror/80–3.htm#b40
59. A special court for the ruling caste has precedent in Iran's history. During Achaemenids, the member of the royal family and many Persian nobles had at their disposal their own judicial-administrative system (Dandamaev & Lukonin, 1989: 123).
60. Amnesty International's 1986 annual report recorded an estimated 6,500 executions in Iran between February 1979 and the end of 1985 (http://reference.allrefer.com/country-guide-study/iran/iran190.html).
61. These are the cultural versions of economic dependency schools. According to these schools, the cultural development of the periphery and its identity is inversely related to its contacts with the Western cultures.

62. In 1978, the judges of Sanandaj Court resigned to protest the killing of protesters by the military (Green, 1982: 112); In May of 1977 a group of 53 lawyers called for investigation of the absence of impartiality in the judicial system (Green, 1982: 65).
63. In this case even the condemned's right to escape during the stoning on the basis of Islamic law was violated.
64. This is very similar to natural law doctrine with its characteristic dualism of true law behind the positive law.
65. *Ejtehād,* what Islamic jurist do, is a technical term of the Islamic Law and means the process of making a legal decision by independent interpretation of the sources of the law, which in Shi'ite tradition are the Quran, the *Sunnah, ejmā'* (consensus of *'ulamā*) and reason. .
66. Jamāl Karimi Rād, the candidate of Ahmadinejād administration for Ministry of Justice-and later the Minister of Justice, refers to ambiguities in the mission of the Minister of justice (http://www.kayhannews.ir/840530/4.htm) and a need for a new law to define Article 160 of the Constitution, where it says "The Minister of Justice owes responsibility in all matters concerning the relationship between the judiciary, on the one hand, and the executive and legislative branches, on the other hand."
67. This desire came through in the second decade with establishment of General Courts. The judiciary officials could dissolve the office of public prosecutor in 1994 but they could not get rid of lawyers.
68. The same phenomenon can be observed in French Revolution (Merryman, 1969: 28).
69. The Judiciary Police that was established right after the Islamic Revolution in 1979 by the Supreme Judiciary Council and merged into new police organization called the Disciplinary Forces in 1989 was revived in 2006. The revival of judiciary police was to differntiate between two main missions of police: prevention and prosecution (http://www.bbc.co.uk/persian/iran/story/2006/08/060829_oh-police.shtml). This force was supposed to undertake a variety of action under the direction and supervision of the judiciary. They include pursuing and arresting suspects, interrogating suspects in some phases of judicial enquiries, gathering evidence and serving search warrants. This force was expected to undertake some of the functions of public prosecutor office that was diminished by the generalization of the courts. The bill for establishing this force was sent to the parliament in 2005 but it was still under discussion when the judiciary took action and shaped the force. Considering the behavior of the judiciary, this police force would be used to search activists' residence and work places without warrants.

NOTES TO CHAPTER SIX

1. The best examples are the acceptance of the U. N. Resolution No. 598 by the Iranian government in 1988 to end the Iraq-Iran war in spite of eight years propaganda that Iraq should and will be conquered and Saddam should and will be overthrown, and privatization of trade that was totally against Article 44 of the Constitution.

2. In chapters 3 (the rights of the people), 6 (the legislative power), 7 (councils), and 9.1 (the executive power, the presidency) there are a dozen of Articles that explicitly or implicitly refer to modern individual and group's rights. The jurist according to Articles 5 and 110 can override all these chapters or simply ignore them without any consequences.
3. The treatment of activists and dissidents in this period, particularly by the security forces, militia and the judiciary, displays a fearful intolerance of alternative views. Religious and ethnic minorities continue to face official and societal discrimination and in some cases, persecution. Iranians are categorized as insiders and outsiders by the ruling caste, and outsiders, i.e. majority, are deprived of most of their political rights.
4. Hierocracy is the government by the clergy. In this doctrine the religious institution is supreme over the state in governmental matters while caesaropapism is the doctrine that the state is supreme over the church in ecclesiastical matters (dictionary.com). Both hierocracy and caesaropapism are the phenomena of combining the power of secular government with the spiritual authority of the religious institution and most especially, the inter-penetration of the theological and spiritual authority of the religious institution with the legal/juridical authority of the government; in their extreme form, caesaropapism is a political theory in which the head of state is also the head of the religious institution while hierocracy is a political theory in which the supposedly head of the religious institution is also the head of the state. What happened in post-Khomeini era was to put a jurist with no high religious authority in the position of the head of the religious institution. In Iran's case, after the death of Āyatollāh Arāki in 1994, Khāmenei tried to suppress all independent religious authorities and this project achieved its goal with suppression of religious intellectuals after 2000. Before 2000, hierocracy was the ideology of the ruling clerics with some resistance from democratic forces but after this year, this ideology almost smashed its dissidents and began to be enforced in almost all public arenas.
5. After the approval of the Constitution of 1989 his authority is defined and is therefore 'rational-legal' in Weberian terms.
6. The amount of tax is one-fifth of the extras that true-believers have them for more than a year, whether funds in the bank or grains in stock.
7. http://www.montazeri.ws/
8. This association is totally different from what was working with the same name before the victory of Islamic Revolution. Before the Revolution, this association was an independent association, mostly professional and based on voluntary membership, while in Khāmenei era it is nothing other than a political organization in the hands of ruling authoritarians and is totally closed to clerics who have different ideas about *marja'iyyah,* rule of the guardian and how to rule the country and seminaries.
9. There has been a pattern of restrictions placed on Shi'ite religious leaders that oppose to fundamental tenets of the Iranian political system such as *velāyat-e faqih* or governmental policies, and the arrest and detention of their followers (AI Index: MDE 13/WU 08/92).

10. Most of violations of religious freedom in Shi'ite section of the population have their roots in illegitimacy crisis of the Khāmenei leadership. The Government carefully monitors the statements and views of the country's senior Shi'ite religious leaders. It has restricted the movement of several Shi'a religious leaders who have been under house arrest for years, including Āzari Qomi and Hussein Ali Montazeri. The declared function of the Special Clerical Court, established in 1987, has been to investigate offenses and crimes committed by clerics. The Leader oversees this court directly to put pressure on Shi'ite clergy who criticize the ruling guardian and express controversial ideas. This court is not provided for in the Constitution and totally operates outside the domain of the judiciary (Hussein Ali Montazeri on Eshkevari's case, news.gooya.com/2002/10/13/1310–10.php; Mohammad Sharif, *Neshat* Daily, March 9, 1998; Ahmad Qabel, *Khordad* Daily, March 7, 1998). On the other side, some clerics has defended the existing situation of this court based on legality of special courts in the Constitution, special status of the clergy in the society(Ali Rāzini and Mohammad Mohammadi Rayshahri: Daryābāri, 2004: 46), clerics' political and religious authority and the Islamic regime's expediency (Daryābāri, 2004: 120–175). This court even wants to be independent from the judiciary; it has always asked for an independent budget section in the Budget Bills.
11. The breach of the autonomy of the church is the main religious aspect of caesaropapism (Angold, 1995: 49). In this kind of political regime, the ruler is not necessarily bound by canon law. In almost all the matters of religious institutions like promotions of clerics, the ruler can set aside the canons and proceed without a preliminary vote of the clerics. The ruler also has the power to appoint a cleric to a secular office (Angold, 1995: 102–3). In a hierocratic regime, the ruler has the same powers but through his religious authority. Khāmenei has benefited from all these privileges because of his position as the jurist. There is no reference to these subjects in Article 110 of the Constitution of IRI.
12. Although political participation dramatically increased between 1997 and 2001, voter participation figures for Iranian elections since 2001 show a remarkable decrease. The public elected Mohammad Khātami on May 23, 1997 with 69% of the popular vote, and it re-elected him in June 2001 with almost 77% of the vote. Approximately 88% of the electorate turned out for that first election, and about 63% turned out for the second election. 69% of the electorate voted in February 2000 parliamentary elections and chose a predominantly reformist—215 out of 290 members—legislature, although the Guardian Council declared 700,000 votes of Tehranians void and nullified elections in some areas that reformists won. Turnout for the country's first local council elections in February 1999 was impressive just under 65% nationwide, 30–50% in major cities, and "much higher" in rural areas. But participation in the February 2003 council elections was noticeably lower 50% nationwide and only 12–20% in metropolitan areas like Tehran, Isfahān, Shiraz, and Mash-had. In the February 2004 parliamentary elections, only 49 % of eligible voters reportedly cast their ballots,

compared to 69% four years earlier. Moreover, almost 1.4 million people, 6% of the voters, cast spoiled or voided ballots.

13. The rigged parliamentary and presidential elections of 2004 and 2005 made the polity unified and Khāmenei could appoint his cronies in Majles and presidential office by fraudulent elections and show of democracy.
14. Kiān was a bi-monthly magazine that was being published ideas of religious intellectuals about the relationship of religion to democracy, human rights, pluralism, feminism, liberalism and rationalism I 1990's. Abd ul-Karim Soroush, Mohammad Mujtahed Shabestari, Akbar Ganji, Sa'id Hajjarian, Ahmad Narāqi, Ebrāhim Sultāni, and Majid Mohammadi were among the writers of different issues of this magazine. The judiciary closed this magazine in Jan. 17, 2001.
15. These organizations were totally or partially funded by the state but they were not organizationally part of the sate structure and they had no obligation to be accountable to the state. Some examples are Daftar-e Tablighāt-e Eslāmi-ye Howzeh-ye 'Elmiyyeh Qom (the Qom Seminary's Office of Islamic Propaganda) and Sāzmān-e Tablighāt-e Eslāmi (Islamic Propaganda Organization)
16. Some examples of these state-made associations are Muslim Journalist Association (vs. Press Association), Sacred Defense Cinema Association (vs. Cinema House that is the umbrella syndicate for all people who work in cinema), Pen Society (vs. Iranian Writers Association), Islamic Student Society and Basiji Students (vs. Islamic Student Associations), etc.
17. After closing the independent newspaper, suppressing the student movement, imprisoning reformist journalists and political activists, filtering websites (here is a list of filtered sites: http://forum.persiantools.com/showthread.php?t=8140) and other Internet outlets and silencing websites and Web-log editors and writers (http://65.54.186.250/cgibin/linkrd?lang=EN&lah=dd2bf9cbb335fbbdcf7b3608ef6aee67&lat=1100177014&hm___action=http%3a%2f%2fhrw%2eorg%2fenglish%2fdocs%2f2004%2f11%2f08%2firan9631%2ehtm), the last remaining outlet for freedom of expression in the country, it was the NGO activists' turn to be punished. The authorities were arresting NGO activists and bloggers in order to cripple the country's growing network of independent nongovernmental organizations. In Oct. 2004, the most active women NGO activists were jailed, accused of taking action against the regime (http://akhbar.gooya.com/politics/archives/018809.php). Ruzbeh Mir-Ebrāhimi(http://akhbar.gooya.com/politics/archives/019826.php),Omid Me'māriān (http://akhbar.gooya.com/politics/archives/019973.php) and Shahram Rafi'zādeh's letters of contrition (http://akhbar.gooya.com/politics/archives/019972.php) as the price for their release were what authoritarian faction want from all Iranian activists.
18. There have been lots of cases in the judiciary that the power of government has been used to push people to pay their religious taxes (for example, Seyyed Hamid Kaffāshān). . According to some ideologized readings of *shari`ah,* collection of religious taxes is on the shoulder of the Islamic ruler and it is not only the duty of innocent *imam* to do the job (http://www.

nezam.org/persian/books/huqooq_va_vazayefe_shahrvandan_va_dawlatmardan/18.htm). In some cases, when wealthy individuals have come forward to pay their religious taxes they have been confronted with new charges.

19. A bill to ban torture in Iran became law after its approval by the Guardian Council. It was the only bill related to people's right approved by the Parliament and not vetted by the Council (http://www.rferl.org/featuresarticle/2004/5/F01AAD71-F3F8–48B0-A285–08CAC46B9DBC.html). The reason that the bill was not vetted was the issuance of a circular by the Head of the Judiciary a week before including the same materials. Parliament passed the anti-torture bill after the head of the judiciary, Mahmoud Hāshemi Shāhrudi, issued an order to police and security officials, calling for an end to torture. This order was a way for authoritarian faction, after conquering Seventh Majles, to preempt European complaints over human rights and to improve economic bonds. Iran's Constitution outlaws the use of torture, but the Islamic Republic's security forces, police, IRGC, and judiciary officials routinely use it to extract confessions. Even after the confirmation of the Anti-Torture Bill by the Guardian Council, torture has been routinely used to suppress the dissidence and make prisoners to confess (http://mag.gooya.com/politics/archives/020270.php). A revealing report about tortures of Internet editors and weblog writers is Abtahi's, one of the members of the Board of Constitutional Watch (http://mag.gooya.com/politics/archives/021147.php).
20. Weber believes "where patrimonial authority lays primary stress on the arbitrary will free of traditional limitations, it will be called sultanism" (Weber, 1947: 347). The absoluteness of guardian rule and weakness of the civil society made the context susceptible for arbitrary free will of the ruler after the consolidation of Khomeini's hierocratic regime in 1981 and consolidation of Khāmenei's regime after the revision of the Constitution in 1989.
21. Meshkini, the Speaker of the Assembly of Leadership Experts; ISNA, June 11, 2004.
22. Alirezā Alavi Tabār, http://rooydad.com/2004/09/blog-post_109431525172349840.html.
23. The Revolutionary Guard and Disciplinary Force commanders have been involved with major financial investments during Khāmenei's leadership and personally benefited from them. In the Imam Khomeini Airport crisis, the IRGC's intervention was mainly because of the competition between one of the military related companies and Transportation Ministry's selected Turkish company. For detailed story look at http://khabarnameh.gooya.com/politics/archives/015392.php, and http://khabarnameh.gooya.com/politics/archives/011138.php, and http://khabarnameh.gooya.com/politics/archives/010255.php
24. Some of the signs are the closing of the Imam Khomeini Airport immediately after opening, the nuclear aspiration, arrest of British sailors in Iran-Iraq border after occupation of Iraq by the U.S. and British forces,

and anti-American and pro-insurgent Revolutionary Guard comments and positions about the Iraqi crisis, all in 2004.

25. These factors do not change the category of the regime from hierocratic sultanism to a bureaucratic-military authoritarian one. Military officers still have the secondary power compared to clergy in this period, and they usually interfere in politics when they are asked to support the authoritarian faction or to suppress the dissidents. Nevertheless, the military is politically heterogeneous and the relevant political actors do not grant legitimacy to the military to act as moderators of the political process under certain circumstances.
26. www.isna.ir/Main/NewsView.aspx?ID=News-568735; roozonline.com/08interview/009903.shtml
27. http://www.kadivar.com/Htm/Farsi/Books/Book01/Sec052.htm
28. Other than the period of 1980–1989, when the judges used to elect three members of the Supreme Council of the Judiciary, the judgeship has been an appointed position in the whole history of Iran.
29. There is a government-approved list of acceptable Islamic names.
30. http://akhbar.gooya.com/politics/archives/006460.php
31. The latest was created before the seventh parliamentary election, i.e. Abād Garān (the Developers). Other examples are Kargozārān-e Sāzandegi (Agents of Construction) and Jam'iyat-e Isār Garān-e Enqelāb-e Eslāmi (Sacrifice for Islamic Revolution Society).
32. Karroubi, the Sixth Parliament Speaker: *Āftāb* Daily, Sep. 4, 2002; Article 90 Committee, *Āftāb* Daily, Sep. 17, 2002
33. The clearest link between the legal and illegal institutions is seen in the secret detention centers. The illegal detention centers (like Prison 59 and Towheed, Mersād, Seol, Abdollāh Ansāri, Motahhari, Foroudgāh, Emām-e Zamān, No. 64, No. 36, No. 66, American Club) are not officially registered as prisons, do not record the names of their prisoners, and information about their budgets, administration, and management is not known even by relevant government authorities. The treatment in the illegal detention centers has been far worse than in any section of Evin Prison. Transport of prisoners to these detention centers usually begins with being told to put their heads down or being forcibly pushed down in the back of a car with a blindfold on, followed by at least forty-five minutes of circling around Tehran in order to confuse the prisoners' directional bearings. Family members recalled that this is the point at which they lost contact with the prisoner, hearing nothing more until or unless they had been moved to a formal prison. Political prisoners are kept in absolute solitary confinement in the illegal detention centers, Prison 59 and Prison 66, allowed to visit the bathroom and pray three times a day while blindfolded, and faced the harshest interrogations of his imprisonment. All said that the staff they were allowed to see did not wear uniforms, and were members of the *lebās shakhsi-ha,* or "the plainclothes ones." Most of these illegal detension centers are under the authority of military powers, police and security forces which work directly under Khamenei and his office. (http://hrw.org/reports/2004/iran0604/7.htm; http://r0ozonline.com/01newsstory/018243.shtml).

34. Section 209 is under the control of the Ministry of Intelligence. Section 240 is under the control of the intelligence services of the judicial authority (*Hefāzat-e Etelā'āt-eh Ghoveh-ye Ghaza'iyyeh*), and it appears that Section 325 and section A2 are under the control of the Intelligence Services of the Iranian Revolutionary Guards Corps (*Hefāzat-eh Etelā'āt-eh Sepāh Pāsdārān*) (http://khabarnameh.gooya.com/politics/archives/016264.php#more). Some believe that Section 209, while nominally under the control of the Ministry of Intelligence, is also under the control of the IRGC agents.
35. The shut down was mostly based on Articles 12 and 13 of Precautionary Measures Act.
36. Hussein Ansāri Rād, the chair of Article 90 Committee of the Sixth Parliament, *Nou Rouz* Daily, Oct. 28, 2001 & Dec. 21, 2001; the judiciary officials did not even respond to letters of the Article 90 Committee, *Āftāb* Daily, Aug. 15, 2001.
37. *Hayāt-e Nou* Daily, Jan. 19, 2001; *Āftāb* Daily, Dec. 21, 2002.
38. In Jan. 30th 2006, Ahmadinejad administration declared the dissolution of this Board. The speaker of the government declared that "the administration does not need [the service of] this board." (http://www.sharghnewspaper.ir/841111/html/iran.htm#s364683).
39. The national survey on Iranians' attitudes (2003) shows that 60 percent of Iranians do not think that rulers and ruled are treated in a same way in front of law (*Arzeshhā va Negareshhā-ye Iraniān,* 2000). (http://khabarnameh.gooya.com/society/archives/014070.php).
40. Most Islamic countries around the world base their legal codes on a set of religious laws known as "*shari`ah,*" based on the Quran and the sayings of the Prophet Mohammad. But countries vary greatly in their application of *shari`ah*. For example, adultery is a serious breach of Islamic law. But in Egypt, the punishment is six months to 2 years in jail whereas in Iran, a woman convicted of adultery may be stoned to death.
41. In lots of press and political cases, the accused were deprived of having attorney or their attorneys could not have access to the files. One example is the National Religious Forces' members whose lawyers could not have access to their files (*Nou-Rouz* Daily, Dec. 31, 2001; *Nou Rouz* Daily, March 6, 2002).
42. https://www1.columbia.edu/sec-cgi bin/gulf/dataplug.pl?dir=/wwws/data/cu/sipa/GULF2000/chronology/pat&ddfile=chron&display=p&hh=b&sp=354294798&qw
43. https://www1.columbia.edu/sec-cgi-bin/gulf/dataplug.pl?dir=/wwws/data/cu/sipa/GULF2000/chronology/pat&ddfile=chron&display=p&hh=b&sp=360431174&qw
44. In 1997 and 2001 presidential, 1998 municipal and 2000 parliamentary elections, the authoritarian camp could get only 10 to 15 percent of the vote (http://moi.gov.ir/fStatisticsList.aspx?ellectionType=1; http://moi.gov.ir/fStatisticsList.aspx?ellectionType=3; http://moi.gov.ir/fStatisticsList.aspx?ellectionType=4).
45. Independent newspapers and magazines have been closed, and leading publishers and journalists were imprisoned on vague charges of "insulting

Islam" or "calling into question the Islamic foundation of the Republic." In only two years between 1999 and 2001, more than 100 newspapers and magazines were closed down and banned by the judiciary (*Bonyān* Daily, May 3, 2001; *Nou Rouz* Daily, May 4, 2001). A handful of journalists and political activists are also deprived of their social rights (*Bonyān* Daily, April 29, 2002). The judiciary kept open the files of journalists even when they were indicted and were spending their time behind bars (*Hayāt-e Nou* Daily, Nov. 7, 2001) to keep them silent. The Sixth Parliament tried to change the restrictive press law shortly after its inauguration. The Leader, however, quashed the debate scheduled for August 2000 in a letter read out to the Parliament.

46. http://www.wilayah.net/pr/bayanat/speeches/68–69/bayan189.htm#link484
47. http://www.wilayah.net/pr/bayanat/speeches/78/bayana12.htm#link23; http://www.wilayah.net/pr/bayanat/speeches/79/ali-2010.htm#link18
48. http://r0ozonline.com/11english/014303.shtml; according to the speaker of the Judiciary, the number of prisoners in Iran was 151 thousands in 2006: http://news.gooya.eu/politics/archives/2006/12/056068.php.
49. For a report on situation of prisons in Iran look at the yearly report of the Association for Defending Prisonors' Rights.(*Sharq* Daily, June 10 & 12, 2006; http://www.sharghnewspaper.ir/850321/html/right.htm, http://www.sharghnewspaper.ir/850323/html/right.htm)
50. *Nou Rouz* Daily, July 11, 2001 (For a video of stoning in 1991 look at http://www.apostatesofislam.com/media/stoning.htm#video. For recent stoning, look at azadizan.com, Nov. 15, 2003; http://www.iranvajahan.net/cgi-bin/news_fa.pl?l=fa&y=1381&m=8&d=4&a=9).
51. Radiofarda.com/transcripts/iran/2003/05/20030513_1330_0743_0901_fa.asp
52. As an example, a court in southwest Iran condemned a young woman to be blinded after she blinded a man who was allegedly harassing her by throwing acid at him. Azam (21) a resident of Behbahān village in Khuzestan province told the court that Abol Ali (37) would come and "harass" her at night while her husband was away at work. Azam was quoted as saying during her trial. The judge sentenced her "to be made blind in public," due to Iran's civil and criminal law's "eye-for-an-eye" principle. (Sapa-AFP Jul. 28, 2002).
53. There are reports of beheading and stoning. According to press reports, an Afghan man was publicly decapitated in Zābol in June 2001. The practice of stoning, which finally appeared to be declining in the late 1990's was resumed in the 2000's. According to reports in the press, an unnamed woman was stoned to death at Evin prison, Tehran, on 20 May 2001. The woman, aged 35, was arrested in 1993 on charges of acting in pornographic films. In January 2001, the Supreme Court reportedly upheld the death sentence by public stoning of Maryam Ayyubi, 38, convicted for the murder of her husband. Iranian press reported her stoning to death in Evin prison, Tehran, on 11 July 2001. A third woman, named Robābeh, was also reportedly sentenced to death by stoning in June 2001 for the

murder of her husband. (http://www.hri.ca/fourtherecord2001/documentation/genassembly/a-56–278.htm). Women activists have been trying to push the government to remove article 82 (b), concerning stoning, from the Islamic Criminal Code.

54. According to the Head of Iran's Disciplinary Forces (police), two members of this force were executed for financial corruption: emruz.info/ShowItem.aspx?ID=6132&p=1 (Accessed April 3, 2007).
55. Following the election of Mahmoud Ahmadinejad in the ninth presidential election in 2005, the number of executions in Iran increased sharply. Between January 20 and February 20 alone, the judicial authorities executed 10 prisoners and condemned another 21 to the death sentence (http://hrw.org/english/docs/2006/02/27/iran12724.htm).
56. *Nou Rouz* Daily, Jan. 5, 2002.
57. *Nou Rouz* Daily, Oct. 29, 2001; http://www.peacelink.nu/KVINNER/iran_woman_execution_2001.html
58. http://www.sharghnewspaper.com/830603/law.htm#s105285
59. Country Reports on Human Rights Practices, Iran–200; Released by the Bureau of Democracy, Human Rights, and Labor March 4, 2002 (http://www.state.gov/g/drl/rls/hrrpt/2001/nea/8251.htm)
60. As reported in the Iranian press on 29 May 2001, Mehrdād Yusefi, an 18-year-old boy, was hanged in the South Western region of Ilam for a crime, which he had committed when he was 16 years old. In June 2001, the press reported the decision of an Iranian court to sentence to death Azizollāh Shenwāri, a 14-year-old Pakistani convicted on drug charges. In August 2004, a 16-year-old girl was hanged in Neka for adultery (http://www.sharghnewspaper.com/830603/law.htm#s105285).
61. One of the accused persons in a car bomb that led to explosion of an IRGC bus in Zahedan, Sistan-Baluchestan province in southeastern Iran was hanged in less than a week from the accident (http://1384.g00ya.com/politics/archives/2007/02/057426.php). Thirteen IRGC members were killed and 36 were injured in the accident (http://www.radiofarda.com/Article/2007/02/21/f2_Zahedan-Bomb-Update.html). According to the judiciary officials in Zahedan, the accused who confessed to his crime was tried by the Revolutionary Court and sentenced to death. The explosion happened in Feb. 14th 2007 and the accused was hanged in Feb. 19th 2007. The whole judicial procedure from arrest to execution took only five days. Although this is a very short period of time, the Revolutionary Court shows a little bit of progress compared to similar cases in the past. In previous cases, the Revolutionary Court has had similar procedures in about two hours or a day.
62. Mohammad Taqi Mesbāh Yazdi, *Dourān-e Emrooz* Daily, Dec. 10, 2000; *Nou Rouz* Daily, Aug. 26, 2001; Mahmoud Shāhrudi, *Hayat-e Nou* Daily, Aug. 8, 2001 and *Resālat* Daily, Aug. 27, 2001; Mohammad Mohammadi Gilāni, *Nou Rouz* Daily, Aug. 29, 2001; Esmā'il Shushtari, the Minister of Justice, *Nou Rouz* Daily, Aug. 19, 2001)
63. *Āftāb* Daily, Aug. 18, 2001.
64. A report prepared by the judiciary of Tehran Province implicitly confirms the spreading of torture in Iran's prison. The press secretary of the judiciary

denied this report as false (http://roozonline.com/01newsstory/008821.shtml).

65. www.mellimazhabi.org/yadasht/100902alijani.htm
66. www.emadbaghi.com/archives/000151.php; http://www.bbc.co.uk/persian/news/030714_a-abdi-letter.shtml; http://www.hamshahri.net/hamnews/1377/770318/shari.htm; http://news.gooya.com/politics/archives/022548.php; http://roozonline.com/01newsstory/008747.shtml
67. Ali Afshāri: http://azad.gooya.name/politics/archives/2005/08/034749print.php; Ezzatullāh Sahābi: http://www.polpiran.com/sahab.htm; Omid Me'māriān, Shahrām Rafi'zādeh, Ruzbeh Mir Ebrāhimi, and Javād Tamimi: http://www.bbc.co.uk/persian/iran/story/2005/01/050104_abtahi-webnevesht-text-15-dey.shtml; Rouzbeh Mir Ebrāhimi: http://raha.gooya.name/politics/archives/037946.php; Mehdi Shirzad: http://www.advar-news.com/university/1031.aspx; Mehdi Amini-zādeh: http://news.gooya.eu/politics/archives/2007/02/057351.php
68. *E'temād* Daily, Aug. 19. 2006
69. Akbar Ganji, as of the middle of June 1999, spent 105 days of his 15 months in jail in solitary confinement (www.polpiran.com/situationhuman-rights.pdf).
70. The bails for political activists and intellectuals prominently increased in this period (*Nou Rouz* Daily, July 31, 2001: *Nou Rouz* Daily, Aug. 4, 2001; news.gooya.com/2002/04/23/2304–22.php; *Nou Rouz* Daily, May 5, 2002; *Nou Rouz* Daily, Jan. 31, 2002)
71. The full name is the Establishment of Revolutionary and General Courts Law.
72. According to Article 49 "The government has the responsibility of confiscating all wealth accumulated through usury, usurpation, bribery, embezzlement, theft, gambling, misuse of endowments, misuse of government contracts and transactions, the sale of uncultivated lands and other resources subject to public ownership, the operation of centers of corruption, and other illicit means and sources, and restoring it to its legitimate owner; and if no such owner can be identified, it must be entrusted to the public treasury. This rule must be executed by the government with due care, after investigation and furnishing necessary evidence in accordance with the law of Islam."
73. The bill reflecting the principles of this law was first approved by the Third Majles in 1992 that was then redrafted and approved by the Fourth Majles. The last draft was approved by the Fourth Majles on July 6, 1994.
74. This kind of court has precedent in different parts of the Islamic world; See Powers, 1994.
75. http://akhbar.gooya.com/politics/archives/019696.php; http://www.hamshahri.org/vijenam/tehran/1382/820513/hoghog.htm; a very good example of this arbitrary justice is collective swearing of murdered individual's family against the defendant (http://www.sharghnewspaper.ir/850614/html/newssoc.htm)
76. *Nou Rouz* Daily, April 20, 2002.
77. Seyyed Hasan Mar'ashi, the Deputy of the Head of Judiciary http://www.iranvajahan.net/cgi-bin/news_fa.pl?l=fa&y=1381&m=12&d=08&a=3

78. Mahmoud Hāshemi Shāhrudi, *Nou Rouz* Daily, June 22, 2002.
79. *Hamshahri* Daily, Sep 24, 2002.
80. *Hamshahri* Daily, Sep 24, 2002.
81. http://akhbar.gooya.com/society/archives/015951.php
82. http://akhbar.gooya.com/politics/archives/017743.php
83. mellimazhabi.org/articles/kadivar_1.htm
84. http://www.hamshahri.org/hamnews/1380/800308/ejtem.htm
85. Mahmoud Hāshemi Shāhrudi, *Āftāb* Daily, Jan. 16, 2003.
86. *Āftāb* Daily, Jan. 1, 2003
87. *Nou Rouz* Daily, Nov. 5, 2001; *Nou Rouz* Daily, Oct. 8, 2001; *Nou Rouz* Daily, Feb. 26, 2002; *Nou Rouz* Daily, July 14, 2001
88. *Hayāt-e Nou* Daily, Jan. 3, 2002.
89. http://216.239.39.104/u/undpsearch?q=cache:667JaHD1PF4J:www.undp.org/governance/cd/documents/32.ppt+judicial+reform&hl=en&ie=UTF-8
90. This term, i.e. religious security is totally new in Persian literature and the writer does not define it.
91. http://216.239.39.104/u/undpsearch?q=cache:v4TYh_E-fW8J:www.undp.org/oslocentre/docsjuly03/Rule%2520of%2520Law%2520and%2520Access%2520to%2520Justice_Perspectives%2520from%2520UNDP%2520experience1.doc+judicial+reform+objectives&hl=en&ie=UTF-8
92. This happened immediately after appointment of Shāhrudi as the head of the judiciary (www.emrouz.ws, Aug. 26, 2003). He did this by getting the interpretation of the Guardian Council on the executive power's authorities.
93. The Head of the Judiciary, Hāshemi Shāhrudi, downgraded one of the judges of the Administrative Justice Court who had annulled the decision of the Central Bank to dismiss the CEO and the board members of Parsiān Bank, a private bank that was accused by the authoritarian camp for illegal activities (http://emruz.info/ShowItem.aspx?ID=4571&p=1).
94. According to the Country's Prisons Health Office Director, "the density of the prisons in Iran has been 10 times more than the standard . . . . The per capita area for each prisoner is 5.5 m including dining, hygiene and sport areas" (*Āftāb* Daily, Sep. 7 2002)
95. *Āftāb* Daily, Jan. 10, 2002;
96. *Hayāt-e Nou* Daily, Aug. 7, 2002; emrooz.org/pages/date/81–12/07/news01.htm; *Nou Rouz* Daily, Feb. 3, 2001
97. *Bonyān* Daily, July, 29, 2001
98. *Hayāt-e Nou* Daily, Nov. 9, 2001; the judiciary officials have been trying to get the same ideas from religious authorities (http://www.kayhannews.ir/831010/3.HTM#other302).
99. http://www.hri.ca/fortherecord2001/vol3/iranga.htm
100. http://www.roozonline.com/archives/2007/02/002486.php
101. http://www.sharghnewspaper.com/830130/disast.htm#s44337
102. There are tens of letters from prisoners' family members to the judiciary officials and MPs: Zohreh Horri (Sa'id Montazari's wife) to Majles Speaker, June 1, 2001; Mohtaram Golbābāii (Eshkevari's wife) to the chair of the Islamic Human Rights Committee and the head of Tehran's Revolutionary Court, June 10 and 19, 2001 respectively.

103. http://www.hri.ca/fourtherecord2001/documentation/genassembly/a-56–278.htm
104. http://mag.gooya.com/politics/archives/020627.php
105. The judiciary charged the Presidents' economic team immediately after the start of Khātami's second term, i.e. the ministers of oil, mines and minerals and the governor of the Central Bank: FT Times, Dec. 7. 2001.
106. An example for this peace court was the idea of "House of Justice." The judiciary officials believed that 80 % of the 4–5 millions of cases filed every year can be dealt with in this kind of courts (*Nou Rouz* Daily, May 31, 2002). Another unsuccessful experience was the implementation of the Arbitration Councils based on Article 189 of the Third Development Plan Bill (*Bonyān* Daily, April 28, 2002)
107. *Yās-e Nou* Daily, April 21, 2003.
108. http://www.iranjudiciary.org/persian/jud-dev/policies.htm
109. Fāzel Khodādād was scapegoated for Mortezā Rafiqdust, the brother of Mohsen Rafiqdust, director of the "Foundation of the Mostaz'afin (Downtrodden)" at the time and the former commander and later the Minister of IRGC. Khodadad was among eight men convicted in August of 1995 "sabotaging the country's economic system" by misappropriating money from the state-run Bank Saderat (http://www.payk.net/mailingLists/iran-news/html/1995/msg00222.html). The 123 billion Rials embezzlement case concluded with a death decree for the first row convict, Fāzel Khodādād, and a life sentence for Mortezā Rafiqdust. He had been provided with some extra facilities in the prison (http://www.macalester.edu/courses/russ64/sites/www.salamiran.org/media/IranNews/980210.html). Husein Dārugheh case in 2006 was very similar to Khodādād case (http://r0ozonline.com/01newsstory/014324.shtml).
110. In Mash-had, Shiraz and Bojnurd Serial Killings (19, 16 and 7 respectively) different groups of loyalist militia killed prostitutes to clean the streets from vice. Shiraz and Bojnurd cases were never tried in the courts. In Mash-had case, the Appeal Court overturned the capital punishment based on an Islamic law that any Muslim can execute *shari`ah* law if he/she can present enough evidence to the court. The killer had access to the files of the slain women (*Nou Rouz* Daily, Aug. 1, 2001; *Āftāb* Daily, Aug. 16, 2001)
111. In Kerman Serial Killing case in which a group of loyalists to Khāmenei killed the people who were considered morally corrupted in 2002. The Supreme Court overturned the capital punishment verdicts for the perpetrators in 2003 (emrooz.ws/showitem.aspx?c==1&serial=647). Being forced by the authorities, three families of the victims forgave the perpetrators. According to victims' families' attorneys, two of the accused have been freed: bbc.co.uk/persian/iran/story/2007/04/070414_mf_kerman_killings.shtml.
112. Seyyed Hasan Mar'ashi, the Deputy of the Head of Judiciary, *Nou Rouz* Daily, Sep. 28, 2001.
113. Karbāschi and other high ranking officials of Tehran Municipality were arrested and tried in 1998. This was apparently the heavy price that they paid for supporting Khātami during his campaign for presidential office in

1997. The leader offered open support for the actions of judiciary against reform minded officials (*Resālat* Daily, June 29, 1998).

114. A definitive example of this effort is the judiciary's role in annulling the role of the Parliament in selection of lawyer members of the Guardian Council. According to Article 91 of the Islamic Republic's Constitution, six of twelve members of the Council should be professional and experienced jurists. The six jurists are nominated by the judiciary and appointed by the parliament, the other six are appointed by the Leader. After nomination by the judiciary, the majority of Majles should approve their appointment. In 2001, only one of the 6 nominees of the judiciary for three vacant positions of the Guardian Council's jurists could get the majority vote of the parliament (Ebrāhim Azizi, 150 out of 238: *Hayāt-e Nou* Daily, Aug. 4, 2001). When other nominees of the judiciary could not earn the majority vote of the parliament, it was only with inference of the Leader and a vote by the Expediency Council that allowed a relative majority in the Majles to be sufficient enough for their confirmation. The Expediency Council lowered the threshold and stated that earning the most votes among the nominees was enough (Abbās Ali Kadkhodā'i and Mohsen Esmā'ili with 67 and 64 out of 244 votes: *Āftāb* Daily, Aug. 8, 2001). In late 2003, a member of the Guardian Council resigned to run for the parliamentary election. His replacement became a major point for the challenge between the reformist-dominated Majles on the one hand and the judiciary and the Guardian Council on the other. The Majles rejected the two nominees, Gholām Hossein Elhām and Fazlollāh Mossavi, respectively. Elhām who was the spokesperson of the judiciary and a member of the Ansār-e Hezbollāh, a group of thugs who acts in favor of the Leader in political challenges, proved to be a very unpopular figure even among the authoritarian minority of the Majles. This was the second time that his nomination was rejected. The first time was in year 2000. He got only 4 votes in his favor in 2003. The other nominee got 90 votes, which was 56 votes short of the 146 votes needed. (Elhām and two other nominees of the Judiciary, i.e. Mohammad Reza Alizādeh and 'Abbās Ka'bi, were finally confirm in June 28, 2004 by the Seventh Parliament right after the beginning of its work. They got 169, 195, and 174 votes of the authoritarian faction dominated parliament respectively: http://mellat.majlis.ir/archive/1383/04/07/parlemanttoday.htm.) In 2003, the speaker of Majles strictly demanded that the majority requirement, i.e. half plus one, be observed. In the new phase of the judiciary-Majles conflict, Khāmenei changed his decision and the speaker apparently declared this change when the replacement process was going on in 2003. Therefore, the Judiciary was asked to nominate other candidates. The reformists insisted that the nominees should not only have expertise in law but also be popular and reputable figures. Some reformists argued that the eleven-member Council lacks the required legal authority to decide on the well-known twin bills- The Domain of Presidents' Duties and Responsibilities Bill, and the Elections Reform Bill- and disqualification of one-third of the parliamentary election nominees.

The Leader's order of 2000 that the confirmation required just a relative majority of vote (among the candidates of the judiciary), and not the majority, was completely against the Constitution. One of the members of the Guardian Council got only 25 percent of the votes of the parliament and was appointed as a member of that council.

115. In his first years of leadership, Khāmenei was against politicization of judiciary (his speech on 1369/4/4: http://www.wilayah.net/pr/bayanat/speeches/68–69/bayan355.htm#link1492)
116. I borrowed these definitions of judicialization from Vallinder, 1995: 13.
117. There are lots of political and press cases tried behind closed door without any statement from the judge or the court about the reason of closedness while on basis of the Article 165 of the Constitution " trials are to be held openly and members of the public may attend without any restriction; unless the court determines that an open trial would be detrimental to public morality or discipline, or if in case of private disputes, both the parties request not to hold open hearing"; an example is the trials of the members of National Religious Forces (*Hayāt-e Nou* Daily, Aug. 18, 2002; *Nou Rouz,* Daily, Jan 16, 2002; *Āftāb* Daily, Jan. 8, 2002). In these cases, the trial was behind closed door while the indictments were open (*Āftāb* Daily, Nov. 14, 2001; *Hayāt-e Nou* Daily, Aug. 18, 2002). In some cases, even reporters could not report what had happened in the court (*Nou Rouz* Daily, Dec. 7, 2001)
118. When in 2000, reformers won 70 per cent of the seats in the parliament, the authoritarians continued to oppose them on every front, through the veto on legislation wielded by the Council of Guardians, and through the judiciary, which closed down more than 100 reformist newspapers and jailed progressive thinkers. Iran's conservative judiciary ordered one of the main pro-reform websites, Emrooz, to be filtered, though most of the news websites were already filtered by a governmental commission including members from state-run Radio and TV, the Communication Department, and Ministry of Islamic Culture and Guidance. Ahead of the Seventh parliamentary election in 2004, authoritarians tried to restrict the Internet, which had become one of the main platforms for reformists to challenge their conservative rivals. The relatively vibrant and fragile reformist press had been muzzled through a series of gag orders by the hard-line judiciary. Even this was not tolerated and they have been repeatedly and periodically closed and banned (http://www.rferl.org/featuresarticle/2004/01/ac7f4be9–2138–48b2–9ace-c389b46ebe1f.html). Official reformers' efforts were stymied and they gradually lost the confidence of the Iranian people, who became disillusioned and apathetic.
119. http://hrw.org/reports/2004/iran0604/
120. A news report on a decision in the case of Emāduddin Bāqi, a journalist imprisoned 2.5 years for his writing, typifies coverage of press-related cases: "Judge Bābāii has stressed in the court ruling, a copy of which was faxed to IRNA, that Bāqi had been found guilty of propagating against the Islamic establishment and working to the benefit of the opposition groups after the court considered a report by the Information Ministry,

Bāqi's lectures, notes and interviews, as well as his confessions": IRNA, December 5, 2003.

121. The case of Nāser Zarafshān, a prominent attorney for many imprisoned journalists and writers, is illustrative. He was arrested (*Nou Rouz* Daily, Nov. 3, 2001) and held in Evin until his sentencing in March 2002 after a closed trial to three years in prison for "weapons and alcohol possession" and two years for "disseminating secret information"(FIDH, "Iran," Annual Report 2002). He was tried by the Judicial Organization of the Armed Forces, which does not have jurisdiction over civilians, but seems to be increasingly involved in targeting political prisoners in cooperation with other security agencies. See Human Rights Watch, "Iran: Attempt to Silence Lawyer in Assassinations Case," March 22, 2002. Mohammad Ali Dādkhāh, the Nationalist Religious Forces' attorney, was tried for talking publicly about his work (*Nou Rouz* Daily, Jan. 28, 2002). In another case Mohammad Ali Safari who was Nationalist Religious Forces' attorney was threatened and tortured (news.gooya.com/2002/05/22/2205–19.php).
122. Judge Ali Bakhshi of the 27th branch of Tehran's Appeal Court was pushed to resign when he resisted against the will of some judiciary officials to issue harsh verdicts against journalists and political activists (*Nou Rouz* Daily, Nov. 26, 2001). He was transferred when he overturned a verdict of a primary court against some reformists during Khāmenei leadership. He was later disqualified for parliamentary election nomination (http://www.sharghnewspaper.com/821025/parlim.htm); The judge of Sharbānu Amāni's case was changed when he was at the final stages of issuing verdict (*Bonyān* Daily, March 17, 2002)
123. http://akhbar.gooya.com/politics/archives/018725.php
124. *Hayāt-e Nou* Daily, May 15, 2001.
125. Hāshemi Shāhrudi, *Nou Rouz,* May 11, 2001.
126. In 2002, academic Hāshem Āghājari was sentenced to death for blasphemy against the Prophet Mohammed, based on a speech in which he challenged Muslims not to follow blindly the clergy, provoking an international and domestic outcry. In February 2003, the Supreme Court revoked his death sentence, but the case was sent back to the lower court for retrial. He was retried in July 2003 on charges that did not include apostasy and was sentenced to 5 years, 2 of which were suspended, and 5 years of additional "deprivation of social right" (meaning that he cannot teach or run for public offices). His time served was counted towards his 3-year sentence, with the remainder of the time being converted by the court to a fine. Hassan Yusefi Eshkevari was sentenced to death in 2001 on similar charges following an unfair trial in a special court. It was reduced to two and a half years (Amnesty International's Annual Report 2002 and UAs MDE 13/22/00, 9 August 2000 and MDE 13/016/2001, 21 May 2001).
127. In Siamāk Purzand case, the primary court's verdict was announced to be confirmed by the appeal court by *Resālat* daily one month before the official announcement (Mehrangiz Kār, his wife's letter to Karrubi, the parliament speaker, July 10, 2002); *Jām,* a weekly newspaper, published the verdict of Āghājari, execution, by the primary court one week before the

official announcement by the court (*Āftāb* Daily, Nov. 20, 2002); *Kayhān* Daily has access to all details and documents of critical cases under investigation and prosecution by the judiciary and in some cases has published the details when there was trials behind closed door or gag order; two prominent examples are Jazāyeri's and Internet journalists cases (*Nou Rouz* Daily, Jan. 2, 2002; http://akhbar.gooya.com/politics/archives/016762.php).

128. Amir Farshād Ebrāhimi vs. the Head of Tehran's Judiciary District (Iran, Jan. 30, 2002), Tājzādeh vs. Jannati (*Nou Rouz* Daily, June 30, 2002), Akbar Ganji vs. Alizādeh (*Āftāb* Daily, Sep. 8, 2001), Ganji vs. Mortazavi (*Nou Rouz* Daily, Sep. 19, 2001), Ebrāhim Yazdi vs. *Kayhan* Daily and Ebrāhim Yazdi vs. *Hamshahri* Daily (http://www.emrooz.info/), Press Chief Editors vs. Mesbah (*Nou Rouz* Daily, Dec. 29, 2001), Dādfar (MP in the Sixth Majles) vs. Mortazavi (*Nou Rouz* Daily, Sep. 25, 2001; jebhemosharekat.com/rooydad/library/06/19/p11.hyml), Shamsulvā'ezin vs. Mortazavi (http://akhbar.gooya.com/politics/archives/012186.php) and Saharkhiz vs. Ejeii (http://www.ostvar.com: Jan. 11, 2005)

129. In a cased called Slain in Karaj Subway, where a 20 years male was shot by a cleric working for the Disciplinary Forces, the killer was just sentenced to three years in prison and paying the blood money and even released for New Year vacation to spend the holiday (15 days) with his family. The media did not even disclose the name of the killer (Aftab Yazd Daily, April 4, 2006).

130. Jalāluddin Farsi, presidential nominee of the Islamic Republic Party in the first presidential election, was acquitted of first murder killing accusation while he confessed the slaying of Mohammad Reza Rezākhāni. He did not spent one night in jail or prison. This case was illegally sent from Karaj, where the killing happened, to Tehran (*Nou Rouz* Daily, Feb. 19, 2002); Mohsen Fallāhiān, the son of the former minister of intelligence who admittedly killed a cop was freed on a small amount of bail (compared to the bails asked from intellectuals and political activists) during the trial and acquitted at the end (*Nou Rouz* Daily, Aug. 12 and 18, 2001); in the Makāseb case regarding economic misdemeanors, all the accused who had ties with authoritarian camp were acquitted due to their lack of knowledge of law (*Āftāb Yazd* daily, March 14, 2003); from 17 people (members of Ansār-e Hezbollāh) who were tried for assaulting two cabinet members in Friday Prayer, 16 people got non-fixed and suspended verdicts and the other one (Amir Farshād Ebrāhimi) was exonerated later (news.gooya.com/1101/2511/2511–3.htm); in Hedāyat Protection House of Karaj which its mission was taking care of prostitutes and its authority abused them led to exoneration of all accused except one (*Nou Rouz* Daily, Feb 5, 2001); in Tehran's Dorm case, all the attackers were acquitted and the killed person was convicted (*Āftāb* Daily, Jul. 23, 2001); in Serial Killing of Intellectuals and Political Activists case, no one was convicted for ordering the killing and the operative agents were convicted to imprisonment (*Ettelā'āt* Daily, Jan. 31, 2001). The Intelligence Minister's oath regarding his innocence was accepted in the court due to his connection to ruling clergy stratum while one of the accused, Mehrdad Alikhāni, had already confessed that they got

orders from Dorri Najaf Ābādi to kill the dissidents (*Payām-e Emrooz*, No. 44, 2001). In Iran's Islamic judiciary system, the clerics and other insiders are considered just and their oaths are accepted.

131. Mortezā Rafiq Dust was the prison salesperson and merchandiser when his sentence (*Hayāt-e Nou* Daily, Nov. 18, 2001)
132. The person who shot Hajjāriān, a consultant for President Khātami, was sentenced to imprisonment and soon freed (*Nou Rouz* Daily, July 14, 2002), while the person who tried to assassinate Razini, the former Head of Tehran District Judiciary, was sentenced to death (*Nou Rouz* Daily, Nov. 11, 2001)
133. *Āftāb* Daily, Nov. 21, 2001
134. *Nou Rouz* Daily, June 23, 2001.
135. *Nou Rouz* Daily, Dec. 30, 2001; http://akhbar.gooya.com/politics/archives/013193.php
136. IRGC published a newsletter, Sobh-e Sādeq, without getting license (*Nou Rouz* daily, April 16, 2002)
137. Shahram Jazayeri's case, only the names of reformist MPs were mentioned in the indictment, while he had paid tens of million Tomāns (tens of thousands of Dollars) to both conservatives and reformists (*Iran* Daily, Jan. 22, 2002).
138. *Nou Rouz* Daily, July 18, 2001.
139. news.gooya.com/2002/04/02/0204–3.php
140. Article 331, Civil Procedural Law; Section 1, Article 28, and Section 3, Article 339
141. Between 1989 to 1997, during two terms of Rafsanjani administration, about 80 intellectuals, writers and political activists were killed by the intelligence agents inside Iran and more than one hundred were killed outside the country (Akbar Ganji,1999 and 2000; 'Emād ul-Din Bāqi, 2000). http://www.iranian.com/Books/2000/November/Sorkhpoosh/p125.html; http://www.iranian.com/Books/2000/November/Sorkhpoosh/p76.html).
142. http://mellat.majlis.ir/archive/1382/01/26/parlemanttoday.htm
143. Judiciary with the cooperation of IRGC made some reformers to confess to the crimes that they did not do because of fear to be held more in solitary confinement, sometimes six month, charged with "fighting against God," that that could result in execution. Afshāri, an influential 27-year-old leader in the country's largest student organization, Daftar-e Tahkim-e Vahdat (The Unity Consolidation Organization) began his contrived confession with apologies to Iran's leader, Ali Khāmenei.
144. Nezām, as it is used by ruling clerics, is a sacred entity that should not be touched (criticized, questioned and even analyzed); It is usually companied with "Islamic" as an adjective.
145. A very good example is the Hemophilia Case as a class action. After years of hearing and rehearing the verdict was issued. According to the verdict that was confirmed by the Appellate and the Supreme Court, Blood Transfusion Organization and Ministry of Health have to pay 17.5 billion Tomāns (about 19.5 million Dollars) to the patients and their families and should pay all the treatment expenses (Kayhān, 29 May, 2005). The case

was brought up to the court by 974 patients and their family members who were killed or infected because of transmission of infectious disease (AIDS) by blood transfusion. According to official website of the police, the Ministry of Health officials have refused to submit to the verdict (www.police.ir, 21, Sep. 21, 2005)

146. In 2000's, politically active intellectuals were usually summoned to report to a detention center controlled by Edāreh-ye Amāken-e 'Omumi [Department of Public Places], working hand in hand with the judiciary. Amaken, a division of the Disciplinary Forces tasked with monitoring "morality crimes" such as physical contact between men and women and playing music, apparently provides facilities for the parallel intelligence services to carry out interrogations at its offices in Tehran.

147. In Iran, even discussing the separation of mosque and state can land you in jail. During 2000–2004, many intellectuals, activists, and dissidents were prosecuted and tortured by the security sections of the IRGC and judiciary which were known for its links with plainclothes security agents ready to do the leader's office bidding: pick up dissidents, search homes, and imprison activists and intellectuals in illegal detention centers—without judicial orders or on the basis of vaguely worded prohibitions. Since 2000 the use of plainclothes security agents to attack critics of the government took on a more formal character. They were increasingly armed and violent, and use sophisticated communication and transportation equipment. Interrogations of political prisoners take on an increasingly ideological and substantive angle: probing, insulting, and manipulating the prisoners' writings, speeches, and views for hours. Hours of interrogation at a time, while blindfolded, by alternating interrogators, were used to crush the prisoners held in solitary. The prisoner is cut off from information, from family and political events, leaving total control in the hands of guards, interrogators, and judges. Some of the activist were kidnapped in the streets (Nāzem Zādeh, *Nou Rouz* Daily, Jan. 29, 2002)

148. The spate of court summonses issued to members of the Sixth Parliament. They were mostly summoned to court to answer charges of hurling insults in their pre-debate speeches. The MP from Kuhdasht, Ali Emāmi Rād, filed separate complaints against fellow deputies Mohsen Ārmin, Mahmud Akhavān Bazādeh, Fātemeh Rākei and Mohammad-Reza Ali-Hoseini for allegedly insulting him in the chamber. Emāmi Rād alleged in his complaint that the deputies hurled insults at him after he delivered a speech in Majles. In a related development, the MP from Piranshahr and Sardasht, Hasel Dase was summoned to court for remarks he made in parliament on the performance of the state TV, the Islamic Republic of Iran Broadcasting (IRIB) (*Towse'eh* Daily and IRNA, Aug 21, 2001). Nahāvand representative, Mohammad Reza Ali-Huseini, was also found guilty of insulting election-supervisory boards and the Guardians Council. The Public Prosecutor's Office summoned Tehran parliamentarian Mohammad Reza Khātami on March 16, 2004 for making critical comments about the February parliamentary elections. On the same day, the Public Prosecutor's Office summoned Tehran's Mohsen Ārmin, whose resignation was accepted just days earlier. The complaint relates to his

interviews about the elections. Mash-had's Ali Tājerniā said on 10 March that he has been summoned to appear before the Special Court for Government Employees. Tehran's Mohsen Mirdāmādi and Isfahān's Rajab-Ali Mazru'i were summoned for unknown reasons, "Hambastegi." Kāzerun's Mohammad-Bāqer Bāqeri-Nejād-Fard is to appear in court following a complaint from the police; Sardasht and Pirānshahr's Hāsel Dāseh faces a complaint from the police; Pākdasht's Mohammad Qomi was summoned for unknown reasons; Khavāf and Rashtkhār's Gholām Heidar Ebrāhimbāy-Salami was summoned in relation to his work for the *Hambastegi* daily; and Isfahān's Ahmad Shirzād was summoned for a speech he made in December. The summonses were the result of a conservative grudge that dated back to the beginning of the reform movement. The authoritarians have gone anyone who is not loyal to Khāmenei and his clique (RFE/RL *Iran Report,* Vol. 7, No. 11, 22 March 2004).

149. The militia groups, directly supported by the leader, have attacked reformist newspaper, violently lashed out against students and other protesters in the streets of major cities, kidnapped student leaders, and interrogated political prisoners in custody and have never convicted by the judiciary when they are brought to the courts.

150. There were more than 8,000 nongovernmental organizations operating in Iran in 2004, working on everything from environmental protection and human rights to poverty alleviation, drug treatment and cultural issues (http://www.parstimes.com/news/archive/2004/rfe/ngos_activism.html; www.unodc.org/pdf/iran/ drug_trends_iran_2002–05–31_1.pdf). The number of applications for press license went up to a record high, i.e. 2900, in 2003 (http://www.irankhabar.com/headlines/Detailed/15026.html).

151. The head of the judiciary in this period defines the principle of transparency merely on the basis of court openness (Shāhrudi, 2001: 5), not publishing the transcript of discussions in the Supreme Court or the details of the proceedings of judiciary officials' meetings. At the same time, most of the political activists and intellectuals have been tried behind closed doors.

152. In December 2001, an appeals court imposed a seven-month prison sentence on Mohammad Dādfar, a prominent reformist member of parliament who had made a speech criticizing the courts. That same month, a special court dealing with press offences concluded its prosecution of several leaders of Iran's most prominent left-wing party, the Islamic Revolution Mujāhedin Organization (IMRO). Its secretary general, Mohammad Salāmati, the deputy minister for labor, was sentenced to 26 months in prison, while the party's weekly newspaper, *Asr-e Ma*, joined the list of 100-odd publications that have been banned since the reformists won control of the Majles in general elections in 2000. Another senior IMRO official and deputy of the Majles Speaker, Behzād Nabavi, was under investigation for alleged misuse of funds as head of Petro Pars, a quasi-state oil company. Other Khātami allies, including his cabinet secretary, who is the former governor of Kurdestān, the head of the Petroleum Ministry, and the governor of the Central Bank have also been targeted. The judiciary ratcheted up the pressure still further when the courts took the unprecedented step of imprisoning a member of parliament,

Hussein Loqmāniān. (Dādfar has been sentenced but not yet actually imprisoned.) Loqmāniān, a pro-reform MP, was sentenced to ten months in prison for libeling and slandering the judiciary. In a speech before Parliament in 2001, Loqmāniān expressed the commonly held belief among MPs that the courts are "decapitating freedom and attempting to threaten and intimidate Parliament." He also denounced the imprisonment of Ezzatollāh Sahābi, an esteemed veteran activist who has languished behind bars for months without trial, charged with a host of counterrevolutionary offenses. A third MP, Fātemah Haqiqatjou, also faced charges of defaming the courts. Tehran's top judge, Abbās Ali Alizādeh, has said Parliament has no right to interfere in judicial affairs. He believes the media had a duty not to publish articles "that might weaken or insult the judiciary." Loqmāniān's incarceration caused an uproar in the Parliament. One MP labeled it "a mini-coup," and some called for a national referendum on the separation of powers, the most direct challenge to date by elected officials to the clerics' political dominion. Loqmāniān went to Tehran's Evin Prison, Khāmeini belatedly defused the confrontation by granting him a pardon.

153. Mahmoud Hāshemi Shāhrudi: "as far as political crime is not defined in our law, we do not have political prisoners in the country . . . they are convicted for regular crimes" *Kayhān* Daily, May 1, 2004; http://akhbar.gooya.com/politics/archives/016264.php

154. In the case known as Serial Killing of Political Activists and Writers, the Intelligence Ministry staff members were tortured to confess to the leaders' theory that the killings were ordered by foreigners (*Nou-Rouz* Daily, June 18, 2002; *Āftāb* Daily, Dec. 4, 2001). Among detainees who were tortured and spoken out about this in a way or other are Siāmak Purzand (news.gooya.com/2002/05/10/1005–05.php; *Nou Rouz* Daily, May 26, 2001), Alirezā Jabbāri (rouydad.ws/docview.asp/docid=5394), disciples of Montazeri like Hasan Ali Nurihā, Mahmoud Dordkeshān, Nāser Dezfuli, Dāvoud Karimi (Akhbār-e Iran, March, 9, 2002), Sa'id Montazeri (*Nou Rouz* Daily, Aug. 14, 2001), National Religious Forces members like Ezattollāh Sahābi (emrooz.org/pages/date/82–04/19/news01.htm; news.gooya.com/2003/301/30/3001-h-22.php; news.gooya.com/2003/01/20/20/201-ff-03.php; Families of detainees' letter to the Head of Judiciary and his deputy, Dec. 17, 2001; news.gooya.com/1001/1710/1719–3.htm), members of the Unity Consolidation Body like Ali Afshāri, Sai'd Razavi Faqih, Mehdi Amin Zādeh, Akbar 'Atri, and 'Abdollāh Mo'meni (*Nou Rouz,* Feb. 21, 2002; *Hayāt-e Nou* Daily, Nov. 30, 2002), journalists and political activists (the letter of families of 37 detainees to Khāmenei, dailynews.yahoo.com/h/ap/20010729/wl/iran_dissidents_1.html), Nāzem Zādeh (*Nou Rouz* Daily, Jan. 15, 2002) . The judiciary considers these tortures as legal and Islamic punishments (Qulām Hussein Elhām, the judiciary's press secretary, news.gooya.com/2003/05/09/0905-h-26.php).

155. During trial of Tājzādeh, the deputy of Interior Minister, the charges against him changed from "prohibition of the inspection of National General Inspectorate staff during the election" to "illegal interference in election procedure" (*Hambastegi* Daily, March 17, 2000).

156. Ali Mazru'i in his letter to Khātami told his story about his son's detention in one of the illegal prisons. The detainees in Internet Websites case were not even registered in any prison and their families did not know about their whereabouts: http://mag.gooya.com/politics/archives/020270.php
157. Mehrangiz Kār's letter to Karrubi, the Majles Speaker, dated Jul. 21, 2002, specifies tortures of her husband, Siāmak Purzand; http://akhbar.gooya.com/politics/archives/009173.php; http://akhbar.gooya.com/politics/archives/003413.php
158. http://hrw.org/english/docs/2004/07/07/iran9017.htm
159. *Hayāt-e Nou* daily, Oct. 30, 2001
160. *Hayāt-e Nou* Daily, Oct, 31, 2001; *Nou Rouz* Daily, Oct. 30, 2001; *Nou Rouz* Daily, Nov. 11, 2001; *Nou Rouz* Daily, Nov. 20, 2001
161. *Hayāt-e Nou* Daily, Nov. 18, 2001.
162. *Nou Rouz* Daily, May 27, 2002.
163. Hundreds of political party members has been prosecuted and imprisoned in this period, especially between 1997–2003 (*Āftāb* Daily, Oct. 28 &30, 2001; *Hayāt-e Nou* Daily, July 13 & 21 2002; news.gooya.com/2003/01/02/0102-h-24.php)
164. *Bahār* Daily, Jan. 10, 2003.
165. http://www.farsnews.com/NewsVm.asp?ID=87565.
166. The judiciary has reacted to this survey by calling it as illegal. The appointed bodies of government usually label the unpleasant surveys as illegal (http://www.sharghnewspaper.com/830830/html/iran.htm).
167. The Expediency Council made the blood money of Muslim and non-Muslim equal in Dec. 2003 on the basis of expediency, not principles of *shari`ah* (http://www.payvand.com/news/03/dec/1211.html).
168. http://www.sharghnewspaper.com/821007/parlim.htm
169. A widespread crackdown on the press was instituted by elements in the judiciary between 2000 and 2004. During four years, more than 100 publications, daily newspapers and weekly magazines have been closed down for various periods of time, some indefinitely. In addition, editors and journalists have been charged with various offences and fined, sent to jail or banned from journalism for a period of years or, in some cases, a combination of the above. At least one was sentenced to be lashed, a sentence subsequently overturned. Since April 2000, more than 100 journalists have spent time in jail, in either pre- or post-trial detention. Typical charges are defamation, publishing false information, publishing criminal and sensational material contrary to modesty, collaborating with counter-revolutionary groups and taking action against national security. The complaints against the press are being brought chiefly by state agencies like IRGC, state-run Radio and TV, the Office of Implementing Virtue and Prohibiting Vice, and the Disciplinary Forces that has given rise to the term "serial plaintiffs." The campaign against the press is waged by these agencies with the willing support of a small group of judges.
170. *Vaqāye'-e Eteffāqiyeh* and *Jomhuriat,* two reformist dailies, were closed because of having reformist journalists as their staff and correspondents (www.emrooz.ws/ShowItem.aspx?ID=445&p=1).

171. For a detailed report of the role of lawyers in this respect in other countries, look at Halliday and Karpik (ed.), 1997.
172. Writing letters and protesting the actions of the judiciary against lawyers as a way of collective action has been very rare. Two examples are the letters of 182 lawyers from all around the country and 180 lawyers from Fars province to Shārudi, the Head of the Judiciary, asking him to free Abdulfattāh Sultāni after he was in jail for months. (http://open.g00ya.com/politics/archives/042469.php/http://hasanagha.net/blog3/news/post_1104.html).
173. In an unprecedented and extraordinary collective move, 182 lawyers signed a letter (dated Nov. 27, 2005) to Mahmoud Shāhrudi, the Head of the Judiciary, to protest against keeping Abdolfattāh Sultāni, a lawyer, in solitary confinement; he was held in jail for more than four months. He was refused visits and phone contact and could not access his lawyer. He was denied the possibility of sending or receiving correspondence. The signatories asked for an open and fair trial. (http://mag.gooya.com/politics/archives/040015.php).
174. Born in 1947 in Iraq and a disciple of Mohammad Bāqer Sadr and Abu ul-Qāsem Kho'i, he was the ex-leader of the Supreme Council for the Islamic Revolution in Iraq.
175. http://americanradioworks.publicradio.org/features/iran/htmlversion/segb.html
176. sr-irn-0102.pdf (English, pdf, 235.7 kB)[archive, 93.4 kB]
177. One of the charges against Ahmad Zaid Ābādi, an activist/journalist, was that "he has mentioned the Leader and his appointees as the sources of existing problems of the country" (*Hayāt-e Nou* Daily, Feb. 21, 2000).
178. According to Ahmad Rezā Shiri, a journalist based in Mash-had, he signs the form for being noticed about his verdict, i.e. one year prison, one day and the next day, when he goes for the appeal, the branch 7 of the Revolutionary Court informs him that his verdict has not been issued yet (khabarnameh.gooya.com/politics/archives/016427.php). This statement was not denied by the officials.
179. Alirezā Morādi was tried for the same accusation in Revolutionary Court, then in General Court of Kermānshāh, and then by the Disciplinary Committee of the University (http://www.iran-emrooz.de, Sep. 27, 2004).
180. Most of the disciples of Hussein-Ali Montazeri-a high ranking cleric-and his family members, the most prominent religious dissident who, notwithstanding being under house arrest for five years, have been prosecuted, jailed, and imprisoned for years merely because of their beliefs and opinions. Hasan Yousefi Eshkevari, in a trial related to his participation in a meeting in Berlin in the spring of 2000, was convicted of apostasy, "waging war on God" and "corruption on earth." He was reported at first to have been sentenced to death but that was later overturned. Ahmad Qābel was immediately arrested when he criticized the Leader of I.R.I regarding the prosecution of MPs and said "the Leader should be subject to the people's will" (news.gooya.com/2002/01/02/0201–8.php). He was in solitary confinement for 125 days and had no access to media and phone. He was not even been registered as a detainee (*Nou Rouz* Daily, May 8, 2002). Even

non-clerics who have criticized Khāmenei have been tried by the Special Court for Clerics. University students have been summoned to and tried by the Special Court for Clerics (*Āftāb* Daily, Dec. 19, 2001). Clerics have also been tried in regular courts (*Nou Rouz* Daily, Feb. 12, 2002).

181. The closed military court trial of the alleged perpetrators of serial killings in late 1998 and early 1999, who were the Intelligence Ministry operational agents, convicted 15 persons in January 2001, with three sentenced to death and 12 to imprisonment (*Dourān-e Emrouz* Daily, Jan 30, 2000; http://www.forouharha.com/nav/index/cx32.shtml). The appellate court later annulled most sections of the sentences including death penalties. Journalists who disclosed the case, Emāddudin Bāqi and Akbar Ganji, were tried and convicted to imprisonment for 2.5 and 6 years respectively. Those higher-ups involved in varying degrees in the murders remained unidentified and uncharged (http://www.forouharha.com/nav/index/cx30.shtml). After the conviction of the 15, the families of the victims declared that they disagreed with the verdicts, including both capital punishment and incarceration, as they did not want "a vendetta." The families had boycotted the trial in protest against its closed nature and the removal of key evidence from the court files. The lawyer of the families was briefly detained in December 2000 for comments implying that the serial killings were part of a campaign by death squads aimed at silencing the opposition. Despite the closed nature of the trial, the 17-page judgement was revealing. The murders were justified by the orders of a superior in a long chain and the group came across as "a structured death machine." According to the judge, there was a hit list of 40–45 targets. The intelligence minister's declaration of innocence under oath was enough for the judge to dismiss allegation regarding his role in directing and ordering the killings. There were in fact more than 80 murders and disappearances stretching over a 10-year period that were likely part of a wider campaign to silence dissent (Akbar Ganji, *Khordād* Daily, Feb. 12, 1998).

182. *Dourān-e Emrouz* Daily, Jan. 31, 2002.

183. In the rights literature we can find three generations of rights; the first generation is the generation of religious, civil and political rights. In the second generation, the social rights were on the agenda, i.e. right to education and welfare. The third generation is the age of ecological movements (Bobbio, 1996: xi, xii). In Bobbio's view "religious freedom resulted from the religious wars, civil liberties from the parliamentarian struggles against absolutism, and political and social freedoms from the birth, growth and experience of movements representing workers, landless peasants and small holders" (Bobbio, 1996: xi). Bobbio also discusses three evolutionary processes of positivization, generalization, and internationalization in the history of human rights ((Bobbio, 1996: 32–33))

184. Between 1994 and 2002, the function and structure of the public prosecutor office was totally changed due to the General Courts Law.

185. Āle Es-hāq, the Attorney of Judges' Disciplinary Court, who called implementing these Articles for closing press "against the regulations and clear violation of law" (http://www.hamshahri.net/hamnews/1381/811112/ejtem.

htm; *Āftāb* Daily, Feb. 3, 2003) was transferred to one of the branches of the Supreme Court (*Hamshahri* Daily, April 29, 2003) because of his opinion on the banning of the press with resort to the Precautionary Measures Act (Article 13, Qānun-e Eqdāmāt-e Ta'mini) of 1960. Immediately after the publication of his idea, Alizādeh, Tehran's District Public Attorney, sarcastically said that "he gave a new year gift to anti-revolutionaries" (*Yās-e Nou* Daily, April 19, 2002). Despite the fact that the existing, rather conservative press law provides for a maximum suspension of six months, many papers have been sentenced to longer periods of closure and some have remained closed even after the expiry of the prescribed closure period. The judges involved have gone outside the press law and invoked other legislation, particularly the Precautionary Measures Law, which both refer to the prevention of crime. One journal was closed for insulting the President, who replied that he knew of no law that prescribed a punishment for such an act.

186. *Payām-Houzeh,* No.1, Spring 1994.
187. The term statute in this text is used in a different sense from ordinances; statutes are regulations that are passed by the parliament; ordinance in this work is used as any authoritative command or order.
188. http://www.irisn.com/akhbar/1383/13830127/13830127_irisn.com_00001.htm. http://www.irisn.com/akhbar/1383/13830127/13830127_irisn.com_00004.htm.http://www.irisn.com/akhbar/1383/13830124/13830124_SIASI08_HAMSHAHRI.HTM.
189. The Guardian Council usually sends signals for annulling the bills that are unpleasant to its powerful members before the legislation in the Parliament. There are also several cases that the Expediency Council has positively passed laws instead of taking the parliament or the Guardian Council side.
190. http://irisn.com/ketabkhaneh/majles_shoray_negahabn_mjama/137901_MAJLES_SHORAY_NEGAHABN_MJAMA.HTM.HTM. http://irisn.com/ketabkhaneh/majles_shoray_negahabn_mjama/138105_MAJLES_SHORAY_NEGAHABN_MJAMA.HTM.HTM. The Expediency Council usually calls these positive legislations "correction and completion."
191. Under Article 1 of the Regulations governing the Prosecutors Offices and Special Courts for the Clergy (Official Gazette, 7 October 1990), the court is under the supreme supervision of the Leader, who also appoints the Chief Prosecutor (Article 3) and the Judge of the First Branch of the court (*Hākem-e Shar'*) (Article 10). Other judges are appointed with the consent of the Leader (Article 11). The competence of the Court is defined in Article 13 as: a) all general offences committed by clerics, b) all acts which are incompatible with the status of the clergy, c) all local disputes which can undermine public security when one of the parties to the dispute is a cleric, d) all affairs which the eminent Leader has assigned the special courts to deal with. The last clause means that, theoretically, the competence of the court is unlimited.
192. IRNA, Nov. 17, 2004.
193. Born in Yazd, Iran in 1934, he teaches Islamic philosophy in Qom Seminary. Since 1975 he established, directed, and taught in different academic institutes

such as the education department in Dar Rah-e Haq Institute, Baqir al-'Ulum Cultural Foundation, Daftar-e Hamkāri Houzeh va Dāneshgāh (the Office for Cooperation between Seminary and University), and the Imam Khomeini Education and Research Institute in Qom. Since 1990, he is a member of the Council of Experts in Leadership). He is the ideologue of Islamic authoritarianism and the most famous enemy of religious intellectuals in Iran.

194. The murderers of a dozen persons in Kerman justified their actions on the basis of Mesbāh's preaching in the court (IRNA, Nov. 19, 2004)
195. The reporters and essayist used this term was to refer to the killings of ordinary citizens by true believers who were supported by the ruling clerics. They claimed that they had permission from some *mujtaheds* to do these murders (IRNA, Nov. 21, 2004).
196. In responding to the letter of Mohammad Yazdi, the former Head of Judiciary, about the decision of the court on people who kill others whose blood may be shed with immunity (*mahdoor al-dam*), Khāmenei wrote: " the officers of the Disciplinary Force, Basij forces and others who kill someone on purpose and do this because they consider them as people whose blood may be shed with immunity or on the basis of preventing vice, their retaliation verdict should be changed to paying the blood money." (IRNA, Nov. 17, 2004). This statement was quoted by one of the accused and never rejected by Khāmenie's office.
197. The Supreme Court rejected the decree of the primary court (capital punishment) in the case of serial killings in Kerman with resort to the same *shari`ah* ordinance (http://66.34.206.139/13830420/Page-7.html).
198. The Capital of Khorāsān Province in the northeast of Iran
199. *Nou Rouz* Daily, July, 25, and Aug. 15, 2001
200. http://www.emadbaghi.com/archives/000335.php
201. In the case of *Gorgān-e Emrouz* Daily, the jury acquitted the editor-in-chief and the court issued a verdict in contradiction with the jury's opinion (*Āftāb-e Yazd* Daily, April 8, 2004).
202. The Sixth Parliament increased the number and diversified the jury in press court (http://www.magiran.com/article.asp?AID=1291; http://www.kayhannews.ir/830118/other3.htm#other308) but the judiciary did not enforced the law that was exceptionally confirmed by the Guardian Council. Seventh Parliament annulled this law (http://www.bbc.co.uk/persian/iran/story/2004/12/041212_a_jb_glance.shtml).
203. Before the election of Seventh parliament, two reformist newspapers, *Shargh* and *Yās-e No* Dailies, were closed because of publishing the MPs' letter to Khāmenei. *Shargh* daily was disbanned when the editor in chief wrote a public letter to the judiciary and confessed that the move was not right at the time (emrouz.ws:81/showitem.aspx?serial=7379&c=1)
204. http://www.mazandnume.com/?PNID=V1570; http://www.isna.ir/news/NewsCont.asp?id=461118; *Hamshahri* Daily, Jan 22, 2004.
205. Khāmenei (http://www.shareh.com/leadership/rahbari/bayanat/77/14_77.htm), Shāhrudi (http://www.iraninstitute.net/1380/800710/html/politic.htm)
206. Yazdi and Shāhrudi as the head of judiciary in this period have always complained about these problems in the judiciary and included their obviation in their policies (Shāhrudi, 2001; 9; *Yās-e Nou* Daily, Sep. 14, 2003).

207. http://donya-e-eqtesad.com/83–08–30/020830.htm
208. In this study when I use this term I have Erikson and Tedin's definition of pubic opinion, i.e. "the preferences of the adult population on matters of relevance to the government" in my mind (2005: 6).
209. According to one of these surveys in May 2005, the job approval rate for the judiciary was 90 percent (http://www.ghest.com/news_view.asp?news_id=15965). Another survey by the judiciary shows that only 19 percent of respondents are satisfied with the anti-corruption activities of the judiciary (http://www.irisn.com/shora/tahgig/Gozaresh/7004.htm).
210. http://www.hamshahri.net/hamnews/1378/780820/shrst.htm: http://www.hamshahri.org/vijenam/tehran/1380/801206/HSHAHR.HTM
211. For the first draft and changes inflicted by the Guardian Council, see http://www.irisn.com/ketabkhaneh/nazarat_ghavanin/13730415_ghavanin_00001.htm
212. http://www.iranbar.com/pm94.php
213. http://www.mehrnews.com/fa/NewsDetail.aspx?NewsID=1626; http://mehrnews.com/fa/NewsDetail.aspx?NewsID=145273.
214. http://www.irjpr.ir/News/News/q141083.htm
215. http://www.irisn.com/ketabkhaneh/nazarat_ghavanin/13770629_ghavanin_00001.htm
216. http://www.hamshahri.org/hamnews/1384/840222/Irshahr/armansh.htm
217. http://www.hri.ca/fourtherecord2001/documentation/genassembly/a-56–278.htm
218. The independent Bar Association objected to this initiative as a severe assault on the independence of the Bar: *Āftāb* Daily, Nov. 5 and 13, 2002
219. *Āftāb Yazd* Daily, March 14, 2003.
220. *Nou Rouz* Daily, Nov. 7, 2001.
221. *Nou Rouz* Daily, Nov. 28, 2001.
222. Mohammad Hasan Mar'ashi, *Āftāb* Daily, Nov. 7, 2002.
223. www.irna.ir/fa/news/view/line-9/8407171719124621.htm; www.irjpr.ir/News/News/q040784–3.htm; www.rooznamehrasmi.ir/Detail.asp?CurPage=&isParent=0&Level=1&CategoryID=510000&NewsID=914
224. http://hoqooq.com/article.php3?id_article=76
225. http://www.hamshahri.net/vijenam/Mahal/1384/Mahele18/840612/pish.htm; http://www.irna.ir/fa/news/view/menu-155/8406236141142100.htm; http://www.kayhannews.ir/840227/3.HTM; www.ghest.com/news_view.asp?news_id=14988
226. http://www.hamshahri.org/hamnews/1381/811214/news/hoghogsh.htm; Iran has been world leader in juvenile executions (Iran: Juvenile Offenders Face the Hangman's Noose, HRW, September, 23, 2006; http://www.hrw.org/english/docs/2006/09/22/iran14247.htm).
227. http://www.baztab.com/news/24007.php; www.sharghnewspaper.com/821104/disast.htm
228. He was shot and dead in Aug. 2, 2005 (http:/azad.gooya.ws/politics/archives/034228.php)
229. http://www.state.gov/g/drl/rls/hrrpt/2000/nea/index.cfm?docid=786
230. http://www.baztab.com/news/19550.php

231. An adjudicated issue that cannot be relitigated (dictionary.com)
232. http://www.unhchr.ch/huridocda/huridoca.nsf/AllSymbols/C6D20CD90B8EDF57C1256AD4003321F5/$File/N0150649.pdf?OpenElement.
233. www.unhchr.ch/Huridocda/Huridoca.nsf/ 0/c6d20cd90b8edf57c1256ad4003321f5/ $FILE/N0150649.doc
234. http://www.sharghnewspaper.com/830806/index.htm
235. http://www.hamshahri.net/hamnews/1382/820304/world/lifew.htm
236. "Iran continues to sentence child offenders to death, despite signing up to international treaties that expressly prohibit this heinous practice . . . Iran executed eight child offenders in 2005. It carried out its first child execution of 2006 on 13 May with the hanging of an unnamed 17-year-old boy." (http://web.amnesty.org/web/wire.nsf/October2006/Iran). Husein Qarabāqi's death sentence was conformed by the Supreme Court in Dec. 2006. He was 16 years old when he committed crime (http://www.radiofarda.com/Article/2006/12/22/f5_iran_execution_amnesty_international.html)
237. According to some human rights activists, about 40 people under 18 years old have been executed: http://roozonline.com/01newsstory/008722.shtml
238. In a case in Tehran a 14 year old boy's eyeballs were plucked out of his sockets (http://roozonline.com/01newsstory/008722.shtml).
239. news.gooya.com/1001/0810/0810–8.php
240. Mahmoud Hāshemi Shāhrudi, *Nou Rouz* Daily, Nov. 28, 2001
241. http://www.bbc.co.uk/persian/iran/story/2004/11/041107_a_iran_judiciary.shtml
242. In spite of a decision by the Court of Administrative Justice to restate the illegality of inspection of cars by militia forces, the extensive inspection has been going on all around the country for a quarter of a century: *Nou Rouz* Daily, Sep. 19 & 12, 2001; *Hayāt-e Nou* Daily, Aug. 26, 2001; *Nou Rouz* Daily, July 31, 2001.
243. The Court of Administrative Justice nullified the executive circular regarding licensing of NGOs and transferred the authority of enacting regulations with regard to these institutions to the judiciary (news.gooya.com/2003/03/15/1503-ff-03.php).
244. This is done by ideological and political profiling. Almost all the reformers who have occupied a high ranking position in executive power have had an existing file in the judiciary. Some examples are cabinet members (*Nou Rouz* Daily, Dec. 1, 10, 18, 2001; *Bonyān* Daily, March 2, 2002), deputy ministers (*Hayāt-e Nou* Daily, Oct. 23, 2001), governors (), and deputy governors (*Hayāt-e Nou* Daily, Sep. 26, 2001)
245. Other than hundreds of journalists from different areas of reporting like cinema and show business (*Iran* Daily, Aug. 8, 2002; news.gooya.com/2002/02/16/1602–9.php), thousands of university students (*Nou Rouz* Daily, Sep. 19, 2001; news.gooya.com/2002/02/25/2502–21.php; *Nou Rouz* Daily, Feb. 6, 2002; *Nou Rouz* Daily, May 28, 2002; *Nou Rouz* Daily, Oct. 8, 2001; *Nou Rouz* Daily, Nov. 21, 2001; *Āftāb* Daily, Oct. 21, 2001; *Nou Rouz* Daily, Nov. 24, 2001; *Nou Rouz* Daily, Nov. 26, 2001; http://www.emrooz.info/), reformist MPs (60 representatives were

summoned between 1–4 times: emrooz.ws/showitem.aspx?id=1719&p=1) and city council members, and other political activists who were kidnapped or summoned by the judiciary and other disciplinary and military forces in a regular basis (despite a law that grants MPs impunity), almost every intellectual, artist, scholar, teacher and writer who has been active in public sphere and has had a different lifestyle or way of thinking other than the ruling clerics has been arraigned to the courts, prosecuted, jailed or imprisoned, fined, and deprived of working in a special period of time in this period; in some cases, the artworks or books are banned; here are some examples from each category:

Artists-Ali Rafi'i, (director, *Hayāt-e Nou,* Aug. 18, 2002), Gowhar Khair Andish (actress, iran-emrouz.de/khabar/khabar810712.html), Hussein Zamān (Singer, *Nou-Rouz* Daily, Jul. 8, 2002), Bahman Farmān Ārā (director, *Hayāt-e Nou,* De. 10, 2002), Bahrām Baizā'i (director), Kiumars Derambakhsh (director), Kaveh Gulestān (photographer, later killed in Iraq in April 3, 2003) (news.gooya.com/2002/02/16/1602–9.php), Paymān Hushmand Zādeh (Photographer, *Hayat-e Nou* Daily, Nov. 6, 2001), Mohammad Khordadian (Los Angeles based dancer, http://archives.cnn.com/2002/WORLD/meast/07/08/iran.dancer.ap/index.html) , Ideen Āqdāshlu (painter), Behruz Gharibpur (director) (*Nou Rouz* Daily, Feb. 19, 2002), Mohammad Reza Shajariān (Singer, gooya.com/news/2002/03/14/1403–01.php) Scholars-Mohammad Hāshemi (Law School, Shahid Beheshti University, emrooz.org/pages/date/81–11/01/news01.htm) Producers-Morteza Shāyesteh, Husein Farah-Bakhsh, Dāriush Bābāian, Gholām Hasan Blurian, Kaffāsh 'Erāqi, Soheili (webgard. Blogspot.com/2002_08_11_webgard_archive.html), Tahmineh Milāni (*Nou Rouz* Daily, Aug. 28, 2001) Gallery director-Ma'sumeh Saihun (*Nou Rouz* Daily, Feb. 19, 2002) Writers and translators-Toukā Maleki (*Yās* Daily, April 21, 2002), Mas'oud Behnoud (*Nou Rouz* Daily, Sep. 11, 2001), Maqāze'i (translator, news.gooya.com/2003/08/10/1008-x-25.php); even after censorship of books by the Ministry of Culture and Islamic Guidance, some books' licenses are revoked (*Second Sex* by Simone De Beauvoir, *Nou Rouz* Daily, June 12, 2002; *Prisonlike Archipelago* by Akbar Ganji, *Nou Rouz* Daily, May 26, 2002) Teacher- convicted to 40 lashes for criticizing his supervisor (*Nou-Rouz* Daily, Aug. 5, 2001) Publishers-Humāyi (Nai Publisher, *Yās* Daily, April 21, 2002), Lawyers-Mohammad Ali Dādkhāh (convicted to ten years deprivation of working as a lawyer, *Nou Rouz* Daily, May 18, 2002), Nāser Zarafshan (convicted to 5 years of imprisonment and 50 lashes in the Appeal Court, isnagency.com/news/newscontent.asp?id=140951&lang=p) Dervishes (*Hayat-e Nou* Daily, Oct. 28, 20010

Some of these people were tried and jailed without knowing their accusations (Eshkevari, *Nou Rouz* Daily, Sep. 15, 2002; Alirezā Rajā'i, *Nou Rouz* Daily, Oct. 15, 2001). In some cases, the family members of the accused are arrested because of their protest and speaking out against the judiciary (Hodā Sāber's sister, Āftāb Daily, July 11, 2001; Sinā Motallebi's father, http://akhbar.gooya.com/politics/archives/016038.php); lots of the detainees' family members are threatened by the courts (National Religious Forces case, IFP, June 11, 2001)

246. To do this, the courts have not ignored any criticism of the judiciary; an editor (of *Iran* daily) was summoned because of publishing an interview of the Minister of Culture and Islamic Guidance who has criticized the judiciary for the trial of directors and researchers of poll survey institutions (emrooz.org/pages/date/81–11/01/news01.htm).
247. *Dowrān-e Emrouz* Daily, Feb. 12, 2000.
248. In 2001, there were over 12,000 people in jails all over the country for bounced checks (about 8 percent of the prisoners); an additional 5,000 people are incarcerated on embezzlement charges (http://www.payvand.com/news/01/nov/1016.html). The bills to reform the country's banking by-laws have been rejected by different parliaments.
249. http://www.kayhannews.ir/830807/2.htm#other1403
250. http://www.sharghnewspaper.com/830205/disast.htm
251. http://www.today.ir/news/?id=93500
252. http://www.nimrooz.com/html/791/news.htm
253. http://www.kayhannews.ir/840228/15.htm
254. www.hamshahri.org/vijenam/javan/1384/840404/ebteda4.htm; www.hamshahri.org/vijenam/javan/1384/840404/ebteda4.htm
255. In the process of militarization of the three branches of government by Khāmenei and his cronies, while Marvi and Mir Sadeqi (ex Press Secretary of the judiciary) were leaving this organization an ex-pāsdārs and members of IRGC were being appointed in high ranking judiciary positions (http://khabarnameh.gooya.com/politics/archives/013251.php).
256. http://www.kadivar.com/Htm/Farsi/Speeches/Isna-811219.htm.
257. http://www.iranbar.com/pt1315.php
258. http://www.bashgah.net/modules.php?name=News&file=article&sid=8667; http://hoqooq.com/article.php3?id_article=360

NOTES TO CHAPTER SEVEN

1. Linz defines an authoritarian regime in this manner: "authoritarian regimes are political systems with limited, not responsible, political pluralism: without elaborate and guiding ideology (but with distinctive mentalities); without intensive nor extensive political mobilization (except some points in their development); and in which a leader (or occasionally a small group) exercises power within formally ill-defined limits but actually quite predictable ones" (Linz, 1970: 255). I cannot agree with the second part of his definition, i.e. "without elaborate and guiding ideology," since there is no political regime without elaborate and guiding ideology in modern times, though some political ideologies are more elaborate than others
2. . H. E. Chehabi and Juan Linz, Richard Snyder, and Homa Katouzian categorize the Pahlavi regime as a sultanistic one (Chehabi and Linz, 1998: chap. 1, 2, 3. & 8), while, in this regime, "the circle of clients [was] wider [compared to Khāmenei's regime] and the discretion of the ruler [was] less

extensive" (Chehabi & Linz, 1998: 9). Chehabi and Linz call this kind of regime neo-patrimonial (1988: 10). Manuchehri categorizes Reza Shah's regime as a modern sultanistic one (1998: 14).

3. Amuzegar describes Pahlavi regime as autocratic (1991, 149). Chehabi characterizes this regime as an authoritarian one with strong sultanistic tendencies (1990: 17–18, 33 & 39). Milani describes Mohammad Reza Shah's personality as authoritarian (2000: 270).
4. Weber differentiates patrimonial regimes from sultanistic ones by considering their basis of operation as tradition and discretion respectively (1978: 231–232).
5. There is some evidence for the intensification of personalization of power in Iran under Khāmenei; one evidence is his high degree of interference in governmental matter. A very good example is the waivers for obligatory conscription. According to the Deputy of Public Conscription Organization, between 2002 and 2006, 45 percents of the waivers and releases are because of direct interventions and orders of Khāmenei; only 32 and 14 percent of the cases are due to medical and guardianship reasons respectively (http://1384.g00ya.com/society/archives/045052.php). Other than funds coming from Foundations and endowments with yearly revenues and budgets in the range of billion dollars, Khāmenei has a share in public budget (for 2006, about $200 million for his trips to provinces; http://web.peykeiran.com/new/articles/article_body.aspx?ID=8147). He is not supposed to be accountable to any elected bodies of government in his financial affairs.
6. All these characteristics of sultanism are borrowed from Chehabi and Linz (1998: chap. 1)
7. The implicit definition of sultanism in this discussion is taken from Chehabi and Linz (1998; 7)
8. Khāmenei has strongly discredited any party and political faction in the country (http://64.233.161.104/search?q=cache:dSuuTN2gQHwJ:www.wilayah.net/pr/bayanat/82/t83.php)
9. By dividing polity members to two groups: the leader's loyalists (*payrowān-e rahbari*) and outsider (*ghair-e khodihā*) (http://216.239.39.104/search?q=cache:Ai08eNVq8doJ:www.wilayah.net/pr/bayanat/82/t55.php). Khamenei explains this idea in details in his speech among members of Mohammad Rasul ul-Lah Army or Army No. 27 (http://www.wilayah.net/pr/bayanat/archive.php). This categorization has its roots in clerical culture that divides people to common people and religious elite (clerics). This has been the base for dividing Iranian citizens to first and second order citizens. Second order citizens (women, non-believers) are deprived of lots of their civil and constitutional rights.
10. *Khāleseh* or conditional *Toyul*
11. The progenies and family members of the ruling clerics and the sources of emulations (*marāje'*)
12. Some of the reformers filed against the members of appointed bodies of government and Khāmenei's appointees between 1997 and 2004 but they never heard from the courts. A famous case is Tājzādeh (former deputy of

Interior Ministry) vs. Jannati (member of the Guardian Council) after the Sixth Parliamentary election.

13. Whenever the National Consultative Assembly (the parliament) and the Senate separately, whether independently or due to the suggestion of the cabinet, approve the revision of one or some articles of the constitution with tow third majority and the king confirm their decision, the royal order for establishment of the constituent assembly and the election of its members will be issued.
14. The revision of the Constitution of the Islamic Republic of Iran, whenever needed by the circumstances, will be done in the following manner: The Leader issues an edict to the President after consultation with the Nation's Expediency Council stipulating the amendments or additions to be made by the Council for Revision of the Constitution.
15. According to natural law legal theory, the authority of at least some legal standards necessarily derives, at least in part, from considerations having to do with the moral merit of those standards. These standards are in some sense derived from, or entailed by, the nature of the world and the nature of human beings (Aquinas, S. T., 1988: I-II, Q.90, A.I).
16. The distinction between civil and common law systems is now in crisis (Merryman, 1969: 94). This does not mean that we cannot use this distinction to explain a legal system in early 20th century Iran.
17. This can be compared to the legal transplantation process in Eastern Europe and Russia during the Socialist era (Ajani, 1995: 93–95)
18. This strategy was used by fascist regime in Italy and Franco in Spain from 1950's (Guarnieri & Pederzoli, 2002: 79).
19. Divān-e Kaifar-e Kārkonān-e Dowlat (The Governmental Officials' Penal Court) under Reza Shah rule and Dādgāh-e Vijeh-ye Kārkonān-e Dowlat, ordinary court branch of 1410 (Special Court for Governmental Officials) in Khāmenei rule; Almost all newspapers and magazines and most of the political activists and writers were tried in the latter one between 1993–2003. The former one had a limited jurisdiction in the beginning; after its establishment in 1928, it was to try governmental officials who were accused of embezzlement and bribery. But its jurisdiction was always increasing to the point that it could try any individual's crime (Zerang, Vol. I, 2002: 456)
20. Although the difference between two types of law, i.e. civil and common law, is no longer distinct as it was (Jacobs, 1996: 4), it is still distinct when we talk about late 19th and early 20th century Iran.
21. *Vaqāye'-e 'Adliyeh* in March 1871 mentions these problems as the main issues of judicial reforms; these are still the main issues of any judicial reform at the end of 20th and beginning of 21st century.

NOTES TO THE CONCLUSION

1. The use of the term here "refers to ideas, values, expectations, and attitudes toward law and legal institutions which some public or some parts of the public holds" (Friedman, 1997: 34).

NOTES TO THE APPENDICES

* http://www.sci.org.ir/portal/faces/public/sci/sci.gozide

1. Where the reference is not mentioned the material is taken from newspapers.
2. The result of the surveys indicated that nearly 75% of respondents were in agreement with starting "negotiations between Iran and the U.S.."
3. Difference spheres of life that each develops separately

Bibliography

BOOKS AND JOURNAL ARTICLES

Abdollāhi, Fereshteh

1990 *Din-e Zartoshti va Naqsh-e 'an dar Jāme'eh-ye Sasanian (Zoroastrian Religion and its Role in Sasanian Society),* Tehran: Qoqnoos Publishers.

Abrahamian, Ervand

1999 *Tortured Confessions: Prisons and Public Recantations in Modern Iran,* LA: University of California Press.

1982 *Iran between Two Revolutions,* NJ: Princeton University Press.

Abrams, Philip

1982 *Historical Sociology,* NY: Cornell University Press.

Ackerman, Bruce

1997 "The Rise of World Constitutionalism," *Virginia Law Review,* May 1997, No. 83.

Ādamiyyat, Fereydun

1976/1991 *Ideology-ye Nehzat-e Mashrutiyyat* (*The Ideology of Constitutional Revolution*), Vol. I&II, Tehran: Payām/Rowshangarān.

1973 *Andisheh-ye Taraqqi va Hukumat-e Qānun: 'Asr-e Sepah Sālār* (*The Idea of Progress and the Rule of Law during Sepah Sālār Era*), Tehran: Khārazmi.

1972 *Siāsat-e Eslāh dar Iran: 1237–1259* (*The Politics of Reform in Iran: 1858–1880*), Tehran: Khārazmi.

1970 *Andishehhā-ye Mirzā Fat'h Ali-ye Akhoond-Zādeh* (*The Fundamental Thoughts of Mirza Fat'h Ali Akhoond-Zādeh*), Tehran: Khārazmi.

1969 *Amir Kabir va Iran* (Amir *Kabir and Iran*), Tehran: Khārazmi.

1961 *Fekr-e Āzādi va Moqaddameh-ye Nehzat-e Mashrutiyyat* (*The Idea of Freedom and Preliminary of Constitutional Revolution*), Tehran: Sokhan.

Afshari, Reza

2001 *Human Rights in Iran: The Abuse of Cultural Relativism,* Philadelphia: University of Pennsylvania Press.

Ajani, Gianmari

1995 "By Chance and Prestige: Legal Transplants in Russia and Eastern Europe," *American journal of Comparative Law,* Vol. 43, No. 1: 93–117.

Albrow, Martin

1975 "Legal Positivism and Bourgeois Materialism: Max Weber's View of the Sociology of Law," *British Journal of Law and Society,* Vol. 2: 14–31.

Alford, Robert & Friedland, Roger

1985 *Powers of Theory: Capitalism, the State and Democracy,* Cambridge University Press.

Algar, Hamid

1991 "Religious Forces in Eighteenth- and Nineteenth- Century Iran," in P. Avery, G. Hambly and C. Melville (ed.), *The Cambridge History of Iran,* vol.7: *From Nadir Shah to the Islamic Republic,* Cambridge: Cambridge University Press. 1991

1969 *Religion and State in Iran, 1785–1906,* Berkeley and Los Angeles: University of California Press.

Amanat, Abbas

1997 *Pivot of the Universe: Nasir al-Din Shah Qajar and the Iranian Monarchy 1831–1896,* Washington, D.C.: Mage Publishers.

Amin, Seyyed Hasan

2003 *Tārikh-e Hoquq-e Iran* (*The History of Law in Iran*), Tehran: The Encyclopedia of Iran Publication.

Amin ul-Dowleh, Mirzā Ali Khan

1962 *Khāterāt-e Siāsi (Political Memoirs),* Tehran: Persian Book Company.

Amirahmadi, H.

1982 "Roots of Dependent Development and Dictatorship in Iran: 1800–1920," Cornell University PhD. Dissertation.

Amuzegar, Jahangir

1991 *The Dynamics of the Iranian Revolution: The Pahlavis' Triumph and Tragedy,* NY: State University of New York Press

Angold, Michael

1995 *Church and Society in Byzantium under the Comneni,* Cambridge: Cambridge University Press

'Āqeli, Bāgher

1995 Nokhost Vazirān-e Iran; Az Mashruteh tā Enqelāb-e Eslāmi (Iranian Prime Ministers: From Constitutional Movement to the Islamic Revolution), Tehran: Jāvidān.

1990 *Dāvar va 'Adlieh* (*Dāvar and the Judiciary*), Tehran: 'Elmi.

Aquinas, Thomas

1988 *On Law, Morality and Politics,* Indianapolis: Hackett Publishing Co.

Arendt, Hannah

1973 *The Origins of Totalitarianism,* New York: Harcourt Brace Jovanovich.

Arjomand, Sa'id Amir

2005 "Political Ethic and Public Law in the Early Qājār Period," in Robert M. Gleave, ed., *Religion and Society in Qājār Iran,* London: Curzon, pp. 21–40.

2003 "Law, Political Reconstruction and Constitutional Politics," International Sociology, 18.1: 9–34.

2000a "Authority in Shi'ism and Constitutional Developments in the Islamic Republic of Iran," in W. Ende & R. Brunner, eds., *The Twelver Shia in Modern Times: Religious Culture & Political History,* Leiden: Brill, pp. 301–32.

2000b "Civil Society and the Rule of Law in the Constitutional Politics of Iran under Khātami," *Social Research,* Vol. 67, No. 2.

1993 "Shi'ite Jurisprudence and Constitution Making in the Islamic Republic of Iran," in *Fundamentalisms and the State: Remaking Polities, Economies, and Militance,* ed. By Martin E. Marty and R. Scott Appleby, Chicago: The University of Chicago Press.

1992 "Constitutions and the Struggle for Political Order," *European Journal of Sociology,* 33, pp. 39–82.

1988 *The Turban for the Crown: The Islamic Revolution in Iran,* NY: Oxford University Press.

1988a "The Mujtahid of the Age and Mullabashi: An Intermediate Stage in the Institutionalization of Religious Authority in Shi'ite Iran," in S. A. Arjomand (ed.) *Authority and Political Culture in Shi'ism,* Albany: SUNY Press.

1985 "Religion, Political Order and social Change," *Current Perspectives in Social Theory,* Vol. 6: 1–15.

1984 *Shadow of God & the Hidden Imam: Religion, Political Order, and Societal Change in Shi'ite Iran from the Beginning to 1890,* Chicago: University of Chicago Press.

Arjomand, Sa'id, A. (ed)

1993 *Political Dimensions of Religion,* NY: University of New York Press.

Arnold, Thomas Walker

1931 "Law and Society," in *The Legacy of Islam,* Oxford: The Clarendon Press.

Aron, Raymond

1968 *Main Currents of Sociological Thought: Montesquieu, Comte, Marx, Tocqueville, and the Sociologists and the Revolution of 1848,* Vol. 1, Transaction Publishers.

Austin, John

1954 *The Province of Jurisprudence Determined,* Prometheus Books (1832).

Azimi, Fakhreddin

1989 *Iran: The Crisis of Democracy, 1941–1953,* London: I.B.Tauris & Co.

'Azmeh, 'Aziz Al-

1998 *Al-'Almaniya min Manzur Mukhtalif,* Beirut: Markaz Darasat al-Wahda al-'Arabiya.

Baihaqi, Abu al-Fazl Mohammad ebn-e Hasan

1945 *Tārikh-e Baihaqi* (*Baihaqi's History*), ed. By Ghani and Fayyāzi, Tehran.

Bakhash, Shaul

1984 *The Reign of the Ayatollahs: Iran and the Islamic Revolution,* NY: Basic books, Inc.

Banani, Amin

1961 *The Modernization of Iran,* Stanford: Stanford University Press.

Barāti Nia, Mahmud

2002 "Barresi-ye Chāleshha va Rāhkārhā-ye Asāsi barāye Vosul be Towse'eh-ye Qazāii dar Quvveh-ye Qazāiyyeh-ye Iran" ("Review of Challenges and Strategies for Judicial Reform in Iran's Judiciary"), in Towse'eh-ye Qazāii (Judicial Reform), ed. by Markaz-e Matbu'āt va Enteshārāt-e Quvveh-ye Qazāiyyeh, Tehran: Mo'āvenat-e Ejtemā'i va Ettelā' Resāni-ye Quvveh-ye Qazāiyyeh.

Bashiriyeh, Hossein

1984 *The State and Revolution in Iran: 1962–1982,* NY: St. Martin's Press.

Bayat, Mangol

1991 *Iran's First Revolution: Shi'ism and the Constitutional Revolution of 1906–1909,* NY: Oxford University Press.

Bāzargān, Mehdi

1998 *Be'that va Ideology* (*Prophetic Mission and Ideology,* written in 1964), Tehran: Enteshār

Beck, Lois

1986 *The Qashqa'i of Iran,* New haven: Yale University Press.

Beckfort, James A.

1986 *New Religious Movements and Rapid Social Change,* Sage Publications / UNESCO Publishing.

Beckford, James A. & Thomas Luckman

1989 The Changing Face of Religion, *International Sociology,* Vol. 37.

Bendix, Reinhard, (ed)

1968 *State and Society,* Berkeley: University of California Press.

1962 *Max Weber: An Intellectual Portrait,* Berkeley: University of California Press.

Benton, Lauren

2001 *Law and Colonial Cultures: Legal Regimes in World History, 1400–1900,* Cambridge University Press.

Berger, Peter

1973 *The Social Reality of Religion*, Penguin Book

Berman, Harold J.

1985 *Law and Revolution,* Mass: Harvard University Press.

Berkes, Niazi

1964 *The Development of Secularism in Turkey,* Montreal: McGill University Press.

Bill, James Alban

1972 *The Politics of Iran: Groups, Classes and Modernization*, Columbus, Ohio: Merrill

Binder, Leonard

1978 *Iran: the Illusion of Power,* NY: St. Martin's Press.

1962 *Iran: Political Development in a Changing Society,* Berkeley: University of California Press.

Bobbio, Norberto

1996 *The Age of Rights,* Cambridge: Polity Press.

Bohannan, P.J.

1965 "The Differing Realms of Law," in Nader, L. (ed.), *The Ethnography of Law,* supplement to *American Anthropology,* 67(2): 3–32.

Bosworth, C.E.

1975(a) "The Tahirids and Saffarids," in *The Cambridge History of Iran,* Vol. 4: *From the Arab Invasion to the Seljuqs,* ed. by R.N. Frye, Cambridge: Cambridge University Press: pp.90–135.

1975(b) "The Early Ghaznavids," in *The Cambridge History of Iran,* Vol. 4: *From the Arab Invasion to the Seljuqs,* ed. by R.N. Frye, Cambridge: Cambridge University Press: pp. 162–197.

1968 "The Political and Dynastic History of the Iranian World (A.D. 1000–1217)," in *The Cambridge History of Iran,* Vol. 5: *The Seljuq and Mongol Periods,* ed. by J. A. Boyle, Cambridge: Cambridge University Press: pp. 1–202.

Bozeman, Adda B.

1971 *The Future of Law in a Multicultural World,* NJ: Princeton University Press.

Brinton, Crane

1938 *The Anatomy of Revolution,* NJ: Prentice-Hall Inc.

Brinton, Jasper Y.

1926 "The Mixed Courts of Egypt," *American Journal of International Law,* Vol. 20, 4: 670–688.

Brown, Nathan J.

2002 *Constitutions in a Nonconstitutional World; Arab Basic Laws and the Prospects for Accountable Government,* NY: State University of New York Press.

1997 *The Rule of Law in the Arab World: Courts in Egypt and the Gulf,* Cambridge University Press.

Browne, Edward G.

1966 *The Persian Revolution of 1905–1909*, Barnes & Noble

Brunner, Rainer & Werner Ende

2001 *The Twelver Shia in Modern Times: Political Culture and Political History,* Leiden: Brill.

Bulsara, Sohrab Jamshedjee

1937 *Matikan-e Hazar Datastan* in *The Laws of the Ancient Persians,* Bombay, Repr. Teheran 1976.

Burbank, Stephen B. & Friedman, Barry (ed.)

2002 *Judicial Independence at the Crossroads: An Interdisciplinary Approach,* Thousand Oaks, CA: Sage Publications.

Burchell, G., C. Gordon & P. Miller

1991 *The Foucault Effect,* Chicago: University of Chicago Press

Busse, Heribert

1975 "Iran under the Buyids," in *The Cambridge History of Iran,* Vol. 4: *From the Arab Invasion to the Seljuqs,* ed. by R.N. Frye, Cambridge: Cambridge University Press: pp. 250–304.

Cannon, Byron

1988 *Politics of Law and the Courts in Nineteenth-Century Egypt,* Salt Lake City: University of Utah Press.

Carey, John A.

1981 *Judicial Reform in France before the Revolution of 1789,* Massachusetts: Harvard University Press.

Casanova, Jose

1994 *Public Religion in the Modern World,* Chicago: University of Chicago Press.

Chazan, Naomi, ed.

1991 *Irredentism and International Politics,* Boulder, CO: Lynne Rienner.

Chehabi, H.E.

2001 "The Political Regime of the Islamic Republic of Iran in Comparative Perspective," *An International Journal of Comparative Politics,* Vol. 36, No 1.

1990 *Iranian Politics and Religious Modernization: The Liberation Movement of Iran under the Shah and Khomeini,* NY: Cornell University Press.

Chehabi, H.E. and Linz, J.J. (eds.)

1998 *Sultanistic Regimes,* Baltimore and London: The Johns Hopkins University Press.

Chodosh, Hiram E.

2003 "Emergence from the Dilemmas of Justice Reform," *Texas International Law Journal,* 38, No3, pp. 587–620

Christensen, Arthur

1989(1944) *Iran dar Zamān-e Sasanian* (*L'Iran Sous les Sasanides*), tr. By Rashid Yasami, 6th reprint, Tehran: Donya-ye Ketab.

Clifford-Vaughan, M. and Scotford-Norton, M.

1967 "Legal Norms and Social Order: Petrazycki, Pareto, Durkheim," *British Journal of Sociology,* Vol. 18, No. 3: 269–277.

Collier, Jane F.

1996 "Intertwined Histories: Islamic Law and Western Imperialism," in *SEHR,* Vol. 5, No. 1.

Coulson, Noel

1964 *History of Islamic Law,* Edinburgh: Edinburgh University Press.

Cronin, Stephanie

2000 "Riza Shah and the Disintegration of Bakhtiyari Power in Iran, 1921–1934," *Iranian Studies,* Vol. 33, Nos. 3–4: 349–376.

Crystal, J.

1994 "Authoritarianism and its Adversaries in the Arab World," *World Politics*, 46: 262–89.

Curzon, G.N.

1982 *Iran va Qaziyyeh-ye Iran (Persia and the Persian Question)*, tr. by Gholam Reza Vahid Māzanderāni, 2 Vols., Tehran: 'Elmi va Farhangi.

Dakolias, Maria

1995 *Judicial Reform in Latin America and the Caribbean*, Proceedings of a World Bank Conference, ed. by Waleed Haider Malik, Maria Dakolias and Malcolm Rowat, World Bank Technical Paper, No 280.

Dandamaev, Muhammad A. & Vladimir G. Lukonin

1989 *The Culture and Social Institutions of Ancient Iran*, MA: Cambridge University Press

Daryābāri, Seyyed Mohammad Zamān

2004 *Dādsarā va Dādgāh-e Vijeh-ye Rowhāniyat* (*The Clergy's Special Court and Office of Attorney*), Tehran: Markaz-e Asnād-e Enqelāb-e Eslāmi.

Dehkhodā, Ali Akbar

1986 *Loghat Nāmeh-ye Dehkhodā* (*Dehkhodā Dictionary*), Tehran: Ministry of Culture ans Islamic Guidance.

Della Porta, Donatella

1999 *Social movements*, Oxford: Blackwell.

Denbeli, Abd ul-Razzāq Maftoon

1827 *Ma'āser Soltānieh (Kingly Heritages: The History of Russia-Iran Wars)*, Tehran: Ebnā-e Sin.

Devereux, Robert

1963 *The First Ottoman Constitutional Period: A Study of the Midhat Constitution and Parliament*, Baltimore: John Hopkins Press.

Diamond, A. S.

1965 *The Comparative Study of Primitive Law*, London: Athlone Press.

1951 *The Evolution of Law and Order*, London: Watts.

1935 *Primitive Law*, London: Watts.

Dowlat Ābādi, Yahyā

1992 *Hayāt-e yahyā* (*Yahyā's Life*), Tehran: 'Attar in association with Ferdows Press,

Dubios, Philip, L. (ed)

1982 *The Analysis of Judicial Reform*, Toronto: Lexington Books.

Durant, Will

1954 *The Story of Civilization:* Part 1, *Our Oriental Heritage,* NY: Simon and Schuster

Durkheim, Emile

1933 *The Division of Labor in Society* (tr. G. Simpson), Free Press.

Dyzenhaus, David

1997 *Legality and Legitimacy: Carl Schmitt, Hans Kelsen and Hermann Heller in Weimar,* Oxford: Clarendon Press.

Dwyer, Daisy Hilse

1990 *Law and Islam in the Middle East,* London: Bergin & Garvey Publishers.

Ehrlich, Eugen

1975 *Fundamental Principles of Sociology of Law,* Foreword, Trans. Walter L. Mall, New York: ArnoPress. Originally published by Harvard University Press, 1936.

Elster, Jon, Offee, Claus & Preuss, Ulrich

1998 *Institutional Design in Post-communist Societies: Rebuilding the Ship at the Sea,* Cambridge University Press.

Elster, Jon

1995 "Forces and Mechanisms in the Constitution-making Process," *Duke Law Journal,* 45.2: 364–96.

Elster Jon & Rune Slagstad

1993 *Constitutionalism and Democracy,* Cambridge: Cambridge University Press.

Ensāfpur, Gholām Rezā

1977 *Sākht-e Dowlat dar Iran: Az Islam ta Yuresh-e Moghol (The State Structure in Iran: From Islam to Mogul's Invasion*), Tehran: Amir Kabir.

Epp, C.R.

1998 *The Rights Revolution,* Chicago: University of Chicago Press.

Eqbāl Āshtiani, Abbās

1976 *Mirzā Taqi Khan-e Amir Kabir,* Tehran: Sokhan.

E'temād ul-Saltaneh, Mohammad Hasan Khan

1877–80 *Mir'āt al-Buldān-e Nāseri* (*The Mirror of the Cities*), Tehran.

1966 *Ruznāmeh-ye Khāterāt-e E'temād ul-Saltaneh (Journals of E'temād ul-Saltaneh*), Tehran: Amir Kabir.

Erikson, Robert S & Kent Tedin

2005 American Public Opinion: Its Origins, Content and Impact, 7th ed, Pearson Longman.

Ewald, William

1995 "Comparative Jurisprudence (II): the Logic of Legal Transplants," The American Journal of Comparative Studies, Vol. 43, No. 4: 489–510.

Farhi, Farideh

1990 *States and Urban-Based Revolutions: Iran and Nicaragua,* IL: University of Illinois Press.

Fazlollāh, Rashid ul-Din

1989 *Tārikh-e Mubārak-e Ghāzāni* (*The History of Ghāzān*), ed. by Carl Ian, Esfehān: Nashr-e Porsesh.

Firouz, Maryam

1994 *Khāterāt-e Maryam-e Firuz* (*Maram Firouz's Memoirs*), Tehran: Ettelā'āt.

Floor, Willem

2003 *Agriculture in Qajar Iran,* Washington DC: Mage, 2003.

1983 "Change and Development in the Judicial System of Qajar Iran (1800–1925)," in *Qajar Iran: Political, Social and Cultural Change,* ed. by Boseworth, C.E., Carole Hillenbrand, Edinburgh: Edinburgh University Press: 113–147.

Fluehr-Lobban, C

1986 *Islamic Law and Society in the Sudan,* London: Cass.

Foucault, Michel

1991 *The Foucault Effect: Studies in Governmentality,* Chicago: The University of Chicago Press.

Foroughi, Mirzā Mohammad Ali Khan-ebn-e Zokā' ul-Molk

1906 *Hoquq-e Asāsi yā 'Ādāb-e Mashrutiyyat-e Doval* (*The Constitutional Law*), Tehran: published by the author.

Franzinetti, Guido

2005 "Long Waves of State-building in the Balkans, 1878–1950: A Retrospective and Comparative View," www.cishsydney.com.

Frerejohn, J., Rakove, J.N. & Riley, J., (eds.)

2000 "Editors' Introduction" to *Constitutional Culture and Democratic Rule,* Cambridge University Press.

Friedman, Lawrence M.

1997 "The Concept of Legal Culture: A Reply," in *Comparing Legal Cultures,* ed. by David Nelken, Dartmouth Publication Co.

1994 "Is There a Modern Legal Culture?" *Ratio Juris,* Vol. 7, No. 2: 117–131.

1975 *The Legal System: A Social Science Perspective,* NY: Russell Gage.

Fuller, Lon L.

1964 *The Morality of Law,* New Haven: Yale University Press.

Gambitta, Richard A.L. & May, Marlynn L.

1982 "Judicial Reform, the Myth of the Triad, and the Decline of Confidence in the Courts," in *The Politics of Judicial Reform,* ed. by Philip L. Dubois, Massachusetts: Lexington Books.

Gay, Peter

1966 *The Enlightment: An Interpretation, The Rise of Modern Paganism,* W. W. Norton & Company

Geertz, Clifford

1968 *Islam Observed: Religious Development in Morocco and Indonesia,* New Haven: CT: Yale University Press.

Geertz, Clifford, (ed)

1963 *Old Societies, and New States: A Quest for Modernity in Asia and Africa* (ed.), NY: The Free Press.

Gerber, Haim

1999 *Islamic Law and Culture, 1600–1840,* Leiden: Brill Academic Publishers.

1994 *State, Society, and Law in Islam,* NY: State University of New York Press.

Ghaffāri, Haibatollāh

1989 *Sākht-e Ejtemā'i-ye 'Ashāyer-e Booyer Ahmad (Social Structures of Booyer Ahmad Nomads*), Tehran: Nashr-e Nai.

Ghani, Cyrus

1998 *Iran and the Rise of Reza Shah: from Qajar Collapse to Pahlavi Rule,* NY: I.B. Tauris Publishers.

Gibb, H.A.R.

1953 *Mohammedanism,* NY: Oxford University Press.

Ghirshman, R.

1954 *Iran: from the Earliest Times to the Islamic Conquest,* Penguin Books (*Iran az Āghāz tā Islam,* tr. by Mohammad Mo'in, Tehran: Bongāh-e Tarjomeh va Nashr-e Ketāb, 1960).

Gluckman, M.

1965 *Politics, Law and Ritual in Tribal Society*, Chicago: Aldine Press.

Goldzieher, Ignaz

1981 *Introduction to Islamic Theology and Law*, NJ: Princeton University Press.

Graham, Robert

1978 *Iran: The Illusion of Power*, London: Croom Helm.

Green, Jerrold D.

1982 *Revolution in Iran: The Politics of Countermobilization*, NY: Praeger.

Green, Michael Steven

2003 "Hans Kelsen and the Logic of Legal Systems," *Alabama Law Review*, Vo. 54, No. 2: 365–413

Guarnieri, Carlo & Patrizia Pederzoli

2002 *The Power of Judges: A Comparative Study of Courts and Democracy*, Oxford: Oxford University Press.

Gulliver, P.H.

1963 *Social Control in an African Society*, London: Routledge and Kegan Paul.

Gusfield, Joseph R.

1962 "Mass Society and Extremist Politics," *American Sociological Review*, Vol. 27, No. 1: pp. 19–30.

Habermas, Jurgen

1996 *Between Facts and Norms: Contributions to a Discourse Theory of Law and Democracy*, trans. by William Rehg, Cambridge: MIT Press.

Hairi, Abd ul-Hadi

1977 *Shi'ism and Constitutionalism in Iran*, Leiden: E.J. Brill.

Hāji Sayyah

1967 *Khāterāt-e Hāji Sayyāh*, ed. by Hamid Sayyāh, Tehran: Ebn-e Sinā.

Hallaq, Wael B.

1999 *A History of Islamic Legal Theories: An Introduction to Sunni Usul al-fiqh*, Cambridge University Press.

2001 *Authority, Continuity and Change in Islamic Law*, Cambridge University Press.

Halliday, Terence C. Lucian Kaprik (eds.)

1997 *Lawyers and the Rise of Western Political Liberalism: Europe and North America from the Eighteenth to the Twentieth Centuries*, Oxford: Clarendon Press and New York: Oxford University Press.

Hamilton, Peter

1991 *Max Weber: Critical Assessment,* London: Routledge.

Hammond, Phillip E.

1985 *The Sacred in a Secular Age: Toward Revision in the Scientific Study of Religion,* Berkeley: University of California Press.

Harley, Herbert

1915 "Present Tendencies in Judicial Reform," *The American Political Science Review,* Vol. 9, 3: 529–542.

Harper, P., Aruz, J, & Tallon, F

1992 *The Royal City of Susa: Ancient Near Eastern Treasures in the Louvre,* NY: The Metropolitan Museum of Art.

Hart H.A.L.

1961 *The Concept of Law,* Oxford: Oxford University Press.

Hayek, F.A.

1973 *Law, Legislation and Liberty, Vol. 1: Rules and Order,* London: Routledge & Kegan Paul.

Haykel, Bernard

2002 *Revival and Reform in Early-Modern Islam: The Legacy of Muhammad al-Shawkani,* Cambridge: Cambridge University Press.

2001 "Reforming Islam by Dissolving the *Madhahib:* Muhammad al Shawkani and his Zaydi detractors in Yemen," in *Studies in Islamic Legal Theory,* Bernard Weiss (ed.), Leiden: Brill.

1994 "Shawkani and the Jurisprudential Unity of Yemen," in *Revue du Monde Musulman et de la Méditerraneé,* No. 67.

Herf, Jeffrey

1984 *Reactionary Modernism: Technology, Culture, and Politics in Weimar and the Third Reich,* NY: Cambridge University Press.

Herodotus

1954 *Tārikh-e Herodot (Herodotus Histories),* tr. by Hādi Hedāyati, Tehran: Tehran University Press.

Hinz, Walter

1973 The Lost World of Elam: Re-creation of a Vanished Civilization, tr. By Jennifer Barns, New York: NY University press.

Hodgson, Marshall G. S.

1993 *Rethinking World History: Essays on Europe, Islam and World, Cambridge University Press.*

1977 *The Venture of Islam: Conscience and History in a World Civilization*, University of Chicago Press, Vols. I & II.

Hoebel, E. Adamson

1954 *The Law of Primitive Man: A Study in Comparative Legal dynamics*, MA: Harvard University Press.

Holmes, Oliver Wendell

1963 *The Common Law*, Cambridge: Harvard University Press.

Horowitz, Donald L.

1994 "The Qur'an and the Common Law: Islamic Law Reform and the Theory of Legal Change," *The American Journal of Comparative Law*, Vol. 42, 233–293 & 543–580.

Huff, E. & Schluchter, Wolfgang

1999 *Max Weber and Islam*, London: Transaction Publishers.

Ibn-e Abi Ādam, Shahāb ul-din Ebrāhim

1982 *Adab al-Qazā' va Hova al-dorar ul-Manzumāt fi al-'aqziah va al-Hokumāt*, Damascus.

Issavi, Charles & Polk, William R.

1971 *The Economic History of Iran, 1800–1914*, Chicago: University of Chicago Press.

Jacobs, Herbert et al

1996 *Courts, Law and Politics in Comparative Perspective*, New Haven: Yale University Press.

Jacobson, David

1996 *Rights across Borders*, Baltimore: The Johns Hopkins Press.

Ja'fari Langrudi, Mohammad Ja'far

NA *Tārikh-e Hoquq-e Iran* (*Iran's Legal History*), Tehran: Ma'refit.

Kadivar, Mohsen

1998 *Hokumat-e Velaii* (*Guardian's Government*), Tehran: Nai.

1997 *Nazariyehā-ye Dowlat dar Feqh-e Shi'eh* (*The Theories of State in Shi'ite Jurisprudence*), Tehran: Nai.

Kahn, Paul W.

1999 *The Cultural Study of Law: Reconstructing Legal Scholarship*, Chicago: The University of Chicago Press.

Kaiser, Daniel

1980 *The Growth of the Law in Medieval Russia*, NJ: Princeton University Press.

Kalberg, Stephen

1994 *Max Weber's Comparative-Historical Sociology*, Cambridge: Polity Press.

Kamali, Masoud

1995 *The Modern Revolutions of Iran: Clergy, Bazaris, and the State in the Modernization Process*, Uppsala: Uppsala University Press.

Kantorowitz Ernst H.

1957 *The King's Two Bodies: A Study in Medieval Political Theology*, NJ: Princeton University Press.

Kashani, Mahmood

1992 Barresi-*ye Qānun-e Eslāh-e Kānun-e Vokalā-ye Dādgostari-ye Jomhouri-ye Eslāmi* (*Review of the IRI Bar Association Reform Law*), Tehran: Author.

Kasravi, Ahmad

1977 *Tārikh-e Mashrutiyyat-e Iran* (*The History of Iranian Constitutional Revolution*), Tehran: Amir Kabir.

1944 *Dah Sāl dar 'Adlieh* (*Ten Years in the Judiciary*), Tehran: Bonyād.

Kāzem Zādeh, 'Ali

2002 "Towse'eh-ye Qazāii bar Pāyeh-ye 'Āsib Shenāsi" ("The Judicial Reform Based on Pathology [of the judiciary"), in *Towse'eh-ye Qazāii* (*Judicial Reform*), ed. by Markaz-e Matbu'āt va Enteshārāt-e Quvveh-ye Qazāiyyeh, Tehran: Mo'āvenat-e Ejtemā'i va Ettelā' Resāni-ye Quvveh-ye Qazāiyyeh.

Keddi, Nikki & Aamanat, Mehrdad

1991 "Iran under Later Qajars, 1848–1922," in *The Cambridge History of Iran*, Vol. 7: *From Nadir Shah to the Islamic Republic*, ed. by Peter Avery, Gavin Hambley, and Charles Melville, Cambridge: Cambridge University Press.

Keddie, Nikki & Richard, Yann

1981 *Roots of Revolution: An Interpretive History of Modern Iran*, New Haven: Yale University Press.

Kelsay, John & Twiss, Sumner B.

1994 *Religion and Human Rights*, NY: The Project on Religion and Human Rights.

Kelsen, Hans

1992 *Introduction to the Problems of Legal Theory*, tr. of 1934 edition by Bonnie Litschewski Paulson and Stanley L. Paulson, Oxford: Oxford University Press.

1961 *General Theory of Law and State*, NY: Russell & Russell.

1875 *Ketābcheh-ye Tanzimāt-e Hasāneh-ye dowlat-e 'Āliyeh va mahruseh-ye Iran*, Tehran; Majles-e Shurā-ye Eslami Library.

Khadduri, Majid

1984 *The Islamic Conception of Justice,* London: John Hopkins University Press.

Khājeh Nouri, Ebrāhim

1961 *Bāzigarān-e 'Asr-e Talāii* (*Actors of the Golden Age*), Tehran: Jibi

Khal'atbary, Amir Arsalān

1933 *Qānun-e Tejārat* (*Commercial Law*), Tehran: Ettelā'āt Publisher House.

Khomeini, Ruhollah

1991 *Sahifeh-ye Nur* (*Scroll of Light*), Tehran: Sāzmān-e Madārek-e Farhangi-ye Enqelāb-e Eslāmi.

1984 *Tali'eh-ye Enqelāb-e Eslāmi* (*The Dawn of Islamic Revolution: Interviews Given by Khomeini in Najaf, Paris and Qom*), Tehran: Markaz-e Nashr-e Dāneshgahi.

1981 *Islam and Revolution: Writings and Declarations of Imam Khomeini,* trans. by Hamid Algar, Berkeley: Mizan Press.

1978 *Velāyat-e Faqih* (*Guardianship of the Jurist*), Tehran: Amir Kabir.

1943 *Kashf ul-Asrār* (*Uncovering the Secrets*), Qom.

Khoury, Philip S. & Kostiner, Joseph

1990 *Tribes and State Formation in the Middle East,* Berkeley: University of California Press.

Kornhauser, William

1959 *The Politics of Mass Society,* Glencoe, Ill: The Free Press.

Kritzeck, James

1960 "'Urf and Law in Islam," in *The World of Islam: Studies in Honor of Philip K. Hitti,* London: Macmillan, 60–67.

Kronman, Anthony T.

1983 *Max Weber,* CA: Stanford.

Krygier, Martin

2001 Transnational Questions about the Rule of Law: Why, What, and How? Presented in International Institute of Sociology, 35th Conference in Jagiellonian University.

Ladjevardi, Habib

1988 "Constitutional Government and Reform under Musaddiq," in *Musaddiq, Iranian Nationalism, and Oil,* ed. by James A. Bill and WM. Roger Louis, Austin: University of Texas Press.

1985 *Labor Unions and Autocracy in Iran,*Syracuse, NY: Syracuse University Press

Lambton, Ann Katharine Swynford

1988 *Continuity and Change in Medieval Persia: Aspects of Administrative, Economic and Social History: 11th–14th Century,* N.Y.: Bibliotheca Persica.

1987 *Qajar Persia: Eleven Studies,* Austin: University of Texas.

1968 "The Internal Structure of the Seljuq Empire," in *The Cambridge History of Iran,* Vol. 5: *The Seljuq and Mongol Periods,* ed. by J. A. Boyle, Cambridge: Cambridge University Press: pp. 203–282.

1967 "The Evolution of the Iqta in Medieval Iran," *Iran,* 5: 41–50.

1953 *Landlord and Peasant in Persia,* London: Oxford University Press.

Lambton, A.K.S., Lewis, B., *et al.*

1965 "Dustur," in *Encyclopedia of Islam,* 2nd ed., Vol. 3, Leiden: Brill.

Lapidus, Ira M.

1988 *A History of Islamic Societies,* Cambridge: Cambridge University Press.

Layish, Aharon & Warburg, Gabriel R.

2002 *The Reinstatement of Islamic Law in Sudan under Numayrī Studies in Islamic Law and Society: An Evaluation of a Legal Experiment in the Light of its Historical Context, Methodology, and Repercussions,* Leiden: Brill.

Levy, Rueben

1971 *The Social Structure of Islam,* Cambridge: The Cambridge University Press.

Linz, Juan J.

2000 *Totalitarian and Authoritarian Regimes,* London: Boulder.

1975 "Totalitarian and Authoritarian Regimes," *Handbook of Political Science,* Vol. 3, CA: Addison Wesley: 175–350.

1970 "An Authoritarian Regime: Spain," in *Mass Politics: Studies in Political Sociology,* ed. Erik Allardt and Stein Rokkan, New York: Free Press.

Lukes S. & A. Scull

1984 *Durkheim and the Law,* Malden: Basil Blackwell.

Luckmann, Thomas

1967 *The Invisible Religion: The Problem of Religion in Modern Society,* MacMillan Publishing Company.

MacDaniel, Robert A.

1974 *The Shuster Mission and the Persian Constitutional Revolution,* Minneapolis: Bibliotheca Islamica.

Mackey, Sandra

1996 *The Iranians: Persia, Islam, and the Soul of a Nation,* NY: Dutton.

Madan, T.N.

1998 *Modern Myths, Locked Minds: Secularism and Fundamentalism in India,* Delhi: Oxford University Press.

Mahboubi Ardekāni, Hussein

1999 *Tārikh-e Mo'assesāt-e Tamaddoni-ye Jadid (The History of New Civilizational Institutions),* 3 Vols., Tehran: Tehran University Press.

Maine, H.S.

1990 *Ancient Law,* AZ: University of Arizona Press (1861).

Malinowski, B

1926 *Crime and Custom in Savage Society,* London: Kegan Paul.

Mallat, Chibli

1993 *The Renewal of Islamic Law: Muhammad Baqer as-Sadr, Najaf and the Shi'i International,* NY: Cambridge University Press.

Manuchehri, Abbās

1998 "Kudetā-ye Sevvum-e Esfand-e 1299 va Sultanism-e Irani" (Esfand 3th 1299 Coup and Iranian Sultanism), *Tārikh-e Mo'āser-e Iran* (*Iran's Contemporary History Journal*), Vol. I, No. 3: 9–18.

Mann, Michael

1993 *The Sources of Social Power: The Rise of Classes and Nation-states, Vol. 2, 1760–1914,* Cambridge: Cambridge University Press.

Mansur ul-Saltaneh 'Adl, Mirzā Mostafā

Basic Rights or the Principles of Constitutional Movement and Interpretation of the Constitution, Tehran: Fāroos.

Mario Diani & Doug McAdam

2003 *Social movements and networks: Relational Approaches to Collective Action,* New York: Oxford University Press.

Markaz-e Tahqiqāt-e Feqhi-ye Qovveh-ye Qazāiyyeh

2002a *Majmu'eh-ye 'Ārā-ye Feqhi-ye Qazā'i dar 'Omoor-e Hoquqi (The Collection of Juristic Verdicts on Legal Affairs),* VoL .I, Qom.

2002b *Majmoo'eh-ye Nazariyāt-e Mashvarati-ye Feqhi dar 'Omoor-eHoquqi (The Collection of Juristic Consultative Opinions on Legal Affairs),* Vol. .I, Qom.

2002c *Majmu'eh-ye 'Ārā-ye Feqhi-ye Qaza'i dar Omoor-e Kaifari (The Collection of Juristic Verdicts on Criminal Affairs),* VoL .I, Qom.

2002d *Majmu'eh-ye Nazariyyāt-e Mashvarati-ye Feqhi dar 'Omoor-e Kaifari (The Collection of Juristic Consultative Opinions on Criminal Affairs),* VoL .I, Qom.

Markoff, John

1996 *Waves of Democracy: Social Movements and Political Change,* London: Pine Forge Press.

M'aroufi Bozorgi, N.

1967 "Population Projection for Iran, 1956–1976," *Proceedings of the World Population Conference,* Belgrade, 30 August-10 September 1965, United Nations, Department of Economic and Social Affairs, Vol.3, Selected Papers and Summaries: Projections, Measurement of Population Trends, New York, UN, 19–22.

Marshall, T.H.

1964 *Class, Citizenship and Social development,* Chicago: University of Chicago Press.

Martin, Vanessa

1989 *Islam and Modernism: The Iranian Revolution of 1906,* NY: Syracuse University Press.

Matin Daftari, Ahmad

1945 *Ā'een-e Dādresi-ye Madani va Bāzargāni* (*Civil and Commercial Court Procedure*), Tehran.

Mattei, Ugo

1997 "Three Patterns of Law: Taxonomy and Change in the World's Legal Systems," *The American Journal of Comparative Law,* Vol. 45: 5–44.

Mathews, John M.

1922 "State Administrative Reorganization," *The American Political Science Review,* Vol. 16, No. 3: 387–398

Maududi, Sayyid Abul 'Ala

1960 *The Islamic Law and Constitution,* trans. & ed. by Khurshid Ahmad, Lahore: Islamic Publications LTD.

Mehrpour, Husein

2005 *Vazifeh-ye Doshwār Nezārat bar Qānun Asāsi* (*Difficult Task of Monitoring the Execution of the Constitution*), Tehran: Sāles.

Merriman, John Henry

1969 *The Civil Law Tradition: An Introduction to the Legal Systems of Western Europe and Latin America,* CA: Stanford University Press.

Merry, Sally Engle

2000 *Colonizing Hawaii: The Cultural Power of Law,* NJ: Princeton University Press.

Messick, Richard E.

1999 "Judicial Reform and Economic Development: A Survey of the Issues," *The World Bank Research Observer*, Vol. 14, No. 1.

Messick, Brinkley

1993 *The Calligraphic State: Textual Domination and History in a Muslim Society,* Berkeley: University of California Press.

Milani, Abbas

2000 *The Persian Sphinx: Amir Abbas Hoveyda and the Riddle of Iranian Revolution,* Washington DC: Mage Publishers.

Milani, Mohsen M.

1992 "Shi'ism and the State in the Constitution of the Islamic Republic of Iran," in *Iran: Political Culture in the Islamic Republic,* ed. by Samih K. Farsoun and Mehrdad Mashayekhi, NY: Routledge.

1988 The *Making of Iran's Islamic Revolution: From Monarchy to Islamic Republic,* London: Westview Press.

Mills, C. Wright

1956 *The Power Elite,* New York: Oxford University Press.

Mills, C. Wright & H.H. Gerth

1967 *From Max Weber: Essays in Sociology,* London: Routledge & Kegan Paul Ltd.: Ch. XI, "Social Psychology of World Religions"& "On Religious Rejection of the World,"

Millspaugh, Arthur C.

1946 *Americans in Persia,* Washington D.C. ; The Brooking Institution.

Minorsky, V.

1965 *Sāzmān Edāri-ye Hokumat-e Safaviān* (*The Administrative Organization of Safavids*), Tehran: Anjoman-e Ketāb.

1913–38 *Encyclopedia of Islam,* 1st ed., "Tuyul," 4: 799–801.

Mir-Hosseini, Ziba

1993 *Marriage on Trial: A Study of Islamic Family Law, Iran and Morocco Compared,* London: I. B. Tauris.

Mirsepassi, Ali

200 *Intellectual Discourse and the Politics of Moderations*, Cambridge: Cambridge University Press

Mirzā Sami'ā

1989 *Tazkerat ul-Molook (Kings' Biographies),* ed. by Seyyed Mohammad Dabir Siāqi, Tehran: Amir Kabir.

Mobārakiān, 'Abbās

1998 *Chehreh hā dar Tārikhche-ye Nezām-e Amoozesh- 'Āli-ye Hoquq va 'Adlieh-ye Novin* (*Figures in the History of Modern Higher Educational System of Law and Judiciary*), Tehran: Nashr-e Paidāyesh.

Montazeri, Hussein Ali

1988 *Derasāt fi Welāyat-e Faqih va Feqh u- Dowlat al-Islamiah (Seminars on Islamic Jurist Guardianship and Islamic* State Jurisprudence), Vol. I & II, Qom: Almarkaz al-'Ālami led-Derāsāt ul-Islamiah.

2000 *Online Memoirs,* montazeri.com.

Moore, Sally Falk

1978 *Law as Process: An Anthropological Approach,* London: Routledge & Kegan Paul.

Morgan, David

1988 *Medieval Persia: 1040–1797,* NY: Longman.

Moslem, Mehdi

2002 *Factional Politics in Post-Khomeini Iran,* NY: Syracuse University Press.

Motahhari, Mortezā

1989 *Āshnaii bā 'Oloom-e Eslāmi (Introduction to Islamic Sciences),* Vol. II, Qom: Sadrā

Mottahedeh, Roy

1987 *The Mantle of the Prophet: Religion and Politics in Iran,* New York: Simon and Schuster.

1975 "The Abbasid Caliphate in Iran," in *The Cambridge History of Iran,* Vol. 4: *From the Arab Invasion to the Seljuqs,* ed. by R.N. Frye, Cambridge: Cambridge University Press: pp. 57–89.

Mouhit Tabātabāii, Seyyed Mohammad

1968 *Dādgostari dar Iran az Enqerāz-e Sassani ta Ebtedāy-e Mashrutiyyat (The Judiciary in Iran from the Collapse of Sassanids to Early Constitutional Era),* Tehran: Vahid.

Musavi Zādeh, Jahāngir

2001 *Mohākemeh: Reza Shah dar Barāber-e Tārikh (Trial: Reza Shah in Front of History),* Tehran: Musavi-Zādeh Publisher.

Mousnier, Roland

1979 *The Institutions of France under the Absolute Monarchy, Society and State,* Chicago: The University of Chicago Press.

Nadolski, Dora Glidewell

1977 "Ottoman and Secular Civil Law," *International Journal of Middle East Studies,* Vol. 8, No. 4: 517–543.

Nafisi, Sa'id

1965 *Tārikh-e Siāsi va Ejtemā'i-ye Iran (Social and Political History of Iran),* Tehran: Bonyād Publisher.

Nā'ini, Shaikh Mohammad Hussein

1955/1334 *Tanbih ul-'Ommah va Tanzih ul-Mellah* (*Enlightening the Islamic Community and Purification of Religion*), Tehran: Sherkat-e Sahāmi-ye Enteshār.

Na'im, Abdollahi An-

1992 *Human Rights in Cross-Cultural Perspective,* Philadelphia: University of Pennsylvania Press.

Najmi, Nāser

1958 *Iran dar miyan-e Tufan, ya Sharh-e Zendegani-ye 'Abbas Mirza dar Jangha-ye Iran va Rus* (*Iran in Turmoil, or the Life of 'Abbas Mirza in Iran-Russian Wars*), Tehran: Kanun-e Ma'refat.

Nashat, Guity

1982 The *Origins of Modern Reform in Iran, 1870–1880,* Chicago: University of Illinois Press.

2000 *Negareshhā va Arzeshhā-ye Iranian* (*Iranian Opinions and Values*), Tehran: Tarhhā-ye Melli.

Nezām ul-Eslam-e Kermāni, Mohammad Shari'atmadār

1982 *Tārikh-e Bidāri-ye Iranian* (*History of Iranians' Awakening*), Tehran: Āgāh.

Nezam-Mafi, Mansoureh Ettehadieh

"The Council for the Investigation of Grievances: A Case Study of Nineteenth Century Iranian Social History," *Iranian Studies,* Vol. XXII, No. 1, 51–61.

Oberling, Pierre

1974 *The Qashqa'i Nomads of Fars,* The Hague: Mouton.

O'Dea, Thomas, F.

1961 "Five Dilemmas in the Institutionalization of Religion," *Journal for the Scientific Study of Religion* 1,1: 30–39.

Offe, Claus

1996 *Modernity and the State: East, West,* Mass.: The MIT Press.

Olmstead, A.T.

1948 *History of the Persian Empire,* Chicago: The University of Chicago Press.

Omid, Homa

1994 *Islam and the Post-revolutionary State in Iran,* NY: St. Martin Press

Orucu, Esin

1996 "Mixed and Mixing Systems: A Conceptual Search," in *Studies in Legal Systems: Mixed and Mixing,* Boston: Kluwer Law International: 335–352.

Pakzad, Sima

1994 "The Legal Status of Women in the Family in Iran," *in* Afkhami & Friedl, eds., *In the Eye of the Storm: Women in Post-Revolutionary Iran,* London; I. B. Tauris.

Parsa, Misagh

1989 *Social Origins of the Iranian Revolution,* New Brunswick: Rutgers University Press.

Perikhanian, Anahit

1983 "Iranian Society and Law," in *The Cambridge History of Iran,* Vol. 3(2): *The Seleucid, Parthian and Sasanian Periods,* ed. By Ehsan Yarshater, Cambridge: Cambridge University Press.

1977 *The Book of A Thousand Judgment: A Sasanian Law Book,* Mazda Publishers & Bibliotheca Persica, CA: Costa Mesa.

Perkins, John A.

1951 "Reflections on State Reorganizations," *The American Political Science Review,* Vol. 45, No. 2: 507–516.

Petrushevsky, I. .P.

1968 "The Socio-economic Condition of Iran Under the Ilkhan," in *The Cambridge History of Iran,* Vol. 5, ed. by J. A. Boyle, Cambridge: Cambridge University Press: pp. 483–537.

Pirniā, Mirzā Hasan Khan (Moshir ul-Dowleh)

1983 *Tārikh-e Iran-e Bāstān* (*The History of Ancient Iran*), Tehran: Donyā-ye Ketāb.

Piscatori, James P.

1986 *Islam in a World of Nation-States,* Cambridge: Cambridge University Press.

Poggi, Gianfranco

2003 "The Formation of the Modern State and the Institutionalization of Rule," in *Handbook of Historical Sociology,* ed. By Gerard Delanty, London: Sage Publication.

1990 *The state: Its Nature, Development and Prospects,* Stanford: Stanford University Press.

1978 *Development of Modern State: A Sociological Introduction,* CA: Stanford University Press.

Priban, Jiri

2002 *Dissidents of law: on the 1989 Velvet Revolutions, Legitimations, Fictions of Legality, and Contemporary Version of the Social Contract,* Aldershot, Hampshire, UK: Ashgate/Dartmouth.

Pound, R.

1910 "Scope and Purpose of Sociological Jurisprudence," *Harvard Law Review*, 24, 1/8: 591–619.

Powers, David S.

1994 "Kadijustiz or Qadi-Justice? A Paternity Dispute from Fourteenth Century Morocco," *Islamic Law and Society*, Vol. 1, No. 3, 332–366.

Qā'em Maqāmi, Jahāngir

1969 *Sad-o Yek Sanad-e Tārikhi (One Hundred and One Historical Documents)*, Tehran.

Qāsemi Puyā, Eqbāl

1998/1377 *Madāres-e Jadid dar Dowreh-ye Qājāriyyeh: Bānian va Pishrouvān (Modern Schools in Qājār Era: Founders and Pathfinder)*, Tehran: Markaz-e Nashr-e Dāneshgahi.

Quigley, John

1990 "Law Reform and the Soviet Courts," *Columbia Journal of Transnational Law*, Vol. 28, No. 1: 59–76.

Rafsanjani, Akbar Hāshemi

1999 *'Obur az Bohrān (Memiors)*, Tehran: Daftar-e Nashr-e Ma'aref-e Enqelāb.

Ragin, Charles C.

2000 "The Place of Case Study Research," *Comparative and Historical Sociology*, Vol.13.1: 1–2.

1987 *The Comparative Method: Moving beyond Qualitative and Quantitative Strategies*, CA: University of California Press.

Ramazani, Nesta

1993 "Women in Iran: The Revolutionary Ebb and Flow," *Middle East Journal*, Vol. 47, No. 3: 409–428.

Rāvandi, Morteza

1961 *Tārikh-e Ejtemā'i-ye Iran (Social History of Iran)*, Vols. 1, 2 & 3, Tehran: Amir Kabir.

Rayshahri, Mohammad Mohammadi

1990 *Khāterāt-e Siāsi (Political Memoirs)*, Tehran: Mo'asseseh-ye Motāle'āt va Pajuheshhā-ye Siāsi.

Ringer, Monica M.

2004 "Negotiating Modernity: Ulama and the Discourse of Modernity in Nineteenth-Century Iran," in *Iran between Tradition and Modernity*, ed. By Ramin Jahanbegloo, NY: Lexington Books.

Rohrborn, Klaus, M. *Nezām-e Ialāt dar Dowreh-ye Safaviyeh*, tr. by Kaikāvoos Jahāndāri, Tehran: 1357/1978

Robertson, B.A.

2003 *Shaping the Current Islamic Reformation,* London: Frank Cass.

Robertson, Roland

1970 *The Sociological Interpretation of Religion,* Oxford: Basil Blackwell.

Rosen, Lawrence

2000 *The Justice of Islam: Comparative Perspectives on Islamic Law and Society,* Oxford: Oxford University Press.

1989 *The Anthropology of Justice: Law as Culture in Islamic Society,* Cambridge University Press.

Rosenberg, Hans,

1958 *Bureaucracy, Aristocracy and Autocracy: The Prussian Experience, 1660–1815,* Boston: Beacon Press.

Roth, Guenther

1979 "Charisma and the Counterculture," in Guenther Roth & Wolfgang Schluchter, *Max Weber's Vision of History: Ethics and Methods,* Berkeley: University of California Press: 119–143.

Russell, Peter H. & O'Brien, David M. (ed.)

2001 *Judicial independence in the age of democracy: Critical perspectives from around the world,* Charlottesville: University Press of Virginia.

Sadr, Mohsen

1985 *Khāterāt-e Sadr ul-Ashrāf* (*Sadr ul-Ashrāf Memoirs*), Tehran: Wahid.

Saifi Fami Tafreshi, Morteza

1988 *Police-e Khofyeh-ye Iran* (*Iran's Secret Police*), Tehran: Qoqnoos.

Sajo, Andras

1999 *Limiting Government: An Introduction to Constitutionalism,* Budapest: Central European University Press.

Sāket, Mohammad Hussein

1986 *Nahad-e Dādresi dar Eslām* (*Court Structure in Islam*), Mashad: Āstān-e Qods-e Razavi.

Salame, Ghassan

1996 *Democracy without Democrats? The Renewal of Politics in the Muslim World,* London: I.B. Tauris Publishers.

Sāleh, Ali Pāshā

1969 *Tārikh-e Huquq-e Iran* (*Iran's Legal History*), Tehran University Press: Tehran.

Sander, Frank E. A.

1979 "Varieties of Dispute Processing," in A.L Levin and R. R. Wheeler (eds.), *The Pound Conference on Justice in the Future*, ST. Paul: West Publishing Company.

Sangelaji, Shari'at

1961 *Kelid-e Fahm-e Quran (Key to Understanding Quran)*, Tehran: Dānesh (reprinted in 2001).

1944 *Mahv al-Mowhum (Obliteration of Fictitious)*, Tehran: Tābān.

Savory, Roger M.

1987 "Some Reflections on Totalitarian Tendencies in the Safavid State," in *Studies on the History of Safawid Iran,* London: Variorum Reprints, X: 226–241.

Schacht, Joseph

1984 *Introduction to Islamic Law,* Clarendon Press.

Schiller, Arthur A.

1958 "Jurist's Law," *Columbia Law Review,* Vol. LVIII.

Schirazi, Asghar

1997 *The Constitution of Iran: Politics and the State in the Islamic Republic,* NY: I.B.Tauris Publishers.

Schluchter, Wolfgang

1981 *Development of Western Rationalism,* Berkeley: University of California Press.

Schneider, Irene

2005 "Religious and State Jurisdiction during Nasir al-Din Shah's Reign," in Robert M. Gleave, ed., *Religion and Society in Qajar Iran,* London: Curzon: 84–110.

Shāhrudi, Mahmoud Hāshemi

2001a *Manshur-e Towse'eh-ye Qazā'i, No.2 (Judicial Development's Charter)*, Tehran: Markaz-e Matboo'āt va Enteshārāt.

2001b *Rāhboardhā va Barnāmehhā-ye Quvveh-ye Qazāiyyeh (The Judiciary Power's Strategies and Plans)*, Tehran: Mo'āvenat-e Ejtemā'i va Ettelā' Resāni-ye Quvveh-ye Qazāiyyeh.

Shaikholeslami, Reza

1997 *The Structure of Central Authority in Qajar Iran: 1871–1896,* Atlanta, GA: Scholars Press.

1971 "The Sale of Offices in Qajar Iran: 1856–1898," *Iranian Studies* IV: 104–118.

Shambayati, Hootan

2004 "A Tale of Two Mayors: Courts and Politics in Iran and Turkey," *International Journal of Middle East Studies,* 36: 253–275.

Shapiro, Barry M.

1992 "Revolutionary Justice in 1798–1790: The Comite des Recherches, the Chatelet, and the Fayettist Coalition," *French Historical Studies,* Vol. 17, 3: 656–669.

Shari'ti, Ali

1979 *Red Shiism,* trans. by Habib Shirazi, Tehran: The shariati Foundation and Hamdami Publishers.

Shaw, J. Stanford & Ezel Kurl Shaw

1977 *History of the Ottoman Empire and Modern Turkey, Vol. II: Reform, Revolution, and Republic: The Rise of Modern Turkey, 1808–1975,* Cambridge: Cambridge University Press.

Shāyegan, 'Ali

1996(45) *Hoquq-e Madani-ye Iran (The Iranian Civil Code)*, Tehran: Tāhā.

Sherif, Adel Omar

1999 "Separation of Powers and Judicial Independence in Constitutional Democracies: The Egyptian and American Experiences," in *Democracy, the Rule of Law and Islam,* ed. by Eugene Cotran and Adel Omar Sherif, Boston: Kulwer Law International.

Skocpol, Theda & Margaret Somers

1994 "The Uses of Comparative History in Macrosocial Inquiry," in *Social Revolutions in the Modern World,* New York: Cambridge University Press.

Smelser, Neil J.

1973 "The Methodology of Comparative Analysis," in *Comparative Research Methods* ed. by Warwick, Donald P. & Samuel Osherson, N.J.: Prentice-Hall, Inc.

Smith, Donald E. (ed.)

1974 *Religion and Political Modernization,* New Haven, CT: Yale University Press.

Smith, Nicole

1997 *Constitutional Watchdogs,* London: The Constitution Unit.

Soroush, Abdolkarim

2000 *Reason, Freedom, and Democracy in Islam,* NY: Oxford University Press.

1996 Tahlil-e Mafhum-e Hokumat-e Dini (An Analysis of the Concept of Islamic State), *Kiān* 6, 32: 2–13.

1994 *Farbeh tar az Ideoluzhi (Plumper than Ideology)*, Tehran: Serāt.

Sousa Santos, Boaventura de

1999 "The Gatt of Law and Democracy: (Mis)Trusting the Global Reform of Courts," in *Globalization and Legal Cultures,* ed. by Johannes Feest, Onati: Graficas Santamaria, pp. 49–86.

Spuler, Bertold

1969 *The Mongol Period: History of the Muslim World,* Princeton: Markus Wiener Publishers.

Starr, June

1992 *Law as Metaphor: From Islamic Courts to the Palace of Justice,* Albany: State University of New York Press.

Stinchcombe, Arthur

1999 "Certainty of Law: Reasons, Situation-Types, Analogy, and Equilibrium," *The Journal of Political Philosophy,* Vol. 7, 3: 209–224.

Sutton, John R.

2001 *Law/Society: Origins, Interaction, and Change,* London: Pine Forge Press.

Sykes, Ella C.

1910 *Persia and Its People,* London: Methuen & Co. Ltd.

Tabari, Ehsān

1977 *Jāme'eh-ye Iran dar 'Asr-e Reza Shah* (*Iranian Society in Reza Shah Era*), Tehran: Hezb-e Tudeh-ye Iran.

Tabari, Keyvan

2003 "The Rule of Law and the Politics of Reform in Post-Revolutionary Iran," *International Sociology,* March, 18: 96–113.

Tabātabā'i, Mohammad Mohit

1966 Tahavvol-e Dādgostari az Eslām ta Enqelāb-e Mashruteh, (The Development of Judiciary from Advent of Islam to the Constitutional Revolution), *Vahid Journal,* No. 41–47.

Tamanaha, Brian Z.

2001 *A General Jurisprudence of Law and Society,* NY: Oxford University Press.

Tapper, Richard et al (ed.)

1997 *Frontier Nomads of Iran: A Political and Social History of the Shahsevan,* NY: Cambridge University Press.

Tate, C. Neal

1992 "Courts and Crisis Regimes: A Theory Sketch with Asian Case Studies," *Political Research Quarterly:* 311–38.

Tate, C. Neal & Stacia L. Haynie,

2001 "Comparative Judicial Politics: Intellectual History and bibliography," presented at the Annual Meeting of the American Political Science Association, San Francisco.

Tate, C. Neal & Torbjorn Vallinder

1995 *The Global Expansion of Judicial Power,* NY: New York University Press.

Taylor, Charles

1995 *Philosophical Arguments,* Cambridge, Mass.: Harvard University Press, Chs. 7. 11–13.

Teitel, Ruti G.

2000 *Transitional Justice,* Oxford: Oxford university Press.

Terrence, C. & Lucien Karpik (ed.)

1997 *Lawyers and the Rise of Western Political Liberalism: Europe and North America from the Eighteenth to Twentieth Centuries,* Oxford: Clarendon Press.

Tetlock, Philip E. & Aaron Belkin

1996 "Counterfactual Thought Experiments in World Politics: Logical, Methodological, and Psychological Perspectives," *Items,* Vol. 50, No. 4, pp. 77–85

Teubner, Gunther (ed.)

1997 *Global Law without a State,* Sydney: Dartmouth.

Tilly, Charles, (ed.)

1975 *The Formation of National States in Western Europe,* Princeton, N.J.: Princeton University Press.

Tocqueville, Alexis de

1955 *The old régime and the French Revolution,* Garden City, NY: Doubleday.

Trubek, David M.

1972 "Max Weber on Law and the Rise of Capitalism," *Wisconsin Law Review,* Vol. 3: 720–753.

Turkamān, Eskandar Baig

1971 *Tārikh-e 'Ālam 'Ārā-ye 'Abbāsi,* Tehran: Amir Kabir.

Turkamān, Mohammad

1989 "Sair-e Tatavvor-e Asl-e Dovvom-e Motammem-e Qānun-e Asāsi," (How the Second Article of the Supplement to the Constitution Developed), *Majalleh-ye Tārikh-e Mo'āser-e Iran* (*Iran's Contemporary History Journal*), No. 1: 74.

Turner, Bryan

1974 *Weber and Islam: A Critical Study,* London: Routledge & Kegan Paul.

Tyan, Emile

1955 "Judicial Organization: The General Characteristics of the Judicial Function," in *Law in the Middle East,* Vol. I, *Origins and Development of*

Islamic Law, ed. by Majid Khadduri and Herbert J. Liebesny, Washington D.C.: Middle East Institute: 236–78.

Unger, Roberto Manqabeira

1976 *Law in Modern Society,* Free Press.

Vallinder, Torbjorn

1995 "When the Courts Go Marching In," in *The Global Expansion of Judicial Power,* ed. by C. Neal Tate and Torbjorn Vallinder, NY: New York University Press, 13–26.

Vago, Steven

2006 *Law and Society,* NY: Pearson.

Vanderbilt, Arthur T.

1976 *The Challenge of Law Reform,* Princeton University Press, Greenwood Publishing Group.

Vesey-Fitzgerald, S. G.

1955 "Nature and Sources of Shari'a," in *Law in the Middle East,* Vol. I: *Origins and Development of Islamic Law,* ed. by Majid Khadduri and Herbert J. Liebesny, Washington D.C.: Middle East Institute: 85–112.

Vogel, Frank Edward

1993 *Islamic Law and Legal System: Studies of Saudi Arabia,* Doctor of Philosophy Dissertation, Cambridge: Harvard University.

Warwick, Donald P. & Samuel Osherson

1973 *Comparative Research Methods,* N.J.: Prentice-Hall, Inc.

Watson, Alan

1998 *Sources of Law, Legal Change, and Ambiguity,* Philadelphia: University of Pennsylvania Press.

1993 *Legal Transplants,* Athens: University of Georgia Press.

1983 "Legal Change: Sources of Law and Legal Culture," *University of Pennsylvania Law Review,* Vol. 131: 1121–1157.

Weber, Max

1978 *Economy and Society: An Outline of Interpretive Sociology,* ed. By Guenther Roth & Claus Wittich, Los Angeles: University of California Press.

1965 "Religion and Social Status" & "On Religious Rejection of the World," in *Theories of Society: Foundations of Modern Sociological Theory,* ed. by Talcott Parsons, Edward Shils, Kaspar I. Naegele and Jesse R. Pitts, NY: The Free Press: 1120–1161.

1964 *The Theory of Economic and Social Organization,* tr. by A. M. Henderson and Talcott Parsons, the Free Press of Glencoe.

Weinstein, Jack B.

1977 *Reform of Court Rule-Making Procedures,* Ohio: Ohio State University Press.

Wheeler, Russell R. & Howard R. Whitcomb

1977 *Judicial Administration: Text and Readings,* NJ: Prentice-Hall, Inc.

Wilbur, Donald N.

1963 *Iran: Past and Present,* Princeton: Princeton University Press

Wilson, Bryan

1948 *Religion in Secular Society: A Sociological Comment,* Penguin.

Wimmer, Andreas

2002 *Nationalist Exclusion and Ethnic Conflict: Shadows of Modernity,* Cambridge: Cambridge University Press.

Wood, Gordon S.

1991 *The Radicalism of the American Revolution,* NY: Alfred A. Knopf.

Zakeri, Mehdi

2002 "Towse'eh-ye Qazāii dar Qānun Asasi-ye Jomhouri-ye Eslāmi-ye Iran" ("Judicial Reform in the Islamic Republic of Iran's Constitution"), in *Towse'eh-ye Qazāii* (*Judicial Reform*), ed. by Markaz-e Matbou'āt va Enteshārāt-e Quvveh-ye Qazāiyyeh, Tehran: Mo'āvenat-e Ejtemā'i va Ettelā' Resāni-ye Quvveh-ye Qazāiyyeh.

Zargari Nejād, Gholām Husein

1998/1377 *Manābe'-e Andisheh-ye Siāsi dar Tārikh-e Iran: Rasā'el-e Mashrutiyyat* (*Sources of Political Thought in Iran's History: Constitutional Treatises*), Tehran: Kavir.

Zarrinkub, Abd al-Husain

1975 "The Arab Conquest of Iran and Its Aftermath," in *The Cambridge History of Iran,* Vol. 4: *From the Arab Invasion to the Seljuqs,* ed. by R.N. Frye, Cambridge: Cambridge University Press: pp. 57–89.

Zerang, Mohammad

2002 *Tahavvol-e Nezām-e Qazā'i in Iran* (*The Development in Iran's Judiciary System*), Vol. I & II, Tehran: Markaz-e Asnād-e Enqelāb-e Eslāmi,

Zurcher, Arnold John,

1951 *Constitutions and Constitutional Trends since World War II: An Examination of Significant Aspects of Postwar Public Law with Particular Reference*

to the New Constitutions of Western Europe, New York: New York University Press.

WEBSITES

1.columbia.edu
4.worldbank.org
advarnews.com
americanradioworks.publicradio.org
apostatesofislam.com
aviny.com
bartleby.com
bartleby.com
bashgah.net
baztab.com
bbc.co.uk
britannica.com
brown.edu
cais-soas.com
cia.gov
ciaonet.org
cnn.com
donya-e-eqtesad.com
emadbaghi.com
emrooz.info
emrouz.ws
ergosum.uaemex.mx
farsnews.com
forouharha.com
forum.persiantools.com
ghest.com
hamshahri.net/hamshahri.org
hasanagha.net
home.att.net
hoqooq.com
hri.ca
hrw.org
iranbar.com
iran-emrooz.de
Iranian.com

iraninstitute.net
iranjudiciary.org
iranjudiciary.org
irankhabar.com
iranprisons.org
iransoc.dircon.co.uk
iranvajahan.net
irib.ir
irica.com
irisn.com
irisn.com
irjpr.com
irjpr.ir
isna.ir
itsa.ucsf.edu
itsa.ucsf.edu
jomhourieslami.com
kadivar.com
kayhannews.ir
lankarani.com
macalester.edu
mag.gooya.com/akhbar.gooya.com/khabarnameh.gooya.com/news.gooya.com/open.g00ya.com/ azad.gooya.name/azad.gooya.ws/ raha.gooya.name/1384.g00ya.com (these are different addresses for only one website that has repeatedly changed its name due to filtering policies of the Iranian government.)
magiran.com
mazandnume.com
mehrnews.com
mellat.majlis.ir
mellimazhabi.org
moi.gov.ir
montazeri.ws
nezam.org
nimrooz.com
nytimes.com
ostvar.com
Parstimes.com
payk.net
payvand.com
peacelink.nu
peykeiran.com
polpiran.com

r0ozonline.com/roozonline.com
rferl.org
rooydad.com
sci.org.ir
sedona.net
shareh.com
sharghnewspaper.ir/sharghnewspaper.com
shariati.com
state.gov
today.ir
ukconstitution.net
unhchr.ch
unodc.org
wilayah,net
wordnet.princeton.edu

PERIODICALS (OTHER THAN JOURNALS)

Official Magazine of Justice Department (Majalleh-ye Rasmi-ye Vezārat-e 'Adlieh)

Official Magazine of Properties and Documents Registration (Majalleh-ye Rasmi-ye Sabt-e Amlāk va Asnād)

Parliamentary Proceedings (Surat-e Mashruh-e Mozākerāt-e Majles)

Record of Parliamentary Legislation (Majmu'eh-ye Qavānin-e Mowzu'eh va Mosavvabāt-e Majles)

Majles Chronicle (Ruznameh-ye Majles)

Judiciary News (Vaqāye'-e 'Adlieh)

Index

D

E

K

N

S

T

For Product Safety Concerns and Information please contact our EU
representative GPSR@taylorandfrancis.com
Taylor & Francis Verlag GmbH, Kaufingerstraße 24, 80331 München, Germany

www.ingramcontent.com/pod-product-compliance
Ingram Content Group UK Ltd.
Pitfield, Milton Keynes, MK11 3LW, UK
UKHW022114190926
475702UK00013B/1438
* 9 7 8 0 4 1 5 5 1 2 9 1 6 *